THAILAND

BUSINESS AND INVESTMENT OPPORTUNITIES YEARBOOK

VOLUME 1
PRACTICAL INFORMATION AND OPPORTUNITIES

International Business Publications, USA
Washington DC, USA - Thailand

THAILAND
BUSINESS AND INVESTMENT OPPORTUNITIES YEARBOOK
VOLUME 1 PRACTICAL INFORMATION AND OPPORTUNITIES

UPDATED ANNUALLY

Cover Design: International Business Publications, USA

We express our sincere appreciation to all government agencies and international organizations which provided information and other materials for this guide

2014 Edition Updated Reprint International Business Publications, USA
ISBN 1-4387-4783-7

This guide provides basic information for starting or/and conducting business in the country. The extraordinary volume of materials covering the topic, prevents us from placing all these materials in this guide. For more detailed information on issues related to any specific investment and business activity in the country, please contact Global Investment Center, USA
Please acquire the list of our business intelligence and marketing guides and other business publications. We constantly update and expand our business intelligence and marketing materials. Please contact the center for the updated list of reports on over 200 countries.

in the USA: **Global Investment Center, USA.**
P.O.Box 15343, Washington, DC 20003
Phone: (202) 546-2103, Fax: (202) 546-3275, E-mail: rusric@erols.com

For additional analytical, marketing and other information please contact
Global Investment Center, USA

Printed in the USA

For additional analytical, business and investment opportunities information,
please contact Global Investment & Business Center, USA
at (202) 546-2103. Fax: (202) 546-3275. E-mail: rusric@erols.com

THAILAND

BUSINESS AND INVESTMENT OPPORTUNITIES YEARBOOK

VOLUME 1
PRACTICAL INFORMATION AND OPPORTUNITIES

TABLE OF CONTENTS

For additional analytical, business and investment opportunities information,
please contact Global Investment & Business Center, USA
at (202) 546-2103. Fax: (202) 546-3275. E-mail: rusric@erols.com

**For additional analytical, business and investment opportunities information,
please contact Global Investment & Business Center, USA
at (202) 546-2103. Fax: (202) 546-3275. E-mail: rusric@erols.com**

**For additional analytical, business and investment opportunities information,
please contact Global Investment & Business Center, USA
at (202) 546-2103. Fax: (202) 546-3275. E-mail: rusric@erols.com**

**For additional analytical, business and investment opportunities information,
please contact Global Investment & Business Center, USA
at (202) 546-2103. Fax: (202) 546-3275. E-mail: rusric@erols.com**

For additional analytical, business and investment opportunities information,
please contact Global Investment & Business Center, USA
at (202) 546-2103. Fax: (202) 546-3275. E-mail: rusric@erols.com

STRATEGIC & DEVELOPMENT PROFILES

Capital (and largest city)	Bangkok 13°45′N 100°29′E13.75°N 100.483°E
Official language(s)	Thai
Official scripts	Thai alphabet
Demonym	Thai
Government	Parliamentary democracy and Constitutional monarchy
- Monarch	Bhumibol Adulyadej (Rama IX)
- Prime Minister	Abhisit Vejjajiva
Legislature	National Assembly
- Upper House	Senate
- Lower House	House of Representatives
Formation	
- Sukhothai Kingdom	1238 - 1448
- Ayutthaya Kingdom	1351 - 1767
- Thonburi Kingdom	1768 - 1782
- Rattanakosin Kingdom	6 April 1782
- Constitutional Monarchy	24 June 1932
- Later Constitution	24 August 2007
Area	
- Total	513,120 km^2 (50th) 198,115 sq mi
- Water (%)	0.4 (2,230 km^2)
Population	
- 2010 estimate	63,878,276 (21th)
- 2000 census	60,606,947
- Density	132.1/km^2 (88th) 342/sq mi
GDP (PPP)	2010 estimate
- Total	$573.607 billion (24th)
- Per capita	$8,643 (89th)
GDP (nominal)	2010 estimate
- Total	$312,605 billion (30th)
- Per capita	$4,620 (89th)
Gini (2002)	42
HDI (2010)	▲0.654 (medium) (92nd)
Currency	Baht (฿) (THB)
Time zone	(UTC+7)
Drives on the	left
ISO 3166 code	TH
Internet TLD	.th
Calling code	+66

Thailand officially the **Kingdom of Thailand** formerly known as **Siam** is a country located at the centre of the Indochina peninsula in Southeast Asia. It is bordered to the north by Burma and Laos, to the east by Laos and Cambodia, to the south by the Gulf of Thailand and Malaysia, and to the west by the Andaman Sea and the southern extremity of Burma. Its maritime boundaries

For additional analytical, business and investment opportunities information, please contact Global Investment & Business Center, USA at (202) 546-2103. Fax: (202) 546-3275. E-mail: rusric@erols.com

include Vietnam in the Gulf of Thailand to the southeast, and Indonesia and India in the Andaman Sea to the southwest.

The country is a constitutional monarchy, headed by King Rama IX, the ninth king of the House of Chakri, who, having reigned since 1946, is the world's longest-serving current head of state and the longest-reigning monarch in Thai history. The king of Thailand is titled Head of State, Head of the Armed Forces, Adherent of Buddhism, and Upholder of religions.

Thailand is the world's 51st-largest country in terms of total area, with an area of approximately 513,000 km^2 (198,000 sq mi), and is the 20th-most-populous country, with around 64 million people. The capital and largest city is Bangkok, which is Thailand's political, commercial, industrial and cultural hub. About 75–85% of the population is ethnically Tai, which includes the four major regional groups, consisting of Central Thai (Khon Pak Klang): 30%; Northeastern Thai (Khon [Lao] Isan): 22%,Northern Thai (Khon Lanna): 9%; and Southern Thai (Khon Tai): 7%. Thai Chinese, those of significant Chinese heritage, are 14% of the population and up to 40% possess part-Chinese ancestry. Thai Malays represent 3% of the population and the rest belong to minority groups, including Mons, Khmers and various "hill tribes". The country's official language is Thai and the primary religion is Buddhism, which is practised by around 95% of the population.

Thailand experienced rapid economic growth between 1985 and 1996, and is presently a newly industrialized country and a major exporter. Tourism also contributes significantly to the Thai economy. The country was ranked second in the 2014 United Nations Human Development Index (HDI), which measures quality of life according to areas such as life expectancy and income.

There are approximately 2.2 million legal and illegal migrants in Thailand, and the country attracts a significant number of expatriates from developed countries.

THAILAND PROFILE

Location: Thailand is situated in the heart of the Southeast Asian mainland, covering an area of 513,115 sq.km. and extends about 1,620 kilometres from north to south and 775 kilometres from east to west. Thailand borders the Lao People's Democratic Republic and the Union of Myanmar to the North, the Kingdom of Cambodia and the Gulf of Thailand to the East, the Union of Myanmar and the Indian Ocean to the West, and Malaysia to the south.

Capital: Bangkok

Major Cities: North : Chiangmai, South: Songkla, Central region : Ayutthaya and Chonburi, North Eastern : Nakhon Ratchasima and Khon Kaen

Climate: Thailand is a warm and rather humid tropical country with monsoonal climate. Temperatures are highest in March and April with average temperature of 28 degree Celsius to 38 degrees Celsius and humidity averaging between 82.8 percent to 73 percent.

Seasons: Dry : March to May, Rainy: June to October, Cool: November to February.

Population: The population in Thailand is approximately 60 million, of which around 6 million live in the capital city, Bangkok.

Language: The national and official language is Thai while English is widely spoken and understood in major cities, particularly in Bangkok and in business circles.

Religion: Buddhism is the national religion. In Thailand, there is total religious freedom and all faiths are allowed to practice. Under the Thai constitution, the King is Buddhist and upholder of all religions: Buddhism (95 per cent); Islam (3.9 per cent); Christianity (0.5 per cent); and others (0.6 per cent).

Government: Thailand is governed by a democratically elected government with H.M. Bhumibol Adulyadej as Head of State. Under the constitution, the Parliament comprises 270 appointed senators and 391elected Members of Parliament. The Prime Minister is an elected MP and is selected from among the members of the House of Representatives.

Bangkok Metropolitan Administration comes under an elected governor and is divided into 36 districts. Besides Bangkok, there are 76 provinces, administered by appointed governors and divided into districts, sub-districts, and villages.

Regulations for Foreign Visitors to Thailand: Foreign nationals visiting Thailand must possess valid passports or accepted travel documents and appropriate visas before entering the country. Visitors from certain countries are permitted to stay up to 15 days without visas, provided they possess tickets confirming departure within 15 days, while visitors from several other countries are allowed to apply for tourists visas at all ports of entry. Transit visas are granted for up to 30 days and tourist visas for up to 60 days. Non-immigrants, diplomatic and official visas are valid for up to 90 days.

Customs: Narcotics and pornographic materials are strictly prohibited. Permits must be obtained for firearms and certain species of animals and plants. The export of Buddha images, images of deities and antiques is strictly forbidden without prior approval from the Fine Arts Department. Any amount of foreign currency may be brought in for personal use.

Currency: The Baht is the standard currency unit.

> 1 Baht = 100 satangs
> Bank Notes : 10, 20, 50, 100, 500, 1,000 baht
> Coins : 1, 5, and 10 baht

Banks: The country's central bank is the Bank of Thailand. Major Thai commercial banks include the Bangkok Bank, Siam Commercial Bank, Krung Thai Bank, Thai Farmers Bank and Thai Military Bank. Business hours are 10:00 - 17:00 hours, Monday to Friday. Several international banks also have offices in Thailand.

Business Hours: Government and business offices are open from 8:30 to 16:30 hours, Monday to Friday.

Electricity: 220 volts 50 cycles throughout the country

Newspaper & Media: There are over 20 Thai morning dailies in Bangkok. Some of the leading Thai papers include Thai Rath, Daily News, Siam Rath, Matichon, Naew Na, Siam Post, Ban Muang, Krung Thep Turakij, Wattachak and the Manager. Two major English-language dailies are the Bangkok Post and The Nation. There are numerous English-language magazines and local publications in Japanese, Chinese and other European languages. Many major international newspapers, magazines and books are also widely available.

Five television stations, Channels 3, 5, 7, 9 and 11 broadcast local variety shows, newscasts and live coverage of special events. Cable TV is also available by subscription.

For additional analytical, business and investment opportunities information, please contact Global Investment & Business Center, USA at (202) 546-2103. Fax: (202) 546-3275. E-mail: rusric@erols.com

There are over 100 radio stations in Bangkok. All are state-owned but private companies are given air time concessions for their programmes. Broadcasting is done in both Thai and English, with news broadcasting every hour.

Thailand's freedom of the press is considered the strongest in Southeast Asia as evidenced by hundreds of Thai-language publications on virtually every subject.

Health and Medical Facilities: Bangkok has numerous clinics and hospitals catering to a variety of needs. Major public and private hospitals are equipped with the latest medical technology and internationally qualified specialists. Almost all pharmaceuticals are widely available. Drinking of tap water should be avoided.

Telephone Services:

> Direct Assistance: 13 (Bangkok) and 183 (upcountry)
> Long Distance Service: 100
> IDD: 001+country code+area code+phone number
> AT&T USA Direct Service:001-999-11111

Emergency Calls:

> Mobile Police: 191
> Fire Brigade: 199
> Ambulance(BKK): 252-2171-5
> Tourist Information (TAT Head Office): 694-1222 ext. 1000-1004, 282-9773-6
> Tourist Information (Airport Office): Terminal I : 523-8972-3 , Terminal II :535-2669
> Tourist Police: 195, 1155
> Tourist Service Centre: 1155

What To Wear: Light, cool clothes are sensible and a jacket is needed for formal meetings and dining in top restaurants.

Eating Out: Bangkok boasts a dazzling variety of restaurants serving just about every national cuisine from around the world. Thai cuisine is rich and spicy and seafood is considered a national speciality. Thai-grown tropical fruits are legendary.

Shopping: At the top of the shopping list should be Thai silk and gems. It is advisable to buy silk at Jim Thompson, Thaipun or other certified stores which guarantee quality at competitive prices, such as Narai Phan and Thailand Duty - Free shops. Gems should be purchased only from TAT-approved stores to ensure quality. An export permit should be obtained from the government office or shop concerned when purchasing items such as Buddha images, antiques, ivory and leather products or other wildlife products. Main shopping areas are Siam Square, Mah Boon Krong, Central Plaza, World Trade Centre, Silom Complex, Robinson, etc. Normal shopping hours are 10:00-21:00hours.

STRATEGIC INFORMATION

GEOGRAPHY

Location: Southeastern Asia, bordering the Andaman Sea and the Gulf of Thailand, southeast of Burma
Geographic coordinates: 15 00 N, 100 00 E

Map references: Southeast Asia

Area:
total: 514,000 sq km
land: 511,770 sq km
water: 2,230 sq km

Area—comparative: slightly more than twice the size of Wyoming

Land boundaries:
total: 4,863 km
border countries: Burma 1,800 km, Cambodia 803 km, Laos 1,754 km, Malaysia 506 km

Coastline: 3,219 km

Maritime claims:
continental shelf: 200-m depth or to the depth of exploitation
exclusive economic zone: 200 nm
territorial sea: 12 nm

Climate: tropical; rainy, warm, cloudy southwest monsoon (mid-May to September); dry, cool northeast monsoon (November to mid-March); southern isthmus always hot and humid

Terrain: central plain; Khorat Plateau in the east; mountains elsewhere

Elevation extremes:
lowest point: Gulf of Thailand 0 m
highest point: Doi Inthanon 2,576 m

Natural resources: tin, rubber, natural gas, tungsten, tantalum, timber, lead, fish, gypsum, lignite, fluorite

Land use:
arable land: 34%
permanent crops: 6%
permanent pastures: 2%
forests and woodland: 26%
other: 32%

Irrigated land: 44,000 sq km

Natural hazards: land subsidence in Bangkok area resulting from the depletion of the water table; droughts

Environment—current issues: air pollution from vehicle emissions; water pollution from organic and factory wastes; deforestation; soil erosion; wildlife populations threatened by illegal hunting

Environment—international agreements:
party to: Climate Change, Endangered Species, Hazardous Wastes, Marine Life Conservation, Nuclear Test Ban, Ozone Layer Protection, Tropical Timber 83,

For additional analytical, business and investment opportunities information,
please contact Global Investment & Business Center, USA
at (202) 546-2103. Fax: (202) 546-3275. E-mail: rusric@erols.com

Tropical Timber 94
signed, but not ratified: Biodiversity, Climate Change-Kyoto Protocol, Law of the Sea

Geography—note: controls only land route from Asia to Malaysia and Singapore

PEOPLE

Population: 60,609,046

Age structure:
0-14 years: 24% (male 7,364,411; female 7,095,428)
15-64 years: 70% (male 20,878,602; female 21,493,735)
65 years and over: 6% (male 1,664,113; female 2,112,757)

Population growth rate: 0.93%
Birth rate: 16.46 births/1,000 population
Death rate: 7.16 deaths/1,000 population
Net migration rate: 0 migrant(s)/1,000 population

Sex ratio:
at birth: 1.05 male(s)/female *under 15 years:* 1.04 male(s)/female *15-64 years:* 0.97
male(s)/female *65 years and over:* 0.79 male(s)/female
total population: 0.97 male(s)/female

Infant mortality rate: 29.54 deaths/1,000 live births

Life expectancy at birth:
total population: 69.21 years
male: 65.58 years
female: 73.01 years

Total fertility rate: 1.82 children born/woman
Nationality:
noun: Thai (singular and plural)
adjective: Thai
Ethnic groups: Thai 75%, Chinese 14%, other 11%
Religions: Buddhism 95%, Muslim 3.8%, Christianity 0.5%, Hinduism 0.1%, other 0.6% (1991)
Languages: Thai, English (secondary language of the elite), ethnic and regional dialects

Literacy:
definition: age 15 and over can read and write
total population: 93.8%
male: 96%
female: 91.6% (1995 est.)

GOVERNMENT

Country name:
conventional long form: Kingdom of Thailand
conventional short form: Thailand

**For additional analytical, business and investment opportunities information,
please contact Global Investment & Business Center, USA
at (202) 546-2103. Fax: (202) 546-3275. E-mail: rusric@erols.com**

Data code: TH
Government type: constitutional monarchy
Capital: Bangkok

Administrative divisions: 76 provinces (changwat, singular and plural); Amnat Charoen, Ang Thong, Buriram, Chachoengsao, Chai Nat, Chaiyaphum, Chanthaburi, Chiang Mai, Chiang Rai, Chon Buri, Chumphon, Kalasin, Kamphaeng Phet, Kanchanaburi, Khon Kaen, Krabi, Krung Thep Mahanakhon (Bangkok), Lampang, Lamphun, Loei, Lop Buri, Mae Hong Son, Maha Sarakham, Mukdahan, Nakhon Nayok, Nakhon Pathom, Nakhon Phanom, Nakhon Ratchasima, Nakhon Sawan, Nakhon Si Thammarat, Nan, Narathiwat, Nong Bua Lamphu, Nong Khai, Nonthaburi, Pathum Thani, Pattani, Phangnga, Phatthalung, Phayao, Phetchabun, Phetchaburi, Phichit, Phitsanulok, Phra Nakhon Si Ayutthaya, Phrae, Phuket, Prachin Buri, Prachuap Khiri Khan, Ranong, Ratchaburi, Rayong, Roi Et, Sa Kaeo, Sakon Nakhon, Samut Prakan, Samut Sakhon, Samut Songkhram, Sara Buri, Satun, Sing Buri, Sisaket, Songkhla, Sukhothai, Suphan Buri, Surat Thani, Surin, Tak, Trang, Trat, Ubon Ratchathani, Udon Thani, Uthai Thani, Uttaradit, Yala, Yasothon

Independence: 1238 (traditional founding date; never colonized)
National holiday: Birthday of His Majesty the King, 5 December (1927)
Constitution: new constitution signed by King PHUMIPHON on 11 October 2002
Legal system: based on civil law system, with influences of common law; has not accepted compulsory ICJ jurisdiction
Suffrage: 18 years of age; universal and compulsory

Executive branch:

chief of state: King PHUMIPHON Adunyadet, also spelled BHUMIBOL Adulyadej (since 9 June 1946)

head of government: Prime Minister YINGLAK Chinnawat also spelled YINGLUCK Shinawatra (since 8 August 2011); Deputy Prime Minister KITTIRAT Na Ranong (since 28 October 2012); Deputy Prime Minister PHONGTHEP Therkanchana also spelled PHONGTHEP Thepkanchana (since 28 October 2012); Deputy Prime Minister PLODPRASOP Suraswadi (since 28 October 2012); Deputy Prime Minister PRACHA Promnok (since 24 March 2013); Deputy Prime Minister SURAPHONG Towijakchaikun also spelled SURAPONG Tovichakchaikul (since 28 October 2012); Deputy Prime Minister YUKHON Limiaemthong (since 25 March 2013)

cabinet: Council of Ministers
note:there is also a Privy Council advising the king

elections: the monarchy is hereditary; according to the 2007 constitution, the prime minister is elected from among members of the House of Representatives; following national elections for the House of Representatives, the leader of the party positioned to organize a majority coalition usually becomes prime minister by appointment by the king; the prime minister is limited to two four-year terms

Legislative branch:
bicameral National Assembly or Rathasapha consisted of the Senate or Wuthisapha (150 seats; 76 members elected by popular vote representing 75 provinces and 1 metropolitan district (Bangkok), 74 appointed by the Senate Selection Committee; members serve six-year terms) and the House of Representatives or Sapha Phuthaen Ratsadon (500 seats; 375 members elected from 375 single-seat constituencies and 125 elected on proportional party-list basis; members serve four-year terms)

elections: Senate - the Constitutional Court declared the 2 February 2014 election valid (the date of the new election has not been announced); House of Representatives - last election held on 3 July 2011 (next to be held by July 2015)

election results: Senate - percent of vote by party - NA; seats by party - NA; House of Representatives - percent of vote by party - NA; seats by party - PTP 265, DP 159, PJT 34, CTP 19, others 23

note:74 senators were appointed on 19 February 2008 by a seven-member committee headed by the chief of the Constitutional Court; 76 senators were elected on 2 March 2008; elections to the Senate are non-partisan; registered political party members are disqualified from being senators

Judicial branch: Constitutional Court, Supreme Court of Justice, and Supreme Administrative Court; all judges are appointed by the king; the king's appointments to the Constitutional Courtare made upon the advice of the Senate; the nine Constitutional Court judges are drawn from the Supreme Court of Justice and Supreme Administrative Court as well as from among substantive experts in law and social sciences outside the judiciary

Political parties and leaders: Chat Thai Phattana Party or CP (Thai Nation Development Party) [CHUMPON Silpa-archa]; Democrat Party or DP (Prachathipat Party) [ABHISIT Wetchachiwa, also spelled ABHISIT Vejjajiva]; Motherland Party (Phuea Phaendin Party) [CHANCHAI Chairungrueng]; Phuea Thai Party (For Thais Party) or PTP [CHAWALIT Yongchaiyut]; Phumchai (Bhumjai) Thai Party or PCT (Thai Pride) [CHAWARAT Chanvirakun]; Royalist People's Party (Pracharaj) [SANOH Thienthong]; Ruam Jai Thai Party (Thai Unity Party) [WANNARAT Channukun]

International organization participation: APEC, AsDB, ASEAN, CCC, CP, ESCAP, FAO, G-77, IAEA, IBRD, ICAO, ICFTU, ICRM, IDA, IFAD, IFC, IFRCS, IHO, ILO, IMF, IMO, Inmarsat, Intelsat, Interpol, IOC, IOM, ISO, ITU, NAM, OPCW, PCA, UN, UNCTAD, UNESCO, UNHCR, UNIDO, UNIKOM, UNMIBH, UNU, UPU, WCL, WFTU, WHO, WIPO, WMO, WToO, WTrO

Diplomatic representation in the US:
chief of mission: Ambassador NIT Phibunsongkhram
chancery: 1024 Wisconsin Avenue NW, Washington, DC 20007
telephone: (202) 944-3600
FAX: (202) 944-3611
consulate(s) general: Chicago, Los Angeles, and New York

Diplomatic representation from the US:
chief of mission: Ambassador Richard HECKLINGER
embassy: 120 Wireless Road, Bangkok
mailing address: APO AP 96546
telephone: [66] (2) 205-4000
FAX: [66] (2) 254-2990
consulate(s) general: Chiang Mai

Flag description: five horizontal bands of red (top), white, blue (double width), white, and red

ECONOMY

Economy - overview:

With a well-developed infrastructure, a free-enterprise economy, generally pro-investment policies, and strong export industries, Thailand enjoyed solid growth from 2000 to 2008 - averaging more than 4% per year - as it recovered from the Asian financial crisis of 1997-98. Thai exports - mostly machinery and electronic components, agricultural commodities, and jewelry - continue to drive the economy, accounting for as much as three-quarters of GDP. The global financial crisis of 2008-09 severely cut Thailand's exports, with most sectors experiencing double-digit drops. In 2009, the economy contracted about 2.8%. The Thai government is focusing on financing domestic infrastructure projects and stimulus programs to revive the economy, as external trade is still recovering and persistent internal political tension and investment disputes threaten to damage the investment climate.

GDP (purchasing power parity):
$538.6 billion (2009 est.)
country comparison to the world: 25
$554.1 billion (2008 est.)
$540.6 billion (2007 est.)
note: data are in 2009 US dollars

GDP (official exchange rate):
$269.6 billion (2009 est.)

GDP - real growth rate:
-2.8% (2009 est.)
country comparison to the world: 160
2.5% (2008 est.)
4.9% (2007 est.)

GDP - per capita (PPP):
$8,100 (2009 est.)
country comparison to the world: 120
$8,400 (2008 est.)
$8,300 (2007 est.)
note: data are in 2009 US dollars

GDP - composition by sector:
agriculture: 12.3%
industry: 44%
services: 43.7% (2009 est.)

Labor force:
38.24 million (2009 est.)
country comparison to the world: 15

Labor force - by occupation:
agriculture: 42.4%
industry: 19.7%
services: 37.9% (2008 est.)

Unemployment rate:
1.6% (2009 est.)
country comparison to the world: 9
1.4% (2008 est.)

Population below poverty line:

9.6% (2006 est.)

Household income or consumption by percentage share:
lowest 10%: 1.6%
highest 10%: 33.7% (2006)

Distribution of family income - Gini index:
43 (2006)
country comparison to the world: 50
42 (2002)

Investment (gross fixed):
21% of GDP (2009 est.)
country comparison to the world: 76

Budget:
revenues: $40.9 billion
expenditures: $51.5 billion (FY10 est.)

Public debt:
45.9% of GDP (2009 est.)
country comparison to the world: 57
37.9% of GDP (2008 est.)

Inflation rate (consumer prices):
-0.9% (2009)
country comparison to the world: 8
5.5% (2008 est.)

Central bank discount rate:
1.75% (31 December 2009)
country comparison to the world: 129
3.25% (31 December 2008)

Commercial bank prime lending rate:
6.05% (31 December 2009)
country comparison to the world: 127
7.04% (31 December 2008)

Stock of money:
$35.35 billion (31 December 2009)
country comparison to the world: 27
$28.76 billion (31 December 2008)

Stock of quasi money:
$283.6 billion (31 December 2009)
country comparison to the world: 14
$237.5 billion (31 December 2008)

Stock of domestic credit:
$301 billion (31 December 2009)
country comparison to the world: 27
$274.1 billion (31 December 2008)

For additional analytical, business and investment opportunities information,
please contact Global Investment & Business Center, USA
at (202) 546-2103. Fax: (202) 546-3275. E-mail: rusric@erols.com

Market value of publicly traded shares:
$176.7 billion (31 December 2009)
country comparison to the world: 43
$101.8 billion (31 December 2008)
$196 billion (31 December 2007)

Agriculture - products:
rice, cassava (tapioca), rubber, corn, sugarcane, coconuts, soybeans

Industries:
tourism, textiles and garments, agricultural processing, beverages, tobacco, cement, light manufacturing such as jewelry and electric appliances, computers and parts, integrated circuits, furniture, plastics, automobiles and automotive parts; world's second-largest tungsten producer and third-largest tin producer

Industrial production growth rate:
-8.7% (2009 est.)
country comparison to the world: 134

Electricity - production:
148.2 billion kWh (2008 est.)
country comparison to the world: 24

Electricity - consumption:
134.4 billion kWh (2008 est.)
country comparison to the world: 24

Electricity - exports:
846 million kWh (2009 est.)

Electricity - imports:
2.313 billion kWh (2009 est.)

Oil - production:
1.073 million bbl/day (2009 est.)
country comparison to the world: 22

Oil - consumption:
690,400 bbl/day (2008 est.)
country comparison to the world: 26

Oil - exports:
269,100 bbl/day (2009 est.)
country comparison to the world: 43

Oil - imports:
1.695 million bbl/day (2009 est.)
country comparison to the world: 13

Oil - proved reserves:
441 million bbl (1 January 2009 est.)
country comparison to the world: 48

Natural gas - production:

For additional analytical, business and investment opportunities information,
please contact Global Investment & Business Center, USA
at (202) 546-2103. Fax: (202) 546-3275. E-mail: rusric@erols.com

28.76 billion cu m (2008 est.)
country comparison to the world: 27

Natural gas - consumption:
37.31 billion cu m (2008 est.)
country comparison to the world: 23

Natural gas - exports:
0 cu m (2008 est.)
country comparison to the world: 108

Natural gas - imports:
8.55 billion cu m (2008 est.)
country comparison to the world: 25

Natural gas - proved reserves:
317.1 billion cu m (1 January 2009 est.)
country comparison to the world: 40

Current account balance:
$20.29 billion (2009 est.)
country comparison to the world: 15
-$113 million (2008 est.)

Exports:
$150.9 billion (2009 est.)
country comparison to the world: 26
$175.3 billion (2008 est.)

Exports - commodities:
textiles and footwear, fishery products, rice, rubber, jewelry, automobiles, computers and
electrical appliances

Exports - partners:
US 10.9%, China 10.6%, Japan 10.3%, Hong Kong 6.2%, Australia 5.6%, Malaysia 5% (2009
est.)

Imports:
$131.5 billion (2009 est.)
country comparison to the world: 27
$157.3 billion (2008 est.)

Imports - commodities:
capital goods, intermediate goods and raw materials, consumer goods, fuels

Imports - partners:
Japan 18.7%, China 12.7%, Malaysia 6.4%, US 6.3%, UAE 5%, Singapore 4.3%, South Korea
4.1% (2009 est.)

Reserves of foreign exchange and gold:
$138.4 billion (31 December 2009 est.)
country comparison to the world: 10
$111 billion (31 December 2008 est.)

For additional analytical, business and investment opportunities information,
please contact Global Investment & Business Center, USA
at (202) 546-2103. Fax: (202) 546-3275. E-mail: rusric@erols.com

Debt - external:
$66.3 billion (31 December 2009 est.)
country comparison to the world: 41
$65.09 billion (31 December 2008)

Stock of direct foreign investment - at home:
$93.84 billion (31 December 2009 est.)
country comparison to the world: 36
$88.52 billion (31 December 2008)

Stock of direct foreign investment - abroad:
$10.52 billion (31 December 2009 est.)
country comparison to the world: 45
$7.013 billion (31 December 2007 est.)

Exchange rates:
baht per US dollar - 34.318 (2009), 33.37 (2008), 34.52 (2007), 37.882 (2006), 40.22 (2005)

COMMUNICATIONS

Telephones - main lines in use:	7.035 million
Telephones - mobile cellular:	27.379 million
Telephone system:	*general assessment:* high quality system, especially in urban areas like Bangkok; WTO requirement for privatization of telecom sector is planned to be complete by 2006 *domestic:* fixed line system provided by both a government owned and commercial provider; wireless service expanding rapidly and outpacing fixed lines *international:* country code - 66; satellite earth stations - 2 Intelsat (1 Indian Ocean and 1 Pacific Ocean); landing country for APCN submarine cable
Radio broadcast stations:	AM 204, FM 334, shortwave 6
Television broadcast stations:	111
Internet country code:	.th
Internet hosts:	786,226
Internet users:	8.42 million

TRANSPORTATION

Railways:
total: 4,623 km
narrow gauge: 4,623 km 1.000-m gauge (99 km double track)

Highways:
total: 64,600 km

For additional analytical, business and investment opportunities information,
please contact Global Investment & Business Center, USA
at (202) 546-2103. Fax: (202) 546-3275. E-mail: rusric@erols.com

paved: 62,985 km
unpaved: 1,615 km

Waterways: 3,999 km principal waterways; 3,701 km with navigable depths of 0.9 m or more throughout the year; numerous minor waterways navigable by shallow-draft native craft

Pipelines: petroleum products 67 km; natural gas 350 km

Ports and harbors: Bangkok, Laem Chabang, Pattani, Phuket, Sattahip, Si Racha, Songkhla

Merchant marine:
total: 293 ships (1,000 GRT or over) totaling 1,848,626 GRT/2,989,382 DWT
ships by type: bulk 41, cargo 135, chemical tanker 5, combination bulk 1, container 13, liquefied gas tanker 17, multifunction large-load carrier 3, oil tanker 61, passenger 1, refrigerated cargo 11, roll-on/roll-off cargo 2, short-sea passenger 1, specialized tanker 2

Airports: 107

Airports—with paved runways:
total: 56
over 3,047 m: 6
2,438 to 3,047 m: 9
1,524 to 2,437 m: 17
914 to 1,523 m: 20
under 914 m: 4

Airports—with unpaved runways:
total: 51
1,524 to 2,437 m: 1
914 to 1,523 m: 15
under 914 m: 35

Heliports: 3

MILITARY

Military branches: Royal Thai Army, Royal Thai Navy (includes Royal Thai Marine Corps), Royal Thai Air Force, Paramilitary Forces

Military manpower—military age: 18 years of age
Military manpower—availability:
males age 15-49: 17,486,014
Military manpower—fit for military service:
males age 15-49: 10,536,417
Military manpower—reaching military age annually:
males: 585,562
Military expenditures—dollar figure: $1.95 billion
Military expenditures—percent of GDP: 2.5%

TRANSNATIONAL ISSUES

For additional analytical, business and investment opportunities information, please contact Global Investment & Business Center, USA at (202) 546-2103. Fax: (202) 546-3275. E-mail: rusric@erols.com

Disputes—international: parts of the border with Laos are indefinite; maritime boundary with Vietnam resolved, August 2002; parts of border with Cambodia are indefinite; maritime boundary with Cambodia not clearly defined; sporadic conflict with Burma over alignment of border

Illicit drugs: a minor producer of opium, heroin, and marijuana; major illicit transit point for heroin en route to the international drug market from Burma and Laos; eradication efforts have reduced the area of cannabis cultivation and shifted some production to neighboring countries; opium poppy cultivation has been reduced by eradication efforts; also a drug money-laundering center; minor role in amphetamine production for regional consumption; increasing indigenous abuse of methamphetamines and heroin

IMPORTANT INFORMATION FOR UNDERSTANDING THAILAND

There are conflicting opinions as to the origins of the Thais. Three decades ago it could be said with presumed certainty that the Thais originated in northwestern Szechuan in China about 4,500 years ago and later migrated down to their present homeland. However, this theory has been altered by the discovery of remarkable prehistoric artifacts in the village of Ban Chiang in the Nong Han District of Udon Thani Province in the Northeast. These include evidence of bronze metallurgy going back 3,500 years, as well as other indications of a far more sophisticated culture than any previously suspected by archaeologists. It now appears that the Thais might have originated here in Thailand and later scattered to various parts of Asia, including some parts of China.

"Siam" is the name by which the country was known to the world until 1939 and again between 1945 and 1949. On May 11, 1949, an official proclamation changed the name of the country to "Prathet Thai", or "Thailand", by which it has since been known. The word "Thai" means "free", and therefore "Thailand" means "Land of the Free".

PROFILE

Geography
Area: 513,115 sq. km. (198,114 sq. mi.); equivalent to the size of France, or slightly smaller than Texas.
Cities: *Capital*--Bangkok (population 9,668,854); Nakhon Ratchasima (pop. 437,386 for Muang district and 2,565,685 for the whole province), Chiang Mai (pop. 247,672 for Muang district and 1,595,855 for the whole province).
Terrain: Densely populated central plain; northeastern plateau; mountain range in the west; southern isthmus joins the land mass with Malaysia.
Climate: Tropical monsoon.

People
Nationality: *Noun and adjective*--Thai.
Population (2009 est.): 67.0 million. (Data based on the Thailand National Statistic Office and the National Economic and Social Development Board.)
Labor force (2009 est.): 38.4 million.
Annual population growth rate (2009 est.): 0.5%.
Ethnic groups: Thai 89%, other 11%.
Religions: Buddhist 93%-94%, Muslim 5%-6%, Christian 1%, Hindu, Brahmin, other.
Languages: Thai (official language); English is the second language of the elite; Malay and regional languages and dialects.
Education: *Years compulsory*--9. *Literacy*--94.9% male, 90.5% female.
Health (2008 est.): *Infant mortality rate*--18.23/1,000. *Life expectancy*--70.51 years male, 75.27 years female.

Government
Type: Constitutional monarchy.
Constitution: Thailand adopted its current constitution following an August 19, 2007 referendum.
Independence: Never colonized; traditional founding date 1238.
Branches: *Executive*--King (chief of state), Prime Minister (head of government). *Legislative*--bicameral, with a fully-elected House of Representatives and a partially-elected Senate. *Judicial*--composed of the Constitutional Tribunal, the Courts of Justice, and the Administrative Courts.
Administrative subdivisions: 77 provinces, including Bangkok municipality, subdivided into 877 districts, 7,255 tambon administration, and 74,944 villages.
Political parties: Multi-party system; Communist Party is prohibited.
Suffrage: Universal and compulsory at 18 years of age.

Economy
GDP (2010 prelim.): $317 billion. (Data based on the National Economic and Social Development Board)
Annual GDP growth rate (2010 prelim.): 7.8%.
Inflation rates (2010): 3.3% (headline) and 0.9% (excluding energy and food prices).
Per capita income (2010 prelim.): $4,716.
Unemployment rate (2010 prelim.): 1.0% of total labor force.
Natural resources: Tin, rubber, natural gas, tungsten, tantalum, timber, lead, fish, gypsum, lignite, fluorite.
Agriculture (12% of GDP): *Products*--rice, tapioca, rubber, corn, sugarcane, coconuts, soybeans.
Industry: *Types*--tourism, textiles, garments, agricultural processing, cement, integrated circuits, jewelry, electronics, petrochemical, and auto assembly.
Trade (2010 preliminary): *Merchandise exports*--$188.8 billion. *Products*--automatic data processing machines and parts, automobiles and parts, precious stones and jewelry, refined fuels, rubber, electronic integrated circuits, polymers of ethylene and propylene, rice, iron and steel and their products, rubber products, chemical products. *Major markets*--ASEAN, EU, China, U.S., Japan, and Hong Kong. *Merchandise imports*--$175.5 billion. *Products*--crude oil, machinery and parts, electrical machinery and parts, chemicals, iron and steel and their products, electrical circuits panels, computers and parts, other metal ores and metal waste scrap, ships and boats and floating structure, jewelry including silver and gold. *Major suppliers*--Japan, ASEAN, China, the Middle East, EU, and U.S.

PEOPLE

Thailand (previously Siam) has always been a multi-ethnic, multi-confessional society. More than 85% speak a variant of Thai and share a common culture, though there is a strong sense of regional identity and pride in many areas of Thailand. Roughly one-third of the population is in central Thailand, including Bangkok; one-third in the northeast, with significant Lao and Khmer heritage; 20% in the north; and 15% in the south. Ethnic Malay Muslims comprise a majority in the three southernmost provinces.

Central Thai is the language taught in schools and used in government. Lao, as well as "Isaan dialect", is spoken widely in northeastern Thailand; "Gam Muang" or northern dialect is spoken in the north; and a southern Thai dialect in the mid-south. Several other Tai dialects are spoken among smaller groups, such as the Shan (Tai Yai), Lue, and Phutai.

Up to 12% of Thai are of significant Chinese heritage, but the Sino-Thai community is the best integrated in Southeast Asia. Other groups include the Khmer in border provinces with Cambodia; the Mon, who are substantially assimilated with the Thai; and the Vietnamese. Smaller mountain-dwelling tribes, such as the Hmong, Mein, and the Karen, number about 788,024.

The population is mostly rural, concentrated in the rice-growing areas of the central, northeastern, and northern regions. However, as Thailand continues to industrialize, its urban population--31.6% of total population, principally in the Bangkok area--is growing.

Thailand's highly successful government-sponsored family planning program has resulted in a dramatic decline in population growth from 3.1% in 1960 to less than 1% today. Life expectancy also has risen, a positive reflection of Thailand's public health efforts. Thailand's model intervention programs in the 1990s also averted what could have been a major AIDS epidemic. Even so, today, approximately 1.4% of the adult population lives with HIV/AIDS.

The constitution mandates at least 12 years of free education; however, only 9 years are compulsory. In early 2009, the Abhisit administration put into effect a program to provide 15 years of free education (3 years in preschool and grades 1-12). Education accounts for approximately 18.0% of total government expenditures.

Theravada Buddhism is the major religion of Thailand, practiced by about 90% of its people. The government permits religious diversity, and other major religions are represented, with Muslim communities scattered throughout Thailand, and in larger numbers in the southern region. Spirit worship/animism and Hindu-Brahmic rituals are widely practiced.

HISTORY

Southeast Asia has been inhabited for more than half a million years. Archaeological studies suggest that by 4000 BC, communities in what is now Thailand had emerged as centers of early bronze metallurgy. This development, along with the cultivation of wet rice, provided the impetus for social and political organization. Research suggests that these innovations may actually have been transmitted from there to the rest of Asia, including to China.

The Thai are related linguistically to Tai groups originating in southern China. Migrations from southern China to Southeast Asia may have occurred in the 6th and 7th centuries. Malay, Mon, and Khmer civilizations flourished in the region prior to the arrival of the ethnic Tai.

The Thai traditionally date the founding of their nation to the 13th century, though kingdoms of Thai peoples existed in the north and in the south before then. According to tradition, in 1238, Thai chieftains overthrew their Khmer overlords at Sukhothai and established a Thai kingdom. After its decline, a new Thai kingdom emerged in 1350 on the Chao Praya River at Ayutthaya. At the same time, there was the equally important Tai kingdom of Lanna, centered in Chiang Mai, which for centuries rivaled Sukhothai and Ayutthaya, and still defines northern Thai identity; a southern kingdom centered in Nakhon Si Thammarat in the south also pre-dated Sukhothai.

The first ruler of the Kingdom of Ayutthaya, King Rama Thibodi, made two important contributions to Thai history: the establishment and promotion of Theravada Buddhism as the official religion--to differentiate his kingdom from the neighboring Hindu kingdom of Angkor--and the compilation of the Dharmashastra, a legal code based on Hindu sources and traditional Thai custom. The Dharmashastra remained a tool of Thai law until late in the 19th century. Beginning with the Portuguese in the 16th century, Ayutthaya had some contact with the West, but until the 1800s, its relations with neighboring kingdoms and principalities, as well as with China, were of primary importance.

After more than 400 years of power, in 1767, the Kingdom of Ayutthaya was brought down by invading Burmese armies and its capital burned. After a single-reign capital established at Thonburi by Taksin, a new capital city was founded in 1782, across the Chao Phraya at the site of present-day Bangkok, by the founder of the current Chakri dynasty. The first Chakri king was crowned Rama I. Rama I's heirs became increasingly concerned with the threat of European colonialism after British victories in neighboring Burma in 1826.

For additional analytical, business and investment opportunities information, please contact Global Investment & Business Center, USA at (202) 546-2103. Fax: (202) 546-3275. E-mail: rusric@erols.com

The first Thai recognition of Western power in the region was the Treaty of Amity and Commerce with the United Kingdom in 1826. In 1833, the United States began diplomatic exchanges with Siam, as Thailand was called until 1938. However, it was during the later reigns of Rama IV (or King Mongkut, 1851-68), and his son Rama V (King Chulalongkorn (1868-1910), that Thailand established firm rapprochement with Western powers. The Thais believe it was the diplomatic skills of these monarchs, combined with the modernizing reforms of the governments, that made Siam the only country in South and Southeast Asia to avoid European colonization.

In 1932, a bloodless coup transformed Thailand from an absolute to a constitutional monarchy. King Prajadhipok (Rama VII) initially accepted this change but later surrendered the kingship to his 10-year-old nephew. Upon his abdication, King Prajadhipok said that the obligation of a ruler was to reign for the good of the whole people, not for a select few.

Although nominally a democracy with a constitutional monarchy after 1932, Thailand was ruled by a series of military governments interspersed with brief periods of democracy. Following the 1932 revolution that imposed constitutional limits on the monarchy, Thai politics was dominated for a half-century by the military and bureaucratic elite. Changes of government were effected primarily by means of a long series of mostly bloodless coups. Thailand was occupied by the Japanese during the Second World War until Japan's defeat in 1945.

Beginning with a brief experiment in democracy during the mid-1970s (the so-called "October generation" between 1973-76), civilian democratic political institutions slowly gained greater authority, culminating in 1988 when Chatichai Choonhaven--leader of the Thai Nation Party-- assumed office as the country's first democratically elected Prime Minister in more than a decade. In 1991, yet another bloodless coup ended his term. After a year-long largely civilian interim government and inconclusive elections, former army commander Suchinda Krapayoon was appointed Prime Minister. The military violently suppressed demonstrations in May 1992, with at least 50 protesters killed. Reaction to the violence, including a televised meeting with King Bhumibol, forced Suchinda to resign, leading to new elections in September 1992.

Political parties that had opposed the military in May 1992 won by a narrow majority, and Democrat Party leader Chuan Leekpai served as Prime Minister until May 1995. The Thai Nation Party won the largest number of parliamentary seats in subsequent elections, with party leader Banharn Silpa-Archa serving as Prime Minister for little more than a year. New Aspiration Party leader Chavalit Youngchaiyudh formed a coalition government after November 1996 elections. The onset of the Asian financial crisis caused a loss of confidence in the Chavalit government, led to a new constitution, and returned Chuan Leekpai to power in November 1997.

In January 2001, telecommunications billionaire Thaksin Shinawatra and his new Thai Rak Thai (TRT) party won a decisive plurality victory on a populist platform of economic growth and development. Thaksin's premiership was marked by a confident foreign policy, implementation of his populist policies, and accusations of anti-democratic actions, including undermining independent bodies, limiting freedom of the press, and a 2003 war on drugs which led to 1,300 unsolved murders. In February 2005, Thaksin was re-elected by an overwhelming majority, sweeping 377 out of 500 parliamentary seats for Thailand's first-ever single-party outright electoral victory. Soon after Prime Minister Thaksin's second term began, allegations of corruption emerged against his government. Peaceful anti-government mass demonstrations grew, and hundreds of thousands marched in the streets to demand Thaksin's resignation. Prime Minister Thaksin dissolved the parliament in February 2006 and called snap elections in April. The main opposition parties boycotted the polls, and the judiciary subsequently annulled the elections.

Before new elections could be held, in September 2006 a group of top military officers overthrew the caretaker Thaksin administration in a non-violent coup d'etat, repealed the 1997 constitution, and dissolved both houses of parliament. The coup leaders promulgated an interim constitution and appointed Surayud Chulanont as interim Prime Minister. In a national referendum in August 2007, a majority of Thai voters approved a new constitution drafted by an assembly appointed by the coup leaders. The interim government held multi-party elections under provisions of the new constitution in December 2007, and the pro-Thaksin People's Power Party (PPP) won a plurality of 233 of the 480 seats in the lower house of parliament. PPP leader Samak Sundaravej formed a coalition government and formally took office as Prime Minister in February 2008.

Samak was forced from office in September 2008 by a Constitutional Court ruling that he had violated the constitution's conflict of interest provisions by hosting a televised cooking show. His successor, Somchai Wongsawat, PPP leader and brother-in-law of former Prime Minister Thaksin, also was forced from office by the Constitutional Court when it dissolved the PPP and two other coalition parties on December 2, 2008 for election law violations in the December 2007 elections. A split among ex-PPP members of parliament paved the way for parliament's election of Democrat Party leader Abhisit Vejjajiva as Prime Minister on December 15, 2008.

Efforts by the two PPP leaders to amend the 2007 constitution and provide amnesty to banned politicians, including ex-Prime Minister Thaksin, led to a renewal of street protests in mid-2008, some of which resulted in violence between security forces and protesters and between pro- and anti-government demonstrators. In 2008, anti-government "yellow-shirt" protesters occupied Government House from late August until early December; blockaded parliament in October; and occupied and forced the closure of Bangkok's airports for several days in late November through early December. "Red-shirt" protests against the Abhisit government commenced in early 2009, leading to the disruption of a major Asian summit in Pattaya and riots in Bangkok in April 2009.

The "red-shirts" continued to hold short demonstrations through 2009 and into 2010 and intensified their protests on March 12, 2010, 2 weeks after the Supreme Court ruled that the government seize $1.4 billion of Thaksin's assets. Demonstrators occupied an area near Democracy Monument and Government House; a few weeks later they established a second protest site in the heart of Bangkok's shopping district. The tense standoff between government security forces and protesters came to a head on April 10; 25 people were killed in street clashes, 5 of them security personnel. The protesters subsequently consolidated their presence around the Ratchaprasong intersection in central Bangkok, effectively shutting down the commercial heart of the city.

Government efforts to negotiate a settlement with "red-shirt" leaders ultimately failed, and on May 14 troops began to seal off the protest site. A week of street battles ensued, climaxing on May 19 when the "red-shirt" leaders surrendered to police and in the aftermath several buildings, including Thailand's largest shopping mall, were torched by elements of the "red-shirt" demonstrators. Protesters also set fire to government offices in several provinces. Ninety-two people were killed and over 1,800 injured during the 2-month protest. Roughly half of the "red-shirt" leaders were arrested or surrendered, with others fleeing abroad, presumed to be hiding in Cambodia. "Red-shirt" protests continued at regular intervals throughout the rest of 2010, though none approached the violence seen in the first half of the year.

Thailand's southern border provinces have long been host to an ethno-nationalist Malay Muslim separatist movement rallying around a regional "Patani" identity. Since 2004, separatists have conducted an increasingly violent insurgency in the provinces of Narathiwat, Yala, Pattani, and Songkhla against symbols and representatives of central government authority, as well as against civilians, both Buddhist and Muslim, which has resulted in thousands of deaths.

GOVERNMENT AND POLITICAL CONDITIONS

Thailand is a constitutional monarchy. From 1992 and until the 2006 coup, the country was considered a functioning democracy with constitutional changes of government. Generally free and fair multi-party elections held in December 2007 subsequently restored democratic governance 1 year after the coup. The King has little direct power under Thailand's constitutions but is a symbol of national identity and unity. King Bhumibol (Rama IX)--who has been on the throne since 1946--commands enormous popular respect and moral authority, which he has used on occasion to resolve political crises that have threatened national stability.

Under the 2007 constitution, the National Assembly consists of two chambers--the Senate and the House of Representatives. The Senate is a non-partisan body with 150 members, 76 of whom are directly elected (one per province). The remaining 74 are appointed by a panel comprised of judges and senior independent officials from a list of candidates compiled by the Election Commission. The House has 480 members, 400 of whom are directly elected from constituent districts and the remainder drawn proportionally from party lists. Constitutional amendments that would change the number and manner of election of House members were under consideration as of January 2011, in anticipation of elections later in 2011.

Thailand's legal system blends principles of traditional Thai and Western laws. Under the constitution, the Constitutional Court is the highest court of appeals, though its jurisdiction is limited to clearly defined constitutional issues. Its members are nominated by a committee of judges, leaders in parliament, and senior independent officials, whose nominees are confirmed by the Senate and appointed by the King. The Courts of Justice have jurisdiction over criminal and civil cases and are organized in three tiers: Courts of First Instance, the Court of Appeals, and the Supreme Court of Justice. Administrative courts have jurisdiction over suits between private parties and the government, and cases in which one government entity is suing another. In Thailand's southern border provinces, where Muslims constitute the majority of the population, Provincial Islamic Committees have limited jurisdiction over probate, family, marriage, and divorce cases.

Thailand's 77 provinces include the metropolis of greater Bangkok. Bangkok's governor is popularly elected, but those of the remaining provinces are career civil servants appointed by the Ministry of Interior.

Principal Government Officials

Portfolio	Minister	Deputy Minister
Prime Minister	Yingluck Shinawatra	
Deputy Prime Minister	Yongyuth Wichaidit (resigned 30 September 2012)	
Deputy Prime Minister	Pol. Capt Chalerm Yubamrung	
Deputy Prime Minister	Gen Yuthasak Sasiprapha	
Deputy Prime Minister	Kittiratt Na-Ranong	
Deputy Prime Minister	Chumpol Silpa-archa	
The Office of the Prime Minister	Woravat Au-apinyakul	
	Nalinee Taweesin	
	Niwatthamrong Boonsongpaisan	

Ministry of Interior	Yongyuth Wichaidit	Chuchat Hansawat
		Thanit Thienthong
Ministry of Justice	Pol. Gen Pracha Promnok	
Ministry of Defence	ACM Sukampol Suwannathat	
Ministry of Finance	Kittiratt Na-Ranong	Tanusak Lek-uthai
		Wirun Techapaiboon
Ministry of Foreign Affairs	Surapong Towijakchaikul	
Ministry of Social Development and Human Security	Santi Prompat	
Ministry of Agriculture and Cooperatives	Theera Wongsamut	Nattawut Saikua
Ministry of Transport	Charupong Ruangsuwan	Pol. Lt Gen Chat Kuldilok
		Chadchart Sittipunt
Ministry of Natural Resource and Environment	Preecha Rengsomboonsuk	
Ministry of Information and Communication Technology	Grp Cpt Anudith Nakornthap	
Ministry of Energy	Arak Chonlathanont	
Ministry of Commerce	Boonsong Teriyapirom	Phum Saraphol
		Siriwat Kachornprasart
Ministry of Labour	Padermchai Sasomsap	
Ministry of Culture	Sukumol Kunplome	
Ministry of Science and Technology	Dr. Plodprasop Suraswadi	
Ministry of Education	Suchart Thadathamrongvej	Sakda Khongphet
Ministry of Public Health	Witthaya Buranasiri	Surawit Khonsomboon
Ministry of Industry	MR Pongsavas Svasti	
Ministry of Tourism and Sports	Chumpol Silpa-archa	

Thailand maintains an **embassy** in the United States at 1024 Wisconsin Ave. NW, Washington DC 20007 (tel. 202-944-3600). Consulates are located in New York City, Chicago, and Los Angeles.

ECONOMY

The Thai economy is export-dependent, with exports of goods and services equivalent to nearly 70% of GDP in 2010. Thailand's recovery from the 1997-1998 Asian financial crisis (which brought a double-digit drop in GDP) relied largely on external demand from the United States and other foreign markets. From 2001-2006, the administration of former Prime Minister Thaksin embraced a "dual track" economic policy that combined domestic stimulus programs with Thailand's traditional promotion of open markets and foreign investment. Real GDP growth strengthened sharply from 2.2% in 2001 to 7.1% in 2003 and 6.3% in 2004. In 2005-2007, economic expansion moderated, averaging 4.9% real GDP growth, due to domestic political uncertainty, rising violence in Thailand's three southernmost provinces, and repercussions from the devastating Indian Ocean tsunami of 2004. Thailand's economy in 2007 relied heavily on resilient export growth (at an 18.2% annual rate), particularly in the automobile, petrochemicals, and electronics sectors.

Political uncertainty and the global financial crisis in 2008 weakened Thailand's economic growth by reducing domestic and international demand for both its goods and services (including tourism). Due to minimum exposure to toxic assets, Thai banks experienced limited direct impact from the global financial crisis. Nonetheless, Thai economic growth slowed to 2.5% in 2008, with fourth-quarter growth dropping below zero. In 2009, the contraction continued. Over the first three quarters, GDP contracted by 5.0% year-on-year on average and hit bottom in the first quarter. To offset weak external demand and to shore up confidence, the Abhisit administration introduced two non-budgetary stimulus packages worth $43.4 billion focusing on key sectors such as mass transit and transportation, irrigation, education, public health, and energy. The Thai economy reversed to positive growth in the fourth quarter (5.9% year-on-year), improving the 2009 full-year average to minus 2.3% year-on-year.

In the first quarter of 2010, the Thai economy surged by 12.0% year-on-year, the highest quarterly growth since 1995. The uptick was mostly due to strong exports (up 32%) from continued global recovery; despite the March-May political protests in Bangkok, growth continued through the second and third quarter of the year. The Thai economy expanded by 9.3% (year-on-year) during the first three quarters of 2010, the second-strongest performance in Southeast Asia, second only to Singapore. The government estimated nearly 8% growth (year-on-year) for full-year 2010 and expects growth to continue into 2011, but at a lower rate (3%-5%). Growth in 2011 is expected to be driven by exports and also domestic demand. Political risk related to the anticipated 2011 general elections, continued appreciation of the baht, and the uncertainties of Thailand's major trading partners' economic recovery also could affect the economy. Inflation is expected to gradually climb from the 2010 level (3.3%) to between 3% and 5%, due in large part to higher world commodity prices.

The Royal Thai Government welcomes foreign investment, and investors who are willing to meet certain requirements can apply for special investment privileges through the Board of Investment. U.S. investors may qualify for additional privileges under the Treaty of Amity and Economic Relations. To attract additional foreign investment, the government of Prime Minister Abhisit has promised to look for ways to expand investment opportunities, focusing more on green technology/manufacturers.

The organized labor movement remains weak and divided in Thailand. Less than 2% of the total work force is unionized, although nearly 10% of industrial workers and more than 59% of state enterprise workers are unionized. In 2009, efforts to restructure the State Railway authority met resistance from the powerful railways union, including a short strike that halted trains nationwide, showing that organized labor still has potential political clout. As a result of the global financial crisis and business restructuring, employers hired large numbers of short-term contract workers. While employers claimed to have done this in order to maintain business flexibility for greater competitiveness during financially uncertain times, labor advocates viewed these actions as reducing job security and attempts to weaken the organized labor movement.

Roughly 40% of Thailand's labor force is employed in agriculture, although agriculture accounts for only 12% of GDP (data based on the Thai National Statistics Office.) Rice is the country's most important crop; Thailand is the largest exporter in the world rice market. Other agricultural commodities produced in significant amounts include fish and fishery products, tapioca, rubber, corn, and sugar. Exports of processed foods such as canned tuna, canned pineapples, and frozen shrimp are also significant.

Thailand's increasingly diversified manufacturing sector is the largest contributor to growth. Industries registering rapid increases in production have included computers and electronics, furniture, wood products, canned food, toys, plastic products, gems, and jewelry. High-technology products such as integrated circuits and parts, hard disc drives, electrical appliances, vehicles, and vehicle parts are now leading Thailand's growth in exports. With stronger exports and a rise in inflationary pressure, the Bank of Thailand started to tighten its monetary policy in mid-July 2010 after having followed a low interest rate policy since April 2009. Large surpluses in both the current and capital accounts contributed to the Thai baht's appreciation relative to the dollar throughout 2009 and 2010. Machinery and parts, vehicles, electronic integrated circuits, chemicals, crude oil and fuels, and iron and steel are among Thailand's principal imports.

Through 2010, the United States was Thailand's third-largest single-country export market after China and Japan, and the third-largest supplier after Japan and China. Thailand's traditional major markets have been the United States, Japan, Europe, and ASEAN member countries (Singapore, Malaysia, Indonesia, the Philippines, and Vietnam). Growing export markets include China, Hong Kong, Australia, the Middle East, South Africa, and India. Due to the global economic recovery, Thai exports in 2010 surged by 25.1% from 2009. Thailand is a member of the World Trade Organization (WTO) and the Cairns Group of agricultural exporters.

Tourism contributes significantly to the Thai economy (approximately 6%). The tourism industry began to recover in the last quarter of 2009, but the protests in Bangkok in April and May 2010 drove away some foreign tourists. The heavy floods during October and November and the strong Thai baht had minimal impacts on the industry. Tourism from January to November was on average 12.7% higher than 2009 levels.

Bangkok and its environs are the most prosperous part of Thailand, and the seasonally barren northeast is the poorest. An overriding concern of successive Thai governments has been to reduce these regional income differentials, which have been exacerbated by rapid economic growth in and around Bangkok. The government has tried to stimulate provincial economic growth with programs such as the Eastern Seaboard project and various populist and crop price support policies.

Although the economy has demonstrated moderate positive growth in recent years, future performance depends on moving up on the value-added ladder away from low-wage industries where regional competition is growing. Key reforms are needed to open the financial sector; improve the foreign investment climate, including updating telecommunications capabilities; and stimulate domestic investment and consumption to balance reliance on exports. Logistics networks and electricity generation increasingly run the risk of bottlenecks and may pose a challenge to growth. Thailand's relative shortage of engineers and skilled technical personnel may limit its future technological creativity and productivity, even as the government is pushing for an increase in the proportion that creative industries contribute to GDP from 12% to 20% by 2015.

FOREIGN RELATIONS

Thailand's foreign policy includes a close and longstanding security relationship with the United States. It also strongly supports ASEAN's efforts to promote economic development, social integration, and stability throughout the region. Relations with China are steadily increasing across the board. Thailand served as the chair of ASEAN from July 2008 to December 2009 and served as host to the ASEAN Summit (heads of government meeting) in February 2009, as well as the ASEAN Ministerial Meeting, Post Ministerial Conference, and Regional Forum in July 2009. At the July 2009 meeting in Phuket, the United States acceded to the Treaty of Amity and Cooperation with ASEAN.

Thailand participates fully in international and regional organizations. It has developed increasingly close ties with other ASEAN members--Indonesia, Malaysia, the Philippines, Singapore, Brunei, Laos, Cambodia, Burma, and Vietnam--whose foreign and economic ministers hold annual meetings. Regional cooperation is progressing in economic, trade, banking, political, and cultural matters.

On the international stage, Thailand contributed troops and UN force commanders to the international peacekeeping effort in East Timor; in late 2010, it sent naval ships to the anti-piracy task force off the coast of Somalia and troops to the UN peacekeeping mission in Darfur. As part of its effort to increase international ties, Thailand has reached out to such regional organizations as the Organization of American States (OAS) and the Organization for Security and Cooperation in Europe (OSCE). Thailand has contributed troops to reconstruction efforts in Afghanistan and Iraq. In May 2010 Thailand was chosen to serve on the UN Human Rights Council for a 3-year term; in June 2010 Thailand was elected as chair of that body for 1 year.

U.S.-THAI RELATIONS

On March 20, 1833, the United States and Thailand, then Siam, signed the Treaty of Amity and Commerce, the United States' first treaty with a country in Asia.

Since World War II, the United States and Thailand have significantly expanded diplomatic and commercial relations, as reflected in several bilateral treaties and by both countries' participation in UN multilateral activities and agreements. Thailand and the U.S. became treaty allies in 1954 (Manila Pact). The 1966 Treaty of Amity and Economic Relations, the most recent iteration of the 1833 Treaty of Amity and Commerce, is the principal bilateral arrangement; the 1966 treaty facilitates U.S. and Thai companies' economic access to one another's markets. Other important agreements address civil uses of atomic energy, sales of agricultural commodities, investment guarantees, and military and economic assistance. In June 2004, the United States and Thailand initiated negotiations on a free trade agreement but these negotiations were suspended in September 2006 following the military-led coup against the government of then-Prime Minister Thaksin.

The United States and Thailand are among the signatories of the 1954 Manila Pact of the former Southeast Asia Treaty Organization (SEATO). Article IV(1) of this treaty provides that, in the event of armed attack in the treaty area (which includes Thailand), each member would "act to meet the common danger in accordance with its constitutional processes." Despite the dissolution of the SEATO in 1977, the Manila Pact remains in force and, together with the Thanat-Rusk communique of 1962, constitutes the basis of U.S. security commitments to Thailand. Thailand continues to be a key security ally in Asia, along with Australia, Japan, the Philippines, and South Korea. In December 2003, Thailand was designated a Major Non-NATO Ally.

Thailand's stability and growth are important to the maintenance of peace in the region. The Thai-U.S. Creative Partnership proposed during 2010 will build on existing public-private and intergovernmental relationships, seeking to emphasize innovative industry and to identify new opportunities for collaborative ingenuity between the two countries. In alignment with the Thai

Government's Creative Economy policies, this formal partnership effort intends to spur increased productivity while re-emphasizing the beneficial aspects of American presence in Thailand. Economic assistance has been extended in various fields, including rural development, health, family planning, education, and science and technology. The formal U.S. Agency for International Development (USAID) bilateral program, ended in 1995, was rejuvenated in 2010. There are also a number of targeted assistance programs which continue in areas of mutually defined importance, including: health and HIV/AIDS programming, civil society capacity-building, reconciliation efforts in southern Thailand, refugee assistance, and combating trafficking in persons. The **U.S. Peace Corps** in Thailand began operating in 1962 and has had over 5,000 volunteers since that time. Peace Corps currently has approximately 100 volunteers in country, focused on primary education, with an integrated program involving teacher training, health education, and environmental education. In late 2003, the Peace Corps also established an organizational development program aimed at promoting sustainable rural development in Thai communities. The United States and Thailand, through programs with USAID, the U.S. Centers for Disease Control and Prevention (CDC), and the Armed Forces Research Institute of Medial Sciences (AFRIMS), cooperate closely on a range of public health initiatives, including efforts to fight malaria, tuberculosis, dengue, HIV/AIDS, and avian/pandemic influenza.

Thailand has received U.S. military equipment, essential supplies, training, and assistance in the construction and improvement of facilities and installations for much of the period since 1950; since then more Thai have been trained under the International Military Education and Training (IMET) program than any other country. Over recent decades, U.S. security assistance included military training programs carried out in the United States and elsewhere. A small U.S. military advisory group in Thailand oversaw the delivery of equipment to the Thai Armed Forces and the training of Thai military personnel in its use and maintenance. As part of the mutual defense cooperation over the last 3 decades, Thailand and the United States have developed a vigorous joint military exercise program, which engages all the services of each nation and averages 40 joint exercises per year.

Thailand and the U.S. have longstanding cooperation in international law enforcement efforts. The large-scale production and shipment of opium and heroin shipments from Burma of previous years have largely been replaced by widespread smuggling of methamphetamine tablets, although heroin is still seized along the border. The United States and Thailand continue to work closely together and with the United Nations on a broad range of programs to halt illicit drug trafficking and other criminal activity, such as trafficking in persons. Thailand cooperates fully in efforts to return felons fleeing justice to the U.S. In addition to bilateral civil law enforcement and security capacity-building through the Transnational Crime Affairs Section and the Regional Security Office, the U.S. supports the International Law Enforcement Academy (ILEA) in Bangkok, which provides counter-narcotics and anti-crime capacity-building programs to law enforcement and judicial officials from a number of regional countries.

Trade and Investment
The United States is Thailand's third-largest single-country trading partner after Japan and China; from January to November 2010, merchandise imports from Thailand totaled $20.7 billion, and merchandise exports totaled $8.1 billion, according to the U.S. Commerce Department. Japan, Hong Kong, Singapore, the U.S., and the European Union are Thailand's largest foreign investors. U.S. investment, concentrated in the petroleum and chemicals, finance, consumer products, computer components, and automobile production sectors, is estimated by the American Chamber of Commerce at over $35 billion.

Many U.S. businesses enjoy investment benefits through the U.S.-Thailand Treaty of Amity and Economic Relations (AER), originally signed in 1833. The 1966 iteration of the treaty allows U.S. citizens and businesses incorporated in the U.S., or in Thailand that are majority-owned by U.S. citizens, to engage in business on the same basis as Thai companies, exempting them from most

For additional analytical, business and investment opportunities information, please contact Global Investment & Business Center, USA at (202) 546-2103. Fax: (202) 546-3275. E-mail: rusric@erols.com

of the restrictions on foreign investment imposed by the Foreign Business Act. Under the treaty, Thailand restricts American investment only in the fields of communications, transport, fiduciary functions, banking involving depository functions, the exploitation of land or other natural resources, and domestic trade in agricultural products. Notwithstanding their treaty rights, many Americans choose to form joint ventures with Thai partners, allowing the Thai side to hold the majority stake because of the advantages that come from familiarity with the Thai economy and local regulations. In recent decades, Thailand has been a major destination for foreign direct investment, and hundreds of U.S. companies have operated there successfully.

Principal U.S. Embassy Officials
Ambassador--Kristie A. Kenney
Deputy Chief of Mission--Judith B. Cefkin
Management Counselor--Gregory Stanford
Political Affairs Counselor--George Kent
Economic Affairs Counselor--Julie Chung
Public Affairs Counselor--Kenneth Foster
Consul General--Ronald Robinson
Commercial Counselor--Cynthia Griffin
Chiang Mai Consul General--Susan Stevenson

The **U.S. Embassy** in Thailand is located at 120/22 Wireless Road, Bangkok (tel. 66-2-205-4000). There is a **Consulate General in Chiang Mai**, 387 Wichayanond Road (tel. 66-53-107-700).

TRAVEL AND BUSINESS INFORMATION

The U.S. Department of State's Consular Information Program advises Americans traveling and residing abroad through Country Specific Information, Travel Alerts, and Travel Warnings. **Country Specific Information** exists for all countries and includes information on entry and exit requirements, currency regulations, health conditions, safety and security, crime, political disturbances, and the addresses of the U.S. embassies and consulates abroad. **Travel Alerts** are issued to disseminate information quickly about terrorist threats and other relatively short-term conditions overseas that pose significant risks to the security of American travelers. **Travel Warnings** are issued when the State Department recommends that Americans avoid travel to a certain country because the situation is dangerous or unstable.

For the latest security information, Americans living and traveling abroad should regularly monitor the Department's Bureau of Consular Affairs Internet web site at http://www.travel.state.gov, where the current Worldwide Caution, Travel Alerts, and Travel Warnings can be found. Consular Affairs Publications, which contain information on obtaining passports and planning a safe trip abroad, are also available at http://www.travel.state.gov. For additional information on international travel, see http://www.usa.gov/Citizen/Topics/Travel/International.shtml.

The Department of State encourages all U.S. citizens traveling or residing abroad to register via the State Department's travel registration website or at the nearest U.S. embassy or consulate abroad. Registration will make your presence and whereabouts known in case it is necessary to contact you in an emergency and will enable you to receive up-to-date information on security conditions.

Emergency information concerning Americans traveling abroad may be obtained by calling 1-888-407-4747 toll free in the U.S. and Canada or the regular toll line 1-202-501-4444 for callers outside the U.S. and Canada.

For additional analytical, business and investment opportunities information, please contact Global Investment & Business Center, USA at (202) 546-2103. Fax: (202) 546-3275. E-mail: rusric@erols.com

The National Passport Information Center (NPIC) is the U.S. Department of State's single, centralized public contact center for U.S. passport information. Telephone: 1-877-4-USA-PPT (1-877-487-2778); TDD/TTY: 1-888-874-7793. Passport information is available 24 hours, 7 days a week. You may speak with a representative Monday-Friday, 8 a.m. to 10 p.m., Eastern Time, excluding federal holidays.

PRACTICAL INFORMATION FOR CONDUCTING BUSINESS

STARTING A BUSINESS IN THAILAND

REGISTRATION A COMPANY

	Procedure	Time to complete:	Cost to complete:
1	Apply for permission to use company name	2 days	no charge or Bht20 for applying application to the Registrar at the Department of Business Development ("DBD")
2	Deposit paid-in capital in a bank	1 day	no charge
3	Obtain a corporate seal	4 days	THB 300-500
4	Get approval for memorandum of association and apply to register the company as a legal entity (final registration) at the Private Limited Companies Registrar.	1 day	Bht700 (Bht200 for duty stamp affixed on the original Memorandum of Association, Bht500 minimum and Bht25,000 maximum for government fee) + THB 5,200 minimum (Bht200 for duty stamp affixed on the original Articles of Association, Bht5,000 minimum and Bht2
5	Register with the Revenue Department for tax	2 days	no charge
6	Register for social security and Workmen's Compensation Fund at the Social Security Office, Ministry of Labor	1 day	no charge
7	Submit company work regulations to the Office of Labor Protection and Welfare of the Ministry of Labor at the district where the head office of the company is located	21 days	no charge

REGISTRATION REQUIREMENTS DETAILS

Procedure 1.

    Apply for permission to use company name

Time to complete:

    2 days

Cost to complete:

    no charge or Bht20 for applying application to the Registrar at the Department of Business Development ("DBD")

Name of Agency:

Comment:

    Promoters can search and reserve a company name on the Department of Business Development's Web site (www.thairegistration.com or www.dbd.go.th). Otherwise, they can apply for a name reservation in person at the Department's Registrar.

Procedure 2.

    Deposit paid-in capital in a bank

Time to complete:

    1 day

Cost to complete:

For additional analytical, business and investment opportunities information, please contact Global Investment & Business Center, USA at (202) 546-2103. Fax: (202) 546-3275. E-mail: rusric@erols.com

no charge
Name of Agency:
Comment:
>Once the company gets approval for the memorandum and the articles of association, it must hold a statutory meeting, and shareholders must pay in at least 25% of the registered capital.

Procedure 3.
>Obtain a corporate seal

Time to complete:
>4 days

Cost to complete:
>THB 300-500

Name of Agency:
Comment:
>According to Thai law, a company is not required to have a corporate seal except for affixation on company share certificates. In practice, however, a Thai company usually affixes its corporate seal to other documents.

Procedure 4.
>Get approval for memorandum of association and apply to register the company as a legal entity (final registration) at the Private Limited Companies Registrar.

Time to complete:
>1 day

Cost to complete:
>Bht700 (Bht200 for duty stamp affixed on the original Memorandum of Association, Bht500 minimum and Bht25,000 maximum for government fee) + THB 5,200 minimum (Bht200 for duty stamp affixed on the original Articles of Association, Bht5,000 minimum and Bht2

Name of Agency:
Comment:
>The application for registration of the memorandum of association must contain (a) the company names in Thai and in a foreign language (for certificate of company name, see Procedure 1); (b) nature of business; (c) capital to be registered; (d) number and par value of shares; (e)
>address of the headquarters; (f) names, ages, and addresses of promoters; (g) number of shares subscribed by each promoter; and (h) signatures of all promoters.
>- The promotors prepare the application for registration of the memorandum of association containing the details specified in procedure 2;
>- The first statutory meeting shall still be convened, provided that the notice to summon the first statutory meeting is not required;
>- The shareholders must pay at least 25% of the registered capital;
>- The promotors and authorized signatory director must sign the applications for registration of memorandum of association and for registration of incorporation, respectively, before Private Limited Companies Registrar, attorney at law, or auditor registered with the Registrar.

>However, if the company has adopted complicated articles of association, the Registrar may take a few days to review the company's articles of association. In such case, the registration of company incorporation may be prolonged for a few days or more.

Procedure 5.
>Register with the Revenue Department for tax

Time to complete:
>2 days

Cost to complete:
>no charge

Name of Agency:

Comment:

Within 60 days of incorporation, the company must register with the Revenue Department to obtain a taxpayer identification card. The same tax number appears on the VAT certificate and on the taxpayer identification card, which are normally obtained on the same date of application filing. However, the VAT certificate will be mailed separately to the company's registered address. Businesses earning more than THB 1,800,000 per year must register for VAT within 30 days from the date the income was earned. The company must also file VAT returns within the 15th day of each month. This is required even if no income was derived in the proceeding month. VAT registration must be filed in person at the same office as for income tax registration. The procedure takes 1–3 days.

Procedure 6.

Register for social security and Workmen's Compensation Fund at the Social Security Office, Ministry of Labor

Time to complete:

1 day

Cost to complete:

no charge

Name of Agency:

Comment:

Employers (with one or more employees) must register their employees for social security and workers' compensation insurance by in person at the Social Security Office, Ministry of Labor.

Procedure 7.

Submit company work regulations to the Office of Labor Protection and Welfare of the Ministry of Labor at the district where the head office of the company is located

Time to complete:

21 days

Cost to complete:

no charge

Name of Agency:

Comment:

The company work regulations are reviewed by the Office of Labor Protection and Welfare, and the company is advised on the required revisions. An employer with 10 or more regular employees must establish written rules and regulations (in Thai) that comply with the amendments of theLabor Protection Act B.E. 2541 on work performance. The regulations must be displayed at the work premises within 15 days of hiring 10 or more employees. This procedure takes 2–4 weeks.

REGISTERING A PROPERTY

REGISTRATION REQUIREMENTS SUMMARY:

	Procedure	Time to complete:	Cost to complete:
1	Obtain certified copies of companies' documents from the Ministry of Commerce	1 day	THB 200 (Affidavits) + THB 700 (MoA, AoA)
2	Parties submit application for registration at the Land Office	1 day	THB 10 (title search) + 0.01% of appraised value (registration fee) + 1% of sale price or appraised value, whichever is higher (withholding tax) + 0.11% of sale price or appraised value, whichever is higher (Specific

Procedure 1.
> Obtain certified copies of companies' documents from the Ministry of Commerce

Time to complete:
> 1 day

Cost to complete:
> THB 200 (Affidavits) + THB 700 (MoA, AoA)

Name of Agency:
> Ministry of Commerce

Comment:
> Parties obtain from the Ministry of Commerce the following documents:
> 1. Companies' Affidavits confirming the name, address, the amount of registered capital, names of directors and the authorized signatories. (THB 100)
> 2. Certified copies of the Memorandum and Articles of Association of each party (THB 50 per page, cost of certification)
> 3. List of shareholders of the company from the Ministry of Commerce to prove their nationality.
> On average, the Memorandum of Association (MoA) has 2 pages and the Articles of Association (AoA) about 5 pages.

Procedure 2.
> Parties submit application for registration at the Land Office

Time to complete:
> 1 day

Cost to complete:
> THB 10 (title search) + 0.01% of appraised value (registration fee) + 1% of sale price or appraised value, whichever is higher (withholding tax) + 0.11% of sale price or appraised value, whichever is higher (Specific Business Tax)

Name of Agency:
> Land Office

Comment:
> The seller and the buyer, or their representatives, must go to the Land Office where the land is located, and submit an application to register the sale of the land and the buildings thereon.
> The Land Officer checks all the documents (from both the seller and the buyer) submitted with the application. He will also compare the original title deed with the original copy kept at the Land Office. All information in both original title deeds must be the same. If everything is consistent, he will proceed with the registration of the transfer of ownership. An official sales agreement is prepared and signed by the authorized representatives of the seller and buyer. The officer then records the sales transaction at the back of the original land title deeds (both the land owner's and the Land Office's copies).
> The Land Officer calculates all the registration fees and expenses and asks the parties to pay and submit to him the receipts.
> The Ministry of Interior reduced the registration fee to 0.01% of the appraised value calculated by the Central Valuation Authority (CVA). This registration was applicable for one year until March 2009, but was this year extended for another year until March 2010.
> The seller has to pay a 1% withholding tax on sale price or CVA- whichever is higher. (Seller may apply this as a credit towards their corporate income tax on any capital gain.) As the seller is a company, withholding tax is calculated on the greater of the appraised value and the sale price.
> The seller has to pay a 0.5% stamp duty, unless he is subject to the Specific Business Tax. The Royal Decree No 472 reduced the Specific Business Tax (SBT) to 0.11% of sale price or CVA, whichever is higher. The 0.11% Specific Business Tax includes the

municipality tax.

The Specific Business Tax is imposed on persons who sell their property for trade or a profit-seeking purpose. Companies who sell real property in Thailand are deemed to be selling for trade or profit and are subject to specific business tax. Even if a company sells property in order simply to move to a new place, it is still deemed to have sold for a trade or profit seeking purpose.

Accordingly, the company who is the seller in this example will be subject to Specific Business Tax.

The registration fee, withholding and specific business taxes are collected by the Land Office. The cheques for the taxes are payable to the Ministry of Finance but collected by the Land Office.

The Land Officer then attaches the receipts to the application, and submits all documents to the Chief in charge who is authorized to approve the registration of the transfer. Once the registration is approved, it is deemed completed. The seller will receive one copy of the registered sale agreement. The buyer will receive another copy of the registered sale agreement and the original Land Title Deed.

As the Seller owns both the land and the buildings upon the land, the transfer of the building occurs in the same process at the same registry as for the transfer of the land. The Seller will need to produce the construction permit and household registration of the building to transfer the building.

PAYING TAXES

Tax or mandatory contribution	Payments (number)	Notes on Payments	Time (hours)	Statutory tax rate	Tax base	Total tax rate (% profit)	Notes on TTR
Corporate income tax	1	online filing	160	25.0%	taxable income	26.1	
Social Security contributions	12		48	5.0%	gross salaries	5.4	
Business specific tax	1	online filing	-	3.3%	taxable income	2.9	
Property Tax	1		-	12.5%	assessed property value	1.6	
Advertising tax	1		-	2% and 3%	service cost	0.4	
Fuel Tax	1		-	2.4 Baht per liter	fuel consumption	0.3	
Workmen compensation fund	1		-	0.2% to 1%	gross salaries	0.2	
Stamp duty	1		-	0.1%	transaction value	0.1	
vehicle tax	1		-	fixed fee (Baht 3,600)		0.1	
Tax on interest	0		-	1.0%	interest income	0	included in other taxes
Tax on check transactions	1		-	3 Baht per check		0	
Property transfer tax	1		-	2.0%	sale price	0	
Value added tax	1	online filing	56	7.0%	value added		not

Tax or mandatory contribution	Payments (number)	Notes on Payments	Time (hours)	Statutory tax rate	Tax base	Total tax rate (% profit)	Notes on TTR
(VAT)							included
Totals:	23		264			37.2	

Notes:

Name of taxes have been standardized. For instance income tax, profit tax, tax on company's income are all named corporate income tax in this table.

The hours for VAT include all the VAT and sales taxes applicable.

The hours for Social Security include all the hours for labor taxes and mandatory contributions in general.

ESTABLISHING BUSINESS IN THAILAND BASICS

There are three kinds of business organizations in Thailand: Sole proprietorships, partnerships, and limited companies.

The most popular form of business organization among foreign investors is the private limited company.

Private limited companies require a minimum of three promoters and must file a memorandum of association, convene a statutory meeting, register the company, and obtain a company income tax identity card. They must also follow accounting procedures specified in the Civil and Commercial code,the Revenue Code and the Accounts Act.

A balance sheet must be prepared once a year and filed with the Department of Revenue and Commercial Registration.

In addition, companies are required to withhold income tax from the salary of all regular employees.

The Ministry of Industry administers The Factory Act, which governs factory construction and operation, as well as safety and pollution-control requirements.

In some cases, factories do not require licenses, in other instances the requirement is simply to notify officials in advance of start-up, and in some cases licenses are required prior to commencing operations. Licenses are valid for five years, and are renewable.

Thailand recognizes three kinds of intellectual property rights: patents, trademarks, and copyrights.

The Patent Act protects both inventions and product designs and pharmaceuticals.The Copyright Act protects literary, artistic works, and performance rights, by making it unlawful to reproduce or publish such works without the owner's permission. The Trademark Act governs registration of, and provides protection for, trademarks.

The Alien Occupation Law requires all foreigners working in Thailand to obtain a Work Permit prior to starting work in the Kingdom, except when they are applying under the Investment Promotion Law, in which case they have 30 days to apply.

Non-Immigrant visas provide the holder with eligibility to apply for a work permit, and allow the holder to work while the work permit application is being considered.

Through the links below, you can learn more about topics such as industrial licensing, taxation, patents and trademarks , and the cost of doing business in Thailand. You can also find out about the status of Thai infrastructure, including facilities such as airports, deep sea ports, and highways, and the availability of power, water and telecommunications.

In addition, there is a link to a page of statistics, which displays tables of utility, communications and labor costs, tax rates, information about air, sea, rail and road freight pricing, and information about availability and cost of land within industrial estates. Other charts and tables provide costs of establishing and running an office in Bangkok, and the results of a survey of expatriate living costs in Bangkok.

This page also contains information about industrial production of selected products in Thailand, tables breaking down Thai imports and exports by product and a table displaying interest rate movements for the past 5 years.

By the time you have finished visiting all these pages, you will have a complete picture about the business climate in Thailand.

COMPANY FORMATION

1. Forming a Company

Company promoters are responsible for registering the company with the Ministry of Commerce (MOC). The promoters must be individuals (not juristic persons) who are 20 years of age or older, and they must be available to sign documentation during the registration process. There must be a minimum of 3 promoters for a private limited company and at least 15 promoters for a public limited company.

Each of the promoters is required to be among the company's initial shareholders immediately after the company's registration and is required to hold a minimum of one share upon the company's registration. However, they are generally free to transfer those shares to existing shareholders or third parties, thereafter, if they wish. It is not required for the individuals serving as promoters to reside in Thailand.

Promoters' potential legal liability is generally limited to the par value of the shares they will hold after registration is completed. The promoters are also responsible for paying expenses associated with the company's registration. After registration, however, the company may choose to reimburse the promoters for those expenses.

Registration of the company occurs at the MOC and can be accomplished on the same day as the registration of the memorandum of association provided that:

All registered shares have been subscribed for

A statutory meeting is held to transact the business with the presence of all promoters and subscribers, and all promoters and subscribers have approved the transacted business

The promoters have handed over the business to the directors and

For additional analytical, business and investment opportunities information,
please contact Global Investment & Business Center, USA
at (202) 546-2103. Fax: (202) 546-3275. E-mail: rusric@erols.com

The payment of at least 25% of the total shares has been paid by the shareholders.

If the company falls under the definition of "foreign" (as defined in the Foreign Business Act (FBA)), it will normally be required to obtain Cabinet approval or a Foreign Business License prior to commencing operations.

Applying for and obtaining the company's tax ID card and VAT certificate (if required) takes place after registration with the MOC and can normally be accomplished within seven to 10 days after providing all required information and documents to the Revenue Department.

All documents associated with the company's registration must be submitted to the registrar of the Department of Business Development of the MOC; or, if the company's office is to be located outside of Bangkok, they must be submitted to the filing office of the province where the office will be located.

All documents associated with the registration of the company's tax ID card and VAT certificate must be submitted to the Central Filing Office of the Revenue Department in Bangkok; or, if the company's office is to be located outside of Bangkok, to the Revenue Office of the province where the office will be located.

REGISTRATION PROCESS

1 Corporate Name Reservation

The first step of the company registration process is name reservation. To reserve a name, one of the promoters is required to submit a signed Name Reservation Form to the Department of Business Development of the MOC.

The promoter is required to supply the requested company name together with two alternative names. The registrar will then examine the application in order to ensure that:

No similar company names have previously been reserved; and

The names do not violate any ministerial rules.

If the applicant's intended name is in conflict with either of the above, that name will be rejected and the registrar will consider the alternative names submitted. This process can normally be completed within two to three days. If all three names submitted are rejected, the applicant will be required to re-submit the form with three new names.

The registrar has considerable discretion with regard to the matter of company names. Many times, the first name or even the first two names are rejected for violating one of the two rules stated above. Once the name is approved, the corporate name reservation is valid for 30 days, with no extensions.

2 Filing a Memorandum of Association

After the name reservation has been approved, the company must then submit its Memorandum of Association (MOA). The MOA must include the name of the company, the province where the company will be located, the scope of the company's business, the capital to be registered, and the names of the promoters. The capital information must include the number of shares and their par value. At the formation step, the authorized capital, although partly paid, must all be issued.

The memorandum registration fee is 50 baht per 100,000 baht of registered capital. The minimum fee is 500 baht and the maximum fee is 25,000 baht. Although there are no minimum capital requirements, the amount of capital should be respectable and adequate for the intended business operation. However, if the company falls under the definition of a foreign company, the following rules apply:

If the company engages in activities specified in the FBA, its minimum registered capital would be the greater of 25% of the company's average per year expenses for its first three years of operation and 3 million baht (exceptions apply) fully (100%) paid up.

If the company does not engage in activities specified in the FBA, its minimum registered capital would be 2 million baht fully (100%) paid up.

If the company is to employ foreigners, other minimum registered capital requirements may also apply.

3 Convening a Statutory Meeting

Once the share structure has been defined, a statutory meeting is called, during which the following are determined:

The adoption of the Articles of Association (by-laws)

Ratification of any contracts entered into and any expenses incurred by the promoters in promoting the company

Fixing the amount of remuneration, if any, to be paid to the promoters

Fixing the number of preferred shares, if any, to be issued, and the nature and extent of the preferential rights accruing to them

Fixing the number of ordinary shares or preferred shares to be allotted as fully or partly paid-up other than in money, if any, and the amount up to which they shall be considered as paid-up.

Appointment of the initial director(s) and auditor(s) and determination of the respective powers of the directors.

The promoters shall over the business to the directors.

4 Registration

Within three months of the date of the statutory meeting, the directors must submit the application to establish the company. If not registered within the specified period, the company statutory meeting shall be void and if would like to register to establish the company, shall arrange the meeting for persons who reserve to buy the shares again.

During the registration process, the promoters will be required to supply the name, license number, and remuneration of the auditor the company is planning to hire. The company registration fee is 500 baht per 100,000 baht of registered capital. The minimum fee is 5,000 baht and the maximum fee is 250,000 baht.

The directors shall then cause the promoters and subscribers to pay forthwith upon each share payable in money such amount, not less than 25%, as provided by the prospectus, notice, advertisement, or invitation. The company is then registered as a legal entity (or juristic person).

If all necessary documents are complete and duly signed by all promoters, directors, and shareholders, the above steps can be completed in one day.

5 Registering for Tax Documents

Companies liable for income tax must obtain a tax ID card and number from the Revenue Department within 60 days of incorporation or the start of operations. Companies that have turnover in excess of 1.2 million baht must also register for VAT with the Revenue Department within 30 days of the date the annual turnover exceeded that threshold.

2. FINANCIAL REPORTING REQUIREMENTS

1 Books of Accounts and Statutory Records

Companies must keep books and follow accounting procedures as specified in the Civil and Commercial Code, the Revenue Code, and the Accounts Act. Documents may be prepared in any language, provided that a Thai translation is attached. All accounting entries should be written in ink, typewritten, or printed. Specifically, Section 12 of the Accounts Act of 2000 provides rules on how accounts should be maintained:

"In keeping accounts, the person with the duty to keep accounts must hand over the documents required for making accounting entries to the bookkeeper correctly and completely, in order that the accounts so kept may show the results of operations, financial position according to facts and accounting standards."

2 Accounting Period

A newly established company should close accounts within 12 months of its registration. Thereafter, the accounts should be closed every 12 months. If a company wishes to change its accounting period, it must obtain written approval from the Director-General of the Revenue Department.

3 Reporting Requirements

All juristic companies, partnerships, branches of foreign companies, and joint ventures are required to prepare a financial statement for each accounting period. The financial statement must be audited by and subjected to the opinion of a certified auditor, with the exception of the financial statement of a registered partnership established under Thai law, whose total capital, assets, and income are not more than that prescribed in Ministerial Regulations. The performance record is to be certified by the company auditor, approved by shareholders, and filed with the Commercial Registration Department of the MOC and with the Revenue Department of the Ministry of Finance (MOF) within 150 days of the end of the fiscal year.

4 Accounting Principles

In general, the basic accounting principles practiced in the United States are accepted in Thailand, as are accounting methods and conventions sanctioned by law. The Institute of Certified Accountants and Auditors of Thailand is the authoritative group promoting the application of generally accepted accounting principles.

Any accounting method adopted by a company must be used consistently and may be changed only with approval of the Revenue Department. Certain accounting practices of note include:

Depreciation: The Revenue Code permits the use of varying depreciation rates according to the nature of the asset, which has the effect of depreciating the asset over a period that may be shorter than its estimated useful life. These maximum depreciation rates are not mandatory. A company may use a lower rate that approximates the estimated useful life of the asset. If a lower rate is used in the books of the accounts, the same rate must be used in the income tax return.

Accounting for Pension Plans: Contributions to a pension or provident fund are not deductible for tax purposes unless they are actually paid out to the employees, or if the fund is approved by the Revenue Department and managed by a licensed fund manager.

Consolidation: Local companies with either foreign or local subsidiaries are not required to consolidate their financial statements for tax and other government reporting purposes, except for listed companies, which must submit consolidated financial statements to the Securities and Exchange Commission of Thailand .

Statutory Reserve: A statutory reserve of at least 5% of annual net profit arising from the business must be appropriated by the company at each distribution of dividends until the reserve reaches at least 10% of the company's authorized capital.

Stock Dividends: Stock dividends are taxable as ordinary dividends and may be declared only if there is an approved increase in authorized capital. The law requires the authorized capital to be subscribed in full by the shareholders.

5 Auditing Requirements and Standards

Audited financial statements of juristic entities (i.e. a limited company, registered partnership, branch, representative office, regional office of a foreign corporation, or joint venture) must be certified by an authorized auditor and be submitted to the Revenue Department and to the Commercial Registrar for each accounting year.

However, for a registered partnership with registered capital of less than five million baht, total revenue of no more than 30 million baht, and total assets of no more than 30 million baht, financial statements need only be submitted to the Revenue Department and not to the Commercial Registrar.

Auditing practices conforming to international standards are, for the most part, recognized and practiced by authorized auditors in Thailand.

3. TYPES OF BUSINESS ORGANIZATIONS

Thailand recognizes three types of business organizations: partnerships, limited companies and joint ventures.

1 Partnerships

According to the Civil and Commercial Code (CCC), partnerships can be divided into 2 types:

(1) Ordinary Partnerships

(2) Limited Partnerships

1.1 Ordinary Partnership

In an ordinary partnership, all the partners are jointly and wholly liable for all obligations of the partnership. An ordinary partnership may or may not register as a juristic person. Therefore, an ordinary partnership can be divided into 2 types:

(1) Non-registered Ordinary Partnership - has no status as a juristic person and is treated, for tax purposes, as an individual.

(2) Registered Ordinary Partnership - is registered with the Commercial Registrar as a juristic person and is taxed as a corporate entity.

1.2 Limited Partnership

Limited partnerships can take two forms:

(1)One or more partners whose individual liability is limited to the amount of capital contributed to the partnership, or

(2) One or more partners who are jointly and unlimitedly liable for all the obligations of the partnership.

Limited partnerships must be registered and are taxed as a corporate entity.

1.3 Partnership Registration

When two or more people agree to invest in one of the aforementioned types of partnership, the appointed managing partner is responsible for registering the partnership with the commercial registration office of the province that the head office of the partnership is located in.

A limited partnership must be only managed by a partner with unlimited liability.

The fee for registering a partnership is 1,000 baht for every 100,000 baht of registered capital. The minimum fee is 1,000 baht and the maximum fee is 5,000 baht.

2 Limited Companies

There are two types of limited companies: private limited companies and public limited companies. The first is governed by the Civil and Commercial Code and the second is governed by the Public Limited Company Act.

2.1 Private Limited Companies

Private Limited Companies in Thailand have basic characteristics similar to those of Western corporations. A private limited company is formed through a process that leads to the registration of a Memorandum of Association (Articles of Incorporation) and Articles of Association (By-laws) as its constitutive documents.

Shareholders enjoy limited liability, i.e. limited to the remaining unpaid amount, if any, of the par value of their shares. The liability of the directors, however, may be unlimited if stipulated as such in the company's MOA.

Limited companies are managed by a board of directors in accordance with the company's charter and by-laws. All shares must be subscribed to, and at least 25% of the subscribed shares must be paid up. Both common and preferred shares of stock may be issued, but all shares must have voting rights. Thai law prohibits the issuance of shares with a par value of less than five baht. Treasury shares are prohibited.

A minimum of three shareholders is required at all times. Under certain conditions, a private limited company may be wholly owned by foreigners. However, in those activities reserved for Thai nationals, foreigner participation is generally allowed up to a maximum of 49%. The registration fee for a private limited company is 5,500 baht per million baht of capital.

The 49% limit in certain reserved businesses can be exceeded or exempted if a Foreign Business License is granted. If the desired business is unique, does not compete with Thai businesses, or involves dealings among members of an affiliated company, the chance of approval is more probable. Conditions, such as minimum capital, transfer of technology and reporting requirements, may be attached to Foreign Business License

2.2 Public Limited Companies

Subject to compliance with the prospectus, approval, and other requirements, public limited companies registered in Thailand may offer shares, debentures, and warrants to the public and may apply to have their securities listed on the Stock Exchange of Thailand (SET).

Public limited companies are governed by the Public Limited Company Act B.E. 2535 (A.D. 1992), as amended by Public Limited Company Act No. 2 B.E. 2544 (A.D. 2001) and Public Limited Company Act No. 3 B.E. 2551 (A.D. 2008). The rules and regulations concerning the procedure of offering shares to the public is governed by the Securities and Exchange Act B.E. 2535 (A.D. 1992) and the amendments thereto, under the control of the Securities and Exchange Commission (SEC). All companies wishing to list their shares on the SET must obtain the approval of and file disclosure documents with the SEC, and then obtain SET approval to list their shares.

For public limited companies, there is no restriction on the transfer of shares (except to satisfy statutory or policy ceilings on foreign ownership); director's proxies are not allowed; circular board resolutions are not allowed; directors are elected by cumulative voting (unless the MOA provides otherwise); at least 50% of the directors must reside in Thailand; and board meetings must be held at least once every three months. Directors' liabilities are substantially increased.

A minimum of 15 promoters is required for the formation and registration of a public limited company, and the promoters must hold their shares for a minimum of two years before they can be transferred. The Board of Directors must have a minimum of five members, at least half of whom are Thai nationals. Shares must have a face value of at least five baht each and be fully paid up.

Restrictions on share transfers are unlawful, with the exception of those protecting the rights and benefits of the company as allowed by law and those maintaining the Thai/foreigner shareholder ratio. Debentures may only be issued with the approval of three quarters of the voting shareholders. The registration fee is 2,000 baht per million baht of registered capital.

The qualifications for independent directors of listed companies and securities companies that have initial public offerings was amended in April 2009, as follows:

1. At least one-third of the board's complement should be independent directors, and in any case, the number should not be fewer than three. This will apply for listed companies Companies' annual general shareholders' meetings from the year 2010 onwards. In the case of an IPO, the requirement for independent directors has to be complied with from 1 July 2008 onwards.

2. The independent director must not have any business or professional relationship with the head office, subsidiaries, associates, or jurist person in his own interest, whether directly or indirectly, as outlined in the Thai Securities and Exchange Commission Circular No. Kor Lor Tor Kor (Wor) 11/2552 Re: the Amendment of the Regulation regarding the independent director.

2.3 Scrutinization of Thai Shareholders in Limited Companies

In 2006, the Commercial Registrar prescribed new rules for the registration of both public and private limited companies. The rules require that sources of investment by Thai nationals in the following two categories of new companies be scrutinized:

(1) A company in which foreigners hold between 40% and 50% of the shares.

(2) A company in which foreigners hold less than 40% of the shares but a foreigner is a director with the power to bind the company.

All Thai shareholders must disclose the source of their funds to the MOC.

An application for the incorporation of a limited company must now be accompanied by at least one of the following documents evidencing the source of funds of each Thai shareholder:

*	Copies of deposit passbooks or bank statements disclosing transactions over the past 6 months

*	A letter issued by a bank certifying the financial position of the shareholder

*	Copies of other documents evidencing the source of funds (i.e. loan documentation)

In addition, the MOC has issued internal guidelines in support of the rules, which set out the following matters:

* The amounts shown in the documents of each Thai shareholder evidencing the source of funds must equal or exceed the amount of funds invested by that Thai shareholder.

* The rules do not apply if a foreign national(s) has joint authority with a Thai national(s) to act on behalf of the limited company.

" Copies of deposit passbooks or bank statements disclosing transactions that are less than six months old may be submitted to the MOC provided that entries on at least one day identify a balance that is equal to or exceeds the funds invested by the relevant shareholder.

Thai shareholders must provide evidence of their sources of funds regardless of the value of their shares.

3 Other Forms of Corporate Presence

Branches of Foreign Companies

Foreign companies may carry out certain business in Thailand through a branch office. Branch offices are required to maintain accounts only relating to the branch in Thailand.

There is no special requirement for foreign companies to register their branches in order to do business in Thailand. However, most business activities fall within the scope of one or more laws or regulations that require special registration (e.g., VAT registration, taxpayer identification card, Commercial Registration Certificate, Alien Business License, etc.), either before or after the commencement of activities. Therefore, foreign business establishments must follow generally accepted procedures.

It should be borne in mind that the branch is part of the parent company and therefore the parent retains legal liability for contracts, and for tortious acts done. For tax purposes, a branch is considered a permanent establishment, and its revenue is subject to Thai tax. It is important to clarify beforehand what constitutes income that is subject to Thai tax because the Revenue Department may consider revenue directly earned by the foreign head office from sources within Thailand to be subject to Thai tax.

A condition for approval of a Foreign Business License for a branch of a foreign corporation is that minimum capital amounting to no less than five million baht be brought into Thailand within four years of start-up. The branch may be allowed to operate for a period of five years, unless a shorter period is applied for. Extension of the original duration of the license to operate may be granted, provided that the working capital to be brought into Thailand requirement is met.

Representative Offices of Foreign Companies

A representative office is defined as an office in Thailand of a foreign company engaged in the business of international trading. A representative office in Thailand cannot engage in any profit-seeking or profit-making enterprise. The scope of activities of a representative office must be limited to approved activities, or significant Thai tax liabilities can arise. The risk of exceeding the scope of activities is that the income of the parent or affiliated companies may be deemed earned in Thailand and subject to taxation.

If the representative office engages in other activities for which permission is not granted, such as buying or selling goods on behalf of the head office, it will be regarded as doing business in Thailand and may be subject to Thai taxation on all income received from Thailand. Also, the representative office may not act on behalf of third persons. Any such business or income-earning activities could amount to a violation of the conditions of the license to establish and operate a representative office, which in turn could result in revocation of that license.

A representative office which undertakes one or more of the approved activities in Thailand without rendering any service to any other person, and which refrains from prohibited activities, is

For additional analytical, business and investment opportunities information,
please contact Global Investment & Business Center, USA
at (202) 546-2103. Fax: (202) 546-3275. E-mail: rusric@erols.com

not subject to Thai taxation. Such a representative office is understood to be receiving a subsidy from the head office to meet its expenses in Thailand. Gross receipts or revenues received by a representative office from the head office are not characterized as revenue to be included in the computation of juristic person income tax.

Even though they are not subject to taxation in Thailand, all representative offices are still required to obtain a Corporate Tax Identification number and submit income tax returns and audited financial statements to the Revenue Department. They are also required to submit the same to the Department of Business Development.

Scope of Representative Office Activities

"International trading business" means activities concerning:

Sourcing of goods or services for head office

Checking and controlling the quality and quantity of goods purchased or hired to manufacture in Thailand by the head office

Giving advice concerning goods of the head office sold to agents or consumers in Thailand

Dissemination of information concerning new goods or services of the head office

Reporting on business trends in Thailand to the head office.

The above international trading business is regarded as a service activity under Schedule 3 of the Foreign Business Act, and thus the establishment of a representative office requires an alien business license from the Director-General of the Department of Business Development.

Fees for Representative Office

Application fee (nonrefundable) is THB 2,000. If the application is approved, the government fee will be set at the rate of THB 5 for every THB 1,000 or a fraction thereof of the registered capital, with a minimum of THB 20,000 and a maximum of THB 250,000.

Tax Position of Representative Office

The representative office is required to obtain a corporate tax identification number and submit income tax returns and balance sheets, even if nil.

Individual aliens and all local staff are required to obtain taxpayer cards and pay personal income tax.

4 Regional Operating Headquarters (ROH)

A Regional Operating Headquarters (ROH) is a juristic company or partnership organized under Thai law to provide managerial, technical, or other supporting services (see below) to its associated companies or its domestic or foreign branches.

Supporting Services

(1) General administration, business planning, and coordination

(2) Procurement of raw materials and components

(3) Research and development

(4) Technical support

(5) Marketing control and sales promotion planning

(6) Training and personnel management

(7) Corporate financial advisory services

(8) Economic or investment research and analysis

(9) Credit control and administration

(10) Any other services stipulated by the Director-General of the Revenue Department

Associated Company A juristic company or partnership that is related to the   ROH in one of the following manners:

A. Shareholding basis:

i. A juristic company or partnership holding shares in the ROH worth not less than 25% of total capital

ii. A juristic company or partnership in which the ROH is a partner or holds shares worth not less than 25% of total capital

iii. A juristic company or partnership in which a juristic company or partnership under (i.) is a partner or holds shares worth not less than 25% of total capital

B. Control basis:

i. A juristic company or partnership that has the power to control or supervise the operation and management of the ROH

ii. A juristic company or partnership that the ROH has the power to control or supervise the operation and management

iii. A juristic partnership that a juristic company or partnership in (i.) has the power to control or supervise the operation and management

Incentives The government provides tax breaks and incentives to attract foreign companies to set up in the Kingdom.

A. Reductions/exemptions on Corporate Income Tax

For additional analytical, business and investment opportunities information,
please contact Global Investment & Business Center, USA
at (202) 546-2103. Fax: (202) 546-3275. E-mail: rusric@erols.com

i. Business income - ROH will be taxed at the reduced corporate rate of 10% on income derived from the provision of qualifying services to the ROH's associated companies or branches.

ii. Royalties - Royalties received from associated companies or branches arising from R&D work carried out in Thailand will be subject to tax at a reduced corporate rate of 10%. Royalties received from a non-related company can also enjoy this reduced rate.

iii. Interest - Interest income derived from associated companies or branches on loans made by an ROH and extended to its associated companies or branches will be subject to tax at a reduced corporate rate of 10%.

iv. Dividends - Dividends received by an ROH from associated companies will be exempt from tax. Dividends paid to companies incorporated outside of Thailand and which do not carry on business in Thailand will be exempt from tax.

B. Accelerated Depreciation Allowances

25% of asset value is allowed as an initial allowance and the remaining can be deducted for over 20 years for the purchase or acquisition of buildings used in carrying out the operations of the ROH.

C. Expatriates

i. An expatriate who is assigned by the ROH to work outside of Thailand is exempt from personal income tax in Thailand for services outside of Thailand. However, the said income must not be borne by the ROH or its associated company in Thailand.

ii. An expatriate who works for an ROH may choose to be subject to withholding tax at the rate of 15% for up to 4 years. By doing so, the expatriate is allowed to omit such income in the calculation of their annual personal income tax liability.

Requirements In order for an ROH to be eligible for tax benefits, it must fulfill the following conditions:

*   The ROH must be a juristic company or partnership incorporated under Thai law

*   The ROH must have at least 10 million baht in paid-up capital on the closing date of any accounting period

*   The ROH must provide services to its overseas affiliated companies and/or branches in at least three countries excluding Thailand

*   At least half of the revenue generated by the ROH must be derived from service provided to its overseas affiliated companies and/or branches, although this requirement will be reduced to not less than one-third of the ROH's revenue for the first three years

*   The company must submit the notification to the Revenue Department

*   Other requirements may be imposed by the Director-General of the Revenue Department

For additional analytical, business and investment opportunities information,
please contact Global Investment & Business Center, USA
at (202) 546-2103. Fax: (202) 546-3275. E-mail: rusric@erols.com

DOING BUSINESS IN THAILAND

MARKET OVERVIEW

Thailand is the United States' 22nd largest trading partner. Two-way trade in 2010 was about $33 billion, with $23.6 billion in Thai exports to the U.S. and $9 billion in

U.S. exports to Thailand. The figures represent an increase of 24 percent in the value of trade between the two countries. U.S. exports to Thailand increased by 28 percent, while US imports from Thailand increased by about 22 percent for the same period in 2009. In Asia, Thailand ranks as the United States' 8th largest trading partner after China, Japan, South Korea, Taiwan, India, Singapore and Malaysia.

The Thai economy is export-dependent with exports accounting for about 61 percent of its Gross Domestic Product (GDP). Since recovering from the Asian financial crisis in the late 1990s, GDP performance has averaged 5-6 percent. The 2010 GDP grew close to 8 percent, as a result of an increase in exports and the Thai Government's increased spending on its "Thai Khem Khaeng" economic stimulus program. This stimulus package was estimated to have contributed an increase to the Thai GDP of 2.3 percent. The Thai GDP per capita is approximately $8,100 (2009 est.).

Exports from Thailand grew close to 29 percent, reaching $196 billion in 2010, despite the strengthening baht and the relatively weak economies in most regions of the world. A major contribution to this impressive growth in exports has been the shifting of the key export destination from the U.S. market to other countries in Southeast Asia. The countries that comprise the Association of Southeast Asian Nations (ASEAN) are now Thailand's largest export destination, accounting for 23 percent of overall exports. This represents an increase of 44 percent compared with 2009. Following ASEAN, the U.S., Japan and China are the next three largest destinations for Thai exports, with each accounting for 11 percent of Thailand's total exports.

The U.S. and Thailand have enjoyed a special commercial relationship for 177 years under the Treaty of Amity and Commerce. Under the treaty, with the exception of a few sectors, U.S. companies operating in Thailand are afforded national treatment, or an "equal playing field," with Thai companies.

Current risks to Thailand's economy include an uncertain political situation, violence in the three southernmost Muslim-majority provinces, and the effects of the global economic downturn.

MARKET CHALLENGES

Thailand's businesses and consumers are extremely price-conscious, often favoring lower prices over product quality or other benefits. Exporters with products that are competitive for reasons other than price should plan to work with their local partner to undertake an extensive marketing strategy.

While Thailand's average applied MFN tariff rate is 11 percent (24 percent for the agricultural sector and 9 percent for the industrial sector), the highest tariff rates apply to imports competing with locally produced goods, often leading to even further price pressures for U.S. exporters hoping to succeed in the market. Furthermore, Thailand has preferential trade agreements with such countries as Japan, Australia, New Zealand, China and India. U.S. firms with direct competitors from those countries could face additional price pressures.

For additional analytical, business and investment opportunities information, please contact Global Investment & Business Center, USA at (202) 546-2103. Fax: (202) 546-3275. E-mail: rusric@erols.com

Corruption and lack of transparency in government procurement tenders, as well as widespread piracy of intellectual property rights are still major concerns for

U.S. companies.

MARKET OPPORTUNITIES

Thailand's economic growth has created opportunities for U.S. companies in a number of infrastructure sectors, including electrical power, telecommunications, and renewable energy. Thai consumers are creating opportunities for new sales of U.S. medical products, cosmetics, security equipment, food supplements and educational services. Thailand also continues to look for U.S. suppliers of automotive accessories, defense equipment, broadcast equipment, food processing and packaging equipment, and environmental technology.

The Thai government is focusing resources on the development of its transportation network, especially train and high speed train projects and also ongoing infrastructure projects, including the expansion of the Bangkok Skytrain and subway systems. U.S. firms engaged in these sectors will find opportunities for success.

For more information on best prospects, please see Chapter 4.

MARKET ENTRY STRATEGY

Obtaining a local partner, such as an agent or distributor, is still the preferred means of entering the Thailand market for the first time as it is one of the most efficient and effective ways to reach Thai buyers. The agent or distributor can facilitate and expedite market entry with their market knowledge and established networks. Within the business culture of Thailand, interpersonal relationships are a vital factor for successful business transactions.

The Commercial Service in Bangkok provides a variety of services to assist U.S. firms with market entry. Please refer to Chapter 10 of the Country Commercial Guide for further information on our services.

INDUSTRIAL LICENSING AND REGULATIONS

The Factory Act of 1992 (which replaces the Factory Act of 1969, 1975 and 1979) stipulates regulations for factory establishment and operation, factory expansion, and safety requirements. The latest revision of the Act also imposes strict controls on industrial pollution. The Act is administered by the Department of Industrial Works of the Ministry of Industry.

A factory is defined as any premise that uses machinery equivalent to five horsepower or more, or that employs seven or more, with or without any machine, for manufacturing, producing, assembling, packing, repairing, maintaining, testing, improving, processing, conveying, storing or destroying anything included in the classes or types of factories presently listed in the Ministerial Regulations.

The Act does not apply to the Government factory run by the Government for the purpose of national security and safety, except that such factories must use the criteria and procedures of the Act as guidelines for their operations.

FACTORY LICENSE

Factories are divided into three categories:

Factories that do not require licenses.

1. Factories that only require notification to officials in advance of the commencement of operations. The operators may commence operations as soon as they receive a receipt form from the Ministry stating that their report has been received.
2. Factories that require license from the Department of Industrial Works, Ministry of Industry, prior to operation. Subject to the Ministry's discretion, the operators may be granted, prior to the license, a certificate allowing them to build parts of the factory.

The operator of a factory in Category 3 must notify the competent authority at least 15 days before a factory test-run commences, and again at least 15 days before actual manufacturing begins.

Note: In general, the degree of government control required is dependent on the degree of environmental protection deemed necessary. The more likely a factory, based on its output, is to cause pollution, the more that type of factory is regulated.

The Ministry of Industry has the power to issue regulations for all of the categories regarding:

- Description, category, or type of machinery and equipment to be used in the operation of the factory business;

- Location, environment, interior and description of the factory;

- Requirements for workers who have specific knowledge to carry out any duties in the factory;

- Process of manufacture and provision of equipment to prevent, stop, or alleviate danger, damage or disturbances that may occur to the public or property in the factory or nearby premises;

- Standards and procedures for the control or release of waste, pollution or anything else arising from factory operations which may affect the environment;

- Provision of necessary data and documents by the factory operators to ensure compliance with the law

- Provision of anything that may affect the safety of work operations.

If there is an inspection of a factory or machinery to ensure compliance with the Act, a private body may carry out the inspection and report in place of government officials, provided the private persons follow the regulations concerning the Act as per the Government Gazette.

Licenses granted are valid until the end of the fifth calendar year from the year in which the business starts operations, except in the case of the relocation of the factory or of the dissolution of the operation in the factory business (which also refers to the event that the factory is transferred, leased or subjected to hire purchase). In these cases, the license is regarded as having expired on the date of issuance of a license to the factory's new operators, or on the date of dissolution of factory business.

For additional analytical, business and investment opportunities information,
please contact Global Investment & Business Center, USA
at (202) 546-2103. Fax: (202) 546-3275. E-mail: rusric@erols.com

Applications for renewal of license must be submitted prior to the date of expiration, along with a fee of 100,000 baht. Following submission, renewal is considered to have been extended unless there is a specific order otherwise. If the application is submitted within 60 days of the expiration date, it will be processed normally, but an additional fine of 20,000 baht will be levied. Once the expiry date is reached, an application for a renewal must be made within 60 days. Upon expiration of the sixty-day period, the application will be treated as if it were a new application.

FACTORY OPERATIONS

The Ministry of Industry has the power to designate:

> The size and quantity of the type of factory in each category that should be established or expanded or not be established or expanded in any locality in the Kingdom.
> The type, quality, source of origin and ratio of raw materials and/or factors or kinds of energy to be used or produced in a factory.
> The type or quality of products to be manufactured in a factory to be established or expanded.
> The application of the produces from factory being established or expanded in certain types of industry; or the export of all or part of such produces.

If a factory in Category 2 or 3 stops operation consecutively for more than 1 year, the operator must notify the competent authority in writing within 7 days of the date the one-year period has lapsed, and must inform the competent authority of such in writing before restarting the operations. In the case of a factory in Category 3, the operator must first receive written permission from the competent authority before restarting the operations.

If there is an accident that causes death, injury or sickness that incapacitates a worker beyond a 72-hour period, the operator must inform the competent authority of such in writing within 3 days of the date of the death or the lapse of the 72-hour period. If there is an accident that causes the factory to stop operations for more than 7 days, the operator must notify the competent authority of such in writing within 10 days of the date of the accident.

A factory operator must obtain permission from the Permanent Secretary to remove machinery from its original place of installation to another site for temporary operations. The period of permission shall be as per request but shall not be longer than 1 year.

In the case of moving a factory to another site, the operator has to proceed as if establishing a new factory.

Permission must also be obtained to transfer, rent, offer for hire purchase or sell a licensed factory. In these cases, the prior license is considered to have expired, and a new license must be applied for by the transferee, lessee or hire-purchaser within 7 days, although no fee is required. Upon submission of such application, the engagement in a factory business shall be continued pending the receipt of a license as if such applicant were the recipient of the license.

If the licensee dies, the heir or administrator of the estate must submit an application for the transfer of the license within 90 days of the date of death; otherwise, the license shall be deemed to expire. Upon submission of such application, the heir or administrator of the estate engaging in a factory business shall be deemed as if they were the recipient of a license.

FACTORY EXPANSION

No factory expansion is allowed unless permission is obtained. There is a fee of 100,000 baht to apply to expand a factory. As defined in the Act, the following undertakings constitute factory expansion:

> An increase in the number of machines, or change or modification of machines to increase its aggregate power by 50% or more in case where the original machines have their aggregate powers of not more than one hundred horse powers or an equivalent thereof of not more than one hundred horse powers or to increase from fifty horse powers or more in case the original machines have their aggregate powers of more than one hundred horse powers or an equivalent thereof of more than one hundred powers.
> The addition to, or alteration of, any part of the factory building which causes any part of the foundation of the factory to bear a load of an additional 500 kilograms or more.

In the case that a licensee:

> Increases the quantity of machines, changes or modifies the machines used for production or generation of power, but by less than 50% of increased aggregate power, or
> Increases the area of the factory building or constructs the new factory building for the direct benefits of the business of such factory rendering the area of the factory building to be increased from 50% or more in case where the area of the factory building does not exceed 200 square meters or to be increase from 100 square meters or more in case where the area of the factory exceeds 200 square meters,

The notification in writing must be filed with the competent authority within 7 days of the date of the change.

A license as to the expanded part shall be valid for the same period as that of the license.

OTHER PROVISIONS

Any factory that is seriously endangering the public or property in the factory or its vicinity may be ordered to cease operations or to make specified improvements. The Minister has the authority to order removal of all or part of the plant to a location where the public will not be threatened. Officers of the Ministry of Industry have broad powers of inspection, and are authorized to issue written orders requiring a factory to cease operations, modify or repair machinery, or undertake other remedial measures.

Issuance of either a factory establishment license or a factory operator's license does not exempt the licensee from compliance with other central or local government requirements for carrying out a proposed industrial activity. For example, the factories established to produce and sell food and drugs must also apply for production license from the Ministry of Health.

Licenses may be suspended for violations of the Act or for failure to carry out orders issued under the Act by competent officials.

Violation of certain provisions of the Act may incur penalties in the nature of a fine or imprisonment not exceeding 4 years. A Case Settlement Committee of three legal experts is appointed by the Ministry to carry out penalties for violations of the Act. If the offender is a partnership, company or other juristic entity, the directors, managers or other persons responsible for committing the offense are subject to the same punishment unless it can be proved that the offense was committed without their knowledge or consent.

6. PROCEDURES AND TIMETABLE FOR FACTORY PERMITS/LICENSE

Insustrial Estate of Thailand (IEAT)

STEP 1 Permit IEAT 01

STEP 2 Permit IEAT 02

Authorization for new factory construction or rental factory renovations Issue construction permits
(IEAT 02/2-5 based on scope or work activity)

▪IEAT 01 Authorities, document, comments:

> Applicant / User
> Industrial Estate Authority of Thailand (IEAT) OR - Ministry of Industry (MOI) Provincial
> Offices (Dept of Ind. Works) as per applicable "Zone", "Park", "Greenfield" rules if not
> "IEAT"
> (3) copies of application submitted
> 10,000 Thai baht permit fee (excluding VAT may vary on location)

Supporting documentation required

If natural person;

> Copy of house registration, ID card of the operator / landowner
> Layout of the land plot according to the mater plan
> Copy of land title or right to utilize the land (Ref. IEAT 5 Sor 1)

If juristic person;

> Copy of company registration (date no over 6 months)
> Shareholder list (date not over 6 months)
> Copy of land title or document indication right to use the land
> Copy of passport of authorized person, or ID card and house registration if local
> All the above with company seal, signature and / or authorized documents

▪IEAT 02 Authorities, document, comments:

> Applicant / User
> Industrial Estate Authority of Thailand (IEAT) OR - Ministry of Industry (MOI) Provincial
> Offices (Dept of Ind. Works) as per applicable "Zone", "Park", "Greenfield" rules if not
> "IEAT"
> (3) copies of application submitted
> Permit fee will be set according to land and building size

Supporting documentation required

> (3) A1 size copies of plant layout (in correct scale ratio) and (2) in A3 size
> Copy of company registration (date not over 6 moths)
> Shareholder list (date not over 6 months)

For additional analytical, business and investment opportunities information,
please contact Global Investment & Business Center, USA
at (202) 546-2103. Fax: (202) 546-3275. E-mail: rusric@erols.com

Copy of land title or document indication right to use the land
Copy of passport of authorized person, or ID card and house registration if local
All the above with company seal, signature and / or authorized documents

IEAT 03 Authorities, document, comments:

Applicant / User
Industrial Estate Authority of Thailand (IEAT) OR - Ministry of Industry (MOI) Provincial
Offices (Dept of Ind. Works) as per applicable "Zone", "Park", "Greenfield" rules if not
"IEAT"
(3) copies of application submitted

Supporting documentation required

(3) copies of machine list with rated horsepower (obtain form from IEAT)
(3) copies of factory layout (with correct and accurate scale ratio) including machinery
and equipmet placement
(3) copies of list of raw material, product and by-products including production process
(3) copies of land layout showing location of an environment and safety management
system
Copy of company registration (date not over 6 moths)
Shareholder list (date not over 6 months)
Copy of land title or document indication right to use the land
Master plan with land plot number
Copy of passport of authorized person, or ID card and house registration if local

*"Export Processing Zones" and " Customs Free Zones" require additional forms at each step.
The same applies for Food &Pharmaceutical projects. Request such forms at the zone's Customs
Officer or Thai Food & Drug Administration as applicable. Certain Thailand Industrial "Parks" &
"Zones" may have unique permit / licence application procedures in place with the Ministry of
Industry. It is recommended one check with both the operator and the local MOI or Department of
Industrial Work to confirm forms and per procedure.*

ENVIRONMENTAL CONCERNS REGARDING SOURCES OF WATER

Certain areas, currently some districts in Ayutthaya and Pathum Thani Provinces, have been
assigned by the Cabinet to be reserved as sources of water by the Metropolitan Waterworks
Authority. In order to control the establishment or expansion of factories in such areas,
regulations have been imposed forbidding setting up or expanding factories which release
wastewater containing heavy metals or poisonous substances used in agriculture, or other
chemicals such as PCBs, cyanide, arsenic, and phenol.

Factories are forbidden to set up and expand in areas reserved for water supply. The only
exceptions are factories which release wastewater with a biochemical oxygen demand of less
than one kilogram per day or those which are set up in Navanakorn Industrial Estates I and II.
Under Ministerial Regulation No. 3, factories specified by Ministry of Industry notifications as
severely affecting the environment are required to provide environmental impact studies.

ENVIRONMENTAL AND HEALTH IMPACT ASSESSMENTS

**For additional analytical, business and investment opportunities information,
please contact Global Investment & Business Center, USA
at (202) 546-2103. Fax: (202) 546-3275. E-mail: rusric@erols.com**

As per paragraph 2 of Article 67 of the Thai Constitution, any project and activity that may seriously affect the quality of the environment, natural resources and biological diversity shall not be permitted, unless its impacts on the quality of the environment and on health of the people in the communities have been studied and evaluated and consultation with the public and interested parties have been organized, and the opinion of an independent organization have been obtained prior to the operation of such project to activity. By virtue of such Article, the Ministry of Natural Resources and Environment by the approval of the Cabinet and the National Environment Board ("NEB") has announced a list of 11 industrial activities that potentially could create severe impact to local communities in terms of natural resources, environment and health and for which environmental and health impact assessments must be conducted.

The list of 11 potentially severe impact projects Simplified Flowchart for EIA and E/HIA Process

1. Land reclamation projects

2. Mining, defined by the mineral • Underground Mining Method, only the caving method and no backfill • Lead Mining, Zinc Mining or Metal Mining using cyanide or mercury or lead nitrate in lead mining process with arsenopyrite associate material • Coal Mining, specifically coal mineral transportation take out project area by cars • Sea Mining

3. Industrial Estate as defined by the Industrial Estate Authority of Thailand Act or Project with similar feature

4. Petrochemical Industry Upstream Petrochemical Industry Intermediate Petrochemical Industry

5. Mineral Smelting Industry of Metal Industry

6. Production, disposal, or configuration of radioactive substances

7. Hazardous waste disposal or incineration plants (exept concrete incinerator that use hazardous waste as supplementary material ot fuel)

8. Avaition transport system

9. Ports

10. Dams or Reservoirs

11. Thermal Power Plants • Coal-fired Power Plant • Biomass-fired Power Plant • Natural Gas-fired Power Plant • Nuclear Power Plant

SELLING U.S. PRODUCTS AND SERVICES

USING AN AGENT OR DISTRIBUTOR

Although Thai law does not require use of local agents and distributors, it is one of the most efficient and effective ways to enter the market in Thailand. The agent and distributor facilitate and expedite the market entry with their market knowledge and established network. Among many business cultures in Thailand, interpersonal relationships are a vital factor for successful business transactions. Local agents and distributors are accustomed to local business practices and requirements. They are in the market and can deliver what is required for a successful business arrangement that companies in the U.S. cannot conveniently provide from afar. In addition, local agents and distributors will take care of regulatory affairs and acquire import permits for U.S. exporters.

U.S. exporters must invest sufficient time and attention in selecting a qualified agent and provide training for marketing and technical support staff. Frequent contact with local representatives is essential in order to build a good relationship.

Some of the best ways to locate an agent and/or distributor in Thailand are to:

Use the International Partner Search Service (IPS), Gold Key Service (GKS), or Video Gold Key Service available from the U.S. Commercial Service, U.S. Embassy Bangkok (see our website at http://www.buyusa.gov/thailand/en for more information).

We recommend ordering an IPS report, since it provides a listing of Thai companies that have been hand-selected by our Commercial Specialist responsible for your industry sector. These companies have examined your product literature and company profile, been interviewed by our Commercial Specialist, and have expressed strong interest in holding further discussions with you about representing your company. We provide you with a company profile and contact information for each Thai company.

Following your receipt of the IPS report and your company's initial follow-up, should you plan to visit Thailand, we recommend you use our Gold Key Service, whereby we will set up meetings with each potential Thai representative. We will arrange hotel and transportation, and provide the appropriate Commercial Specialist from our staff to accompany you to the meetings. Should you not be in a position to travel from the U.S. to Thailand but wish to have face-to-face discussions with the Thai candidates, we can arrange "virtual" meetings by videoconference under our Video Gold Key Service. If you do not have access to videoconferencing equipment, you would simply go to the nearest U.S. Department of Commerce Export Assistance Center for the video hookup in the United States. A searchable directory of these centers may be found at the following website http://www.export.gov/comm_svc/eac.html.

Participation in related trade exhibitions in Thailand can also be an effective means to test the market and locate serious agents and/or distributors in Thailand visiting the trade exhibitions to find new products and services.

ESTABLISHING AN OFFICE

The primary organizational forms for commercial enterprises are as a sole proprietorship, partnership, limited liability company, joint venture, or foreign branch operation. All are similar in nature to those found in the United States. Limited liability companies, however, are more often privately held rather than public corporations. The majority of foreign corporations operating in Thailand do so through private limited liability companies.

There are three major forms of partnership in Thailand:

an unregistered ordinary partnership

a registered ordinary partnership

a limited partnership.

As in the United States, each form of partnership has different levels of liability for partners and different tax consequences for the partners and partnership. If a firm chooses a more formal type of organization, it may decide to form a private limited company or a public limited company.

Generally speaking, a private limited company is similar to a U.S. privately held corporation while the latter may offer shares to the public.

Thailand also offers the possibility of establishing a representative or regional office for those companies engaged in non-revenue generating activities. These may be offices engaged in market research and assessment, providing quality control or purchasing services to a head foreign office, or providing warranty support services for products sold by its head office to the Thai market.

In any process of establishing an office, individuals and firms are strongly advised to consult at an early stage with legal or other professional advisors to ensure compliance with all applicable laws and regulations and to ensure selection of the optimal business structure for their activities in Thailand. The U.S. Commercial Service website (http://www.buyusa.gov/thailand/en) offers listings of law firms operating in Thailand. Other considerations for American firms are to ensure there are no restrictions on foreign entity participation in a particular sector - whether there are import licenses or other special licenses required and whether there are any special incentives available from Thai organizations such as the Board of Investment (BOI) and the Industrial Estate Authority (IEAT).

The U.S.-Thai Treaty of Amity and Economic Relations of 1966 allows U.S. majority-owned businesses, incorporated either in the United States or in Thailand, to operate on a nearly equal footing with Thai corporate entities. As a result, U.S. corporations may establish wholly owned subsidiaries or branch offices in Thailand without the constraints that other foreign firms face from the Alien Business Law. However, there are still government restrictions in the communications, transport and banking sectors, the exploitation of land and natural resources and the trade of domestic agricultural products. To register under the Treaty of Amity, a U.S. company needs to obtain documents from the U.S. Commercial Service office and to file an application with the Department of Commercial Registration at the Thai Ministry of Commerce. The U.S. Commercial Service at the U.S. Embassy in Bangkok has further information available for interested firms or individuals. Information on the Treaty of Amity may also be found at: http://www.buyusa.gov/thailand/en/treatyofamity

Franchising

The franchise industry is still very popular among Thai investors because it is perceived as an attractive and relatively safe form of investment. According to the Thai Franchise Association, there were approximately 408 franchisers in Thailand in 2010. Of this, 50 percent are homegrown, while the rest are foreign. Every year, about 20 franchisers enter into the business and only half of them stay in business for more than five years. The franchise industry is expected to continue to grow at an average of 15 percent over the next few years due to government policies to support in developing standardization of local franchise industry to meet the international level while banks provide loan support for new franchise entrepreneurs. The quality, standards, brands, and innovations offered by U.S. franchises are well known to potential Thai investors. However, franchising fees required by U.S. companies are perceived as very high and start-ups require a huge capital investment.

There is a 25 percent failure rate for local franchise operations, due to franchisors lack of franchise knowledge, which lead to their poor services and low quality. Nevertheless, local franchises have better growth potential than international franchises due to its lower initial investment and lower offer prices. The number of local franchises is still growing very fast due to the flexibility of franchisers and their ability to know the tastes and purchasing influences of local consumers. Local sources mentioned that most Thai investors are willing to pay about US$2,500-

25,000 for franchise fees and will consider their budget as the priority in making the decision on a franchise.

Many famous American franchises already have a presence in Thailand, such as McDonalds, Burger King, Starbucks, KFC, Pizza Hut, Krispy Kreme, Baskin Robbins, A&W, Post Net, Mail Boxes Etc., Subway, Radio Shack, Outback Steak, Sizzler, Dunkin Donuts, and Gymboree. The best prospects for U.S. franchise concepts are in the following areas: food service business, automotive aftermarket, laundry, and home building & maintenance services.

DIRECT MARKETING

Direct marketing is considered to be an effective means of marketing in Thailand and is expected to grow steadily. Since the onset of the Asian financial crisis in mid-1997, many of those made redundant joined the direct marketing workforce. Often, these people possess business experience and are highly motivated. Direct marketing is used widely in the sale of life insurance, cosmetics, health products, cleaning and household items, and electrical appliances. Major U.S. cosmetics brands that are sold via direct marketing are Amway, Nu Skin, Herbal Life, and Avon. Even though direct marketing has proved to be very successful in the Thai market, many problems still need to be solved such as poor product quality, loss during delivery, imitation, and poor enforcement of consumer protection laws by the government of Thailand.

Direct marketing and mail order sales to some extent have benefited from use of individual credit cards in Thailand. Credit cards stretch the buying power of Thai consumers and facilitate retail sales through non-traditional means, such as mail order and electronic commerce. Leading the market in this sector are American Express (Amex) and Citibank (which issues both Visa and MasterCard). Most major department stores in Thailand conduct direct marketing via mail order campaigns through their own networks of discount cardholders. Installment plan sales of household consumer goods and electrical appliances are gaining popularity among consumers, especially in rural areas.

TV home shopping was introduced several years ago and had been moderately accepted. Within the last few years however, it has been gaining ground. Currently, it generates an annual turnover of over US$50 million. Still, the poor quality of some products has lessened consumer confidence in this channel. The Thai consumers' buying pattern of seeing and touching products that they are buying is another limitation of the TV home shopping.

JOINT VENTURES/LICENSING

Joint ventures (JVs) and licensing agreements are important market entry strategies for American exporters to Thailand. In many cases, the only way to overcome costly freight charges, high tariffs and competition from cheaper local goods is via local production. Thai firms need to become more technologically advanced to offset competition from lower cost producers. Thailand's Civil and Commercial Code has a section on General Contracts, which broadly governs all contractual business relationships and transactions. Depending on the nature of the contract, the Public Companies Act and Alien Business Act include provisions pertaining to joint venture agreements which American firms should be aware of before signing with any local partners. Joint venture partnerships with funding support, technology transfer and training components are effective mechanisms to achieve this.

Many Thai firms are actively seeking U.S. joint venture partners which, along with much needed capital, can also bring technical, marketing and management skills to a business relationship. In turn, Thai firms generally offer assets, valuable local vendor and government contacts, and

For additional analytical, business and investment opportunities information, please contact Global Investment & Business Center, USA at (202) 546-2103. Fax: (202) 546-3275. E-mail: rusric@erols.com

established business relationships throughout the region. A number of aggressive U.S. companies have already entered into strategic joint-venture relationships with Thai partners in Indochina and China.

The U.S. Commercial Service at the U.S. Embassy in Bangkok can provide assistance to American firms seeking potential joint venture partners in Thailand through various marketing services. Visit their website at http://www.buyusa.gov/thailand/en or visit http://www.export.gov for more information.

SELLING TO THE GOVERNMENT

U.S. exporters interested in selling to the Thai government have opportunities in such key fields as petroleum refining and petrochemicals, telecommunications, transportation, information and communications technology, the environment, health care and commercial defense.

Further information may be found with the Commercial Service in Bangkok or on the Royal Thai Government National Economic and Social Development Board's website at http://www.modernizethailand.com/.

The key to successful bidding on Thai government contracts and supply tenders is to have a reputable local representative with good access to the procuring agency and knowledge of specific procurement requirements. Without this intermediary, it is very difficult to win a government project – procurement is decentralized among more than 200 government agencies and state enterprises. Representatives are accepted as legitimate players in the bidding process. Agents often provide an early "heads up" to

U.S. firms when they hear of attractive tenders. Before these tenders are even issued, they can help to ensure that a principal's product will meet all of the required tender specifications.

It should also be noted by companies bidding on government projects that training on all equipment purchases is an important feature considered in the review of all proposals. A U.S. company should expect additional training costs and expenses on top of the product cost and should plan to build these costs into the bid. American firms may find it more cost-effective to send engineers or specialists to train bigger groups of employees at a plant or specialized government facility, such as a military installation.

A specific set of rules, commonly referred to as the "Prime Minister's Procurement Regulations," governs public sector procurement. These regulations require that nondiscriminatory treatment and open competition be accorded to all potential bidders. However, in reality the system is not entirely transparent, and the Thai government is not a signatory to the WTO Agreement on Government Procurement. Some observers feel that the Royal Thai Government does not always provide a level playing field for foreign bidders. Generally, the procuring government agency provides preferential treatment to domestic suppliers who under a "Buy Thai" policy receive an automatic price advantage of 3-7 percent rate (depending on the product) over foreign bidders in initial bid round evaluations. The specific laws that apply to international tenders are Regulations 87 and

89. These adhere to established international procedures. International companies may bid without having an agent if the government agency or state enterprise in charge of the project does not specify in the terms of reference (TOR) to *only* open for bid proposals from Thai companies. If the project is funded by foreign loans, then it will be treated as an international bid. The "two envelope" system is commonly used, with technical evaluations of bids conducted

For additional analytical, business and investment opportunities information, please contact Global Investment & Business Center, USA at (202) 546-2103. Fax: (202) 546-3275. E-mail: rusric@erols.com

separately from cost evaluations. The procuring government agency reserves the right to accept or reject any or all bids at any time, and is not bound to approve the lowest bid. The procuring government agency may also modify the technical requirements during the bidding process. This flexibility can prove frustrating to bidders. Charges leveled that changes are made for special considerations have been common in the past.

On January 13, 2005, in an effort to encourage greater transparency, the Ministry of Finance announced regulations creating electronic auctions for government procurement. E-auction works like a reverse auction, with the purchasing agency announcing that it wants to buy a certain good or service, and prospective suppliers bidding via the Internet. The lowest qualified bidder wins. E-auction must be used on procurements greater than 2 million baht (approximately $50,000), but agencies are free to use e-auction for lesser value procurements as well if they wish to.

The status and powers of the National Counter Corruption Commission (NCCC) have been enhanced, giving it independence from all branches of government. The members of the Commission sit on the NCCC for a term of nine years with no renewal, and report to their own chairperson. Individuals holding high political offices, and members of their immediate families, are now required to list their assets and liabilities before taking office and upon leaving office. It appears that there is an increasing will to enforce transparency in government procurements. However, the autonomy and transparency of the NCCC has not truly been tested; the appointment of individual commission members and accusations of conflicts of interest are still being publicly questioned in the Thai media.

DISTRIBUTION AND SALES CHANNELS

Distribution and sales of industrial goods in Thailand are normally conducted through two channels: 1) from U.S. exporter to Thai importer, to Thai end-user, and 2) from U.S. exporter to Thai end-user. The selection of distribution and sales channels depends largely on the type of product and the end-user. Exporters of products that require after-sales service should have a Thai importer representing them locally. A local agent or distributor can respond more quickly to provide service and parts replacement. Accordingly, the end-user's confidence will increase if there is a place where they can receive near-immediate assistance any time a machine breaks down. Also, the end-user normally feels more comfortable dealing with a local agent or distributor since there are no language or distance barriers. The agent or distributor also facilitates customs procedures for end-users. It should be noted that, in general, only local agents, distributors, or manufacturer's branch offices in Thailand are eligible to enter day-to-day bidding for routine government tenders. Please also see the sections in this chapter on "Selling Factors" and "Selling to the Government" for more detailed information on bidding on projects by international bidders.

For consumer goods, there are generally three distribution and sales channels: 1) from

U.S. exporter, to Thai importer, to Thai retailer, to Thai end-user; 2) from U.S. exporter, to Thai importer, to Thai wholesaler, retailer, and end-user; 3) from U.S. exporter, to Thai retailer, to end-user. Perishable consumer goods tend to go through the first channel, which is the fastest. In this instance, importers tend to act as wholesalers at the same time. Non-perishable consumer goods normally go through the second or third channel. The second channel seems to be the most favored, especially with lower-priced items, since there are over 250,000 (mostly small) retail outlets in Thailand. Working through wholesalers will promote better market coverage.

SELLING FACTORS/TECHNIQUES

For additional analytical, business and investment opportunities information,
please contact Global Investment & Business Center, USA
at (202) 546-2103. Fax: (202) 546-3275. E-mail: rusric@erols.com

To differentiate themselves from local and third country competitors, U.S. firms should emphasize their strengths in quality, innovation, technology enhancements and customer service. Thai customers have come to expect more, and better, styles and designs, regular product upgrades and updated technology from U.S. companies. They will often choose U.S. products and services on the basis of "value for money," not solely on cost factors. To gain a competitive advantage in the marketplace, U.S. firms should develop and maintain good customer relationships and be able to reference success with existing customers when seeking new clients. American companies should also choose strong local partners or distributors offering high service standards and capabilities.

A competent marketing strategy is important for doing business in Thailand because the market structure is changing rapidly in several respects. Successful companies use the following techniques and strategies to maintain and expand their market shares in Thailand:

Identify potential customers in the appropriate business communities;

Understand end users' behavior and their cultural environment in order to offer the most suitable products to them;

Promote themselves in business communities by advertising through the media, participating in trade shows, and organizing seminars to launch new products;

Educate buyers on new technologies, and provide high reliability and unbiased advice through direct sales to end users;

Sell consulting services together with solutions;

Identify the features and benefits of specific product or service solutions;

Use training as an effective means to make potential customers aware of the quality of products and services, and

Create end user awareness in order to expand services.

Large U.S. firms have their own subsidiaries in Thailand to sell products and provide technical services. Opening a representative office and a company-owned support facility will also underscore the company's commitment to the market. Following the 1997-98 Asian financial crisis, most Thai buyers are requiring longer-term or more flexible and creative financing terms. Thai distributors prefer to deal directly with U.S. vendors over regional distributors and to be appointed as a sole distributor in most cases.

Thai law permits all foreign companies, with or without a local representative, to submit bids on public sector tenders. A consortium of U.S. companies is acceptable for the supply of a wide range of products in large tenders. For example, when bidding was conducted for the New Bangkok International Airport, the U.S. bidders were able to submit without having a local agent but many had a joint venture partner in place even though this was not a condition of the tender. Direct international bids have also been accepted for major power plants. Conversely, day-to-day procurements by public sector agencies and ministries almost always make local representation a condition for bidders. The U.S. Commercial Service can certify notarized documents presented by American firms and their local partners prior to bid submissions to meet the requirements of the agency or ministry tendering the bid. Most foreign firms have found it advantageous to appoint a local agent who can deal with problems related to communications, bureaucratic procedures,

For additional analytical, business and investment opportunities information,
please contact Global Investment & Business Center, USA
at (202) 546-2103. Fax: (202) 546-3275. E-mail: rusric@erols.com

local business practices and marketing when competing and bidding on government projects. For more detailed information, please also see the section on "Selling to the Government," in this chapter.

U.S. firms should be aware that while the purchasing company may simply accept the lowest bid that meets specifications, it might also attempt to bargain with one or more of the lowest bidders to negotiate better terms. Therefore, U.S. firms should be prepared to empower their agents to take measures to increase competitiveness. On major contracts, it is advisable to have an American representative involved when such bargaining ensues. In addition, the public agencies may request credit in their procurement tenders. A supplier who offers credit will have a better chance of winning bids. Sales without credit are sometimes made if other factors such as price, quality, and delivery schedules are of greater importance.

The most important requirements for new U.S. suppliers are: continuous upgrading and development of new products; suitable promotional activities; good service, and hiring qualified representatives in the local market. In addition, flexible sales policies are also important to attract potential long-term users. A Thai language manual for users is also important.

ELECTRONIC COMMERCE

The Royal Thai government's support for expanded ICT infrastructure has enabled broader internet penetration and cheaper access to information for the Thai people. This growth has been accompanied by legislation that regulates internet usage; namely the Computer Crime Act of 2007. Several people have been detained in Thailand under this Act in 2009.

E-Commerce technology enables Thai companies to reach more customers around the world, reduce their overhead costs and become more efficient. E-Commerce is expected to become more widely used in Thailand to support "business to business" collaboration (i.e., supply chain management and e-marketplaces). Thai consumers still prefer to see goods before purchasing them.

TRADE PROMOTION AND ADVERTISING

Advertising and trade promotion are important marketing tools in Thailand, especially for the sale of consumer goods. In particular, automobile, insurance services, food supplements, and consumer products should be promoted heavily via a full range of mass media. In 2010, advertising on television is the most popular and commands 60 percent, newspapers 14 percent, radio 7 percent, cinema 6 percent, magazine 5 percent, billboards 4 percent, transit 2 percent, in-store 1 percent and Internet 0.3 percent. New media (satellite/cable TV, mobile TV, website, social media, and digital media) has been projected to increase 50-60 percent as other traditional media in 2011 due to consumers turn to spend more time on digital content on interactive applications. There are six free television channels and 400 local cable television channels. Since the government allowed advertising on satellite/cable TV in early 2008, the advertising agencies has turned to spend more advertising budget on satellite/cable TV services, which are expected to grow 4 – 8 percent of overall advertising budget for free television channels within the next 3 years. Television and newspaper are a very successful medium for the promotion of a wide range of American consumer products. There are two popular English-language newspapers in Thailand, "The Bangkok Post" and "The Nation". For advertising, U.S. companies should also consider Thai-language publications as other essential means to promote their products and services. The most popular daily business newspapers in Thai are "Krung Thep Thurakit" (Bangkok Business News) and "Manager." Special promotional campaigns should be conducted

For additional analytical, business and investment opportunities information,
please contact Global Investment & Business Center, USA
at (202) 546-2103. Fax: (202) 546-3275. E-mail: rusric@erols.com

at local shopping centers, hotels and convention halls. The most popular campaign is giving away free samples at major business and commercial buildings.

The Internet has become a far more dynamic and effective marketing tool and can be developed much more as a selling medium in almost every industry for both durable and non-durable goods. Digital provides incredibly rapid information delivery and real-time updates of happenings and also offers consumers a fast track for getting news. Digital media serve as channels to reach a broader client base, develop stronger customer relations, generate customer feedback, and enhance a company's image.

Commercial promotions are an equally important marketing tool for both consumer and industrial products in Thailand. Consumer trade promotion in Thailand is frequently conducted by using gift premiums, discount coupons, or drawings for items such as package tours, cars, or electrical appliances. Consumer trade promotion events are frequently held in supermarkets and shopping malls. Exhibiting firms repeatedly take part in these events because the cost of attending is much lower than participating in a privately organized trade fair. The Department of Export Promotion in Thailand has been actively holding industry exhibitions to promote Thai exports to international buyer audiences during "trade days" and increase domestic awareness by staging "public days" at such fairs.

Industrial product promotion, on the other hand, varies from industry to industry. The two most efficient methods of promotion for industrial products are trade exhibitions and placement of advertisements in trade magazines. Trade fairs with an industry focus serve as a screening tool since exhibitors can be certain that they will have access to the appropriate group of customers. The U.S. Commercial Service in Bangkok includes a list of suggested industry events staged in Thailand a well as U.S. Pavilions at local events and trade missions in Chapter 9 of this Country Commercial Guide. This information is also published on the Commercial Service website in English (http://www.buyusa.gov/thailand/en or http://www.export.gov) and in Thai at http://www.buyusa.gov/thailand/th . It is advisable to translate all product literature and technical specifications into Thai when advertising in trade journals, participating in trade shows or organizing technical seminars. Successful firms also arrange for their agents to receive specialized training at offices or factories in the U.S.

Major Newspapers:

The Bangkok Post http://www.bangkokpost.net

The Nation http://www.nationmultimedia.com

Krung Thep Thurakit (Bangkok Business News) http://www.bangkokbiznews.com

Post Today (Thai): http://www.posttoday.com

Business Day Newspaper: http://www.bday.net

Magazines:

Business in Thailand Magazine (http://www.businessinthailandmag.com)

Business Web Sites:

http://www.buyusa.gov/thailand/en http://www.ustbc.org http://www.indo-siam.com

Pricing

The market in Thailand is open and very competitive. Thai customers agree that price is a significant factor in selecting which products to purchase. U.S. firms need to study such factors as the channels of distribution, necessary sales and promotional techniques and the current pricing practices of key competitors. Standard credit payments, as in most international trade, apply in Thailand as well.

Importers of large equipment or machinery charge a commission of 5-10 percent and allow their customers to open a letter of credit themselves. Manufacturers or wholesalers normally receive a 5-10 percent profit margin. Retailers and distributors of local products require a 25-35 percent margin. There is a 7 percent V.A.T. charged on consumer goods as well.

Thai consumers are very price conscious. In fact, less than half of Thai consumers report buying based on brand-name recognition and first time buyers often buy on price alone. Consumers are often offered free gifts or extra options with their purchases. In addition, midnight sales or occasional sales have proven to be quite successful. Retailers' pricing depends on the product and the frequency of turnover. In general, the

margin structure is as follows:

Convenience Stores	18-20 %
Discount Stores	8-10 %
Department Stores	40%
Manufacturers or Wholesalers	5-10 %
Distributors of Local Products	10-15 %

Direct sale of specialty products 60-80 % Direct sale of general product 40 % max.

Importers of large equipment or machinery 5-10 % Importers of luxury products 60 % min.

SALES SERVICE/CUSTOMER SUPPORT

Training, after sales service, reliable customer support, and the availability of spare parts are the most important factors cited by Thai customers in evaluating services related to their purchasing decisions. These factors are especially important when marketing industrial products. Buyers seek a quick turnaround time on their requests for technical assistance and perceive such service as being provided by reliable suppliers. In case a local branch cannot provide the service, suppliers should be able to acquire support from overseas branches. Spare parts should also be available in a timely manner.

Better support and after-sales-service have placed U.S. suppliers in a much better position, compared with their European competitors selling products of equal quality or Asian competitors that provide lower priced products. Thai customers generally have greater confidence in U.S. suppliers' service and support, due to their well-trained service and support teams, availability of concisely written manuals, and willingness to modify product offerings. Some Thai buyers would rather invest in higher-quality, more expensive products, in order to save expensive maintenance costs following warranty expirations.

For additional analytical, business and investment opportunities information, please contact Global Investment & Business Center, USA at (202) 546-2103. Fax: (202) 546-3275. E-mail: rusric@erols.com

Suppliers of products that have complicated technologies should hire and train a team of highly qualified and experienced technical people as well as provide technical training to their customers. It is also advisable to set up a customer help desk. High-end Thai customers usually consider quality, service and price respectively when purchasing products. A well-trained after-sales service team can increase the possibility of repeat orders from satisfied customers. In addition, Thai customers appreciate receiving periodic technical updates and information from their suppliers. Often, engineers or specialists are sent by the U.S. firm to stay for extended periods in Thailand to conduct larger scale training of big groups of employees who will operate new equipment.

It is important for U.S. suppliers to appoint a qualified partner who can provide their customers with quality services in the Bangkok area and elsewhere. Major suppliers noted that competitive pressures and slim margins have forced them to place higher priority on service and support in order to retain old customers and gain new ones. Positive word of mouth recommendations from customers can increase the supplier's reputation and sales volume. Conversely, bad service can severely hamper a company's chance for increasing sales in this market.

PROTECTING YOUR INTELLECTUAL PROPERTY

Protecting Your Intellectual Property in Thailand:

Several general principles are important for effective management of intellectual property ("IP") rights in Thailand. First, it is important to have an overall strategy to protect your IP. Second, IP is protected differently in Thailand than in the U.S. Third, rights must be registered and enforced in Thailand, under local laws. Your U.S. trademark and patent registrations will not protect you in Thailand. There is no such thing as an "international copyright" that will automatically protect an author's writings throughout the entire world. Protection against unauthorized use in a particular country depends, basically, on the national laws of that country. However, most countries, including Thailand, do offer copyright protection to foreign works under certain conditions, and these conditions have been greatly simplified by international copyright treaties and conventions.

Registration of patents and trademarks is on a first-in-time, first-in-right basis, so you should consider applying for trademark and patent protection *before* selling your products or services in the Thailand market. It is vital that companies understand that intellectual property is primarily a private right and that the U.S .government generally cannot enforce rights for private individuals in Thailand. It is the responsibility of the rights holders to register, protect, and enforce their rights where relevant, retaining their own counsel and advisors. Companies may wish to seek advice from local attorneys or IP consultants who are experts in Thailand law. The U.S. Commercial Service can provide a list of local lawyers upon request:

http://www.buyusa.gov/thailand/en/bsp.html?bsp_cat=80120000

While the U.S. Government stands ready to assist, there is little we can do if the rights holders have not taken these fundamental steps necessary to securing and enforcing their IP in a timely fashion. Moreover, in many countries, rights holders who delay enforcing their rights on a mistaken belief that the U.S. Government can provide a political resolution to a legal problem may find that their rights have been eroded or abrogated due to legal doctrines such as statutes of limitations, laches, estoppel, or unreasonable delay in prosecuting a law suit. In no instance should U.S. Government advice be seen as a substitute for the obligation of a rights holder to promptly pursue its case.

It is always advisable to conduct due diligence on potential partners. Negotiate from the position of your partner and give your partner clear incentives to honor the contract. A good partner is an important ally in protecting IP rights. Consider carefully, however, whether to permit your partner to register your IP rights on your behalf. Doing so may create a risk that your partner will list itself as the IP owner and fail to transfer the rights should the partnership end. Keep an eye on your cost structure and reduce the margins (and the incentive) of would-be bad actors. Projects and sales in Thailand require constant attention. Work with legal counsel familiar with Thai laws to create a solid contract that includes non-compete clauses, and confidentiality/non-disclosure provisions.

It is also recommended that small and medium-size companies understand the importance of working together with trade associations and organizations to support efforts to protect IP and stop counterfeiting. There are a number of these organizations, both Thailand or U.S.-based. These include:

The U.S. Chamber and local American Chambers of Commerce

National Association of Manufacturers (NAM)

International Intellectual Property Alliance (IIPA)

International Trademark Association (INTA)

The Coalition Against Counterfeiting and Piracy

International Anti-Counterfeiting Coalition (IACC)

Pharmaceutical Research and Manufacturers of America (PhRMA)

Biotechnology Industry Organization (BIO)

Pharmaceutical Research and Manufacturers of America (PhRMA)

Biotechnology Industry Organization (BIO)

IP RESOURCES

A wealth of information on protecting IP is freely available to U.S. rights holders. Some excellent resources for companies regarding intellectual property include the following:

For information about patent, trademark, or copyright issues -- including enforcement issues in the US and other countries -- call the STOP! Hotline: 1866-999-HALT or register at www.StopFakes.gov.

For more information about registering trademarks and patents (both in the U.S. as well as in foreign countries), contact the US Patent and Trademark Office (USPTO) at: 1-800-786-9199.

For more information about registering for copyright protection in the U.S., contact the U.S. Copyright Office at: 1-202-707-5959.

For more information about how to evaluate, protect, and enforce intellectual property rights and how these rights may be important for businesses, a free online training program is available at www.stopfakes.gov.

For US small and medium-size companies, the Department of Commerce offers a "SME IP Advisory Program" available through the American Bar Association that provides one hour of free IP legal advice for companies with concerns in Brazil, China, Egypt, India, Russia, and . For details and to register, visit:

http://www.abanet.org/intlaw/intlproj/iprprogram_consultation.html

For information on obtaining and enforcing intellectual property rights and market-specific IP Toolkits visit: www.StopFakes.gov This site is linked to the USPTO website for registering trademarks and patents (both in the U.S. as well as in foreign countries), the U.S. Customs & Border Protection website to record registered trademarks and copyrighted works (to assist customs in blocking imports of IP-infringing products) and allows you to register for Webinars on protecting IP.

The U.S. Commerce Department has positioned IP attachés in key markets around the world. You can get contact information for the IP attaché who covers Thailand at: http://www.buyusa.gov/thailand/en/contact_us.html

IPR CLIMATE IN THAILAND

Widespread commercial IP counterfeiting and piracy continue to plague intellectual property rights owners in Thailand. The lack of sustained, aggressive, and coordinated enforcement and prosecution remains a substantial problem. U.S. copyright industries reported that losses due to piracy of business software grew to US$367.8 million in 2009, up from US$335 million in 2008 while the music industry reports that piracy has devastated the local creative economy in Thailand. In 2008, physical sales of legitimate music products decreased by 40 percent and faced an additional drop of 17 percent in 2009.

In 2007, Thailand was elevated to the US Trade Representative's Priority Watch List, reflecting an overall deterioration in the protection and enforcement of IPR. The United States and Thailand held extensive consultations on IPR issues under the Trade and Investment Framework Agreement and during the Free Trade Agreement negotiations aimed at strengthening Thailand's regime, but tangible progress has been slow to date.

PATENTS, DATA, TRADE SECRETS, AND PLANT VARIETY PROTECTION

Thailand's patent regime generally provides adequate protection for most innovations. However, Thailand's patent office lacks sufficient resources to keep up with the volume of patent applications, and examination can take more than five years, and eight to ten years or more for pharmaceutical patents. While patent filings have increased in recent years patent issuance numbers have not kept pace, and there is a significant backlog in applications. The Department of Intellectual Property (DIP) is reportedly subject to a hiring freeze that prevents hiring more than the current number of examiners. Thailand joined the Paris Convention and the Patent Cooperation Treaty in recent years and has begun accepting PCT applications.

U.S. industry has expressed concerns that the legislation that Thailand enacted to implement its data protection obligations under the TRIPS Agreement would not provide adequate protection of confidential information from disclosure. On January 30, 2007, the Ministry of Public Health issued implementing regulations for the 2002 Trade Secrets Act. The regulations restrict the government from releasing protected data for a period of five years, but do not provide data exclusivity that would prevent unfair commercial use. U.S. industry is also concerned that Thailand does not have a formal patent linkage system to prevent the regulatory approval of copies of pharmaceuticals that are still patented. There has been a reported increase in the number of such copies receiving Thai FDA approval while the original product is still under patent.

Registration of new plant varieties under the Plant Variety Protection Act began in April 2006. Private sector representatives have expressed concern about the implementation and enforcement of the Act, noting the wide availability of pirated counterfeit seeds and other products in Thailand. In 2010, the first foreign companies applied for protection. The United States has urged Thailand to strengthen the 1999 Act to make it consistent with the 1991 International Convention for the Protection of New Varieties of Plants (UPOV) and to accede to this convention.

COPYRIGHT

Thailand's copyright law, intended to bring Thailand into conformity with international standards under TRIPS and the Berne Convention, became effective in March 1995. The Thai government is in the process of amending the Copyright Law in several ways. A current set of amendments deals with collecting societies and creates fair use exceptions for disabled users. Additional amendments that would create secondary liability for landlords renting to infringing tenants and that would prohibit camcording in cinemas are currently under consideration.

In August 2005, the Optical Disk Manufacturing Control Act went into force. This Act is designed to enhance the authority and capabilities of the Thai government to act against operators of illicit optical disc factories and to control the production materials and machines of legal producers. U.S. copyright industries are concerned that the Optical Disk Act is deficient in several respects, including that penalties are not high enough to deter pirates and do not enhance the Thai government's enforcement and oversight powers sufficiently. There has only been one action taken under the Optical Disk Act since it came into force.

TRADEMARKS AND GEOGRAPHICAL INDICATIONS

The Thai government amended its trademark law in 1992, increasing penalties for infringement and extending protection to service, certification, and collective marks. The Thai government also streamlined trademark application procedures, addressing issues raised by the U.S. Government. Additional amendments designed to bring Thailand's trademark law into compliance with the TRIPS Agreement were enacted in June 2000, broadening the legal definition of a mark. Thailand is in the process of joining the Madrid Protocol and is also considering further amendments to the Trademark Act.

The Geographical Indications Act was passed by the Thai Parliament in September 2003 and went into effect in April 2004. This legislation allows rights holders to seek protection for indications that identify a good as originating in the territory of a member or a region or locality in that territory, where a given quality, reputation, or other characteristic of the good is essentially attributable to its geographic origin. It is not clear how this law will be applied to U.S. geographical indications ("GI"s), because it requires explicit evidence that the GI is protected under the law of the foreign country in order to receive protection in Thailand. In addition, the existence of a similar previously registered trademark does not constitute grounds for refusal of a GI registration in Thailand.

ENFORCEMENT

Thailand's IPR enforcement efforts have been inconsistent. Corruption and a cultural climate of leniency can complicate both enforcement actions and prosecution of cases. The frequency of raids compromised by leaks from many sources remains a concern. Rights holders complain that seized materials disappear and are used to reward enforcement officials and even the press. Pirates, including those associated with transnational crime syndicates, have responded to intensified levels of enforcement with intimidation against rights holders' representatives and enforcement authorities.

In 2009, The Royal Thai Government established the National Intellectual Property Policy Committee which is chaired by the Prime Minister and has the Deputy Minister of Commerce, Mr. Alongkorn Ponlaboot, as Vice-Chair. It now comprises top-level representatives from 11 agencies namely, the Ministry of Commerce, the Ministry of Culture, the Ministry of Education, the Ministry of Finance, the Ministry of Information and Communication Technology, the Ministry of Foreign Affairs, the Ministry of Science and Technology, the Ministry of Public Health, the Royal Thai Police, the Office of the Attorney General and the National Broadcasting and Telecommunication Commission. The responsibilities of the Committee include formulating policies and strategies for promoting intellectual property, fighting against rights violations at all levels and improving the intellectual property laws and their implementation.

The Department of Special Investigations (DSI) was established in 2004 and took on an IPR enforcement role, focusing on major infringing production, warehousing and trafficking operations, as well as those activities associated with organized crime. In January 2006, the threshold for cases to be referred to DSI was lowered to 500,000 baht ($13,400), promising stronger investigative action into more cases.

The Thai government established a specialized intellectual property court in 1997, which has improved judicial procedures and imposed tougher penalties. Criminal cases generally are disposed of within 6 months to 12 months from the time of a raid to the rendering of a conviction. However, courts frequently hand down light sentences that are not considered a deterrent to criminal behavior. Right holders and even the Royal Thai Police complain that the IP Court is increasingly unwilling to issue search warrants and civil search orders. For many right holders, this is the primary obstacle to enforcement.

U.S. copyright industries continue to express serious concerns over optical media piracy in Thailand. Right holders report that enforcement of the Optical Disk Manufacturing Control Act has been sporadic, and only one case has been brought by prosecutors in five years. Industry has noticed a small decline in the amount of pirated product available on the streets, but this is more than matched by an increase in online piracy. Digital copyright issues are not directly addressed in the Thai copyright law, and law enforcement agencies lack sufficient expertise and resources to tackle the problem. Cable and broadcast satellite piracy continue to be a major problem throughout Thailand, as pirate providers expand their reach in the provinces. Book publishers have also raised concerns that the existing copyright law is being interpreted in a manner that allows extensive book piracy to go unchecked. According to industry, annual losses are estimated at about approximately $30 million.

Trademark infringement remains a serious problem. U.S. companies with an established presence in Thailand and a record of sustained cooperation with Thai law enforcement officials have had some success in defending trademarks, but the process remains time-consuming and costly. Penalties for proven trademark violations are insufficiently high to have a deterrent effect.

The Government organization that mainly responsible for IPR matters in Thailand is the Ministry of Commerce, Department of Intellectual Property. Please find their contact information, including the addresses of the responsible enforcement agencies, as follows:

DEPARTMENT OF INTELLECTUAL PROPERTY, MINISTRY OF COMMERCE:

http://www.ipthailand.go.th/ipthailand/ 44/100 Sa Nam Bin Nam Road, Muang Nonthaburi 11000 Tel: (662) 547-4621 Fax: (662) 547-4699

The Central Intellectual Property and International Trade Court The Government Complex Commemorating His Majesty the King's 80th Birthday Anniversary, Building A, 5th -7th Floor. Chaengwattana Rd., Thoongsonghong Subdistrict, Laksi District, Bangkok Tel: (662) 141-1910 Fax: (662) 143-8725

The Department of Intellectual Property and International Trade Litigation, The Office of the Attorney General The Government Complex Commemorating His Majesty the King's 80th Birthday Anniversary, Building A, 4th Floor. Chaengwattana Rd., Thoongsonghong Subdistrict, Laksi District, Bangkok Tel: (662) 246-2100 Fax: (662) 246-2622

The Royal Thai Police; Economic Crime Investigation Division, Central Investigation Bureau

North Sathorn Road, Bangrak District, Bangkok 10110 Tel: (662) 235-2827 Fax: (662) 234-6806

The Customs Department; Policy and Planning Bureau, The Royal Thai Customs Department, Ministry of Finance

Sunthornkosa, Klong Toey, Bangkok 10110 Tel: (662) 240-2617 Fax: (662) 249-4016

DUE DILIGENCE

The 1997-98 financial crisis in Thailand was due, in part, to excessive risks taken in the financial sector that were not discovered or checked because of legal, regulatory, institutional and information deficiencies, and the nation's weak supervisory system.

American buyers/investors considering any ventures in Thailand should be cautious, and exercise extreme due diligence. A number of local companies still lack transparency in their accounting practices. Commercial Service Bangkok offers our International Company Profile (ICP) service that provides basic information on Thai firms such as: date founded; number of employees; officers; bank references; product lines, and foreign business contacts. More information on this service is available on the website http://www.export.gov.

For more in-depth information, U.S. buyers/investors are advised to hire professional accountancy companies, lawyers, asset appraisers, and other experts in due diligence work to check bona fides of the bank or company they want to buy, extend credit to, or with whom they want to form joint partnership or any type of licensing agreement. A number of leading American accounting and consulting companies with expertise in due diligence are active in Thailand.

American firms may also need to check with government agencies which have information on firms listed in the Stock Exchange of Thailand (SET) for their listing status. Organizations worth checking for this type of information are the Stock Exchange of Thailand and the Securities and Exchange Commission (SEC). Each has their own data bank which include mandatory information that all listed firms need to report on a quarterly and/or annual basis. For information related to other non-listed companies or private owned firms, the Department of Business Development at the Ministry of Commerce should be contacted.

LOCAL PROFESSIONAL SERVICES

It is highly recommended that U.S. firms obtain relevant legal advice from a local attorney who can provide guidance on drafting and enforcing commercial agreements, company registration, and applying for requisite permits. The services of a local attorney are required for executing distributorship agreements, setting up offices in Thailand, registering patents and trademarks, and for taking legal measures to protect a product from intellectual property right infringement.

As literature on commercial law in Thailand (in English) is scarce, it is recommended that a firm wishing to do business in Thailand gather information on regulations and legal processes prior to arriving in Thailand. This will also ensure that the firm is aware of practices and benefits that it is entitled to, granted by the Board of Investment (BOI) and the Industrial Estate Authority of Thailand (IEAT).

The U.S. Commercial Service at the American Embassy in Bangkok can provide a list of Thai lawyers and American legal consultants who specialize in Thai commercial law and service international clients. The list can also be downloaded from the Commercial Service Bangkok website at http://www.buyusa.gov/thailand/en.

Although Thai law does not require use of local agents and distributors, it is one of the most efficient and effective ways to enter the market in Thailand. The agent and distributor facilitate and expedite the market entry with their market knowledge and established network. Among many business cultures in Thailand, interpersonal relationships are a vital factor for successful business transactions. Local agents and distributors are accustomed to local business practices and requirements. They are in the market and can deliver what is required for a successful business arrangement that companies in the U.S. cannot conveniently provide from afar. In addition, local agents and distributors will take care of regulatory affairs and acquire import permits for U.S. exporters.

U.S. exporters must invest sufficient time and attention in selecting a qualified agent and provide training for marketing and technical support staff. Frequent contact with local representatives is essential in order to build a good relationship. The Commercial Service Bangkok offers services to assist you in identifying a qualified agent. Please refer to the first section of this chapter.

WEB RESOURCES

U.S. Commercial Service Home Page (English Version): http://www.buyusa.gov/thailand/en

U.S. Government Export Portal: http://www.export.gov

U.S. Commercial Service Home Page (Thai Version): http://www.buyusa.gov/thailand/th

U.S. Department of Commerce Export Assistance Center: http://www.export.gov/comm_svc/eac.html.

Business in Thailand Magazine: http://www.businessinthailandmag.com

Business Web Sites: http://www.ustbc.org, http://www.indo-siam.com

Board of Investment: http://www.boi.go.th

The Bangkok Post: http://www.bangkokpost.net

The Nation: http://www.nationmultimedia.com

Krung Thep Thurakit (Bangkok Business News): http://www.bangkokbiznews.com

Post Today (Thai): http://www.posttoday.com

Business Day Newspaper: http://www.bday.net

TRADE REGULATIONS, CUSTOMS, AND STANDARDS

IMPORT TARIFFS

The Thai Government is behind schedule in its WTO tariff reduction commitments but has significantly eased other barriers for a small, select group of agricultural and food products in the past several years. The United States has benefited from these measures through increased sales and/or additional market share.

Nevertheless, Thailand's high tariff structure remains a major market access impediment. Duties on many high-value fresh and processed food products are especially high. Even though the rates will decline by 33 to 50 percent under the WTO, most items remained in the 30 to 40 percent range by 2005 -- high compared with Malaysia, Singapore and Indonesia. Thus, producers of meats, certain fresh and dried fruits, juices, and other packaged items may still find it difficult to penetrate the Thai market.

Thailand's tariff rate quotas for a selected number of agricultural products were adjusted in 1996. In some cases, Thailand has lowered applied tariffs on agricultural and food products below its WTO commitments. For example, Thailand eliminated the quota for soybeans and reduced tariffs on soybean meal when specific domestic purchase requirements were met. Corn is still subject to a tariff-rate quota based on domestic wholesale corn prices. Rice is subject to a "safeguard" on importation and price levels, pursuant to WTO rules.

TRADE BARRIERS

In addition to high duties, other Thai policies continue to impose tough barriers on imports of products. For example, Thailand's food registration and labeling requirements are time-consuming and costly for suppliers of processed food products.

Phytosanitary (SPS) standards continue to be a source of concern for the United States. SPS Standards for certain agricultural products also often appear to be applied arbitrarily and without prior notification.

IMPORT REQUIREMENTS AND DOCUMENTATION

IMPORT LICENSE REQUIREMENTS

Import licenses are required for 26 categories of items, down from 42 categories in 1995-1996. Licenses are required for the import of many raw materials, petroleum, industrial, textiles, pharmaceuticals, and agricultural items. Imports of some items not requiring licenses nevertheless must comply with applicable regulations of concerned agencies, including, in some cases, extra fees and certificate of origin requirements.

Additionally, a number of products are subjected to import control under other laws:

Importation of processed foods, medical devices, pharmaceuticals, vitamins, and cosmetics require licensing from the Food and Drug Administration, Ministry of Public Health.

Importation of tungsten oxide, tin ores, and metallic tin in quantity exceeding two kilograms require permission from the Department of Mineral Resources, Ministry of Industry.

Importation of arms, ammunition, or explosive devices requires licensing from the Ministry of Interior.

Importation of antiques or objects of art, whether registered or not, require permission from the Fine Arts Department, Ministry of Education.

IMPORT/EXPORT DOCUMENTATION REQUIREMENTS AND CERTIFICATION

General customs clearing procedures for both imports and exports in Thailand require the submission of a Customs' export entry form or import entry form. The form should be accompanied by standard shipping documents, which include: commercial invoice, packing list, bill of lading/airway bill, and letter of credit. Some products may require import/export license and/or authorization from relevant agencies. These include food products (processed or unprocessed), pharmaceuticals, medical devices, healthcare products, cosmetics, hazardous substances, animals, and some agricultural products. As of January 29, 2002, Thailand has already eliminated its requirement of a certificate of origin for information technology imports pursuant to the WTO Information Technology Agreement. In general, use of a freight forwarder to deal with import and export customs clearing in Thailand is highly recommended.

U.S. Export Controls

For information on the latest U.S. export and re-export regulations, please go to the following website: http://www.bis.doc.gov/

TEMPORARY ENTRY

As a member of the World Customs Organization, Thailand has been using A.T.A. Carnet. This treaty facilitates the duty exemption of goods temporarily imported for exhibitions, exposition meetings, training, seminars and international conferences. Imported goods used for free distribution (such as T-shirts, caps, scarves, pens, etc.) or for exchange between attendees of international meetings (related to the development of economy, social and/or technology aspects) are exempt from duty. The goods should have a logo or symbol related to the meeting, and the value of goods should be relatively inexpensive. At present, the Thai Customs grants duty exemption on exhibition goods for use only at exhibition sites, for the repair of professional equipment, product samples, and scientific/technological equipment. If the goods are not re-exported within six months, duties and tax will then be levied. The entry of temporary imported goods and exhibit materials can be handled by freight forwarding companies for customs clearance and other required procedures. For further information, please see chapter 9 –

For additional analytical, business and investment opportunities information, please contact Global Investment & Business Center, USA at (202) 546-2103. Fax: (202) 546-3275. E-mail: rusric@erols.com

Temporary Entry of Goods and Exhibit Materials and visit the section on Customs Procedures at the Thai Customs Department web site: http://www.customs.go.th

WARRANTY AND NON-WARRANTY REPAIRS

U.S. companies based in Thailand can be exempted from import duties for items which are brought into the country and which had left the country before. This is normally the case of repair and service products.

Goods imported for repairing means:

1) Exported goods that were damaged then shipped back to for repair and reexported to the same buyer; 2) Exported goods not meeting required standards shipped back for repair by the vendor and re-exported to the same buyer; 3) Goods sent to Thailand by a foreign customer for repair and then sent back to the customer; 4) Any goods imported for repair and then sent back to any country.

There are two scenarios:

a. Tax of the previous shipment has been reimbursed from the Customs Department. In case the company has applied and been reimbursed for tax from the transaction related to previous shipment, the local company has to process a permit/certificate to allow re-entry of the goods. The said permit application must be placed at the same port as the port of departure from previous outbound shipments. The authorities will check the record of the product to ensure that there has been no modification and changes to product attributes. The goods can stay in Thailand initially up to one year with the possibility of renewal for another year.

b. If the exporter in Thailand did not apply for a tax reimbursement, the exporter can collect the goods. No special permit is required. The same time frame as the above case is allowed. Outbound re-shipment of products involves no duties.

LABELING AND MARKING REQUIREMENTS

Labels must be approved by the Thai Food and Drug Administration and affixed to imported food products. Labels must bear the product name, description, net weight or volume and manufacturing/expiration dates. The label must also identify the manufacturer or distributor's name and address, and the product/label registration number. All labels must be printed in Thai with the exception of alcoholic beverages.

To apply for label approval from the Thai Food and Drug Administration Office, one needs to present a certificate of Food Analysis Report issued by the government of the country of origin or any accredited private laboratory. This certificate should be issued not more than one year from the date of the label approval application. The result of the analysis must comply with the quality or standards specified in the Ministry of Public Health's ministerial notification. A copy of the ministerial notification can be obtained in English, free of charge, from the Food and Drug Administration, Ministry of Public Health, Royal Thai government.

Five copies of the original label, together with the Thai labels attached in the way that the food product will be presented for marketing, must be attached to the application. More information can be found at the Thai Food and Drug Administration website, at: http://www.fda.moph.go.th/

Prohibited and Restricted Imports

Imports of used motorcycles and parts, household refrigerators using CFCs, refurbished medical devices, and gaming machines are prohibited.

CUSTOMS REGULATIONS AND CONTACT INFORMATION

Thai Customs uses value of the imported goods, as specified by the importers and where the transaction value of the goods can be determined, to value the goods for import tax purposes. Where there is a debate between parties on the value of the goods, or where the price of the goods cannot be used as the basis of a Customs valuation, Thai Customs will used the GATT Valuation System (GVS) to determine a value for the goods. Since January 1, 2000, Thai Customs has enforced the GVS to value the goods. Under the GVS, there are 6 methods in order of relevance to calculate the import duty. The price specified by the importer is not used as a reference.

Method 1: Transaction Value of the Imported Goods
Method 2: Transaction Value of Identical Goods
Method 3: Transaction Value of Similar Goods
Method 4: Deductive Value
Method 5: Computed Value
Method 6: Fall Back Value

These regulations have alleviated many valuation problems, although some importers complain of uneven implementation, particularly in the area of intra-company transfers, discounted goods, and promotional items. Progress has been made in reforming payment procedures and broker licensing, but the process continues to be hampered by considerable paperwork and formalities and lack of coordination between customs and other import regulating agencies.

By nature, regulations at the Customs Department are subjected to frequent changes, which may be difficult for foreigners to observe and follow. It is highly advisable for foreign exporters to have reliable freight forwarding and Customs Clearing companies representing them in the goods clearing process and customs relations in Thailand.

Detailed information on the customs regulations can be obtained from the Customs Department's website at http://www.customs.go.th

In addition to import duties handled by the Customs Department, certain import items are also subject to excise tax. These include gasoline and products thereof, automobiles (less than 10 seats), electrical appliances, beverages, perfume, yachts and vessels for entertainment, lead crystal and other crystals, carpets and woven fur items, motorcycles, batteries, marble and granite, liquor, tobacco, and playing cards. It is worth mentioning that an excise tax is also imposed on local products in the same categories as well as on certain entertainment service providers such as horse racing grounds/clubs and golf clubs.

Excise tax is calculated on CIF value plus import duty, special fees pursuant to the Investment Promotion Act and any other taxes or fees as prescribed by Royal Decree (Excluding VAT). Further information on excise taxes can be obtained from the website of the Excise Tax

Department, Ministry of Finance at http://www.mof.go.th/ Import-export statistics and import tax rates can be accessed from the customs website at http://www.customs.go.th

Thai Customs Department of Thailand

Soonthornkosa Road, Klongtoey Bangkok 10110 Tel: (66-2) 249-0442, 249-9494 Fax: (66-2) 249-1279 Website: http://www.customs.go.th/

TRADE STANDARDS

Thailand's emphasis on exporting makes compliance with international standards important to companies manufacturing here. There are now 25 Thai food processors that have been certified as being in compliance with the Hazard Analysis and Critical Control Point (HACCP) system. There are a further 40 food and beverage companies who are in compliance with Good Manufacturing Practices (GMP) standards. The main standards developing organization is the Thailand Industrial Standards Institute (TISI).

STANDARDS ORGANIZATIONS

The Thailand Industrial Standards Institute (TISI) is the central national standards organization under the Ministry of Industry. TISI develops both mandatory and voluntary Thai Industrial Standards (TIS's). TISI publishes a work program once every two years with its plan for standards development for Thailand.

NIST Notify U.S. Service

Member countries of the World Trade Organization (WTO) are required under the Agreement on Technical Barriers to Trade (TBT Agreement) to report to the WTO all proposed technical regulations that could affect trade with other Member countries. Notify U.S. is a free, web-based e-mail subscription service that offers an opportunity to review and comment on proposed foreign technical regulations that can affect your access to international markets. Register online at Internet URL: http://www.nist.gov/notifyus/

Conformity Assessment

The National Accreditation Council (NAC) of Thailand is the part of TISI that administers the accreditation system in Thailand. Through the process of the Thai accreditation system, the National Accreditation Council gives the formal recognition that a conformity assessment body is competent to carry out specific functions or tasks according to relevant international requirements.

TISI is empowered to give product certifications according to established Thai standards and is an accredited body for ISO and HACCP certifications in Thailand.

PRODUCT CERTIFICATION

The government of Thailand requires a compulsory certification of sixty products in ten sectors including: agriculture, construction materials, consumer goods, electrical appliances and accessories, PVC pipe, medical, LPG gas containers, surface coatings, and vehicles. Certification of other products is on a voluntary basis. Industrial products that have TISI's certification are generally regarded as having high standards and good quality. TISI has certified more than 2,000 products on a voluntary basis.

Thailand is part of the ASEAN Economic area, and as part of it, mutual recognition agreements (MRA) become effective for compulsory standards of certain electrical products traded between Thailand, Malaysia and Singapore. Eligible products for MRA must meet the IEC or its equivalent standards.

ACCREDITATION

The National Accreditation Council (NAC) is Thailand's accreditation body (see Conformity Assessment above). Contact information for the NAC is:

National Accreditation Council (NAC) of Thailand **Rama 6 Street, Ratchathewi, Bangkok, 10400, THAILAND Tel: 662-202-3487 Fax: 662-202-3486 Mr. Chaiyong Krittapholchai, Director**

All authorized laboratories are required to be accredited under the scope relevant to such products or product groups by the Thai Laboratory Accreditation Scheme (TLAS) or a laboratory accreditation body that has been approved by the International Product Standards Council (IPSC).

PUBLICATION OF TECHNICAL REGULATIONS

Information can be obtained at TISI; however the official documents are only available in Thai. Basic information can be obtained at http://www.tisi.go.th.

LABELING AND MARKING

For imported foods, a Thai-language label must be affixed to every single retail item of food prior to marketing. Failure to affix the label will lead to product seizure by the Thai Food and Drug Administration. The Thai FDA requires pre-approval of labels only for specifically-controlled foods. For most foods, the food manufacturers or food importers are only required to prepare a product label complying with *Ministerial Notification No. 194 B.E. 2543: Regarding Labeling*. Labels must bear the product name, description, net weight or volume and manufacturing/expiration dates. The label must also identify the manufacturer or distributor's name and address, and the product/label registration number.

For those foods that need to receive label approval from the Thai Food and Drug Administration, company representatives need to present a certificate of food analysis issued by the government of the country of origin or any accredited private laboratory. This certificate should be issued not more than one year before the date of the label approval application. The result of the analysis must comply with the quality or standards specified in the Ministry of Public Health's ministerial notification. A copy of the ministerial notification can be obtained in English, free of charge, from the Food and Drug Administration, Ministry of Public Health, Royal Thai government.

Five copies of the original label must be attached to the application, with one attached to the products in the way that the product will be marketed. More information can be found at the Thai Food and Drug Administration website, at: http://www.fda.moph.go.th/

CONTACTS

Thai Industrial Standards Institute **Rama 6 Street, Ratchathewi, Bangkok 10400, Thailand Tel: (662) 202-3301-4 Fax: (662) 202-3415 E-mail: thaistan@tisi.go.th Website: http://www.tisi.go.th**

Mr. Pairoj Sanyadechakul **Secretary-General Tel: (662) 202-3400 Fax: (662) 245-7802 E-mail: pairoj@tisi.go.th**

Commercial Service Bangkok Contact: **Ms. Wanwemol Charukulthavatch – Commercial Specialist**

U.S. Commercial Service American Embassy E-mail: wcharuku@trade.gov Website: http://www.buyusa.gov/thailand/en

TRADE AGREEMENTS

Thailand is a member of the Association of Southeast Asian Nations (ASEAN). In 1992, leaders of ASEAN governments approved a Thai proposal to establish the ASEAN Free Trade Area (AFTA), which aimed to reduce tariffs on most processed agricultural and industrial products traded among ASEAN countries. The scheduled tariff reductions have continued to be pushed forward; currently, most reductions will be in place by 2015. ASEAN is examining the possibility of expanding this special trade relationship with Australia, New Zealand, China, South Korea, India and Japan.

Thailand has signed a limited bilateral free trade agreement with China and has a partial agreement with India. Thailand implemented an FTA with Australia on January 1, 2005. Thailand has completed FTA negotiations with Japan and the agreement was signed in 2007.

WEB RESOURCES

Thai Customs Department web site: http://www.customs.go.th

U.S. export and re-export regulations: http://www.bis.doc.gov/

Ministry of Finance: http://www.mof.go.th/

TRADE AND PROJECT FINANCING

METHODS OF PAYMENT

The majority of U.S. firms that export to Thailand, conduct business on a documentary basis and use various methods of financing and trade facilitation such as letters of credit (L/Cs), bank drafts and wire transfers. New-to-market exporters and infrequent exporters should require confirmed, irrevocable L/Cs when initiating relationships with new importers and distributors. Once the importer has established a good payment record and the U.S. firm is convinced of the importer's trustworthiness, it is advisable to provide more lenient terms. However, since the 1997-1998 financial crisis, many exporters are retaining tighter control on payment mechanisms than they exercised previously.

HOW DOES THE BANKING SYSTEM OPERATE

In addition to more than 30 commercial banks, both foreign and domestic, the public financial sector includes several "specialized" government banks, namely the Government Savings Bank for small savings deposits, the Bank for Agriculture and Agricultural Cooperatives for farm credits, the Government Housing bank for middle and low income housing mortgages, the Industrial Finance Corporation of Thailand for industrial development projects, and the Export Import Bank for importers and exporters.

In the years before the 1997-98 financial crisis, the Thai financial sector grew rapidly, but it was poorly regulated and mismanaged. However, with the cooperation of the IMF and other multilateral and bilateral donors, the government has done a lot of work to bring financial sector practices in line with international standards and to strengthen the operations and balance sheets of Thai banks. Accounting, auditing standards, and corporate governance have been upgraded. Also regulatory and corporate governance requirements for listed companies have been strengthened. In the banking sector, the Bank of Thailand, with multilateral and bilateral assistance, has improved its examination and supervision functions, and banks are required to meet BIS capitalization standards. As part of its efforts to create fewer, sounder financial institutions, The Bank of Thailand has required all finance companies and credit fanciers to either merge with another bank, convert to a retail or commercial bank, or close operations.

GENERAL AVAILABILITY OF FINANCING

Since the 1997-1998 crisis, local banks and other financial institutions have exercised considerable caution on new lending due to the fear of creating new non-performing loans. New loans are typically offered only to bank customers who have sufficient collateral (land or cash only), for the entire amount of the loan, including interest. Liquidity is ample, and local lending interest rates remain near historic lows for Thailand.

Besides the local commercial, trade, and corporate financing facilities available from local banks, the Thai government maintains facilities, such as direct packing credit, to ease exporters' access to trade financing. The Thai EX-IM Bank, Asian Development Bank, Japanese EX-IM Bank, and the U.S. Export Import Bank also have trade financing facilities.

FOREIGN-EXCHANGE CONTROLS

After the Asian Financial crisis Thailand adopted a managed-float exchange rate regime, by which the value of the Baht is determined by market forces, allowing the currency to move in line with economic fundamentals. The Bank of Thailand regularly intervenes in the market to prevent excessive volatility and achieve economic policy targets that include preventing the Baht from growing too strong or too weak against the currencies of Thailand's major trading partners. The Bank of Thailand prohibits Baht-denominated lending to non-residents where there are no underlying trade or investment activities by the borrower in Thailand.

According to information from the Thailand Board of Investment, non-residents in transit may bring foreign currency and negotiable instruments into Thailand without limit. They may also freely take out of the country all foreign currency they had brought in, without limit. Individuals in transit, however, may not take out Thai currency exceeding 50,000 Baht per person, except for trips to countries bordering Thailand (Burma, Laos, Cambodia, Malaysia and Vietnam), where an amount of up to 500,000 Baht is allowed. There is no restriction on the amount of Thai currency that may be brought into the country.

Regarding investors, there is no restriction on the import of foreign currency such as investment funds, offshore loans, etc. Such foreign currency, however, must be sold or exchanged into Thai Baht, or deposited in a foreign currency account with an authorized bank, within seven days from the date of receipt or entry into the country. An application form F.T. 3 or F.T. 4 must be

For additional analytical, business and investment opportunities information,
please contact Global Investment & Business Center, USA
at (202) 546-2103. Fax: (202) 546-3275. E-mail: rusric@erols.com

submitted to an authorized bank for each transaction involving the sale, exchange or deposit of such foreign currency in an amount exceeding US$5,000 or its equivalent. Repatriation of investment funds, dividends and profits as well as loan repayments and interest payments thereon, after settlements of all applicable taxes, may be made freely. Similarly, promissory notes and bills of exchange may be sent abroad without restriction.

U.S. BANKS AND LOCAL CORRESPONDENT BANKS

Commercial Banks With Correspondent U.S. Banking Arrangements:

Bank of Ayudhya PCL. (http://www.krungsri.com/eng/) 1222 Rama III Road, Bang Pongphang Yannawa, Bangkok 10120 Tel: 662-296-3000 Fax: 662-683-1275

Bangkok Bank Public Co., LTD. (www.bangkokbank.com) 333 Silom Road, Bangrak Bangkok 10500 Tel: 662-231-4333, 231-4665 Fax: 662-236-8288

Kasikornbank PCL (www.kasikornbank.com) 1 Thai Farmer Lane Ratburana Road, Bangkok 10140 Tel: 662-470-1122, 662-470-1199 Fax: 662-470-2749

Krung Thai Bank Public Co., LTD. (www.ktb.co.th) 35 Sukhumvit Road, Klongtoey Nua Wattana, Bangkok 10110 Tel: 662-255-2222 Fax: 662-255-9391/6

Siam Commercial Bank Public Co., LTD. (www.scb.co.th) 9 Rachadapisek Road, Ladyao Chatuchak, Bangkok 10900 Tel: 662-544-1111, 662-937-7777 Fax: 662-937-7550

Thai Military Bank (http://www.tmbbank.com) 3000 Phaholyothin Road, Ladyao Chatuchak, Bangkok 10900 Tel: 662-299-1111 Fax: 662-617-9111

U.S. FINANCIAL / LENDING INSTITUTIONS IN THE LOCAL ECONOMY:
JP Morgan Chase Bank 20 North Sathorn Road, Bubhajit Building
Bangkok 10500 Tel: 662-684-2805
Fax: 662-684-2811

Citibank NA Citibank Tower, 82 North Sathorn Road Bangrak, Bangkok 10500 Tel: 662-639-2000, 662-232-2000 Fax: 662-639-2560, 662-639-2550

Locally or Regionally-based MDB or Other IFI Offices:

Asian Development Bank (ADB) (http://www.adb.org/) Postal Address:

P.O. Box 789 0980 Manila, Philippines Street Address: 6 ADB Avenue, 0401 Mandaluyong City, Philippines Tel: 632-632-4444 (connecting all Offices) Main Fax: 632-636-2444

PROJECT FINANCING

U.S. EXPORT-IMPORT BANK (EX-IM) PROJECT FINANCING

The U.S. Export-Import Bank established its Project Finance Division in June 1994. As developing nations turn away from sovereign-guaranteed borrowing, the Bank's project financing program will assist U.S. exporters to compete in new international growth industries such as the development of private power plants and other infrastructure projects. While such a financing structure has been used successfully in the past for oil and gas, mining, and power projects, the move toward "privatization" by sovereign entities has created new opportunities for U.S. exporters in telecommunication, transportation and other sectors.

The Ex-Im Bank offers short-, medium-, and long-term programs to support U.S. exports to Thailand. The Ex-Im Bank's short-term export credit insurance program will provide for the financing of exports or consumer goods, spare parts, raw materials (on terms up to 180 days) and bulk agricultural commodities and quasi-capital goods (on terms up to 360 days).

OVERSEAS PRIVATE INVESTMENT CORPORTATION (OPIC)'S PROJECT FINANCING

OPIC offers various financing options to assist U.S. businesses investing overseas. OPIC views each project as unique and assesses each transaction individually. All projects seeking OPIC financing must be commercially and financially sound. They must be within the demonstrated competence of the proposed management, which must have a proven record of success in the same or a closely related business, as well as a significant financial risk in the proposed project. OPIC financing can often make the difference when it comes to a project going forward. OPIC can lend up to $250 million per project on either a project finance or corporate finance basis in countries where conventional institutions are often unable or unwilling to lend on such a basis. Generally, OPIC tries to identify three sources of repayment and, therefore, may use a combination of available project cash flow, sponsor support, and collateral to reach a sound financing structure with a prudent security package.

OPIC also finances U.S. business expansion overseas by providing long-term, limited-recourse project financing to ventures involving significant equity participation by U.S. businesses. Financing is available for new ventures as well as expansion or modernization of existing ones. Loan guaranties are typically used for larger projects, while direct loans are reserved for projects involving U.S. small businesses and cooperatives.

U.S. TRADE AND DEVELOPMENT AGENCY (USTDA)

USTDA supports the planning of priority infrastructure projects in developing and middle-income countries worldwide, with special emphasis on economic sectors that represent significant U.S. export potential. USTDA assists in building mutually beneficial partnerships between American companies and overseas project sponsors to complete high quality and successful projects in host countries. USTDA is an independent agency, which works closely with other Federal agencies including the U.S. Trade Representative; the Departments of State, Commerce, Homeland Security and Transportation; the Export-Import Bank of the United States, and the Overseas Private Investment Corporation to advance U.S. commercial interests and host country development objectives.

USTDA advances economic development and U.S. commercial opportunities in Thailand and other developing countries through its cooperation with various private and public entities. The agency's program focuses on two types of activities: 1) project definition and investment analysis; and 2) trade capacity building and sector development activities. The project identification and investment analysis involves activities that support large capital investments that contribute to overseas infrastructure development. Trade capacity building and sector development assistance supports the establishment of industry standards, rules and regulations, trade agreements, market liberalization and other policy reform. USTDA accomplishes its mission through funding project definitional missions, feasibility studies, orientation visits, workshops and conferences, procurement assistance, sector development technical assistance, trade agreement support, training, and trade and industry advisors.

Each year, USTDA funds approximately 125 feasibility studies worldwide. The average USTDA grant is $400,000. In March 2002, USTDA opened its Asia Regional Office in Bangkok to further develop the Thailand opportunities and support USTDA operations throughout South and Southeast Asia. That office is co-located with the U.S. Commercial Service office in Bangkok. Since the inception of the program in the early 1980's, Thailand has received over $45 million for more than 150 projects. While the agency's activities span a wide variety of sectors, many focus on transportation, energy and power, water and the environment, health care, mining and natural resources, telecommunications, and information technology. Emerging opportunities for USTDA involvement in Thailand appear to be in technical assistance and trade capacity building related to mitigating climate change, promoting energy security, improving the transportation and trade infrastructure, ICT modernization and development, and implementation of ASEAN-wide initiatives.

Overall, USTDA's 2010 program in Asia illustrated the unique ability of the agency to meet a wide range of development needs, from supporting energy security and clean energy investments to disaster management initiatives and capacity-building activities designed to foster an environment more conducive to economic growth and trade. USTDA will build on its vigorous program in Asia in 2011 as it continues to enhance their Thailand operations to facilitate commercial partnerships involving U.S. firms that further advance the developmental and trade capacity of the region.

Web Resources Export-Import Bank of the United States: http://www.exim.gov Country Limitation Schedule: http://www.exim.gov/tools/country/country_limits.html OPIC: http://www.opic.gov Trade and Development Agency: http://www.tda.gov/ SBA's Office of International Trade: http://www.sba.gov/oit/ USDA Commodity Credit Corporation: http://www.fsa.usda.gov/ccc/default.htm

U.S. Agency for International Development: http://www.usaid.gov Bank of Ayudhya Pcl: www.krungsri.com Bangkok Bank Public Co., Ltd: http://www.bangkokbank.com Krung Thai Bank Public Co., Ltd: http://www.ktb.co.th Siam Commercial Bank Public Co., Ltd: http://www.scb.co.th Kasikorn Bank Public Co., Ltd.: http://www.kasikornbank.com Thai Military Bank: http://www.tmbbank.com Asian Development Bank (ADB): http://www.adb.org/

BUSINESS TRAVEL

BUSINESS CUSTOMS

Business relationships in Thailand are not as formal as those found in Japan, China, Korea or the Middle East, but neither are they as relaxed and impersonal as is common in the West. Many business relationships have their foundations in personal relationships developed within the social circles of family, friends, classmates and office colleagues. Although Thailand is a relatively open and friendly society, it is advisable to approach potential business contacts with a prior introduction or personal reference. Thais will be more receptive if you arrive with an introduction or letter from a known government official or business contact. Using the Commercial Service's Gold Key Service is also an effective way to gain access to the Thai business community.

The Thai cultural values of patience, respect for status (age, authority, etc.) and not losing face, are significant factors in business relationships as well. Thais feel great pride for their country and have deep respect for tradition. Sometimes, however, observance of traditional formalities may seem inconsistent to the tolerant, relaxed nature of living in Thailand. This can be confusing or frustrating to Westerners who are more informal and more time conscious.

Respect for, and consideration of, one's elders, superiors and patrons is deeply rooted in the Thai cultural and social environments. Thais are very reluctant to hurt the feelings of others or to cause them any dissatisfaction. Losing one's composure is losing face and losing respect in Thailand. It can be difficult for Westerners to be sure they have received accurate and complete answers to questions, or that they have received frank and open opinions. (Source: Thailand Business Basics, Standard Chartered Bank.)

ETIQUETTE

"Khun" is the Thai form of address for Mr., Mrs., and Ms.

The "wai" is a traditional gesture of greeting and respect in Thailand. Practice by placing your palms together in a prayer-like position.

Business cards are an indispensable part of making business contacts in Thailand. Bring lots of your own as a general form of introduction.

Remove shoes before entering a home or temple.

Touching someone on the head or pointing your feet to anything is considered by Thais to be very rude.

Thais hold the Royal Family in high esteem and you are also expected to do so.

TRAVEL ADVISORY

Americans may register on-line with U.S. Embassy Bangkok to obtain updated information on travel and security within Thailand by visiting the U.S. Embassy's website at http://bangkok.usembassy.gov/ . Another place with useful information for travelers is the Royal Thai Embassy in Washington D.C.'s website, http://www.thaiembdc.org/ Travelers visiting Thailand may also wish to review the State Department Consular Information Sheet on Thailand at: http://travel.state.gov/travel/cis_pa_tw/cis/cis_1040.html

VISA REQUIREMENTS

U.S. citizen tourists staying for fewer than 30 days do not require a visa, but must possess a passport and may be asked to show an onward/return ticket. Effective October 1, 2006, persons entering Thailand without a visa will be allowed to stay in Thailand for 30 days per visit. The total duration of stay in Thailand for persons who enter Thailand without a visa cannot exceed 90 days during any six-month period, counting from the date of first entry. Travelers must pay a Passenger Service Charge in Thai baht when departing from any of Thailand's international airports

When a traveler enters the country, Thai Immigration stamps in his or her passport the date on which the traveler's authorized stay in Thailand will expire. Any traveler remaining in Thailand beyond this date without having received an official extension will be assessed an immediate cash fine when departing Thailand. Any foreigner found by police to be out of legal status prior to departure (during a Thai Immigration "sweep" through a guesthouse, for example) will be jailed, fined, and then deported at his or her own expense, and may be barred from re-entering Thailand.

For additional analytical, business and investment opportunities information,
please contact Global Investment & Business Center, USA
at (202) 546-2103. Fax: (202) 546-3275. E-mail: rusric@erols.com

In this regard, American citizens should be aware that private "visa extension services," even those advertising in major periodicals or located close to Immigration offices or police stations, are illegal. A number of Americans are arrested at border crossings each year when the visas and entry stamps they have obtained through these illegal services are discovered to be counterfeit.

Thailand's Entry/Exit information is subject to change without notice. For further information on Thailand's entry/exit requirements, contact the Royal Thai Embassy, 1024 Wisconsin Avenue, N.W., Washington, D.C., 20007, telephone (202) 944-3600, or contact the Thai consulates in Chicago, Los Angeles, or New York City. See our *Foreign Entry Requirements brochure* for more information on Thailand and other countries. Visit the Embassy of Thailand web site at http://www.thaiembdc.org for the most current visa information.

On September 29, 2006, Bangkok's main airport, Don Muang, ceased operations, and all inbound and outbound flights were shifted to the Suvarnabhumi International Airport. Suvarnabhumi International Airport is located 18 miles (30 kilometers) east of downtown Bangkok and is approximately a thirty-minute drive to/from downtown Bangkok in light traffic. Traffic conditions may result in longer drive times. Information on the new airport can be found at: http://www.bangkokairportonline.com/.

See Entry and Exit Requirements for more information pertaining to dual nationality and the prevention of international child abduction. Please refer to our Customs Information to learn more about customs regulations.

• *NON-IMMIGRANT VISA*

Purpose of visit: Business, Conference, Research, Teaching, Mass Media or Missionary work (requires letter from your government, agency or organization sending you on your mission or from your counterpart in Thailand). Education (requires letter from educational institution in Thailand). Family Reunion (requires marriage or birth certificates). Settlement after retirement (requires proof of retirement and financial support). Medical treatment (requires letter from licensed doctor). (Maximum stay is 90 days.)

• *TOURIST VISA*

Purpose of visit: for tourism only. (Maximum stay 60 days.)

• *TRANSIT VISA*

Purpose of visit: Transit (requires proof of confirmed onward ticket to a third country). Sports or Crew (requires letter from organization concerned). (Maximum stay is 30 days).

For more information travelers may contact the Royal Thai Embassy, Visa Section, Suite 101, 1024 Wisconsin Ave., N.W. Washington, D.C. 20007 Tel. (202) 944-3600 Ext. 767 Fax. (202) 944-3611 e-mail: consular@thaiembdc.org

Office Hours: Monday-Friday 9:00 a.m. –1:00 p.m. and 2:30-4:00 p.m. (Walk-in Services: 9:00 a.m. – 1:00 p.m. only) U.S. Eastern Standard Time. Closed on Thai and

U.S.
Official Holidays.

U.S.

Companies that require travel of foreign businesspersons to the United States should be advised that security options are handled via an interagency process. Visa applicants should go to the following links.

U.S.

Companies that require travel of foreign businesspersons to the United States should be advised that security evaluations are handled via an interagency process. Visa applicants should go to the following links.

State Department Visa Website: http://travel.state.gov/visa/

United States Visas.gov: http://www.unitedstatesvisas.gov/ US Embassy Consular Section: http://bangkok.usembassy.gov/visas/visa-services.html

TELECOMMUNICATIONS

Telecommunications for the business traveler in Bangkok and major cities is efficient, with worldwide access for voice, fax and data with international direct dialing. Cellular phones are very common and can be rented for short stays. A foreign cellular phone on GSM roaming service will generally work in Thailand. In rural or remote areas, cell coverage is spotty and only first class hotels have reliable land coverage.

Thailand is a member of the International Telecommunications Satellite Consortium, and maintains 2 ground stations connected to satellites over the Pacific and Indian oceans to provide convenient radio communication services. On December 17, 1992, THAICOM, the first Thai national satellite, was launched into orbit followed by THAICOM 2 on October 8, 1994, and THAICOM 3 on April 16, 1997. A new satellite for high-speed transmission and broadband Internet, iPSTAR has been launched on August 2005 and provides services across the Asia-Pacific region.

Thailand is served by the major international cable television channels including CNN, BBC, CNBC, ABN, Star TV, HBO, ESPN, etc. which are widely available in hotels, residences and other public facilities.

After a long wait, the National Telecommunications Commission (NTC) was set up in October, 2004. The market structure of the telecom sector remains unchanged from the previous year, with the number of operators in both fixed-line and mobile sector the same as in 2004. Fixed-line service providers include TOT Corporation Public Company Limited, True (Previously Telecom Asia Corporation) and TT&T Public Company Limited. The sole international service provider is CAT Telecom Public Company Limited. Mobile phone service operators are Advance Info service Plc (AIS), Total Access Communication Plc (DTAC), Thai Mobile Company Limited, Hutchison CAT Wireless Multimedia Ltd, TOT Corporation Plc., and CAT Telecom Plc.

In the late 1990s, Thailand's cellular phone service grew significantly and overtook the number of subscribers in fixed line telephone service in 2001. Given the continuous fall in handsets prices and attractive sales promotion campaigns, it is no surprise that the cellular phone penetration rate reached 48 percent by the end of 2005, with around 30 million subscribers. The market is presently dominated by GSM-based technologies. By comparison, despite being in operation for nearly 50 years, the fixed line telephone service has a total capacity of over 8 million lines, of which about 7 million are in use. Previously, the competition in the telecom sector tends to be in non-price areas. Major operators, particularly mobile operators, compete using product differentiation through service quality, advertising and value-added services. However price competition is now heating up. Fixed-line operators drastically cut down the price for long distance and international calls. For mobile phones, prices fell for the pre-paid option to as low as two cents per minute.

For a landline telephone, the installation fee is about $90-99, the monthly service fee is $2.52-5.03, and the flat rate for a local call is $0.075. For a cellular phone, an entry-level handset with pre-paid calling card for 60 minutes costs about $70-80, while a handset of the latest technology price ranges from $300 to $700 and more, bundled with attractive post-paid promotion campaigns.

TRANSPORTATION

The business traveler has access to a range of ground transportation in Bangkok and major cities. Metered taxis are common and most hotels offer limousine services. Chauffeured cars can be rented for extended stays. For Bangkok, an extensive public bus network with both air-conditioned and non-air conditioned vehicles serves all areas of the city.

In addition, Bangkok has two mass rail transit systems; the BTS and the MRTA. The BTS, known locally as Sky Train (http://www.bts.co.th), is an elevated train network that opened in Bangkok's most congested business districts, including Silom and Sukhumvit. The MRTA (http://www.mrta.co.th) is a 20 KM subway system that runs between Hua Lamphong (Central Train Station) and Bangsu.

For inter-city travel, public regular and air-conditioned buses are available. These buses run on a regular basis between Bangkok and provincial cities in Thailand. Three regional bus depots serve Eastern region destinations (Ekamai), Northern and North Eastern region destinations (Mor Chit) and the Southern region (Sai Tai Mai).

Thailand has a road network of more than 250,000 kms, of which 51,466 kms is national highways. The 4 major national highways connecting Bangkok and the rest of the country are Highway No 1(North), Highway No 2 (North East), Highway No 3 (central), and Highway No 4 (South).

Inter-city rail services range from comfortable and efficient to primitive. The State Railway of Thailand operates 4,119 kms of rail networks with four main routes: Bangkok-north to Chiang Mai; northeast to Nongkhai and Ubon Rajathani; east to Prachinburi; and, south to the Thai-Malaysian border.

Thailand has 122 ports, wharves, and jetties able to accommodate sea-going vessels engaging in international trade, including eight international deep-sea ports. These deep-sea ports are located in Bangkok, Laem Chabang and Map Ta Phut on Thailand's Eastern Seaboard, and Songkhla, Satun, Narathiwat, Phuket and Ranong in the South, having a total capacity of more than 4.5 million TEU. Laem Chabang Port, Thailand's main port, is expected to be able to handle up to 5.9 million TEU by 2008.

Thailand currently has 28 commercial airports, 5 of which are international and 21 of which are domestic. The five international airports are: Bangkok International Airport, Chiang Mai International Airport, Chiang Rai International Airport, Hat Yai International Airport, and Phuket International Airport. Thai Airways International is Thailand's national airline serving both domestic and inter-continental routes. Thailand also has 28 airports that service domestic flights. Bangkok International Airport (BIA), which is located just north of Bangkok, serves as Thailand's main gateway for air transportation, handling 34 million passengers, 215,000 flights, and 823,000 tons of cargo per year. Suvarnabhumi Airport opened in September 2006 replacing BIA as the country's primary international airport and aviation with an initial passenger capacity of 45 million, and a cargo capacity of 3 million metric tons per year.

LANGUAGE

Thai is the national language. English is the next most commonly spoken language, and is especially prevalent among the business community in Bangkok. (There are four distinct language dialects in Thailand, with the Central Thai dialect being the first language of 75 percent of the population.) Many Sino-Thai also speak Chinese.

HEALTH

Excellent medical treatment is available in Bangkok, with good to adequate treatment available throughout the country. While the general level of health and nutrition is good, some tropical diseases are a problem. Hepatitis is endemic. The incidence of AIDS has leveled off due to educational awareness campaigns by the Royal Thai Government. However, Thailand is still considered a high-risk country, especially among prostitutes and intravenous drug users. Japanese encephalitis and malaria are a problem in rural border areas, but generally not in Bangkok, major cities, or major tourist destinations. Dengue fever outbreaks occur periodically throughout the country. Rabies is also a risk to consider due to the large number of abandoned animals roaming the streets.

Nearly all cases of avian influenza in Thailand and other countries have been associated with close contact with infected poultry. Thailand is among the best prepared countries in the region in terms of prevention and containment of an outbreak. For *information about avian influenza please see the State Department's Bureau of Consular Affairs Avian Flu Fact Sheet at:* http://travel.state.gov/travel/tips/health/health_1181.html

Doctors and hospitals often expect immediate cash payment for services, and U.S. medical insurance is not always valid outside the United States. Many hospitals in Bangkok and other major cities will accept standard credit cards. For additional useful health information, contact the International Travelers' Hotline at the Center of Disease Control at 404-332-4559.

FOOD

Eating is an important part of the Thai group-oriented culture. Thai food has become internationally popular because of its sophistication and variety. The staples of this cuisine include rice, noodles, vegetables, meats, fish, spices and chilies. Thai food can be enjoyed in a wide variety of venues, from street-side kiosks to elegant world-class restaurants. In addition, all other international cuisines are available in the major cities and resort areas ranging from European fine dining, to other Oriental and ethnic restaurants, to American fast food.

Local Time, Business Hours, and Holidays

The common professional workweek in Thailand is 40 hours per week consisting of five, 8-hour days, Monday through Friday. Office hours in Bangkok vary to accommodate flextime travel through the city's notoriously heavy traffic. Common office hours are 8:00 a.m. to 5:00 p.m. Most business offices are closed on Saturdays and Sundays although most commercial establishments remain open. The U.S. Commercial Service Bangkok's hours are 7:00 a.m. - 4:00 p.m., Monday through Friday. The office is closed during lunch from 12:00 noon to 1:00 p.m.

During the calendar, the following are the commercial holidays on which most business and government offices in Thailand will be closed:

			OFFICIAL HOLIDAYS 2011
MONTH	DATE	DAY	OCCASION
January	3	Monday	Substitution for New Year's Day
April	6	Wednesday	King Rama I Memorial and Chakri Day
April	13-15	Wed-Fri	Songkran Days
May	5	Thursday	Coronation Day
May	17	Tuesday	Visakha Bucha Day
August	12	Friday	Her Majesty The Queen's Birthday
October	24	Monday	Substitute for Chulalongkorn Day
December	5	Monday	His Majesty the King's Birthday
December	12	Monday	Substitute for Constitution Day

TEMPORARY ENTRY OF MATERIALS AND PERSONAL BELONGINGS

Thai Customs Department policy and procedures on temporary entry of goods for business practices and exhibitions are described below. Duty exemption is valid for temporary imported goods that will be re-exported within three or six months of the importation date depending on the entry purpose. Traveler entering or departing from Thailand is exempt from duty for accompanying with spirituous liquor (one liter), cigarettes (two hundred), cigars or smoking tobacco (250 grams).

For more specific information on type of goods and steps of customs procedure, please visit the section on "Traveler Information" on the web site http://www.customs.go.th , or contact U.S. Commercial Service Bangkok at tel: (662) 205-5090.

GOODS FOR BUSINESS PRACTICE

Laptop Computers: The Thai Customs Department considers portable computers as reasonable personal effects and not dutiable, restricted or prohibited goods. If travelers carry laptop computers for use while visiting Thailand, they should check the "Nothing to Declare" box on the customs declaration form and submit the form at the Green channel. However, each traveler should carry only one laptop computer at a time and should be prepared to prove at a Customs random inspection that the computer is a personal belonging or for use while doing business in Thailand, and not for re-sale.

Computer Software: Unwrapped computer diskettes and CD-ROMs for use while visiting Thailand are not dutiable. Check the "Nothing to Declare" box on the customs declaration form and submit the form at the Green channel.

EXHIBIT MATERIALS

There are 2 choices of Customs procedures for entering exhibit materials exempted from duty payment into Thailand for A.T.A. Carnet treaty members and nonmembers.

1. Bonded Guarantee (A.T.A.Carnet): A.T.A. Carnet is an international system that provides bonded guarantees on goods imported temporarily. Its purpose is to facilitate customs procedures for temporary import-export of goods that are exempt from payment of duty without

prohibited and restricted conditions. All member states accept and provide this service under their own laws and regulations.

The Thai Customs Department recommends exhibit materials enter into Thailand through a carnet as it cuts down the required Customs procedures. The guarantee issuer and guarantor must be approved by the Customs Department and be a member of the international guarantee issuer organization such as a

U.S. Trade Association or Chamber of Commerce. The guarantee issuer organization can issue a letter of guarantee to exporters in which they agree to pay duty if carnet conditions are not followed.

An importer can use the letter of guarantee as a substitute to the import entry form and the payment guarantee. The importer must complete the carnet import/re-export document and submit it to Customs officers at Thailand's port of entry. The Customs officers will inspect the goods, keep a copy of the import entry form and return the carnet book to the importer. If the goods are not taken out within the period of time stated in the contract, the guarantor will have to pay duty, a 10 percent penalty, and any applicable fees. For further information, please contact the Privilege Goods and Investment Promotion Sub-Division telephone: (662) 249-4150, fax: (662) 249-4212.

2. Imported goods for exhibitions in Thailand (for A.T.A. Carnet non-members): Exhibit materials apply to goods which are imported for public exhibition and goods on which the importer has placed a bonded guarantee and will be reexported within a certain period of time. Goods used up in an exhibition such as printed documents, advertised articles, and distributed materials are not duty-exempted items. The process for temporary importation of exhibit materials into Thailand is as follows:

The importer must provide detailed information on the exhibition including the host, venue, period of time, reasons for importation, and goods category to the Customs Department for temporary import permission;

The importer must submit a duty-exempted application with certification of the exhibition, an import entry form with documents such as invoice, Airway bill, and packing list and a permission form for import of restricted goods. The importer signs for the materials, states the period of temporary entry (must be under 6 months), and places a cash deposit or Bank's guarantee for the following total (duty + 140 percent + VAT);

Customs officers will inspect the goods and return a copy of the special Import Entry Form to the controller of the goods to be presented on the way of taking the goods out of Thailand. The controller may appoint a local firm, as an importer, to deliver the material from the port of entry to the exhibition site;

When taking the materials out of the country, the controller shall present a copy of the special Import Entry Form to the Customs officers and shall withdraw the guarantee contract. If the importer has shown intention of not taking the goods out of the country within the period of time stated in the contract, the guarantee contract will be enforced;

Regarding contract extensions, the importer can request an extension of 6 months from the date of entry. To receive this extension, the importer must submit an application to the Customs House or to the Laws and Regulations Division, Customs Department for approval.

Royal Thai Embassy in Washington D.C.'s website, http://www.thaiembdc.org/

State Department Consular Information Sheet on Thailand at:
http://travel.state.gov/travel/cis_pa_tw/cis/cis_1040.html

State Department Visa Website: http://travel.state.gov/visa/index.html

United States Visas.gov: http://www.unitedstatesvisas.gov/

U.S. Embassy's website: http://bangkok.usembassy.gov/

U.S. Embassy's Visa website: http://bangkok.usembassy.gov/visas.html

IMPORTANT INVESTMENT AND BUSINESS OPPORTUNITIES

LEADING SECTORS FOR EXPORT AND INVESTMENT

AUTOMOTIVE PARTS AND SERVICES/EQUIPMENT

Unit: USD thousands

	2009	2010	2011 (estimated)	2012 (estimated)
Total Market Size	20,113	26,418	32,609	33,494
Total Local Production	27,915	36,796	48,671	54,025
Total Exports	13,553	19,233**	26,769	32,415
Total Imports	5,751	8,174**	10,707	11,884
Imports from the U.S.	124	131**	134	144
Exchange Rate: 1 USD	28	28	28	28

Thailand's vehicle production is expected to total 1.62 million units in 2010 and 1.8 million units in 2011, and exports are estimated to be 52 percent of total output. The export value of automotive products from Thailand for the first nine months of 2010 totaled USD 18.6 billion, an increase of 59 percent from the previous year. Meanwhile, domestic sales of vehicles in 2010 are expected to reach 780,000 units, an increase of 40 percent. Industry experts are optimistic that the Thailand market will grow to 840,000 units in 2011.

Japanese manufacturers have a combined market share in Thailand of ninety percent. The five best-selling brands are Toyota (41 percent), Isuzu (19 percent), Honda (14 percent), Nissan (7 percent), and Mitsubishi (5 percent). Notably, Ford and GM have had impressive growth in 2010, with sales increases of 79 percent and 32 percent, respectively. All of these global manufacturers have assembly operations in Thailand that manufacture for both the domestic and export markets. The industry currently has an overall assembling capacity of 1.8 million units, and is expected to turn out two million units in 2012.

The ASEAN Free Trade Area (AFTA) was implemented in January 2010 and is expected to benefit the automotive industry in Thailand over the long run. With the region's largest and most

For additional analytical, business and investment opportunities information,
please contact Global Investment & Business Center, USA
at (202) 546-2103. Fax: (202) 546-3275. E-mail: rusric@erols.com

sophisticated automotive manufacturing platform, the Thai automotive industry is expected to increase its exports in the region. The increase in intra-regional exchange of vehicle parts, resulting from the zero-to-five percent tariff scheme, lowers production costs for assemblers and creates economies of scale in production for the industry.

SUB-SECTOR BEST PROSPECTS

Best prospects for the automotive parts and service equipment sector include:

Accessories & performance parts

General automotive service equipment & tools

Tire (wheel) & brake service equipment

Body and paint repair service equipment

OPPORTUNITIES

As the Southeast Asian regional automotive manufacturing hub, Thailand presents significant opportunities for U.S. companies. Building on the success of its initial plan to make Thailand one of the world's major pickup truck manufacturers, the Royal Thai Government announced its intention to become a manufacturing hub for the "Eco Car," with the objective of upholding Thailand's competitive position as a production hub in the global market. This will increase opportunities for parts manufacturing, automotive technologies and related services in OEM manufacturing. Additionally, greater integration of vehicle markets among ASEAN countries will result in an expanded regional market for replacement parts and after-market service equipment.

WEB RESOURCES

Thai Automotive Institute

655 Soi 1, Bang Poo Industrial Estate, Moo 2, Sukhumvit Road, Km. 34, Muang, Samutprakarn 10280 Tel: (+66) 0-2324-0710 Fax: (+66) 0-2323-9598 Website: http://www.thaiauto.or.th

The Customs Department

Soonthornkosa Road, Klong Toey, Bangkok 10110 Tel: (+66) 0-2249-0442, 2249-9494 Fax: (+66) 0-2249-1279 Website: http://www.customs.go.th

The Office of Industrial Economics (OIE)

75/6 Rama VI Road, Rajathevee, Bangkok 10400 Tel: (+66) 0-2202-4395 Fax: (+66) 0-2644-7139 Website: http://www.oie.go.th

BROADCAST EQUIPMENT

			Unit: USD thousands
2009	2010	2011 (estimated)	2012 (estimated)

Total Market Size	1,610	1,851	1,945	2,042
Total Local Production	3,319	1,640	1,722	1808
Total Exports	6,999	7,354	7,721	8,107
Total Imports	5,290.5	7,565	7,943	8,340
Imports from the U.S.	200	232	243	255
Exchange Rate: 1 USD	28	28	28	28

The Broadcasting Act of 2008 governs the licensing of all radio and television operations, and licenses for the use of frequency, cable and satellite networks have been allocated to local service providers. The Act allows commercial television businesses to generate revenue from advertising airtime as well as membership fees, stimulating growth in the commercial television sector. In 2010, 50 satellite television channels were launched (compared to 30 channels in 2009), and 50 additional channels are expected to be launched in the Thai market in 2011, an investment of USD 50 million.

The number of households receiving satellite and cable television signals is expected to increase from 9 million in 2010 to 13 million in 2011. This presents a major business opportunity for U.S. suppliers to expand their businesses in Thailand.

Television and radio are the key sub-sectors comprising Thailand's broadcasting industry. Both sectors fall under the control of three major government bodies: the Mass Communications Organization of Thailand (MCOT), the Public Relations Department of Thailand (PRD), and the Royal Thai Army Radio and Television (RTA). These three players own more than two-thirds of the nation's airwaves. The Royal Thai government actively supports the development of communication technologies; it has recently invested in two north-south fiber-optic cable networks, international submarine links with several countries in the region, and domestic satellite communications systems.

The media and broadcasting industry is growing in tandem with the expanding consumer market in Thailand. There are five major media formats that are used for advertising campaigns in Thailand:

Television and Radio (65%)

Newspapers (17%)

Magazines (6.5%)

Outdoor Advertising (5%)

Movie Theaters (5%)

Miscellaneous (2.5%)

Sub-Sector Best Prospects

The best-selling U.S. products for Thailand's broadcast industry include:

-Transmission

For additional analytical, business and investment opportunities information,
please contact Global Investment & Business Center, USA
at (202) 546-2103. Fax: (202) 546-3275. E-mail: rusric@erols.com

Radio

Television

-Radio Consoles
-Studio Equipment

Radio

Television -Software Systems, e.g. Automation and Advertising Solutions

- Microwave Communications Equipment

OPPORTUNITIES

The majority of broadcast communications equipment is imported. The United States, Germany, and Japan are the most popular sources of products for this industry. This is driven by customer perceptions that these manufacturers are the technological innovators providing the highest quality broadcast communications devices.

Most Chinese manufacturers concentrate on non-linear equipment and software automation, which involve low production and R&D costs. The lower prices of Chinese products have a major impact on purchasing decisions.

For broadcast communications equipment, the key competitors are Itelco (Italy), Rohde & Schwarz (Germany), Sony (Japan), NEC (Japan), Dayang (China), and Sobey (China).

WEB RESOURCES

Public Relations Department (PRD)

Rama VI Road, Soi 30, Bangkok 10400 Tel: (+66) 0-2618-2323, Ext. 1700 Fax: (+66) 0-2618-2358 URL: http://www.prd.go.th

Mass Communication Organization of Thailand (MCOT)

63/1 Rama 9 Road, Huay Kwang, Bangkok 10320 Tel: (+66) 0-2201-6000 Fax: (+66) 0-2245-1435 URL: http://www.mcot.net

Royal Thai Army Radio and Television

210 Phaholyotin Rd., Sanampao, Phayatai, Bangkok 10400 Tel: (+66) 0-2278-1697 Fax: (+66) 0-2615-2066 URL: http://www.tv5.co.th

Commercial Service Bangkok Contact: **Ms. Oraphan Boonyalug – Commercial Specialist U.S. Commercial Service American Embassy E-mail: oboonyal@trade.gov Website: http://www.buyusa.gov/thailand/en**

DEFENSE EQUIPMENT

Thai Defense Budget

	2008	2009	2010	2011	2012(e)
					Unit: Million US$
Defense Budget	5,126	6,077	5,501	6,082	6,478
GDP	329,721	350,493	347,364	369,943	381,041
Defense Budget in % to GDP	1.55%	1.73%	1.58%	1.64%	1.70%

Following the military coup in 2006 and the recent civil unrest in 2010, the Thai military has played an important role in both maintaining internal security and protecting national interests and sovereignty. With support from the Thai government for the military's ongoing force development plan, the Thai defense equipment market remains attractive for both local and foreign defense equipment manufacturers and suppliers.

Procurement priorities are dictated by the national security situations and the anticipated threats. Current key military initiatives with major campaigns include: the promotion of national reconciliation, protection of border areas and maritime interests, suppression of illegal immigrants and goods smuggling, anti-terrorism, disaster relief, and anti-riot and internal peacekeeping activities.

The Thai armed forces will continue to follow their 2011-2020 military development plan to improve efficiency and effectiveness; prioritizing maintenance requirements and new procurements are the critical tasks for the Thai armed forces. Under the plan, the annual defense budget will be in the range of 1.6 to 1.7 percent of the Gross Domestic Product (GDP) or approximately 8 percent of the total budget expenditure.

With the recovering Thai economy, the Thai military budget remains relatively high compared to the early 1990s. Over the past four years, the Thai defense budget has remained in the USD four to six billion range. This budget will fund the long-awaited development plan of the Thai armed forces, ensuring Thailand's ability to cope with national security threats, especially for maintaining internal security, fighting terrorist and separatist groups, and coping with border area disputes, all of which have become more prevalent in recent years.

Thailand's defense equipment suppliers come from all over the world and offer fairly competitive pricing and equipment package terms. The United States is one of the prime defense suppliers to Thailand due to commonality with NATO and Thai-U.S. joint military exercises. Local production is limited to conventional weapons, ammunition, and military supplies provided by a few Thai military-owned weapon production units.

SUB-SECTOR BEST PROSPECTS

Under the Thai military development plan, the Thai armed forces have prioritized their military upgrades, reconditioning/refurbishment projects, and new procurements. This is to ease the Thai government's critical budget constraints by spreading the appropriation over several budget years – so called "tied-over" budget allocations.

Based on the development plan for future military projects, the following are items with high procurement potential: C4I tactical communications systems, helicopters (tactical and transport), tanks and armored vehicles, training simulators, Unmanned Aerial Vehicles (UAVs), Air Defense Systems (ADSs), Tactical Data Links (TDLs), Electronic Warfare (EW) equipment, radar systems, and combat communications equipment.

OPPORTUNITIES

The major buyers of defense equipment are the three branches of the Thai armed forces: the Royal Thai Army (RTA), the Royal Thai Air Force (RTAF), and the Royal Thai Navy (RTN), which includes the Marine Corps. Provided below are summaries of the procurement rationales of the Thai defense forces.

Royal Thai Army (RTA)

The RTA is relatively self-sufficient despite its needs for hardware improvements, new equipment, upgrades, and refurbishment. The challenge that the RTA faces is operating aging equipment. Therefore, main focuses of the RTA's development plan include replacing obsolescing hardware, increasing crowd-control capability, improving firepower and mobility, improving the armored air cavalry regiment, and enhancing its ability to fight around the clock (e.g. night mission capability).

Royal Thai Air Force (RTAF)

The RTAF is striving to ensure its combat readiness to respond to the air forces of neighboring countries by keeping pace with regional developments in air power and continuing to develop its force through refurbishment and upgrades of existing equipment. In recent years, new threats requiring RTAF support include: air support for ground troops during anti-terrorist activities in the three Southern provinces, border area conflicts, disaster relief and internal peacekeeping missions.

Royal Thai Navy (RTN)

The RTN is responsible for a relatively large area, including Thai bodies of water as well as other areas such as those involved in its participation with international task forces to suppress pirate activities in the Middle East. However, the RTN's main duty is to protect Thailand's territorial waters, natural resources, fishing areas, and shipping lanes. In peacetime, the RTN also assists with disaster relief and related search and rescue missions. The RTN has introduced a development plan to improve its capability; however, its needs must be prioritized given the limited budget. Currently, there are plans for maintenance work, upgrades and replacement of aging hardware.

WEB RESOURCES

Ministry of Defense

Foreign Affairs Division Office of Policy and Planning Tel: (+66) 0-2225-7414 Fax: (+66) 0-2226-1839 Website: http://www.mod.go.th/eng_mod/index.html

The Royal Thai Armed Forces Headquarters

(formerly The Supreme Command Headquarters) Office of Policy and Plans, Directorate of Joint Operations Tel: (+66) 0-2575-6203 Fax: (+66) 0-2575-6067 Website: http://www.rtarf.mi.th/EN/index_new_en.html

Royal Thai Army

Policy and Plans Division Directorate of Logistics Tel: (+66) 0-2297-7424 Fax: (+66) 0-2297-7420 Website: http://www.rta.mi.th

Royal Thai Air Force

Policy and Plans Division Directorate of Operations Tel: (+66) 0-2534-1457 Fax: (+66) 0-2534-1378 Website: http://www.rtaf.mi.th/index.asp

Royal Thai Navy

Research and Development Division Naval Operations Department Tel: (+66) 0-2475-5533 Fax: (+66) 0-2475-7968 Website: http://www.navy.mi.th/new/index.php

Commercial Service Bangkok Contact: **Mr. Kitisorn Sookpradist – Commercial Specialist U.S. Commercial Service American Embassy E-mail: ksookpra@trade.gov Website: http://www.buyusa.gov/thailand/en**

EDUCATION SERVICES (EDS)

Unit: USD thousands

	2009	2010	2011 (estimated)	2012 (estimated)
Total Sales	1,066	1,219	1,462	1,820
Sales by Local Institutions	59	71	88	110
Sales by International Institutions	1,125	1,290	1,550	1,930
Sales by U.S. Institutions	470	518	695	935
Exchange Rate: 1 USD	28	28	28	28

The demand for overseas education continues to grow among students in Thailand. Thai parents still consider higher education a worthwhile investment for their children, and higher education overseas has become a norm among well-to-do Thai families. Graduates from international and bi-lingual schools across Thailand are studying abroad in larger numbers. Of the Thai students attending overseas academic and degree programs, approximately 50 percent are enrolled in graduate and post-graduate programs, 25 percent are enrolled in undergraduate programs, and the remaining are enrolled in either one-year high school exchange programs or short-term ESL programs. Business administration is the leading subject chosen by Thai students as their major area of study, with engineering, computer science and mass communications being the next most popular majors. ESL programs at universities that allow students to directly enroll into degree programs on a conditional acceptance after passing language requirements are also gaining high acceptance.

In 2010, it is estimated that over 25,000 Thai students were studying in the United States. By comparison, the number of Thai students in Australia is estimated to be from 15,000 to 17,000 students. Australia is also a highly popular destination for short-term (e.g. 4-week) summer cultural and language programs among students in Thailand. The number of Thai students in the United Kingdom is growing, currently estimated to be from 12,000 to 15,000 students. The growing popularity of the one-year MBA degree program, heavily promoted by most of the universities in the United Kingdom, has drawn a lot of interest among Thais during the past few years. Additionally, there are approximately 3,500 Thai students in New Zealand and around 2,500 Thai students in Canada.

There is growing competition from local universities offering degree programs in English, at both the undergraduate and graduate level. Currently, there are approximately 5,000 international students in Thailand, the majority of them from China, studying graduate degree programs. Leading local universities include Assumption University, Mahidol University, Thammasat University, Webster University, and Bangkok University.

SUB-SECTOR BEST PROSPECTS

Major programs and areas of study that Thai students are most interested in pursuing include:

MBA
Computer Science
Engineering
One-Year Exchange Programs (e.g. High School)
Computer Graphics and Design
Summer Language Training and Cultural Programs
Short- and Long-Term ESL Programs
Private High Schools

OPPORTUNITIES

One-year student exchange programs in the U.S. remain quite popular among students in Thailand. Local study abroad agents actively promote these one-year exchange programs as they can earn solid commissions with less work and effort. These programs have high growth potential as more study abroad agents in Thailand are focusing on this market.

The potential for attracting more undergraduate students from Thailand also remains strong because of the continued increase in high school graduates from local international schools. There are about 130 international schools across the country, most located in Bangkok. The expansion of bi-lingual high schools in Bangkok means an increase in the number of potential candidates for undergraduate degree programs abroad. The growing popularity of community colleges among Thai parents and students has also increased the number of undergraduate students studying in the U.S.

The other high potential opportunity involves U.S. high schools. Currently, New Zealand and Australia are major destinations for Thai high school students. School fees in these countries are more competitive than the fees for private schools in the U.S. and the U.K. Moreover, most of the schools in New Zealand and Australia work with agents to promote their institutions, while most of the schools in the U.S. do not.

WEB RESOURCES

OCSC International Education Fair Ms. Ratana Ubonsri – Director Education and Training Abroad Branch Office of the Civil Service Commission Phitsanulok Road Bangkok 10300 Tel: (+66) 0-2281-9549, (+66) 0-2281-3333, Ext. 2132 Fax: (+66) 0-2628-6202 E-mail: ratana@ocsc.go.th

Commercial Service Bangkok Contact: Mr. Nalin Phupoksakul – Commercial Specialist U.S. Commercial Service American Embassy E-mail: nphupoks@trade.gov Website: http://www.buyusa.gov/thailand/en

ELECTRONIC COMPONENTS

Unit: USD thousands

	2009	2010	2011 (estimated)	2012 (estimated)
Total Market Size	31,627	32,830	37,223	42,203
Total Local Production	40,720	41,307	46,834	53,101
Total Exports	32,576	33,046	37,468	42,481
Total Imports	23,483	24,569	27,856	31,584
Imports from the U.S.	2,005	2,151	2,366	2,602
Exchange Rate: 1 USD	28	28	28	28

In 2010, the overall Thai electronic parts and components market grew slightly as a result of new orders for semiconductor devices, transistors, and other integrated circuits from ASEAN countries, China, the United States, and emerging markets such as Hong Kong, Australia and India; reductions and revocations of import and export tariffs on electronics components among the ASEAN countries following the ASEAN Free Trade Area (AFTA) agreement of 2010 have contributed to this growth. The increasing demand for high-tech consumer products that use data storage, such as personal computers, external drives, mobile phones, net books, and notebooks have stimulated the increasing demand of imported electronics parts and components into Thailand.

More than 60 percent of Thailand's imported electronic components consist of integrated circuits (IC) and computer components (CC). Of these imports, USD 10.01 billion are IC (44 percent) and USD 6.2 billion are CC (27 percent), driven my Thailand's current position as the manufacturing base for 4 out of 5 major HDD producers, i.e. Seagate Technologies, Western Digital, Hitachi Global Storage and Fujitsu.

Thailand's Electrical and Electronics Institute (EEI) has projected that electronics manufacturing production will increase 21.61 percent in 2011 due to a strong demand for high-tech products that need a large amount of storage space, high speed processors, and features that are compatible with other IT equipment such as media tablets, smart phones, and automotive electronics. EEI expects the growth of the HDD, IC, and semiconductor markets to be 14.72 percent, 5.72 percent and 4.90 percent, respectively. The Thailand Board of Investment (BOI) has approved 220 projects in the electronics and electrical appliances industries, worth around USD 2.3 billion in 2010. These projects focus on HDD manufacturing, memory storage equipment, digital cameras, automobile electronics and other electronic products.

SUB-SECTOR BEST PROSPECTS

Best prospects for the electronic parts and components sector include:

Integrated Circuits (Wafers, Thin Film Technology, Dice and Chips, Substrates and Lead Frames)

Radio-Frequency Identification (RFID)

Computer Components (CPU, HDD, Media/Platter, Floppy Disk Drive, CD Rom Drive, Tape Drives, Monitors, Printers, LCD Projectors)

Hard Disk Media/Platter, HDD Suspension

Flexible Print Circuit, Multi-Layer PCB

Flat Panel Display, LCD Panel, OLED Panel

OPPORTUNITIES

The Thailand Board of Investment (BOI) grants tax incentives for high-tech investment projects totaling more than USD 2.83 billion that involve the manufacture of products not yet made in Thailand; investors can be exempted from corporate income taxes for up to 8 years as well as qualify for other BOI incentives. For example, a company specializing in wafer production and electronic design may be exempted from import duties on machinery, raw materials and components used for manufacturing its products. Apart from attractive incentives, the BOI also focuses on promoting value-added projects and more advanced technology in the automotive and electronics industries as well as in knowledge-based industries such as biotechnology and renewable energy. Projects involving LEDs, LCD panels and the "Eco Car" are among those currently being supported by BOI. This is in keeping with the government's policy to support the development of the electrical and electronics industry in cooperation with the BOI and EEI.

WEB RESOURCES

Thailand Board of Investment (BOI)

Head Office: 555 Vibhavadi-Rangsit Rd., Chatuchak, Bangkok 10900 Tel: (+66) 0-2553-8111 Fax: (+66) 0-2553-8222 Website: http://www.boi.go.th Email: head@boi.go.th

Electrical and Electronics Institute (EEI)

57 Department of Industrial Works Building, 6th Floor, Phrasumen Road, Banglumphu, Phranakorn, Bangkok 10200 Tel: (+66) 0-2280-7272 Fax: (+66) 0-2280-7277 Website: http://www.thaieei.com Email: general@thaieei.com

The Office of Industrial Economics (OIE)

75/6 Rama VI Road, Rajathevee, Bangkok 10400 Tel: (+66) 0-2202-4395 Fax: (+66) 0-2644-7139 Website: http://www.oie.go.th

The Customs Department

1 Sunthornkosa Road, Klong Toey, Bangkok 10110 Tel: (+66) 0-2249-0431-40 Fax: (+66) 0-2249-1279 Website: http://www.customs.go.th

Mrs. Thanyathorn Voravongsatit – Commercial Specialist U.S. Commercial Service American Embassy E-mail: tvoravon@trade.gov Website: http://www.buyusa.gov/thailand/en

ELECTRICAL POWER SYSTEMS (ELP)

	2009	2010	2011 (estimated)	Unit: USD thousands 2012 (estimated)
Total Market Size	5,200	5,304	5,463	5,626
Total Local Production	3,139	3,202	3,298	3,397
Total Exports	3,047	3,108	3,201	3,297
Total Imports	5,292	5,397	5,559	5,726
Imports from the U.S.	335	341	352	362
Exchange Rate: 1 USD	30	28	28	28

Electrical power accounts for approximately 20 percent of Thailand's total energy consumption and plays an important role in the country's development. The Royal Thai government plans to gradually increase electricity generation capacity in the next 20 years under Thailand's Power Development Plan (PDP). The PDP aims to increase generating capacity from 29,212 megawatts to 65,574 megawatts by 2030, mainly through power plant construction and power purchases from IPPs and neighboring countries. This initiative creates market opportunities for electric power generation equipment using conventional fossil fuels, renewable and alternative energy, and nuclear power.

One of the important objectives of the PDP is to diversify energy resources. The Thai government's policy supports sustainable energy through the development of the electricity supply industry to meet demand and by promoting diversification of fuel types used for power generation. With approximately 71 percent of electric power in Thailand currently being generated from local natural gas, diversification of the energy supply is seen as a necessary step towards enhanced energy security.

Although the growth of energy and electric power demand in Thailand has slowed due to the world economy, the power sector remains relatively attractive. The Thai market is open for electric power generation equipment using various types of fuels, and the energy industry is important to Thailand as the country strives to achieve economic growth while maintaining energy security with a minimum of 15% in power reserves.

Despite strong opposition from NGOs and environmentalists, implementation of nuclear energy for power generation is inevitable in the long run as a means to increase Thailand's competitiveness. Furthermore, regional cooperation is expected in the development of common energy interests among ASEAN countries to form the "ASEAN Power Grid".

SUB-SECTOR BEST PROSPECTS

The best sales prospects are: power generators using fossil fuels, renewable/alternative fuels (especially biomass and nuclear energy), transmission infrastructure, substations, distribution networks, transformers, converters, energy efficiency and conservation equipment, and switching apparatus to maintain existing power systems and to support future expansion.

Major buyers include government-owned electric power authorities such as EGAT, private power producers (IPPs, SPPs, VSPPs), industrial estate developers, the Metropolitan Electricity Authority of Thailand (MEA), and the Provincial Electricity Authority of Thailand (PEA).

**For additional analytical, business and investment opportunities information,
please contact Global Investment & Business Center, USA
at (202) 546-2103. Fax: (202) 546-3275. E-mail: rusric@erols.com**

OPPORTUNITIES

The U.S. plays important roles as equipment suppliers and technology providers, and there are opportunities for U.S. companies to provide products and services related to the energy sector.

The main focuses of Thailand's energy and electrical power system development are energy security, promotion of alternative and renewable energy, energy efficiency improvement, the promotion of environmentally friendly equipment, and enhanced public participation in energy projects. Listed below are business opportunity highlights associated with prospective buyers' energy projects:

-Power generators, clean coal technology, alternative/renewable energy technology, and nuclear power technology (e.g. hydropower, biomass, waste-toenergy, low-speed wind turbines, and solar panels), mainly for the EGAT and Independent Power Producers (IPPs).

-Transmission and distribution line infrastructure and equipment, including underground power cables and submarine cable extensions, for the Metropolitan Electricity Authority of Thailand (MEA) and the Provincial Electricity Authority of Thailand (PEA).

-Legal framework and public relations advisory to pave the way for the development and improvement of green energy and nuclear power technology. This is to support the Ministry of Energy's preparations for future renewable and alternative energy projects and for the development of nuclear power plants.

WEB RESOURCES

Ministry of Energy (MOEN)

Pibultham Villa (1897), 17 Rama 1 Rd., Rongmuang, Pathumwan, Bangkok 10330 Tel: (+66) 0-2225-2468, 0-2226-4123 Fax: (+66) 0-2226-4468 Website: http://www.energy.go.th

Electricity Generating Authority of Thailand

53 Charan Sanitwong Road, Bang Kruay, Nonthaburi 11130 Tel: (+66) 0-2436-3000 Fax: (+66) 0-2436-3090 Website: http://www.egat.or.th

Metropolitan Electricity Authority (MEA)

30 Soi Chidlom, Ploenchit Rd., Lumpini, Pathumwan, Bangkok 10330 Tel: (+66) 0-2256-3094, 0-2251-6691 Fax: (+66) 0-2253-1424 Website: http://www.mea.or.th

Provincial Electricity Authority (PEA)

200 Ngam Wong Wan Road, Chatuchak, Bangkok 10900 Tel: (+66) 0-2953-0670, 0-2590-5100 Fax: (+66) 0-2590-5047, 0-2589-4990, 0-2590-5048 Website: http://www.pea.co.th

Commercial Service Bangkok Contact:

Mr. Kitisorn Sookpradist – Commercial Specialist U.S. Commercial Service American Embassy E-mail: ksookpra@trade.gov Website: http://www.buyusa.gov/thailand/en

FOOD PROCESSING AND PACKAGING EQUIPMENT

Unit: USD thousands

	2009	2010	2011 (estimated)	2012 (estimated)
Total Market Size	1,850	1,615	1,695	1,780
Total Local Production	1,968	2,253	2,087	2,254
Total Exports	1,598	1,930	1,748	1,898
Total Imports	1,480	1,292	1,356	1,424
Imports from the U.S.	129	78	103	128
Exchange Rate: 1 USD	28	28	28	28

In 2010, Thailand ranked as the world's 12th food exporter, and the second biggest in Asia behind China. The country's food exports were valued at USD 24.9 billion, a 4.7 percent increase over 2009. For the majority of food giants, such as Frito-Lay and Kellogg's, Thailand is their processing and distribution center for the Southeast Asian market due to abundant supply and competitive pricing of major agricultural products.

Thailand increasingly depends on high-quality machinery to meet food safety standards for such major importing markets as the EU, Japan and the USA. However, the global economic downturn and domestic political uncertainty have contributed to a reduction in purchases of manufacturing equipment. This has resulted in a slight decrease (5.5 percent) in the imports of food processing and packaging equipment.

SUB-SECTOR BEST PROSPECTS

Best sales prospects for U.S. food processing and packaging equipment include:

Packaging machinery (e.g. film making machines, form-fill-seal machines, heat sealers) and materials

Machines for cleaning, sorting or grading eggs, fruit or other agricultural produce
Bakery equipment
Machinery for the manufacture of macaroni, spaghetti or similar products
Machinery for the manufacture of confectionery, cocoa or chocolate
Meat processing equipment
Machinery for the extraction or preparation of animal or fixed vegetable fats or oils
Machinery used to manufacture wine

OPPORTUNITIES

In 2010, major suppliers of food processing and packaging equipment were China (18.9%), Japan (16%), Germany (8.5%) and the U.S. (6%). In the early stages of setting up their companies, it is common for Thai food processors to invest in cheaper machinery. As they expand and raise more capital, they will start to invest in higher quality equipment. Chinese machinery has been increasingly competitive in the lower-end market.

In terms of high quality machinery, Thailand imports food processing and packaging equipment primarily from Japan. With over 7,000 local manufacturing facilities, Japan is the biggest investor in Thailand, and Japanese companies normally use machinery made in Japan. According to the latest import statistics, Japan is particularly strong in certain product categories such as bakery equipment and packaging equipment. According to the Food Industry Club of the Federation of Thai Industries, in the past few years, Japan has aggressively promoted its machinery. Japan has remained competitive in the market, as seen from its 16 percent market share, which is approximately the same as the previous year.

Machinery from European countries, especially Germany, is generally perceived to have the highest quality by local companies due to establishing a strong presence and brand awareness in the Thai market. Their local agents have continuously introduced and promoted new technology, and European suppliers are more willing to customize their machines to meet the specific requests of end users. However, those who have used both American and European machinery have expressed the view that American machinery is easy to maintain and more durable. The US market share has decreased slightly from 8.7 percent in 2009 to 6 percent in 2010. In this lucrative market, U.S. companies are, therefore, encouraged to showcase their distinctive selling points such as high quality and competitive pricing.

WEB RESOURCES

The Thai Packaging Association

86/6 Soi Trimit, Kluaynamthai, Rama IV Rd., Klong Toey, Bangkok 10110 Tel: (+66) 0-2712-1995 Fax: (+66) 0-2713-6164 URL: http://www/thaipack.or.th E-mail: thaipack@thaipack.or.th

Commercial Service Bangkok Contact **Ms. Kornluck Tantisaeree – Commercial Specialist U.S. Commercial Service American Embassy Email Address: ktantisa@trade.gov Website: http://www.buyusa.gov/thailand/en**

MEDICAL DEVICES

USD thousands

	2009	2010	2011 (estimated)	2012 (estimated)
Total Market Size	1,352	1,495	1,680	1,980
Total Local Production	1,675	1,750	1,900	2,150
Total Exports	1,260	1,505	1,655	1,820
Total Imports	937	1,250	1,435	1,650
Imports from the U.S.	270	333	400	460
Exchange Rate: 1 USD	28	28	28	28

The market for medical devices in Thailand is expected to grow by 15 percent in both 2011 and 2012 due mainly to the continued flow of international patients and to the government plan to increase the number of small community healthcare centers around the country. Healthcare facility upgrades and expansions will be additional factors for growth in this market during the next few years (2011 to 2013). Thailand remains heavily dependent on imported medical devices, which dominate the market with an 84 percent share; local production still concentrates on low technology and less sophisticated medical devices and accessories. Imports from the United States lead the market with a 27 percent share and are expected to experience growth of approximately 15 percent in 2011. Most major international manufacturers are well represented in the Thai market.

Thailand relies on the import of medical devices, especially sophisticated, higher-end devices. Local production is still limited to products that are labor intensive, including reagents, simple disposable test kits, disposable syringes, artificial legs and other orthopedic accessories. In addition, Thailand is a major producer of examination and surgical latex gloves as well as non-disposable medical gowns and uniforms.

Public hospitals are still the major consumer of medical devices and supplies in Thailand, accounting for approximately 60 percent of total purchases. Private hospitals represent the other 40 percent of the demand. The Ministry of Public Health reported that in 2009 there were 999 public hospitals with a combined 105,000 beds and 322 private hospitals with a combined 33,405 beds.

Medical devices are normally imported by and brought to the market through agents and/or distributors. An agent is typically appointed for a limited period of time, with the agreement renewable at the end of each term. Normally, the agent will keep stocks of low-priced items only, and large or more costly items will be ordered on an as-needed basis. The agent's role includes not only marketing of the medical devices but also clearing the items with the Thai Customs Department and taking the necessary steps to arrange for product registration and import authorization from the Thai Food and Drug Administration (FDA). The Thai FDA regulates importation of medical devices and accessories, and product registration with the Thai FDA is required prior to importation.

Use of local agents or distributors is highly recommended for marketing medical devices in Thailand. The agent provides immediate access to an established marketing network and in-depth knowledge about pertinent regulations. Buyers and end-users expect a local representative to handle after-sales service and to stock spare parts; the agent should develop close personal relationships, an important factor in future procurement decisions.

Sub-Sector Best Prospects
Best prospects for medical devices from the U.S. include:
Heart valves and artificial blood vessels
Disposable diagnostic test kits
Quick diagnostic testing devices
Respiratory devices and oxygen therapy
Rehabilitation equipment and accessories
Orthopedic and implant devices and accessories
Minimum invasive surgical devices
Dermatological devices
Neurosurgical and other surgical devices and accessories

OPPORTUNITIES

The market growth in the next two years (2012 to 2013) will continue to be driven primarily by the demands to upgrade and expand existing health care facilities and medical device capacity as well as to replace accessories. The government actively promotes medical tourism as a means to attract more international visitors to the country, and international patients will remain the main target for most leading private hospitals in Thailand. Most hospitals try to expand their specializations and use them as the marketing tools to attract patients; cutting edge medical equipment often forms the basis of promotional campaigns to draw customers' attention.

Investment in new healthcare facilities will still be quite limited due mainly to the heavy financial and capital investment. However, takeovers, mergers and buyouts of private hospitals are used as strategies to expand and to create purchasing and negotiating power with suppliers.

Dermatological clinics will remain a popular sector with solid growth potential. The number of dermatological clinics has increased rapidly during the past few years, and this growth trend is expected to continue over the next two years. This will create higher demand and business potential for electro surgical devices and other dermatological devices and accessories.

Important Website **Food and Drug Administration Ministry of Public Health Website: http://www.fda.moph.go.th**

Commercial Service Bangkok Contact: Mr. Nalin Phupoksakul – Commercial Specialist U.S. Commercial Service American Embassy E-mail: nphupoks@trade.gov Website: http://www.buyusa.gov/thailand/en

PRINTING/GRAPHIC ARTS EQUIPMENT

Unit: USD thousands

	2009	2010	2011 (estimated)	2012 (estimated)
Total Market Size	1,508	1,872	2,059	2,265
Total Local Production	2,022	2,509	2,760	3,036
Total Exports	1,617	2,007	2,208	2,429
Total Imports	1103	1,370	1,507	1,658
Imports from the U.S.	28	33	37	40
Exchange Rate: 1 USD	28	28	28	28

Thailand has been the largest printing hub in ASEAN since 2009. The overall printing industry continues to grow by 10-15 percent annually. In 2010, Thailand imported printing machinery valued at over USD 917 million and printing ink worth approximately USD 170 million; this was the result of a government policy to support the printing industry by removing import tariffs on printing machinery and lowering tariff on imported paper to 0-5 percent. This successful initiative has led several printing houses from the United States, Japan, Singapore, and Europe to shift their printing production bases to Thailand.

Thailand must import 100 percent of its offset and digital printing machinery, while gravure, flexographic and screen printing machinery is both imported and produced domestically. High-quality inkjet printers are the fastest growing segment in the digital printing market and are driving the expansion of color printing, which includes wide-format inkjet printers, digital photography, printer-based multi-function office devices, and digital presses in imaging and graphic space.

Digital printing devices, especially wide-format inkjet printers and digital multi-function printers, are playing an increasing role in the personalized printing business. Presently, more than 10,000 Thai small-to-medium-sized enterprises provide personalized printing or "print on demand" services to customers. The leading suppliers of digital printing devices are HP, Canon, Epson, Kodak, Konica Minolta, Océ and Fuji Xerox.

During the past few years, the United States has become an accepted supplier of high-end digital printers and wide-format printers. HP dominates the wide-format printer market in Thailand, representing more than 80 percent; offset printing machinery is dominated by Japanese and German companies. Key suppliers to local companies include Heidelberg, Manroland, Ryobi, GOSS, Mitsubishi, Komori and Canon. Imports from China have risen dramatically due to its cut off price strategy, and importing second-hand printing machinery from European countries has been increasing recently.

The primary buyers are printing houses, packaging companies, educational institutions, and smart office/home office. Main purchase factors are price, brand, reputation, reliability, quality, speed, color separation, versatility and enhanced capabilities that can add value and create new business possibilities. Budget constraints for some Thai printers have created a market for imported used machinery as well.

SUB-SECTOR BEST PROSPECTS

A promising area is "computer-to-plate" (CtP) technology, which utilizes production software to control the workflow process, reducing labor costs and processing time while increasing accuracy and quality.

High-quality inkjet printers (e.g. digital photography, printer-based multi-function office devices, and digital presses in imaging and graphic space) and high-quality printing ink

Post press printing equipment (e.g. trimming, perforating, gluing, laminating, folding and bindery machinery)

OPPORTUNITIES

An estimated 80 percent of Thai printers are still using offset printing machinery. Thailand has been well accepted as the Printing Hub of ASEAN since 2009, and Thai printers are more interested in enhancing their printing machinery capacities to fulfill their customers' needs. It is likely that only well-established printing houses with strong capital resources will invest in new printing technologies. However, small-to-mediumsized companies are expanding their business lines to digital printing services, such as print on demand and photo books, to offer a diverse set of services to their current customers.

WEB RESOURCES

The Thai Printing Association

311-311/1 Soi Soonvijai 4, New Petchburi Road, Bangkapi, Huay Khwang, Bangkok 10310 Tel: (+66) 0-2719-6685-7 Fax: (+66) 0-2719-6688 Email: thaiprint@thaiprint.org Website: http://www.thaiprint.org

Ministry of Commerce

44/100 Nonthaburi 1 Rd., Amphur Muang, Nonthaburi 10110 Tel: (+66) 0-2507-8000 Fax: (+66) 0-2547-5210, 0-2507-6305 Email: webmaster@moc.go.th Website: http://www.moc.go.th

The Office of Industrial Economics (OIE)

75/6 Rama VI Road, Rajathevee, Bangkok 10400 Tel: (+66) 0-2202-4395 Fax: (+66) 0-2644-7139 Website: http://www.oie.go.th

The Customs Department

Soonthornkosa Road, Klong Toey, Bangkok 10110 Tel: (+66) 0-2249-0442, 0-2249-9494 Fax: (+66) 0-2249-1279 Website: http://www.customs.go.th

Commercial Service Bangkok Contact: **Mrs. Thanyathorn Voravongsatit – Commercial Specialist U.S. Commercial Service American Embassy E-mail: tvoravon@trade.gov Website: http://www.buyusa.gov/thailand/en**

SECURITY AND SAFETY EQUIPMENT

Unit: USD thousands

	2009	2010	2011 (estimated)	2012 (estimated)
Total Market Size	376	395	435	457
Total Local Production	38	40	44	46
Total Exports	-	-	-	-
Total Imports	338	355	391	411
Imports from the U.S.	118	124	130	137
Exchange Rate: 1 USD	28	28	28	28

The market for safety and security equipment is projected to grow 5 to 10 percent over the next few years. The ongoing unrest in Thailand's three southernmost provinces is expected to sustain government spending in this area over the next couple of years. Over the past five years, the Royal Thai government's budget for security operations in the South has been reported to be USD 1.5 billion. Additionally, government spending on city surveillance systems is expected to increase in Bangkok and Thailand's major cities, partly driven by development of mass transit systems. Demand growth in the private sector is also expected given increasing concerns over protecting personal assets and business establishments, especially among large-scale operations and upper segments of the market.

American safety & security equipment compete intensely in the high-end market. Quality and technology that result in greater reliability are the key competitive advantages for U.S. products in a market segment for which the costs of device failures are formidable.

SUB-SECTOR BEST PROSPECTS

Video Surveillance Systems -Digital video recording and network transmission -CCTV and night vision equipment

**Anti-Intrusion Devices
- Alarm systems -Intruder alarm systems
Detection Equipment -Handheld / Walk-through metal detectors
- Motion detectors -X-ray / Screening equipment
Access Control Systems -Card technology systems
- Biometrics devices -Security doors and power fences
Fire Safety Systems**

OPPORTUNITIES

CCTV accounts for 70 percent of the overall spending on security equipment in the market, which has an estimated annual value of USD 90 million. Industry experts believe CCTV will continue to be the most popular form of security equipment and expect this sector to grow 10-15 percent annually. This market segment attracts a large number of players, supplying products with a wide range of quality. Imports from China and Taiwan dominate the lower end of the market, while American, European and Japanese products are at the high-to-medium end.

The market for fire alarms is estimated at USD 60 million, and demand for fire alarm systems is expected to grow by ten-fold with the legal enforcement of the Building Inspection Law in Thailand. Enforcement of this regulation will create a market of 15,000 to 20,000 building units that need new fire alarm systems. Companies in the security industry are optimistic about the growth of this market segment.

WEB RESOURCES

The Customs Department

Soonthornkosa Road, Klong Toey, Bangkok 10110 Tel: (+66) 0-2249-0442, 0-2249-9494 Fax: (+66) 0-2249-1279 Website: http://www.customs.go.th

Commercial Service Bangkok Contact: **Ms. Wanwemol Charukulthavatch – Commercial Specialist U.S. Commercial Service American Embassy E-mail: wcharuku@trade.gov Website: http://www.buyusa.gov/thailand/en**

TELECOMMUNICATIONS EQUIPMENT

Unit: USD thousands

	2009	2010	2011 (estimated)	2012 (estimated)
Total Market Size	12,137	12,600	14,490	15,900
Total Local Production	19,120	13,888	14,860	16,346
Total Exports	27,850	24,241	26,665	29,331
Total Imports	20,867	22,953	25,248	27,773
Imports from the U.S.	1,624	1,786	1,964	2,161
Exchange Rate: 1 USD	28	28	28	28

According to a national market survey conducted by the National Electronics and Computer Technology Center (NECTEC), Thailand's information and communications technology (ICT) spending in 2010 was valued at USD 12.62 billion, reflecting a 7.7 percent increase over the previous year. The ICT market is forecasted to grow by 15 percent in 2011.

Sub-Sector Best Prospects

Telecommunication operators will install new base transceiver stations, radio base stations, supporting facilities, and switching equipment with the introduction of third generation (3G) technology.

U.S.
suppliers who specialize in mobile applications, speech recognition software, billing applications, and network management applications are well positioned to supply this expanding network.
U.S.
exporters are strongly encouraged to appoint local agents to deal with regulation related-issues, bureaucratic procedures, local business practices and marketing. For telecommunications equipment, foreign suppliers require a distributor to submit type approval applications to the National Telecommunications Commission.

OPPORTUNITIES

Stronger competition among telecommunications operators in Thailand will continue through 2011 as companies seek to enhance their existing networks and prepare for 3G technology. Presently, Thailand has a mature second generation (2G) market, but new products, applications and services are continuously changing the industry. Thailand became the fastest-growing Facebook community in Asia in 2010, and this rapid growth directly increased the online-advertising market. The boom in social networking has significantly influenced the growth rate of other segments of Thailand's ITC industry, notably mobile data services and the equipment markets for smart phones and media tablets. These demands are creating ample opportunities for U.S. telecommunications suppliers.

WEB RESOURCES

Ministry of Information and Communications Technology

89/2 Moo 3 TOT Corporation Pcl. Building 9, ICT 2 Floor, Chang Watana Road, Laksi, Bangkok 10210 Tel: (+66) 0-2568-2584 Fax: (+66) 0-2568-2583 Contact: Sue Lor-Uthai, Permanent Secretary

The National Telecommunications Commission

87 Paholyothin Soi 8, Samsennai, Payathai, Bangkok, 10400 Tel: (+66) 0-2279-1842 Fax: (+66) 0-2616-7499 Contact: General Chuchart Promprasid, Chairman of the National Telecommunications Business Commission

Commercial Service Bangkok Contact: **Ms. Oraphan Boonyalug – Commercial Specialist U.S. Commercial Service American Embassy E-mail: oboonyal@trade.gov Website: http://www.buyusa.gov/thailand/en**

WATER POLLUTION CONTROL EQUIPMENT

Unit: USD thousands

	2009	2010	2011 (estimated)	2012 (estimated)
Total Market Size	222	262	288	317
Total Local Production	192	277	274	291
Total Exports	148	224	216	227
Total Imports	178	209	230	253
Imports from the U.S.	24	22.5	24	25
Exchange Rate: 1 USD	28	28	28	28

In Thailand, water and wastewater treatment equipment comprise 50 percent of the environmental equipment market. Solid waste treatment and air pollution control equipment represent 30 percent and 20 percent, respectively. The market for wastewater technologies is growing because of demands from municipal and industrial sectors and a heightened environmental consciousness.

Thailand's total market size for wastewater treatment is estimated at over USD 1 billion, with construction and engineering services accounting for 85 percent of the market. Due to limited local capabilities to produce high-tech products, about 85 percent of wastewater treatment equipment comes from Japan, the United States, and Europe. The environmental technology sector in Thailand, especially wastewater treatment, has solid potential. In the past few years, government, industry and the public have become increasingly concerned with environmental issues.

SUB-SECTOR BEST PROSPECTS

-Pumps (e.g. submersible, centrifugal, aerator/mixer, dosing, vacuum)

-Sludge dewatering equipment (e.g. filter presses, belt press, small dewatering systems)

-Screening machines (e.g. bar screens, shredding screens)

-Consultants and engineering services (e.g. pollution prevention technologies, advanced wastewater treatment, water monitoring systems, biological treatment systems, renewable energy technology)

-Advanced water treatment chemicals

OPPORTUNITIES

The total import market for wastewater treatment equipment was USD 185 million in 2010. Major suppliers for these products were from Japan (26.6%), China (19.2%) and the USA (10.7%). The rest came primarily from European and ASEAN countries. European and Japanese suppliers are major competitors with the U.S. equipment providers. However, U.S. products have a good reputation among Thai engineers and consultants and are typically shortlisted as qualified technologies.

WEB RESOURCES

Pollution Control Department, Ministry of Natural Resources and Environment

92 Soi Phaholyothin 7, Phaholyothin Road, Samsennai, Phayathai, Bangkok 10400 Tel: (+66) 0-2298-2000

Commercial Service Bangkok Contact **Ms. Kornluck Tantisaeree, Commercial Specialist U.S. Commercial Service American Embassy Email: ktantisa@trade.gov Website: http://www.buyusa.gov/thailand/en**

BEST PROSPECTS FOR AGRICULTURAL PRODUCTS

COTTON

Thailand relies on imported cotton due to limited domestic production, which accounts for less than 5 percent of domestic needs. In CY2010, the value of cotton imports increased significantly due to higher world cotton prices and economic recovery in Thailand; key export markets for Thai textiles also increased their purchases. The total value of cotton imported from January to November 2010 increased by 53 percent compared to the previous year, and cotton import volume increased 11.7 percent. Capacity utilization for the Thai spinning industry increased to nearly 80 percent in the second half of the year, as compared to an average of 67 percent in 2009. Thai exports of textile products increased 19.5 percent from the previous year, especially for yarn and fabric. In CY2011, cotton imports are expected to continue to grow as a result of strong demand for Thai textile exports, particularly as China's exportable supplies of yarn and fabric are expected to remain tight.

Despite a 17 percent increase in value, the volume of U.S. raw cotton shipped to Thailand declined 12 percent in 2010; market share dropped to 31 percent, as compared to 41 percent in 2009. Thai spinners have shifted to Australia, which has increased its cotton production since the severe drought in 2008. In 2011, U.S. cotton will likely remain a primary source of high quality fine-count yarn staple and extra-long staple cotton for Thai spinners. Thailand's U.S. cotton import volume should improve in 2011 as the U.S. cotton crop is expected to increase significantly.

WHEAT

Thailand's domestic wheat production is practically non-existent. Thailand therefore relies on imports to meet its wheat flour needs. Ninety percent of Thai flour comes from locally milled imported wheat and the rest is imported directly. In 2010, Thailand's import value of wheat and flour increased significantly by 43.6 percent from the previous year. Wheat imports reached 1.7 million tons, up 53.8 percent from 1.1 million tons in the previous year. Much of the increase in wheat imports reflected the substitution of wheat for corn in feed mills due to high domestic corn prices. In CY2011, wheat import volume is expected to decline as a surge in world wheat prices has made wheat less attractive for feed use in Thailand.

Thai imports of US wheat totaled 529,520 metric tons in 2010, up 6.5 percent from 497,180 metric tons in 2009. The value of U.S. wheat imports increased by 8.1 percent.

Market share for U.S. wheat increased slightly from 47 to 48 percent, and the United States is expected to maintain this market share in 2011.

SOYBEANS

Domestic soybean production remains small at 200,000 tons per annum, supplying only about 10 percent of total Thai demand, and local soybean production is likely remain flat over the next few years. Soybean consumption is forecasted to increase from 1.95 MMT in 2010 to 2.05 MMT in 2011 due to the continued growing demand for both feed and food uses.

The Thai Vegetable Oil Company (TVO), the largest Thai soybean crusher, opened a new facility in May 2010, adding an additional crushing capacity of 2,000 tons/day to its current capacity of 4,000 tons/day. The Thanakorn Vegetable Oil Products Co. (TVOP), the second largest crusher, also started operating a new plant in late 2010 with a capacity of 2,500 tons/day, adding to its current capacity of 1,300 tons/day. This expansion will lower production costs as economies of scale are attained, improving their competitive position in the domestic soybean meal and global soybean oil markets. The Thai soybean crushing industry is dominated by these two companies; of the ten major soybean crushing mills in Thailand, TVO and TVOP utilize 90 percent of the soybeans destined for oil crushing. Smaller crushers are facing difficulties due to financial limitations and fluctuating soybean prices. They have been forced to scale down production, with some running at less than 50 percent of capacity.

In 2011, demand for soy-based food will likely grow steadily as consumers continue to perceive soy products as a healthier alternative. The soy-based food industry prefers domestic soybeans to imported beans due to freshness and their GMO-free status. However, with a growing annual demand of 7-10 percent coupled with a stagnant supply, processors are increasingly relying on

For additional analytical, business and investment opportunities information,
please contact Global Investment & Business Center, USA
at (202) 546-2103. Fax: (202) 546-3275. E-mail: rusric@erols.com

imported soybeans to meet their needs. In 2010, soymilk processors imported between 25,000 and 30,000 tons of non-GM food grade soybeans (mainly from the US and Canada) due to insufficient domestic supplies.

Thailand is a promising market for imported soybeans because of its steadily increasing demand and its small domestic production. It is a relatively well-developed market with sophisticated buyers who can readily source from different origins based on price. Accordingly, U.S. exports are at their height from November to February, immediately after the harvest, while Brazilian and Argentinean exports are strong after their harvests in the spring. Weather or other short-term market changing events can have a large impact on relative market shares. In 2010, the U.S. market share dropped sharply to 14 percent as compared to 28 percent in 2009, largely as a result of record harvests in Argentina and Brazil.

Thailand has a commitment under the WTO to a tariff rate quota (TRQ) of 10,922 tons with a 20 percent tariff rate. However, extending measures that have been in place for many years, on November 25, 2010, the Thai Cabinet approved an unlimited quota at zero tariff for soybeans imported from WTO member countries from 2011 to 2013. If Thailand were ever to impose an out-of-quota tariff on imports, it would be 80 percent.

FRESH FRUIT

Thailand's fresh fruit imports increased by 11 percent to USD 284 million in 2010, as compared to USD 257 million in 2009. The 30-40 percent import tariffs on U.S. fresh fruits are a major constraint hindering growth in this market, and recent Free Trade Agreements between Thailand and China, Australia and New Zealand create an additional challenge for U.S. produce. Despite these difficulties, U.S. fruit exports have continued to increase as demand for fresh fruit consumption in Thailand is large and growing. Fruit is an important part of the Thai diet and is purchased as a gift item during major Thai and Chinese celebrations. Apples, grapes, and cherries are the major U.S. fruits exported to Thailand, followed by strawberries, stone fruits and citrus.

Grapes: California seedless grapes (Flame, Crimson, Autumn Royal, and Summer Royal) are popular among Thai consumers. New grape varieties have also been successfully introduced to Thai consumers such as Scarlet Royal and Princess. Other suppliers of grapes to Thailand are China, Australia, and Chile. Despite strong competition from these countries, imports of California grapes have been increasing each year. Although consumer surveys still show U.S. grapes are firmer, look and taste better, and have a more consistent size and quality than Chinese grapes, China has gained market share due to its tariff advantage and more competitive prices. Less-expensive domestic fruit and low-cost Chinese fruits have eroded the market share of California grapes from 47 percent in 2005 to 22 percent as of 2009.

Cherries: U.S. cherries are very popular among Thai consumers due to their consistently good taste and high quality, and they are a typical gift for special occasions. As Thailand cannot grow cherries, total domestic consumption of cherries is entirely dependent upon imports from other countries. In 2010, U.S. cherry exports to Thailand increased dramatically to USD 2.29 million, a 37 percent increase from 2009 despite a 40 percent tariff. Still, seasonal availability and relatively high prices have limited Thai imports of U.S. cherries. Cherries are commonly available in both modern and traditional retail markets. Major competitors include Australia, Chile and New Zealand; however, the U.S. is still the leading exporter with a 37 percent market share followed by New Zealand with 35 percent and Australia with 16 percent.

Apples: Imports of U.S. apples increased by 26 percent from USD 13 million in 2009 to USD 16 million in 2010. Washington Red Delicious, Gala, and Granny Smith varieties are popular and well-established in Thailand. Other Washington apple varieties available in the market are Fuji, Golden Delicious, and Cameo. Washington organic apples have been continuously imported for up-scale markets while new apple varieties from New York and California such as Empire and Rome have been gradually introduced to the market. However, Chinese apples are the dominant player in the Thai market with a 68 percent market share while the U.S. ranks third with a 13 percent share. Other competitors are New Zealand and France.

WINE

Thailand imports most of its wine from France, Australia, Italy, the United States, and Chile. The value of imported wines has grown from USD 25 million in 2007 to USD 32 million in 2010. France leads with a 40 percent market share, followed by Australia with 32 percent, Italy with 8 percent, Chile with 7 percent, and the United States with 4 percent.

Although drinking beer and spirits is more prevalent among the citizens and residents of Thailand, consumption of wine is increasing. Local wine consumption is forecasted to increase due to growing consumption among mid- and high-income consumers in urban areas and an expanding awareness of wine as a healthy drink in moderation. However, high tariffs, excise taxes and other tax burdens on imported wines restrain growth. Australian wines also have an advantage over U.S. wines due to FTA tariff differentials. Thai consumers perceive U.S. wines as expensive and for the high-end market, while Australian, Italian and Chilean wines are viewed as more affordable. Although consumers now enjoy the greater variety of wine available on the shelves in hypermarkets, supermarkets and wine shops, price is still the key factor determining growth in consumption. In Thailand, red wine accounts for 76 percent of the total wine market, with the balance going to other wines. The most popular varieties for red wines are Cabernet Sauvignon, Shiraz, and Merlot. Chardonnay and Sauvignon Blanc are well known in the white wine category, and there is potential for growth in the still small market segments of dry white, sweet, and dessert wines.

DRIED FRUITS AND NUTS

Thailand's market for imported dried fruits and nuts grew strongly in 2010, with imports totaling 26,035 metric tons (USD 71 million in value). Demand is expected to continue to increase as the Thai bakery and snack food sector expands and bakers and manufacturers increase the proportion of dried fruits and nuts in their recipes. Bakers and manufacturers compete by highlighting the quality of their ingredients and their marketable health benefits. Consequently, demand for U.S. dried fruits and nuts in the Thai market should remain strong, especially for raisins, cranberries, blueberries, almonds, pistachios, and walnuts. However, Thailand's recent Free Trade Agreements with China and Australia have put pressure on U.S. dried fruit exporters as the tariffs on these two countries products have been removed while the U.S. tariff remains at 30 percent.

SNACK FOOD

Thailand's snack food market is one of the largest and most diverse in the Asia-Pacific region, and it has strong potential for further growth. The market is divided into five main segments: potato chips, extruded snacks, fish snacks, prawn crackers, and peas and nuts. The potato chip market is estimated to account for 30 percent of the overall snack market. In 2010, the overall market for imported snacks, excluding nuts, was USD 171 million of which the U.S. holds only a 3 percent share. The market continues to grow annually as consumer tastes and preferences

For additional analytical, business and investment opportunities information,
please contact Global Investment & Business Center, USA
at (202) 546-2103. Fax: (202) 546-3275. E-mail: rusric@erols.com

become increasingly sophisticated. Growth of snack food sales is often fueled by new products with novel flavors and new ingredients. The increased awareness among Thai consumers of healthy eating is expected to increase demand for products that are low in sugar, cholesterol and salt. Opportunities exist for U.S. potato chips, extruded snacks, confectionaries, dried fruits and nuts if the right price and flavor combination is introduced into the market.

Foreign Agricultural Service Bangkok Contact

Ms. Sukanya Sirikeratikul U.S. Department of Agriculture American Embassy Email: Sukanya.Sirikeratikul@fas.usda.gov Website: http://www.buyusa.gov/thailand/en

OIL AND GAS EQUIPMENT MARKET

The oil & gas equipment market in Thailand remains attractive due to an increase in demand for primary energy and petroleum products; however, the oil and gas industry will be affected by the changing environmental policy over the next few years. As the government places more emphasis on renewable and alternative energy, companies will diversify their businesses to encompass these new technologies. Additionally, the Thai government is striving to become less dependent on imports of natural gas and oil, making domestic production more attractive.

US companies looking to operate in Thailand should strive to involve the surrounding communities in their decisions and to help enhance their lifestyles, especially after the Map Ta Phut pollution crisis of the past few years. Attractive markets for US companies will include green energy technologies and clean oil & gas technologies, exploration and production technologies, and services and expertise for the petrochemical market.

MARKET DEMAND

The domestic commercial energy consumption within Thailand is primarily based on oil and natural gas. 37% of this demand is met through oil, and 44% through natural gas. 84% of the oil is imported from the Middle East, and 20% of the natural gas is imported from Myanmar. Domestic petroleum production in Thailand currently comprises 44% of the country's total demand for energy. In order to reduce reliance on imported energy, the Thai government is heavily promoting renewable and alternative energies.

2010 saw an increase in total primary energy, or energy that exists in a natural form before being converted to its end-use form, demand of 7.3% to an equivalent of 1.785 Kilo Barrels Per Day (KBD) of crude oil from 2009. Import volume of crude oil decreased by 0.1%, although its value actually increased because of high import prices.

As 81% of energy demand comes from oil and natural gas, this represents an opportunity for the continued importance of petroleum-related technologies and services. Renewable energies and alternative energies will play greater role in power generation for Thailand. However, these technologies will not completely replace the traditional petroleum industry, and the technologies used in generating power from these sources remains largely untried.

According to the Thai Power Development Plan (PDP) for 2010-2030, the forecasted GDP growth percentage for Thai power demand over the next 20 years will range from 3.58-4.28% per year. The PDP also provides a breakdown of future projections of generating capacity classified by fuel types through 2030. These projections indicate a shift in the types of fuels used to generate power in Thailand over the next 20 years. In 2011, natural gas has the capacity to provide 65.8%

of the power generated in Thailand. By 2030, this percentage is expected to decrease to 24.8% as Thailand utilizes diversifying sources of power and as power needs increase.

In 2010, the demand for petroleum products increased by 2.6% to 708 KBD over 2009 levels. Diesel fuels, LPG, and gasoline comprised a total of 81.6% of this demand, with the remainder coming from jet petroleum, fuel oil, and kerosene. Natural gas vehicles (NGV) have become increasingly popular in Thailand, resulting in a replacement of oil consumption of 6.9%.

MARKET DATA

The following products are examples of equipment imported by Thailand for the oil & gas industry. The products are labeled under the Harmonization System of tariff nomenclature.

Product classifications under the Harmonization System Codes

9026 Instruments and apparatus for measuring or checking the flow, level, pressure or other variables of liquids or gases (for example, flow meters, level gauges, manometers, heat meters), excluding instruments and apparatus of heading No. 90.14, 90.15, 90.28 or 90.32.

8430 Other moving, grading, levelling, scraping, excavating, tamping, compacting, extracting or boring machinery, for earth, minerals or ores; pile-drivers and pile-extractors; snow-ploughs and snow- blowers.

8481 Taps, cocks, valves and similar appliances for pipes, boiler shells, tanks, vats or the like, including pressure-reducing valves and thermostatically controlled valves.

8413 Pumps for liquid, whether or not fitted with a measuring device; liquid elevators.

7304 Tubes, pipes and hollow profiles, seamless, of iron (other than cast iron) or steel.

Import Statistics of Major Importers of Oil & Gas Equipment

MARKET SIZE FOR OIL & GAS EQUIPMENT (US DOLLARS MILLIONS)

	2010	2011 Estimated	2012 Estimated	Projected Annual Growth Rate for Following 2 years (%)
Import Market	2,379.17	2,507.20	2,582.42	3.00%
Local Production	1,251.99	1,200.43	1,236.44	3.00%
Exports	1,226.56	1,189.90	1,225.59	3.00%
Total Market	2,404.60	2,517.74	2,593.27	3.00%
Imports from US	239.26	184.28	189.81	3.00%

Exchange Rate (Baht/US$) 30 30 30 30

BEST PROSPECTS

As Thailand's current energy policy focuses heavily on renewable and alternative energy sources, clean technologies are becoming more important in the marketplace, in addition to traditional oil &

gas equipment and services. Technological equipment for the following applications have high potential.

Carbon Capture and Storage (CCS) – The Asian Development Bank listed CCS as one of the clean technologies to be pursued in its 2009 Energy Policy. In Southeast Asia, this is particularly applicable, as the greenhouse gas emissions in the region are increasing twice as quickly as the rest of the globe. In Thailand, high levels of natural gas production also result in high levels of carbon dioxide production. CCS technology has the potential to mitigate the production of carbon dioxide by injecting the gas back into underground reservoirs and petroleum formations.

Gasohol – Gasohol, a blend of gasoline and ethanol, has seen increased usage in Thailand since 2008, driven by volatile oil prices. The ratio of ethanol to gas in gasohol has also increased. However, when the price of ethanol is higher priced than 95 Research Octane Number gasoline, blending ethanol into gasoline becomes a cost. At times over the past few years, the price of ethanol has actually been higher, making gasohol more expensive to produce than a pure gasoline base.

Biodiesel – The Ministry of Energy (MOEN) has been striving to raise the compulsory biodiesel content by one to two percent, depending on the availability of palm oil in Thailand. The deadline to switch from B3 (3% B100) biodiesel to B5 (5% B100) biodiesel was continuously delayed due to a shortage of palm oil in 2011, and MOEN actually reduced the compulsory mixture of B100 diesel from B3 to B2 (2% B100).

In addition to clean technologies, technology and equipment for accessing the natural gas and oil deposits in the Andaman Sea will continue to play an important role in this market, as many companies continue to explore and produce in this area.

Exploration & production – The remaining hydrocarbon deposits in Thailand are likely located in the Andaman Sea, where deep water (1 km) increases the cost of drilling and exploration. Technologies and expertise to access these deposits will prove valuable for companies looking to drill in this area.

Best prospects for exporters of oil & gas equipment and services include the projects on which that these companies are working, as they will require different types of equipment and services depending on the nature of the project.

Oil & Gas Equipment and Services with High Sales Potential in the Thai Market

> High pressure vessels for natural gas vehicles
> Oil & gas exploration and production services
> Oil field machinery for lifting/handling or unloading
> Boring or sinking machinery/rotary for oil well field drilling
> Oil well and oil field pumps
> Pumps for dispersing fuel or natural gas
> Underground and underwater piping for oil and gas transmission

KEY SUPPLIERS

The United States, once a very important supplier of oil and gas equipment and services to the Thai market, has been losing market share steadily to China and Japan. In 2003, the US was responsible for 37% of the imported oil & gas equipment and services in Thailand. However, as

For additional analytical, business and investment opportunities information,
please contact Global Investment & Business Center, USA
at (202) 546-2103. Fax: (202) 546-3275. E-mail: rusric@erols.com

Chinese and Japanese products have become more cost-effective and competitive, US market share in this industry has eroded to under 8%.

Market Shares of Oil & Gas Equipment Imported (Jan-May 2011)

Country	Market Share in US$	Market Share in Percent
U.S.A.	76,785,085	7.35%
Japan	347,434,941	33.26%
Germany	64,215,749	6.15%
China	198,866,341	19.04%
Republic of Korea	38,973,535	3.73%
Singapore	33,763,700	3.23%
Others	284,629,351	27.25%
Total	1,044,668,701	100.00%

Source: Thai Customs

Market Share In Percent

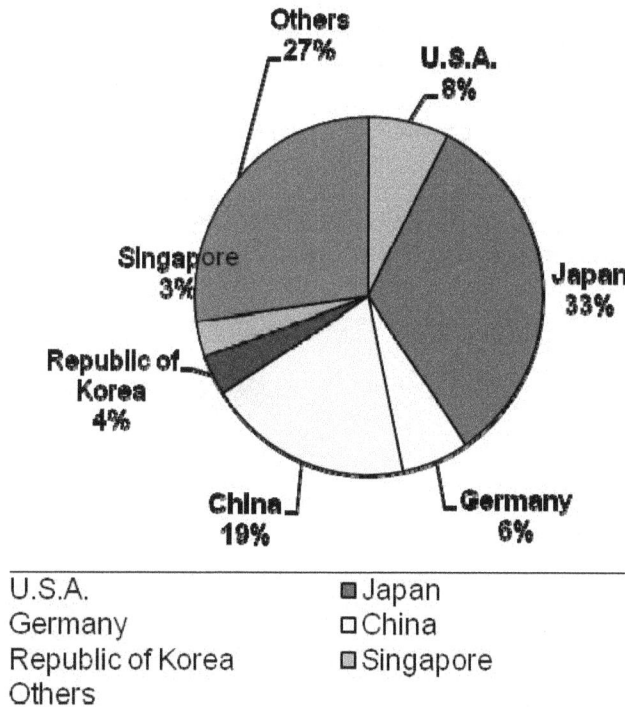

U.S.A.	■ Japan
Germany	□ China
Republic of Korea	■ Singapore
Others	

In order to regain competitiveness in this industry, US companies should focus on providing high-quality products and services that satisfy the green initiatives that are being pushed by the Thai government. After-sales support will remain important, and companies should maintain good relationships with their buyers and agents/distributors within the region.

Key suppliers of the Thai oil & gas equipment and services industry include companies such as Bechtel, Cameron, MI-Swaco, Probe International, Valerus, and Vantage Energy. These companies provide products and services ranging from environmental cleanup to oil refineries to meet their clients' needs. The suppliers of this industry are diverse and varied due to the broad nature of the oil & gas equipment and services market.

PROSPECTIVE BUYERS

Major buyers will include both private companies and government-owned enterprises such as Chevron Thailand, Exxon Mobil, PTT Public Company Limited (PTT Plc.), PTT Exploration and Production (PTT-EP), Pearl Oil, and Hess, which often collaborate on different projects.

PTT Plc. and PTT-EP: They are the national petroleum exploration and production company of Thailand. Both employ over 3000 people and are currently engaged in over 40 projects worldwide.

Chevron Thailand: Chevron is one of Thailand's largest oil and gas producers, supplying approximately one-third of the country's needs through its various operations.

Exxon Mobil: Exxon Mobil produces and sells natural gas in the northeast of Thailand, maintains a service office in Bangkok, and owns the brands Mobil and Esso. Esso is a public company that has operated in Thailand for over a century.

Pearl Oil: Pearl Oil, founded in 2004 in Bangkok, Thailand, engages in exploration, development, and production of oil and gas in Southeast Asia.

Hess: Hess holds interests in Sinphuhorm (formerly known as Phu Horm) in northern Thailand. This plant came on stream in 2006, and currently provides gas-generated power to the region. The company also is involved in a Malaysia/Thailand Joint Development Area with PETRONAS Carigali in the northern Malay Basin; gas production from this venture serves the Malaysian peninsula and the Bangkok region of

Thailand. (http://www.hess.com/operations/default.aspx)

Examples of Current Projects and Collaborations Source: "Our Business." PTT Exploration and Production Plc.

Project	Location	Product	Phase
A4/48, A5/48 & A6/48	Andaman Sea on the western coast of Thailand	natural gas	exploration
G9/43	Gulf of Thailand	natural gas and condensate	exploration
L21/48, L28/48 and L29/48	Khon Kaen and Chaiyaphum provinces of northeastern Thailand	natural gas	exploration
L22/43	Phitsanulok and Pichit provinces	crude oil	exploration
L53/43 & L54/43	Suphan Buri, Kanchana Buri, Ayutthaya, and Ang Thong provinces	crude oil	exploration
Arthit North	Gulf of Thailand	condensate and natural gas	production
B6/27	Gulf of Thailand	crude oil	production

E5	Khon Khaen	natural gas	production
PTTEP 1	Suphan Buri and Nakhorn Pathom provinces	crude oil	production
Bongkot	Gulf of Thailand	condensate, crude oil, and natural gas	production

Source: "Our Business." PTT Exploration and Production (PTT-EP).
http://www.pttep.com/en/ourBusiness_EAndPprojects.aspx

Examples of Current PTTEP Investments

Project	Location	Description
Floating Liquefaction Natural Gas production (FLNG)	Not specified	Commercialize stranded gas and secure natural gas supplies for Thailand
Gas Transmission Business	Myanmar	25.5% participation in Moattama Gas Transportation in 1995 and 19.32% participation in Taninthayi Pipeline

http://www.pttep.com/en/ourBusiness_EAndPprojects.aspx

MARKET ENTRY

For U.S. companies interested in the Thai oil & gas exploration and production industry, the most important Act governing the Thai petroleum industry is the Petroleum Act (B.E. 2514) promulgated by the Royal Thai Government (RTG) in 1971 which laid down rules and procedures for interested parties to apply for petroleum exploration and production concessions from the RTG. The RTG in return obtains benefits in the form of tax and royalty fees from the concessionaires. The following are steps to obtain petroleum exploration and production concessions from the Thai government.

Designation of Exploration Blocks: The Department of Mineral Fuels (DMF) determines the area and invites any interested companies to apply for exploration blocks, selects concessionaires, and awards exploration concessions to companies.

Exploration and Production: Once the concession is awarded to the concessionaire(s), exploration activities may begin. The first few years of the concession period will be used to assess the commercial viability of the granted blocks. If the designated blocks are determined to be commercially feasible, the concessionaire(s) then will apply for a petroleum production license, enter into a production contract with the Thai government, and commission the production facilities. The terms and conditions of the production contract determine the production area, period of the concession, royalty rate, and effective petroleum income tax rate. At this stage the concessionaire normally begins negotiating a long-term sales agreement (off-take contract) with buyers to ensure that the discovered petroleum products can be sold and their investment will be recovered.

Procurement methods: The procurement methods for oil & gas equipment and machinery vary by the nature of the end users. If the end user is a government authority such as PTT Plc. Or PTT-EP, an invitation for bids will be announced and an open-bid method is normally used. On select occasions when an urgent need for products or to procure small orders for routine maintenance and spare part replacements, a direct order to local/overseas suppliers would be placed. Other local non-government buyers normally deal directly with suppliers or agents/distributors of foreign products by asking them to provide quotations, then place orders with the seller with the most favorable offers.

Recommended approach to reach end-users for U.S. companies: Interested oil & gas equipment manufacturers, suppliers or local agents/suppliers should contact each buying authority directly or periodically check with the U.S. Department of Commerce at www.export.gov for updates on procurement announcements.

MARKET ISSUES & OBSTACLES

Tax and customs duties: The import tariff applied to oil and gas equipment and machinery imported from overseas under the normal import tariff imposed by Thai Customs Department typically ranges from 20% to 35% of the CIF price, depending on the type of equipment imported. Import tariff rates are established, maintained, and updated by the Customs Department. The department has established an Integrated Tariff Database website offering Customs-related information to the general public, overseas exporters, and local importers. The site can be used as a primary source of information for Thai customs and tariff rates. It is available in both Thai and English, and can be accessed at http://igtf.customs.go.th/igtf/en/main_frame.jsp

RESOURCES & CONTACTS

The Ministry of Energy (MOEN) http://www.energy.go.th/?q=en/ focuses on the national energy policy, planning, and management of the use of energy in Thailand. The main duty of MOEN is to provide energy security, promote energy conservation, maintain a fair energy pricing mechanism, and develop renewable energy projects. The following four offices and departments of MOEN play the most active roles in the Thai energy industry:

Energy Policy and Planning Office (EPPO) – This office acts as the Secretariat of the National Energy Policy Committee, which formulates policy and regulations and manages oil and energy conservation funds.

Department of Mineral Fuels (DMF) – This department was set up to oversee exploration and production of petroleum and coal products, manage exploration and production concessions for mineral fuels, and cooperate with other countries in exploration and production of petroleum products.

Department of Energy Business (DEB) – Activities related to safety and product quality standards fall under the responsibility of the DEB. It also oversees the issuance of licenses to operate energy related businesses (i.e. petrol stations, oil & gas trading and transportation) in Thailand and issues concessions to operate power plants.

Department of Renewable Energy Development and Conservation – This department conducts research, develops renewable energy projects, and promotes and supports energy conservation schemes.

GREEN BUILDINGS

Experts anticipate increasing numbers of global companies to incorporate LEED certified offices as one element of their CSR on environmental responsibilities. LEED certificates are becoming an increasingly desired quality in office buildings targeting high-end tenants. Owners of existing properties will look to retrofit their buildings to be LEED certified to enhance their ability to maintain and attract their targeted tenants. Similarly, new developments will seek design and construction that will qualify their new properties under the LEED certification systems. At present, approximately 30 buildings in Bangkok have applied for the LEED certification. For example, Park Venture, Bangkok's latest premium commercial complex, is the city's second building to receive the LEED Platinum certification.

In the long term, an increasing number of property owners is expected to place greater importance on green buildings. The Thai Green Building Institute (TGBI) is expected to launch Thailand's own green building standards by the third quarter of this year. Developed based on the LEED certification system, Thailand's green building certification system is expected to increase awareness for energy-efficient building among a wider group of audiences, especially among property owners focused on the local market. Prior to the founding of TGBI, the Association of Siamese Architects, under the Royal Patronage (ASA), created ASA Green Awards to promote the importance of environmentally responsible buildings to the Thai public. These awards were presented to nine buildings, ranging from commercial buildings to a Buddhist temple. ASA's criteria included energy-efficiency, water-conservation, and designs that improve environmental quality.

MARKET OVERVIEW

Commercial property, specifically office buildings in the central business district of Bangkok, offers the best demand potential for U.S. green building exports. There are some 345 buildings in Bangkok's central business district. Most of these buildings were built in the 1980s and 1990s in response to the peak demand for office space that resulted from the economic boom of the early 1990s. These buildings are now requiring renovation to maintain their value. Many owners of these high-valued properties are expected to include environmentally sustainable features in their renovations. Green features are becoming necessary components to attract a growing number of global businesses in Thailand that are adopting green credentials as one of their critical CSR components.

Industry surveys indicate that Bangkok has 1,600 buildings with floor space greater than 2,000 square meters. These buildings include hospitals, educational institutions, offices, condominiums, hotels, cinemas, and shopping complexes. These commercial and residential properties will increasingly employ energy efficient products and technologies in their properties as their energy costs increase. Thus, the projection for the medium and long-term markets for green building products and technologies is positive.

MARKET TRENDS

The Leadership in Energy and Environmental Design (LEED) certificate, developed by the U.S. Green Building Council (USGBC), is the green building standard most sought after among owners of commercial property in the premium segment of the market in Thailand. Large businesses competing in international market are leading the LEED trend in Thailand. For example, the Energy Complex (ENCO) is the first and largest commercial property which was designed to be energy efficient under the LEED system. The complex, owned by Thailand's largest energy corporation, PTT PLC, was awarded a platinum certificate in 2010. A major branch of Kasikorn Bank, Thailand's leading commercial bank, is gold LEED certified. Six Senses, a resort and spa management and development company, has one of its villa suits at Soneva Kiri, a high-end resort in Thailand's Kood islands developed under the LEED certification system.

Experts anticipate increasing numbers of global companies to incorporate LEED certified offices as one element of their CSR on environmental responsibilities. LEED certificates are becoming an increasingly desired quality in office buildings targeting high-end tenants. Owners of existing

**For additional analytical, business and investment opportunities information,
please contact Global Investment & Business Center, USA
at (202) 546-2103. Fax: (202) 546-3275. E-mail: rusric@erols.com**

properties will look to retrofit their buildings to be LEED certified to enhance their ability to maintain and attract their targeted tenants. Similarly, new developments will seek design and construction that will qualify their new properties under the LEED certification systems. At present, approximately 30 buildings in Bangkok have applied for the LEED certification. For example, Park Venture, Bangkok's latest premium commercial complex, is the city's second building to receive the LEED Platinum certification.

In the long term, an increasing number of property owners is expected to place greater importance on green buildings. The Thai Green Building Institute (TGBI) is expected to launch Thailand's own green building standards by the third quarter of this year. Developed based on the LEED certification system, Thailand's green building certification system is expected to increase awareness for energy-efficient building among a wider group of audiences, especially among property owners focused on the local market. Prior to the founding of TGBI, the Association of Siamese Architects, under the Royal Patronage (ASA), created ASA Green Awards to promote the importance of environmentally responsible buildings to the Thai public. These awards were presented to nine buildings, ranging from commercial buildings to a Buddhist temple. ASA's criteria included energy-efficiency, water-conservation, and designs that improve environmental quality.

Additionally, the Thai government's policy on energy efficiency development includes the promotion of energy efficient buildings. These promotions are expected to create public awareness of green building over the long term. The Department of Alternative Energy Development and Efficiency under the Ministry of Energy announced ministerial regulations on energy efficient building codes in 2009. The regulations apply to buildings with floor spaces greater than 2,000 square meters. They set minimum required standards on five components of the buildings, including: thermal performance of building exteriors also known as "envelop," lighting, air-conditioning systems, boilers, and uses of renewable energy.

BEST PROSPECTS

Almost all green projects need overseas consultants and foreign products, according to industry experts. Thus, Thailand offers opportunities for green building design, technologies, products, and maintenance solutions. Best prospects include:

Architectural Design and Engineering Service Energy Saving HVAC Systems Energy Saving Lighting Systems Water Efficiency Waste Water Technologies Building Management Systems Innovative Building Products with LEED Certification

MARKET ENTRY

Identifying qualified local distributor(s) is essential to U.S. exporters in marketing green building products in Thailand. Local distributors have advantages in terms of their local market knowledge. Their proximity to the market allows better and earlier access to information on development of new property projects or renovations of existing properties. In addition, as buyers rely heavily on distributors' product knowledge and services local distributors are instrumental in the distribution of energy-efficient systems and equipment that require technical support during and after the purchase. Distributors view their track record and reputation as one of the key purchasing factors. Thus, reputable distributors significantly increase competitive value of energy-efficient systems marketed in Thailand.

RESOURCES & CONTACTS

Thai Green Building Institute www.asa.or.th

The Department of Alternative Energy Development and Efficiency www.dede.go.th

American Society of Heating Refrigerating and Air Conditioning Engineers (ASHRAE) Thailand Chapter http://www.ashraethailand.org

Pollution Control Department http://www.pcd.go.th

Illuminating Engineering Association of Thailand www.tieathai.org

NET-BASED TECHNOLOGY

After being exposed to the Internet since 1994, Thailand is now prepared to embrace the Internet as an ideal channel to the global marketplace. With the assurance of the current administration and Prime Minister Thaksin Shinawatra vowing that "Science and Technology will be the heart of this government," net-based products and services emerges as the IT area with the most promise. Of which, good market potential for U.S. products is in the area of web hosting, web-enabled e-commerce and e-transaction, call center, electronic data interchange, certification authority services, application service provider, information security, and e-education.

The market for information technology products and services in 2001 is nearly $1.4 billion, representing a 12% growth over year 2000 according to the Association of the Thai Computer Industry. U.S. products are well-accepted and is likely to command a 40% share of the total computer hardware market and 80% of the total computer software and services market. The share of hardware, software and services in the total IT market for 2001 is projected to be 63%, 18%, and 19% respectively. Given the stability of Thai economy and currency, industry sources expect the IT market to grow around 10-15% each year during the next five years. The economic recovery, restructuring of business operations, government support for IT development, booming Internet usage and e-commerce businesses, and the growing number of home offices and edutainment businesses extensively drive the market growth.

MARKET HIGHLIGHTS & BEST PROSPECTS

Market Profile

The new Thai government has promoted IT utilization and expansion of technology throughout the nation. The Thai government has recently initiated its Buy Thai Policy, a movement to compel Thais to purchase domestically made products, to boost the economy. The policy may affect the future of imported PC units, however, domestic manufacturers use imported components to assemble PCs. The vast availability of PCs will lead to an increase in importing software and networking products as well as a demand for highly skilled IT professionals. It is estimated that in 2002, computer software and computer services will establish 40% of the entire market value. Realizing hardware alone cannot eliminate the digital divide, the Thais have replaced this area of importance to sophisticated software and professional services in order to enhance efficiency in the public and private sector.

Most companies in the Thai market use the Internet as a cost-saving method rather than a revenue generator. There were approximately 3,500 accredited Thai owned web-sites, 7% of which use the Internet as trade medium such as e-Commerce. IDC indicated that total revenues from e-Commerce and Internet capabilities would rise from 21.3 billion baht ($473 million) in 2001 to 315 billion baht ($7 billion) by 2005. For example Siam Makro, Thailand's largest wholesale store operator, employed the first online initiative in the local groceries sector to cut costs and enhance efficiency. This leading discount retailer launched its Internet based online system in June 2000. The system offers more than 1,000 Makro suppliers with real-time stock data and automated payments.

Internet Market

Even though only 5.7% of the 62 million people are using the Internet, the number of net users in Thailand within the next few years will exceed those of Singapore and Malaysia, who's Internet users currently account for 56% and 35% of their population respectively. With a population that is 16 times greater than that of Singapore and expected Internet usage to more than double by the end of 2001, Thailand's Internet population will be the largest user within ASEAN. Those who are regular users realize the importance of the Internet for both business and personal reasons, particularly the younger generation.

High speed Internet transmission and broadband technologies are available in Thailand. These include Digital Subscriber Lines (DSL), Cable Modem, Integrated Services Digital Network (ISDN), and satellite. Broadband service providers currently focus on business and high-end customers who require high speed and uninterrupted communications, but not dial-up users. [For more information on communications infrastructure, see industry sector analysis reports on telecommunications services (4/10/2001) and telecommunications equipment (4/10/2001).]

According to AC Nielsen Thailand, 24% of the urban homes in Bangkok have personal computers. Access to the Internet in Bangkok was predominately found in homes 43% while Internet Cafes accounted for 38%. In terms of upcountry urban residents, Internet Cafes is the most common place for access with 47%.

Government Projects

Aware of the importance of the Internet, the Thai government has recently served as a pioneer to create and establish several projects. Currently, the government has taken the initiative in pooling information by government agencies, and transforming government-service provisions under the "one-stop-service" concept to launch "e-Government." Under the e-Government project, there consists of four key development areas, which include online information services, simple transaction services, a payment gateway, and e-Procurement. According to the project plans, all government agencies will need to have a computerized working process and provide online public information services via the Net by 2003. Three agencies, the Cabinet Secretariat, the Office of the Permanent Secretary of the Prime Minister and the Revenue Department have computerized their systems. There are around 200 government agency web-sites, with 20 that are regularly updated. About 10 sites offer e-Services, such as online company registration and tax payments, to the public at present.

The current Thai government has said it would concentrate on the adoption of IT and Internet applications to improve the education and public health sectors. Although no immediate plans have been set forth, the Ministry of Education and the Ministry of University Affairs have stressed the importance to educate the public to create greater IT knowledge and literacy. They have highlighted the Internet as a key medium to speed the learning process and perceive i-learning (Internet Learning) as the focal remedy. In addition, the Ministry of Public Health have illustrated strong interest to modernize public healthcare services in order to compliment the proposed 30 baht-per-visit Health Care Plan.

The most ambitious of the government's Internet developments is the Tambon or Sub-district Internet Project. The Ministry of Interior has started tendering for Internet equipment worth 68 million baht ($1.5 million) as part of its plan to complete its nationwide district Internet project, connecting the Internet to 7,000 districts in 76 provinces by 2003. This year the government intends to network 1,000 districts in 76 provinces and expand to 6,000 districts next year. Furthermore, the government has also set firm goals of putting 10 million Thais online and establishing at least one Internet connection for every district by 2004. To coincide with the new village expansion plan, some 3,000 electronic entrepreneurs are scheduled to receive government assistance in the form of concept development, back-office services, marketing and a government-sponsored electronic marketplace directed at the global market.

About 70% of import and export companies in Thailand currently process customs clearances through EDI networks, while the rest of 30% are still using a manual process. The Thai Customs Department expects to employ a full EDI system for both importation and exportation on October 1, 2001. Thailand has adopted EDI as a fundamental system for the paperless trading that the World Trade Organization is requiring its members to institute in their customs departments. The national EDI service provider, TradeSiam was set up to serve as a gateway linking the Customs Department with exporters and importers in 1996. Commercial EDI service providers serving as a value-added network link, help manage information flows for importers and exporters, and transfer data from their clients to TradeSiam which then links to Customs.

The government aims to allocate 20 billion baht ($450 million) annually for five years to expand Research and Development (R&D) projects to benefit academic institutions and SMEs. The government currently allocates an annual budget of 7 billion baht ($155 million) towards innovative public projects. In addition, the government plans to encourage relationships between universities and the private sector to foster a knowledge network.

New Policies

The government has a policy to offer tax exemptions and Board of Investment incentives to Internet start-up companies, so they can build their business during the first four years of existence. In addition, the Thai government has been considering whether to allow small companies and dotcoms to access capital through the Market for Alternative Investments, where listing requirement are less burdensome than the main stock exchange.

As for the local software development, the government has a policy to provide special conditions on visa applications and work-permit approval for foreign IT professionals as well as investment incentives in order to create a foundation and stimulate technology transfer to the local software industry. Thailand currently faces a shortage of highly skilled IT professionals such as system analyzers, database designers and software architects. There are only 20,000 IT professionals, of which most are in low-skilled level, while the sector requires around 50,000 over the next five years.

The current government has confirmed that it will proceed with the privatization of Communications Authority of Thailand (CAT), which should eventually lead to downward pressure on the cost of international Internet connections and allow fair competition in this market. The Telephone Organization of Thailand (TOT) made an announcement in early this year on providing international and domestic Internet services. On September 1, 2001 the TOT started TOTonline.net, a free Net access service to its pilot homepages for its 3.6 million subscribers nationwide. In preparation for the privatization, both authorities have developed business plans to become ISPs and to continue their involvement in the communications infrastructure.

In addition to technological and demand-based impediments to the development of the Internet in Thailand, improvement of the underlying legal infrastructure has lagged behind Western countries. The government has drafted five basic e-Commerce laws, two of which are currently under consideration, while the other three are either being drafted or will be submitted within a couple of months. The Electronic Transaction Law, a combination of the electronic data interchange and digital-signature drafts, is expected to be approved through the Senate by the end of September 2001. The Universal Access Laws, Computer Crime, and Data Protection are expected to be passed by 2002, while the Electronic Fund Transfer still remains in the drafting process.

The Five e-Commerce Laws:

·   Electronic Transaction Law – the acceptance as legal evidence of all electronic transactions conducted through computer networks.
·   Universal Access Law – making information accessible to all Thai people on as equal basis.
·   Computer Crime Law – the prevention and suppression of crime committed through computer systems, data systems and computer networks.
·   Data Protection Law – protection of information on individuals.
·   Electronic Funds Transfer Law – facilitating electronic fund transfer and the acceptance of use of electronic money.

New Legislation

The government proposed to set up a new organization, the Ministry of Information Technologies, to oversee IT development and take care of pooling information from every ministry. The new body would act as a single command center for the government, allowing the Prime Minister and all ministers to access the information they need from a computer screen, therefore enabling them to make decisions more efficiently.

Statistical Data

The outlook for IT market presented here is based on trade estimates and the Association of Thai Computer Industry's estimates. Value of products that related to the Internet-based business cannot be verified.

IT Market Size Table (US Dollars Millions)

	2000	2001e	2002e	Projected Average Annual Growth Rate for Following 2 years (%)
Import Market	719	825	930	10-15%
Local Production	503	545	620	10-15%
Exports	0	0	0	0%
Total Market	1222	1370	1550	10-15%
Imports from US	428	495	558	10-15%
Exchange Rates	$1=40.16Bt	$1=45Bt	$1=45Bt	

Estimated Future Inflation Rate 1.8%

Last Year's Import Market Share (Percent for US and Major Competitors):

US: 60%, Germany: 20%, Japan: 10%, Taiwan: 10%

Best Sales Prospects

Products
Hand-held computers or pocket PCs
Security-related technologies
Electronic commerce solutions for vertical markets such as government, banking and manufacturing
Business applications software such as ERP (Enterprise Resource Management), SCM (Supply
  Chain Management), SRM (Supplier Relationship Management) and CRM (Customer
Relationship Management)
Networking solutions
Internet-related technologies

Opportunities are vast for U.S. suppliers of sophisticated Internet products and technologies, due to the increase in Internet usage and the government's promotion an e-Society in Thailand. Since the deployment of the "e-government" project, more advance security technologies are needed to ensure that transactions will be made in a safe manner. Credit cards for instance are becoming more prevalent. The number of cards issued by commercial banks at the end of the first-quarter 2001 totaled 1.89 million, a growth of 7.2% from the preceding quarter, according to the Bank of Thailand. Spending totaled 55.2 billion baht ($1.2 billion) in the quarter, an increase of 7.4% from the previous quarter. One of the major deterrents for paying VAT or other taxes and shopping via the Internet is the lack of trust that businesses and the rest of the community has for online dealings.

There has been an increasing demand for business software applications especially for SMEs. To compete effectively against larger companies, SMEs seek to find sophisticated software that can enhance productivity and growth. For example, customer relationship management (CRM) and enterprise resource planning (ERP) would help foster product planning, parts purchasing, maintaining inventory and customer service. Business software applications, however, should be priced in a minimal fashion.

Services
Internet Data Center and web hosting
Highly-skilled IT professionals such as system analyzers, database designers, project leaders and
  designers, software architects, and certified computer auditors
Internet content providers
Internet-related services
Supply chain management
Value-added services such as application service providers, IP telephony, Internet banking
Call center
Certification Authority

Thailand currently faces a shortage of highly skilled IT human resources in the software industry. The types of experts needed include system analyzers, database engineers, project leaders and

For additional analytical, business and investment opportunities information,
please contact Global Investment & Business Center, USA
at (202) 546-2103. Fax: (202) 546-3275. E-mail: rusric@erols.com

designers, and software planners. Thailand has shown great interests in acquiring foreign professionals to narrow the digital divide among its neighboring countries.

Internet content providers could prove as another area of interest. The content and information on Thai web-sites is often outdated or not updated. Furthermore, SMEs who use the Internet as medium for business, need assistance in transforming their information to one that suits the user, for example from Thai to English.

Existing Weaknesses

The leasing of Internet lines for corporate user in Thailand costs six times more than in Hong Kong, four times more than in Japan and over twice as much as in Malaysia and the Philippines. However, the Internet access fee for dial-up individual user is of moderate price. International bandwidths are owned by a monopolistic state-agency, CAT, which leaves little room for any real competitors in the market. Although Internet access rates have fallen, a current Thai GDP of about 3,000 per capita, represents that the Internet is currently aimed towards the rich. After a long awaited process, the government has confirmed that it will proceed with the privatization of CAT.

Nearly 80% of the labor force has only completed a primary-level education or less, and secondary enrollment is still lower than most countries in within ASEAN. A majority of students pursuing higher education are enrolled in professional colleges rather universities. Fewer than 20% of graduates choose science or technology degrees, while only 5,000 graduate as IT specialists. In comparison to the population, the digital divide will persist until there are a sufficient supply of IT experts who can sustain or construct sophisticated software and services. In addition, the country needs to accelerate the development of education, in order to foster the Internet in its fullest form.

Poor security measures have led to several cases of fraud in the recent past, reducing public confidence in the Internet. In March of 2000, a US based hacker allegedly lifted 5,000 credit-card numbers from an unsecured, e-Commerce server at www.shoppingthailand.com.

Government initiative has played a major role when executing IT policy and projects. But in a wider context, it is undeniable that the Internet in Thailand has been stalled because of political power struggle and a lack of support among state agencies. As for the e-government project, the government expects to complete a master plan draft and assign an agency in charge by the end of 2001.

COMPETITIVE SITUATION

Domestic Production

In terms of Thai consumption of PCs, domestically-made models comprise more than 50% of the total market. A domestically made PC however, is regarded as a PC that is assembled in Thailand and but is comprised of imported components, predominantly those from the U.S. In terms of software, domestic companies can develop basic applications such as accounting, medical and educational packages to serve local small-to-medium enterprises. The Thais are more than capable of developing general software but unlike most of the Western countries the Thais are not sufficiently creative in developing intricate software.

3rd-Country Imports

European, Canadian and Japanese companies are strong competitors to the U.S. especially in the computer hardware market. For the Internet and networking environments, competitors are Ericsson (Sweden), Alcatel (France), Siemens (Germany), Nortel and NewBridge (Canada), Fujitsu and NEC (Japan). For business applications, SAP (Germany) registered a remarkable growth of over 80% in 2000 and plans to flood the market with four of its nine main end-to-end solutions – supply chain management, customer relationship management, workplace and marketplace in 2001.

U.S. Market Position

Leading U.S. vendors of Internet products and services have dominated the high-end market for years and are gaining more market share in the lower-end market. U.S. consulting firms will remain prominent within this area. The U.S. will continue to be the leader and maintain its market share in Thailand by offering the distinct quality and advantages based on current research and development (R&D) by U.S. products and service companies. Many of the larger U.S. IT vendors have their own subsidiaries in Thailand to sell products and provide technical services.

Major Vendors: 3COM, AMP, AT&T, Cabletron, Cisco, Compaq, Computer Associates, Dell, Hewlett-Packard, IBM, Intel, Lucent, Microsoft, Novell, Oracle, Sun Microsystems.

Major value-added network providers in Thailand (TIFFA, Thai Trade Net, EXIM Net, and CAT) have been using EDI solutions from the U.S., GE Information System and St. Paul - Harbinger.

END-USER ANALYSIS

End-users in both the public sector and most industries in the private sector have increasingly and broadly adjusted to use net-based services in daily operations. Most end-users of Thailand Internet products are government organizations and business entities, which regularly budget for such expenses. The National Electronics and Computer Technology Center states that 55% of people in Bangkok use the Internet while use of the Internet is 4.9% in the Central provinces, 5.7% in the Northeastern provinces and 8% in the Northern provinces. To increase Internet users, the government needs to initiate more projects driven by demand before supply and to complete Internet links to people in all provinces. Current estimated Internet users are 3.53 million, of which 2.3 million are subscribers.

Most end-users of software products consider prompt- trouble-free implementation and maintenance and availability of support services. End-users prefer customized software as it provides a better fit with their business needs. Software piracy remains a serious problem, particularly among smaller businesses and individual consumers. U.S. companies have dominated the high-end market and can possibly gain market share in the lower-end market by offering services at competitive prices. Due to the lack of local expertise in sophisticated net-based business, there is an opportunity for U.S. consulting firms to enter this market and provide start ups business models to SMEs.

Major end-users of U.S. computer hardware, software and services are government and state enterprises, local and multinational corporations, manufacturing companies and banking & financial institutes, ISPs & Internet solution providers, and SMEs. The Association of Thai Computer Industry provided a breakdown of the IT spending by industry sector as follows:

Segment	1999 US$M	Ratio	2000 US$M	Ratio	2001 US$M (Est.)	Ratio
Government/State Enterprise	195	21%	220	18%	246	18%

Financial		84	9%		86	7%	96	7%
Manufacturing		167	18%		183	15%	205	15%
Health Care		19	2%		12	1%	14	1%
Hotel		9	1%		12	1%	14	1%
Telecommunication		111	12%		208	17%	233	17%
Education		102	11%		195	16%	219	16%
Home uses		111	12%		208	17%	233	17%
Other	130	14%		98	8%		109	8%
Total		928	100%		1222	100%	1369	100%
		(US$1=37.84Baht)			(US$1=40.16Baht)		(US$1=45Baht)	

International telephone services and Internet gateway are now, by law, monopolized by the Communications Authority of Thailand (CAT), a state-owned enterprise under the supervision of the Thai Ministry of Transport and Communications. CAT has granted licenses to 18 private companies to serve as Internet Service Providers (ISP). The Internet Service Provider Club of Thailand estimated that these ISPs generated total revenues of US$17.25 million in 1997, $22.5 million in 1998, $30 million in 1999, and $37.5 million in 2000.

It is expected that the telecommunications laws could be passed by the end of September 2001 and two regulatory bodies (the National Telecommunications Commission and the National Broadcasting Commission) could be established as early as the 4th quarter of 2002. New telecommunications operators will then be allowed to apply for licenses and existing operators will be more encouraged to expand their businesses.

There are now 18 licensed Internet Service Providers (ISP). Fifteen of them are actually operating but only three are believed to be profitable, and about 10 of these companies have been struggling and are still in financial trouble. By law, CAT is given a 35% share in all 18 ISPs and each ISP is limited to having only 14 million baht ($400 thousand) capital. An ISP can increase its capital only if CAT can invest more to maintain its 35% share. In practice, CAT is not willing to do so. Hence, it is difficult for these ISPs to upgrade their equipment.

The top six ISPs of the list below have swiftly expanded international bandwidth from 73.8% in August 2000 to occupy 91% of the total bandwidth in June 2001. ISP that is an affiliate of leading telecommunication company has advantages in marketing Internet services along with their other services. CS Communications of Shin Corporation is the first ISP to link the Internet network to all 76 provincial nodes. Asia Infonet has launched economical Internet service via Telecom Asia phone lines offering unlimited (at present 2-hour) use service.

Internet Service Providers in Thailand (listed by international bandwidth)

Company Name (ISP Name)	Years in Business	Web Site	Bandwidth (Mbps) To USA (June 2001)
C.S. Communications Co., Ltd	3	www.cscoms.com	83
Loxley Information Service Co., Ltd	5	www.loxinfo.co.th	69
KSC Commercial Internet Co., Ltd./ Internet KSC Group	7	www.ksc.net	58

Internet Thailand Co., Ltd	7	www.inet.co.th	55
Asia Infonet Co., Ltd.	4	www.asianet.co.th	54
A-Net Co., Ltd.	4	www.a-net.net.th	45
Jasmine Internet Co., Ltd.	2	www.ji-net.com	8
Samart Infonet Co., Ltd./ Samart Connect Co., Ltd.	5	www.samart.co.th	8
Worldnet & Services Co., Ltd.	3	www.wnet.net.th	5
Cable & Wireless Services (Thailand) Ltd., A Pacific Century Cyber Works Company	1	www.cwasia.net	4.5
The Idea Net Co., Ltd.	4	www.idn.co.th	2
Siam Global Access Co., Ltd.	4	www.sga.net.th	2
Data Line Thai Co., Ltd.	4	www.themead.linethai.co.th	2
Asia Access Internet Service/ Inet (Thailand) Co., Ltd.	4	www.asiaaccess.net.th	2
Chomanan Worldnet Co., Ltd.	3	www.cwn.net.th	0.5
Roynet Co., Ltd.	1	www.roynet.co.th	0.5
Far East Internet Co., Ltd.	3	www.fareast.net.th	0.5
E-Z Net Co., Ltd.	Business activities still under preparation	www.princess1.com	0.375

MARKET ACCESS

Import Climate

Trade Regulations: The Thai market is a free market and there are no special restrictions or regulations on importing U.S. net-based products or trading over the Internet. Internet usage is on the rise and more Thais are likely to order products and services via the worldwide web.

Duty Rate: The reductions in tariffs to 0% have been in effective since January 1, 2000 for computers, telecommunication products, software and CD-ROMs, and goods covered by the WTO ITA-1 agreement. Computer related goods imported in Thailand classified in harmonized codes 8471, 8472, 8524 which have certification of origin from WTO member countries are subject to 0% import duty. However, problems have been reported by some importers to provide the proper certification of origin documents to obtain duty-free entry.

The current tariff system in Thailand is based on the harmonized system, and tariffs are levied on C.I.F. prices. The duty is normally payable to the Thai Customs Department at the time of importation. The Value Added Tax (VAT) is levied at the rate of 7% on the value of goods sold and services rendered at every level, including on importation. Goods imported for re-export are generally exempted from import duty and VAT.

Software (free ware) such as web browsers, server software, and anti-virus can be freely downloaded from the Internet or bundled with hardware/service packages. For electronically transmitted license software, the Thai Revenue Department is charging a 5% withholding tax for software loyalty payments. For a domestic sale, a domestic company would automatically have the 5% withheld from the income as a domestic taxpayer. Software piracy remains a serious problem.

Distribution/Business Practices

A strong local partner is recommended for entering and promoting Internet products and services in Thailand. It is important to appoint a local agent who can deal with problems related to communications, bureaucratic procedures, local business practices and marketing. Potential partners can possibly be a recent start-up company carried out by skilled Thai staff and willing to carry new products. Most existing or long-time established are less flexible in carrying additional new products. Good partners should be able to:

· Educate and advise buyers on business models and benefits from adopting Internet products and services.
· Establish close connections with buyers and decision-makers.
· Closely follow up end-users' requirements and financial status.
· Modify product offerings.
· Understand end-users' behavior and cultural environment.

Thailand's lack of compatibility and efficiency in bureaucracy does not promote entrepreneurial activity. In the Thai business world, personal connections remain highly important business success. Hence, new to market firms are encouraged to have a local partner.

U.S. firms wishing to set up an agency contract or develop a market entry strategy in Thailand are encouraged to contact the Commercial Service Bangkok or the nearest Export Assistance Centers in the U.S. to get a first-hand appraisal.

Financing

Letters of Credit (L/Cs) settles most payments. Credit terms in general business are 60-120 days. However, the longer the trade term offered by suppliers, the lower the cost for holding inventory. A longer trade term is a supportive factor for agents and distributors to save costs on inventory investment.

U.S. vendors in the Thai market may wish to locate a source of financial support, either through a strategic partnership or directly through traditional financial agencies. Third-country competitors, especially Japan and European countries, often offer lower-interest loans, and training and technical assistance to help develop major projects in Thailand.

United States bilateral export financing, loan guarantee and insurance programs are available through the United States Export and Import Bank (EXIMBANK). EXIMBANK is actively involved in medium and long term loans as well as bank guarantees. Their financing covers a wide variety of major project sectors.

For additional analytical, business and investment opportunities information,
please contact Global Investment & Business Center, USA
at (202) 546-2103. Fax: (202) 546-3275. E-mail: rusric@erols.com

The U.S. Trade and Development Agency (USTDA) has provided funding for feasibility studies, orientation visits, conferences, training and other activities that have supported economic priorities in Thailand since 1981.

Trade Promotion Opportunities

IT Trade 2001 (annual), 18-20 July 2001, BITEC, Bangna, Bangkok – Official event of the Association of Thai Computer Industry, the Association of Thai Software Industry, and the IT Network Association

Computer Thai 2001, 28-30 November 2001, the UN Conference Center, Rajdamnern Nok Avenue, Bangkok -- the annual IT event for Government and State Enterprise sectors

POST-CRISIS: LAND TRANSPORT INFRASTRUCTURE PROJECTS

Rail-based mass transit systems are Thailand's land infrastructure development focus. Before the end of 2001 two major studies proposing elevated rail networks system for the Bangkok Metropolitan area will be submitted for Cabinet approval. Pending Cabinet approval, priority routes of networks recommended in the Urban Rail Mass Transportation Master Plan (URMAP) and the Bangkok Railroad Improvement Project are most likely to be implemented. However, the size of priority projects selected from these plans will be scaled down to correspond with the limited Government fund at present. One of the priority lines is the "SBIA Rail Access Project", an airport rail express connecting the new airport to the Central City. Development of the project is likely to have majority private participation and offer major investment opportunities. In addition, an extension plan for the Blue Line Initial System Project (ISP), Thailand's first subway system is also planned for implementation in 2002.

Past and present investment in major land infrastructure development in Thailand is concentrated in Bangkok. Bangkok received 45% of total government transportation budget during 1997-2001. This is because Bangkok contains 20% of Thailand's overall population and generates 51% of the country's Gross Domestic Product. Development of an efficient land transport is critical in a highly populated city such as Bangkok.

Thailand's 1997economic crisis severely impacted Government budget availability as well as the ability to borrow from external sources for land infrastructure developments. Hence, alternative means for project funding like the Build-Operate –Transfer will increasingly be used to fund land infrastructure projects. Private participation is expected to increase even more in the sector. This major change creates opportunities for American firms with know-how in project financing and non-conventional project developments like design-build or turnkey.

This report provides an overview of Thailand land infrastructure development with a focus on upcoming project opportunities. It also attempts to explain competition in the market and overall structure of relevant market sectors.

MARKET OVERVIEW

Land Transportation planning and development is the responsibility of several departments, agencies and state owned enterprises. They are under jurisdiction of three ministries: Ministry of Transport and Communications (MOTC), Ministry of Interior (MOI), and Office of the Prime

Minister (OPM). As a result, land infrastructure development plans often lack coordination and in many cases compete with one another in serving the same set of objectives.

Two planning agencies under the Office of the Prime Minister are in charge of reviewing land infrastructure projects. The National Economic and Social Development Board (NESDB) reviews project feasibility in terms of the overall Government budget allocations and the country's development objectives. Meanwhile, the Office of the Commission for the Management of Land Traffic (OCMLT) an agency set up to coordinate land transportation developments also review project feasibility in terms of traffic demand and management.

Road Networks

Thailand has 158,425 kms. of road networks comprising of 51,775 kms of highways, 59,200 kms of distributor roads and 47,450 kms of rural roads. The Department of Highways, Ministry of Transport and Communication is responsible for the development, construction and maintenance highways nationwide. The Public Works Department, the Office of Accelerated Rural, and Local Administration, Ministry of Interior are responsible for municipal and rural road networks.

The Inter-City Motorway, a toll highway with complete access and exit control, fencing barriers along both sides and a design and specifications enabling a driving speed of 120-140 kms per hour, is the latest type of road networks introduced in Thailand. In 1997, the Cabinet approved the Inter-City Motorway Master Plan. In the plan the Department of Highways proposed to construct 13 Inter-City Motorway over a 20 year period (1997- 2016) and estimates a total investment of Baht 472,360 Million (US$10.735 Billion at US$1= Baht 40). Prospective sources of funds for these projects are Government Budget, loans from foreign assistance institutions, and private investment.

At present, two such motor ways are in operation; the Bangkok-Chon Buri Motor Way (83 kms) and the Eastern Bangkok Outer Ring Road (63 kms). Fee on both tolls are 1Baht per km for 4-wheel vehicles, 1.60 Baht per km for 6-wheel truck and 2.30 Baht per km for other trucks. Both tollways are Government-funded and managed by the Department of Highways.

Four additional tollways have been identified for development in the first phrase (1997-2001) of the plan. They are 1) Network for Eastern Seaboard Development 2) Network for Western Seaboard Development 3) Network for Outer Bangkok Ring Road 4) Connecting Roads between main cities in Northern Part of Thailand and the Greater Maekhong Land Development. However, the Department of Highways does not anticipate that any of these projects will be implemented in the near term.

Expressway Networks

The Expressway and Rapid Transit Authority of Thailand (ETA), a state enterprise under the Ministry of Interior, is responsible for development, maintenance and management of special roadways that provide express transit alternatives to existing road networks. The ETA is authorized to collect fee from expressway users. The Expressway fee varies from Baht 40 to Baht 150 depending on types of vehicles and distances.

At present, the ETA provides five expressway systems with combined distance 171.2 kms. ETA invested in the two earlier systems using Government budget and foreign loans to fund the system construction. However, private investors were invited to invest in later systems in exchange for a 30-year concession to operate the systems.

ETA plans 13 projects with a combined distance of 323 kms for the city of Bangkok, and 8 inter-city expressway projects with a combined distance of 727 kms over the next 10-15 years. ETA is currently undertaking surveys and studies in provincial cities like Nakhonrachasima, Phisanulok, Khonkaen, Phuket, Songkhla, Chacherngsao, and Nakhonsrithummarach in preparation for their future plan to develop expressway systems in these cities. However, no near term development of additional expressway networks is planned.

Rail Transport Networks

Thailand's rail system has a network of about 4,119 kilometers throughout the country consisting of 3,954 kilometers single-track line and 165 kilometers double-track lines. The Government's limited investment in the system and the State Railways of Thailand's continuous operating loss has restricted development and modernization of the system. Hence, Thailand' s rail networks lags behind other transportation modes in the country.

The State Railways of Thailand 's master plan outlines three major projects three major projects. They are: 1) track doubling, 2) track rehabilitation and 3) new railway lines.

Track Doubling Project: In 1993, the Government approved the basic plan for SRT to provide double tracking of the systems major routes, with a total length of 2,744 kms to be covered. Implementation of the plan has been divided into phrases with priorities given to lines that radiate from Bangkok, and the Eastern Seaboard area. Completion of the first phase with a total length of 234 kms is scheduled for 2004. SRT is seeking cabinet approval for the double tracking of the Chachoengsao-Sri Racha line. The line is given implementation priority to serve the continued expansion of the Laem Chabang port. However, further implementation of track doubling of the SRT network will depend on findings of the "Investigation of Capacity Constraints and Determination of the Need for Track Doubling of SRT Network" a study which is scheduled for completion later 2002.

Track Rehabilitation: The rehabilitation project involves replacing existing timber sleepers with mono-block pre-stressed concrete sleepers together with elastic rail fastenings. It will also include improvement works on the ballast and embankment. The SRT is completing the rehabilitation of the first 791 kms, and is seeking Government budget for the detail design of the next 813 kms. Routes planned for rehabilitation are listed below

Phrase 4: 227 km. North Pitsanulok – Ban Dan (110 km) South Bang Sue – Talingchan - Ban Chimplee (18 km) Toongsong - Ban Tondod (99 km)	Consultant Fee	Ballast Wagon and	Track Maintenance Equipment Construction	Total
Million Baht	188.3	914.4	4,897.00	6,000.50

Phrase 5: 308 km Northeast Kaengkoi - Gang Sueten (37km)	Consultant Fee	Ballast Wagon and	Track Maintenance Equipment	Total

Suranarai - Buayai (192km) Chumthang Jira Road - Buayai (79 km)			Construction	
Million Baht	198.6	1,305.30	7,398.60	8,902.50

Phrase 6: 278 km Northeastern: Buayai – Nong Khai (278 km)	Consultant Fee	Ballast Wagon and	Track Maintenance Equipment Construction	Total
Million Baht	207.4	1,232.00	6,993.00	8,432.40

New Railway Lines: Since July 1997, the Cabinet has approved the SRT extension plan of the 4 new lines that extend to Chiang Rai province in the north, Pang-Nga in the south, Rayong province in the Eastern Seaboard, and Nakhon Phnom in the northeast. Detailed engineering design of the first three lines was completed in 1997. Total cost of the project is estimated to be more than Baht 90,000 million (US$2.250 Billion at US$1= Baht 40) . The Government rejected SRT's request to fund the initial phrase of this project.

Urban Rapid Transit Systems

The Bangkok Mass Transit System (BTS), commonly called the Skytrain began operation in December 1999 and is Thailand 's first mass transit system. It is a dual track heavy rail system elevated above the medians of city streets that run through the central business districts of Bangkok. The System consists of two lines, the Sukhumvit Line and Silom Line with a total length of approximately 23.5 km. The Bangkok Mass Transit System Public Company Limited (BTSC) developed the project as part of the concession awarded by the Bangkok Metropolitan Administration. The concession grants BTSC the right to build the system operate and retain all revenue for 30 years.

The estimated cost of system is about US $1.333 Billion with US$ 451.4 million invested in civil works and US$ 601.4 million in electrical and mechanical works. (*Note calculation is based on an exchange rate of US$ 1 = 38 Baht*) Siemens – Italian-Thai Consortium built the system on a turnkey basis. Siemens is a lead supplier for the electrical and mechanical equipment, and responsible for maintenance of the electrical and mechanical equipment for the first five years.

The BTSC proposed plan to extend the Skytrain from Sathorn to Phetkasem and Onnuj to Samrong. In its proposal, the BTSC asked the Government to invest in civil construction. The proposed plan has been rejected on the basis that the plan did not agree with the Cabinet decision to extend the system in three directions that are the two BTSC proposed extension and the extension from Chong Nonsi to Rama 3. In addition, the Government will not invest in civil construction of the system. Thus, the extension plan of the BTSC depends on further negotiations between the BTSC and the Bangkok Metropolitan Administration, the project owner.

The M.R.T. Chaloem Ratchamongkhon Line or known as the Blue Line Initial System Project (ISP) will be Thailand's first underground heavy rail mass transit system (i.e., subway). The system is under the responsibility of the Mass Rapid Transit Authority of Thailand (MRTA) a government enterprise in charge of developing mass transit systems throughout Thailand. The 20kms route aligns principally along the center-line of existing roads, and is approximately 14-30 meters below road surface. The route starts from Hua Lamphong railway station passing along Rama 4 road, Ratchadapisek Road, Lat Phrao Road, and ends at Bang Sue railway station. The MRTA plans for partial opening of the system (the northern section) at the end of 2002, and a full line service by mid of 2003.

The total investment cost of this project is about US$ 2,716 million:

Land Acquisition	613	million US$
- Civil Works	1,591	million US$
- M & E Works	435	million US$
- Consultant	77	million US$
Total	2,716	million US$

Note: Cost is calculated based on an exchange rate of US$ 1 = 40 Baht

Funding for the ISP development comes from both Government and private investment. Government through MRTA invests in civil work including land acquisition while the concessionaire from the private sector invests in the electro-mechanical work and system operation and maintenance. In August, 2000 Bangkok Metro Co., Ltd. (BMCL) won the concession contract to operate the ISP for 25 years. Forecasted revenue for the 25 year concession is about 300,000 million Baht at the fare structure of 12 Baht boarding fare and 2 Baht per kilometre travelling in the year 2002. The revenue sharing scheme of 55% for BMCL and 45% for MRTA, the estimated earning would yield BMCL 15% minimal internal rate of return of and MRTA 4.4 % on investment.

As of November 2001, construction of the depot has been completed while completion of the underground structure for the southern and northern section is about 92.4% and 86%respectively. Trackwork and lift and escaltors is about 88% and 78% completed. Final selection for the M&E equipment supplier was made in October 2001. BMCL granted the contract to the French-Japanese consortium Alstoms-Mitsubishi Electric and Mitsubishi Corporation to supply M&E equipment for the system.

MRTA plans to extend the Blue Line Initial System Project to the south direction from Hua Lumphong to Bang Kae during the next seven years(2002-2007) The extension is planned to serve the demand in the old high density development area and demand in the residential area in the east side of Chao Phraya River (Thonburi side). To reduce the financial burden of the project. MRTA divided the project into two phrases.

			Length (km)	Construction Year	Opening Year
Phase I	:	Hua Lumphong-Bang Wa	8.7	2003-2010	2008
Phase II	:	Bang Wa-Bang Khae	4.9		2010

Implementation of the project would be similar to that of the ISP Blue Line. The government will invest in civil works while a private sector will be invited to invest in the electrical and

For additional analytical, business and investment opportunities information,
please contact Global Investment & Business Center, USA
at (202) 546-2103. Fax: (202) 546-3275. E-mail: rusric@erols.com

mechanical works and to operate and maintain the system for a certain period. Design Build concept will also be use for the project construction.

Schedule

Projects	Schedule
Land Acquisition	2002-2005
Selection of Consultant	2002
Selection of Contractors	2002-2003
Detailed Design and Construction	2004-2006

ESTIMATED PROJECT CAPITAL COST AND SOURCE OF FUNDS

Projects	Fiscal Year	Total
Land Acquisition	2003-2005	3,357
Consultant Fee	2003-2008	1,471
Design/Construction Civil Works	2003-2008	27,771
Design/Construction System	2003-2008	6,434
Contingency	2003-2008	3,260
Total		42,293
Source of Funds		
Government Budget	2003-2008	8,088
Loan	2003-2008	27,771

For additional analytical, business and investment opportunities information, please contact Global Investment & Business Center, USA at (202) 546-2103. Fax: (202) 546-3275. E-mail: rusric@erols.com

Private Investment	2003-2008	6,434
Total		42,293
Note : 1. Excluding cost escalation and VAT 2. Price in year 1997		

MARKET TRENDS

The 1997 economic crisis has significantly diminished the level of investment in land infrastructure projects as it reduced the Government's budget available for large-scale infrastructure projects and the country's ability to borrow from international sources. Government investment in infrastructure is estimated at baht 86.4 billion for this year, as compared with 121.5 billion last year and 145.2 billion in 1997. The severe decline in economic activities and the prolonged pace of recovery have lessened the urgency of many projects and caused many projects to become financial unviable. The postponement of additional expressway network developments is a prime example. Moreover, the restricted availability of Government funds also calls for new financial arrangements to fund projects with a greater role for the private sector.

As a result, development of land infrastructure in Thailand requires a different set of expertise, know-how and investment than has been traditionally available in the local market. The Build, Operate, and Transfer (BOT) model is a recently introduced concept resulting from Government attempts to increase public/private partnership in large land infrastructure projects to overcome its budget limitations. The concept is likely to be used in many future projects. This new concept requires the project contractor to fund the project in addition to doing the constructing work. The contractor would transfer the completed project for operation by the Government who will in turn pay back the money and interest. This new concept requires project financing know-how and potential investment partners.

Moreover, alternative means to conventional project design and construction such as turnkey and design-build have become increasingly popular. Development of recent projects in Thailand such as the Skytrain or the ISP Blue line were carried out under a design-build and turnkey method. Local consultants are in search of know-how as the industry moves away from conventional project development method toward this new concept.

In terms of project opportunities, Thailand's upcoming land transportation developments will emphasize development of its urban rail mass transit system. Two major plans for development of rail mass transit system are in final review. Both the Urban Rail Transportation Master Plan (URMAP) of the Office of the Commission for the Management of Land Traffic (OCMLT) and The Bangkok Railroad Improvement Project (BRIP) by the State Railways of Thailand are plans to develop an elevated rail system network as Bangkok's key mass transit system. URMAP will serve as a master plan outlining overall system developments, while BRIP will serve as a detail plan of the Eastern and Northern lines recommended in the URMAP. SRT and OCMLT expect to submit the two studies for Cabinet approval by the end of this year.

For additional analytical, business and investment opportunities information,
please contact Global Investment & Business Center, USA
at (202) 546-2103. Fax: (202) 546-3275. E-mail: rusric@erols.com

Urban Rail Transportation Master Plan (URMAP): An urban rail mass transit master plan for the Bangkok Metropolitan Area. The plan emphasizes minimizing capital expenditure and increasing private sector participation because of the limited funding of transport sector anticipated in the next 10 years. URMAP outlines plan to develop elevated railway lines along the existing railway alignment to serve as a backbone (inter urban) system bringing passengers from outer suburban locations to the city. Then, the MRTA Blue Line and the BTSC Skytrain would provide a distribution (intra-urban) system for the inner city. Hence, the proposed network would provide suburban commuter service, and intra-urban mass transit service while maintaining the existing rail network's traditional nationwide long distance passenger service.

The study outlines 3 phases of development spanning beyond the next twenty year. An annual investment of Baht 16 billion is estimated for projects listed in the first phrase (2001-2011). Priority projects are as follows:

· Phaya Thai – Nong Ngu Hao (New Bangkok International Airport): This route will be a new rail line parallel to the existing railway line, recommended for completion by 2004 in time for the opening of the new airport. The Japanese Government through JICA is funding a study "SBIA Rail Access Project" which will be completed in December 2001. The study will recommend the system development as an "airport express rail with check in facilities in the city, its engineering structure (partially or completely elevated) and funding alternatives. This project is likely to be developed under the jurisdiction of the State Railways of Thailand with majority private investment.

· Bang Sue – Phaya Thai: an elevated double track connecting eastern line (SBIA) to the new central station
· Hua Lamphong – Bang Sue: elevated tracks along SRT alignment
· Bang Sue – Rangsit: an elevated track using the existing Hopewell Structure
· Southwest Extension (Hua Lamphong – Tha Phra-Bang Wa): an MRTA Blue Line a new alignment, crosses the Chao Phraya River in southwest direction to Phet Kasem/Charan Sanit Wong junction to Bang Wa.
· Southeast Extension (On Nut – Samrong): a BTSC Skytrain extension along Sukhumvit road to Samrong
· Southwest Extension (Saphan Taksin – Mae Klong Interconnection Station – BTSC)

The Bangkok Railroad Improvement Project (BRIP): The State Railway of Thailand initiated the BRIP to address four key issues: inadequate urban rail transport service in Bangkok Metropolitan Region (BMR); intersections between the exisiting rail network and urban roads, resulting in serious traffic congestion in many areas of Bangkok; inadequate commuter train services; and no productive use for the abandoned rail superstructure along the SRT northern and eastern rail corridors. (Note: The superstructure was built under the former Bangkok Elevated Road and Train System, commonly known as the Hopewell Project. BERTS was terminated after construction of the superstructure).

In fact, BRIP is a downscaled supplant of the Hopewell project. It would be an upgrade of the rail infrastructure in BMA through the construction of an elevated track support structure and associated facilities from Hua Lampong to Rangsit on the SRT's northern corridor, and from Yommaraj Junction to Huamark on the eastern corridor. BRIP proposed three transit services that are:

Standard commuter services:

- Hualampong – Rang sit – Ayutthaya
- Hualampong – Hua Mark - Cha Choeng Sao

Express commuter services:

- Hualampong - Rangsit – Ayutthaya
- Bang Sue/Asoke – Hua Mark – SBIA
- Hualampong – Hua Mark – Cha Choeng Sao

Mass Rapid Transit services:

- Don Muang – Yommaraj – Hualampong
- Yommaraj – Hua Mark

The total cost of the Project is estimated at estimated at 159,110 million Baht (US$ 3978 million at $US1= Baht 40), excluding taxes and interest and other charges during construction. The foreign currency component of the project is about 67 percent or Baht 105,847 million (about $2,646 million at $1 to 40 Baht). The total base cost of the Project, excluding consultancy cost would be 108,755 million Baht. Project implementation is about 5 year.

The study proposes an investment structure similar to the MRTA one where the Government funds the cost of the civil work and a private concessionaire invests in the M&E in return for the right to operate the system for a given period of time. Hence, the Government investment in the project is estimated at Baht 69,630 million (US$1741 million at $1 to 40 Baht) approximately 44% of the total cost meanwhile the private concessionaire cost is at Baht 89,480 million (US$ 2237 millionat $1 to 40 Baht) approximately 56% of the total cost.

IMPORT MARKET

Industry estimates import content of large land infrastructure projects to range from 30-60% on average. However, import content level would likely be reduced to a level as low as 30% due to increasing government pressure for projects to minimize imports of both goods and services.

Engineering Consultant Services: Engineering consulting firms from Germany, France, Japan and the U.S. are the major players in land infrastructure development projects in Thailand. Imported content of engineering consultant services for road and expressway projects is estimated to be around 15-20%, while more technological complex projects like a cable stay bridge requires a foreign content as high as 40%, and an even higher import content for the ISP Blue Line underground system.

Construction Contractor Service: The local construction contractors market in Thailand is highly competitive. A few large and capable local contractors and well-established foreign contractors companies control the market for large infrastructure projects. Meanwhile medium sized local contractors control the market for road network construction. Major players among foreign companies are from Japan and Germany. Contractors from Korea and the People's Republic of China are recent entrants in the market. They are viewed as low cost competitors with some limitations in terms of technology. The high local content nature of the construction work and the capable local contractors makes the Thai market difficult for new-to-market foreign competition to enter the market.

COMPETITION

For additional analytical, business and investment opportunities information, please contact Global Investment & Business Center, USA at (202) 546-2103. Fax: (202) 546-3275. E-mail: rusric@erols.com

Major land infrastructure projects in Thailand generally attract competition from leading global players, because Thailand lacks local availability and opens its market for international competition. Project owners generally seek their sources of supply in the international market. For example, they invite companies from list of engineering consultant services maintained by international lending institutions like World Bank, Japan Bank for International Cooperation. Hence, well-known services and equipment companies often are involved in development and implementation of major land infrastructure projects in Thailand.

Technical capability and experience with similar projects are essential in competition among engineering consultant firms. Firms with expertise in different part of the project often form a consortium to work on a project. Their partnership patterns varies from one to the next, and hence they can be partner in one project and competitors in the others.

International engineering consultants with specific expertise often are subject experts are involved in design, construction and management of large and complex land infrastructure projects in Thailand. A most recent example is the Blue Line Initial System Project which involved a number of international engineering consultant firms expert in the subway system. Two groups of consultants led by Halcrow Asia, and Dorsch Consult did the preliminary design for the system. De Leuw Cather International Inc. is a leading consultant working as the Project Management, which involves inspection of engineering design, control of the overall project schedule, and coordination among contractors and concessionaire. Louis Berger International, Inc. is the system construction supervision consultant supervising the civil work construction and preliminary system-wide M&E design interface required for all the designated contractors. Electrowatt Engineering (Thailand) is the M&E supervision consultant supervising the M&E installation works of the concessionaire. In addition, MRTA contracted the Mouchel Group to prepare inter-modal transfer facilities and station development master plan.

For projects financed by Government budget or where specific import expertise is of secondary importance, having a local partner(s) is a key element for success for foreign consultants to obtain the service contract. The State Railways of Thailand commissioned a consortium led by Team Consulting Engineering & Management, Thailand's leading engineering consultant firm to conduct the study on The Bangkok Railroad Improvement Project. The consortium consists of Electrowatt Engineering Ltd,. L.E.K. Consulting Ltd., JMP (Thailand) Ltd., and ASDECON Corporation Ltd. The Government regulations require that for consultants consortium to be qualified to bid for public projects its lead firm must be a Thai firms registered at Thai Consultant Data Base Center, Public Debt Management Office, Ministry of Finance. It is also required that man-months of Thai personnel must be at least 50% of the total service. Though these regulations allow exception on a case by case basis, the importance of local partners can not be disregarded. In addition to the regulation requirement, local participation can also bring the connections and relationship with prospective contract commissioners, a useful element in winning the contract.

To an even greater extent, local participation is essential in large land infrastructure projects market. The few existing foreign construction contractors successful in Thailand often form a consortium with major local contractors to work on large projects. Large local contractors bring to the consortium their market expertise and well-rounded local connections useful to winning the contact. Meanwhile, the foreign firm provides technical expertise and favorable relationship with the project's financier often of their own country. Hence, these few Thai and foreign contractors control the land infrastructure projects market.

Unlike other markets, international land infrastructure equipment and system manufacturers compete mainly on the financial terms proposed as part of their bid to supply the products.

Manufacturers also form a consortium to propose a complete system for prospective projects. Financial package proposed as part of the bid is the deciding factor for contract of this nature, since global equipment and system manufacturers are relatively at par in terms of technology and technical capability. Example is the M&E proposal for ISP Blue Line. The five international manufacturers / consortia that competed to supply the mechanical and electrical works related equipment and system for BMCL, the private concessionare awarded to operate the ISP Blue Line, were: Siemens, Bombardier, Alstom-MELCO, JMC-Mitsui and Adtranz. BMCL selected Alstom-MELCO and according to industry experts, the consortium's financial package was the determining factor in their selection by BMCL.

Moreover, international suppliers also gain competitive advantages in projects that borrow from the prospective supplier country. URMAP, a study commissioned by OCMLT is funded by a JBIC loan. Pacific Consultants International is the lead firm conducting the study. The consortium includes Japan Railway Technical Service (JART), Asian Engineering Consultants Corp., Ltd. (AEC), Transconsult Co., Ltd. (TC) and Wilbur Smith Associates. Suppliers from lending countries have an earlier access to project information. Lending institutions often share project information with prospective suppliers from its country as they received the project information from working on the prospective loan agreement with the project owners. Moreover, the loan contract often includes conditions with favorable implications for service providers or equipment suppliers from the lending country.

For Thailand, the Japan Bank for International Cooperation (JBIC) is its largest lender. According to the Ministry of Finance, JBIC accounts for 40.5% of all Thailand's external borrowing for the fiscal year 2000. The three largest JBIC loan for the year are for MRTA, Department of Highways, and the New Bangkok International Airport. In fact, JBIC's loan to the ISP Blue Line exceeds 90% of the project's civil works and consultant costs.

Key Upcoming Projects

-- MRTA Blue Line Extension: Hua Lamphong - Bang Khae section

-- Development of Airport-Express Rail System (SBIA Rail Access Project)

-- Urban Rail Transportation Master Plan (URMAP)*

--The Bangkok Railroad Improvement Project (BRIP)*

* Note: Priority projects under URMAP and BRIP can not be identified at this point. Priority projects in plans of this nature will be identified only after approval of the plans. Moreover, the Prime Minister has recently requested SRT to scaled down projects proposed in BRIP to accommodate the country's constrained financial capability. It is widely anticipated that project priority and sizes in both URMAP and BRIP will be further reviewed in response to the Prime Minister's latest request.

MARKET ACCESS

Thailand is an open market for global participation in the country's land infrastructure development projects. The Thai Government does not enforce regulations that completely ban or create insurmountable barriers to entry for foreign participation in engineering consultant services, equipment and system or construction contractor service market. As a result, the Thai market is highly competitive with competitors from many countries. Moreover, suppliers and service providers targeting large projects involving large capital investment often draws in their Government for support, often in terms of capital lending for the project.

Partnership with local expertise is a necessary element of successful entry for new-to-market companies. Partners' market expertise can help new to market firms overcome initial difficulty in making market entry. Foreign engineering consultants generally make their initial market entry by being sub-contractors to leading firms in the project. In a process, new-to-market companies acquire market expertise and necessary local connections for their future opportunities. The process could be time consuming but it is an essential mean to successful establishment in the Thai market.

FRANCHISING

Franchising has resulted in substantial successes for numerous Thai investors. In 2000, there were approximately 220 franchise systems operating 7,700 branches and generating annual sales of approximately US$1,697 million. Due to changing consumer buying patterns, urbanization and improvements in Thailand's transportation and communications network, the franchise industry is expected to continue to grow an average of 30 percent over the next few years. Even though the economic crisis in Thailand has slowed the rate of expansion of established franchises since 1997, there are many investors still seeking to launch potentially lucrative franchises in this sector because Thais perceive it as an attractive and relatively safe form of investment.

International franchises account for 70 percent of the total market. Within that figure, American franchises comprise 80 percent of all international franchises operating in Thailand. The quality and innovations offered by U.S. franchises are admired, but franchising fees are regarded as very high and start-ups are perceived as requiring large investments. Flexibility in terms with new franchisees is suggested in order to stimulate development of franchise concepts in Thailand. More recently, local Thai franchises have become very competitive because they require smaller initial investments at lower prices than international franchises. Thus, they have better growth potential than international franchises. Additionally, their payments are denominated in Baht and terms appear more favorable when the Baht exchange rate dips against the dollar.

MARKET HIGH LIGHTS AND BEST PROSPECTS

STATISTICAL DATA

There is no published statistical data available for the market size of the franchise market in Thailand. Therefore, the following estimated statistics were prepared based on interviews with the Thai Franchise Association and both local and international master franchisees, .

Statistical Data
Franchising Market in Thailand
(US$ million)

	1999	2000	2001(e)	Avg. annual growth rate for next 2 years
A. Total franchise sales	1,305	1,697	2,036	+30 %
B. Sales by local firms	261	509	611	+35 %
C. Sales by international firms	1,044	1,188	1,425	+20 %
D. Sales by U.S. firms	835	950	1,114	+17 %
Exchange rate US$1=Baht	45	45	45	
Inflation	3.5	2.5	2.0	

Note: The above statistics are unofficial estimates and (e) represents estimate

MARKET ASSESSMENT

Franchise systems operating in Thailand run the gamut from gas stations and hotels to fast food outlets and convenience stores. Even in the midst of an economic crisis, there is interest in franchises because they are considered a relatively fast, safe and easy way to launch a successful business. Although the crisis slowed growth to 15 percent-20 percent per year for international firms from 30 to 40 percent throughout the last decade, the high growth rate for franchising even in weak economies demonstrates that the industry is still dynamic.

Because of the rapid development of franchising here, Thailand offers many opportunities for U.S. franchisors. The growth in 2001 will continue to be significant but is expected to be lower than in 2000. Total franchise sales in 1999 were US$1,305 million and increased 30 percent to US$1,697 million in 2000. By the end of 2001, growth is estimated to reach 20 percent with total sales of US$2,036 million. The economy is expected to improve in the next few years with typical annual growth rates returning to pre-crisis levels of around 30 percent.

In 2000, trade sources estimated that Thailand had 220 franchises with 7,700 branches. By comparison, there were 200 franchises with 6,500 branches in 1999. Franchises in Thailand make up one fourth of all retail sales. Grossing US$1,188 million in sales in 2000, international franchises in Thailand made up 70 percent of the total franchising market. Franchises from the United States account for an estimated 80 percent share of the international market.

Food franchises comrpise 30 percent of the market while convenience and retail stores total 50 percent. The other 20 percent is comprised of drug and healthcare stores, laundry and cleaning services, auto services, schools, hotel chains, etc.

The franchise industry in Thailand has been characterized by rapid change. Most notably, in 2000, the Minor Group (which owns the Pizza Public Company that had the Pizza Hut franchise) became involved in a bitter court dispute with franchisor Tricon International over certain conditions in the franchising arrangement. The two parties went their separate ways early in 2001, with the former franchisee rebranding his restaurants as The Pizza Company. The issues raised offer important lessons for local firms operating foreign franchises and the U.S. principals as well. Thai franchisees must pay great attention to joint venture agreements and other conditions with foreign franchisors. Local franchisees operating different types of food franchises must be aware of competitive concerns that American, and other, franchisors would have when seeking to protect their brands that may already be operational in Thailand through other local franchisees. Contract renewal conditions should also be clearly stated. Some other franchise contracts with American franchises have been terminated due to slower than planned expansion of outlets, lack of outlet performance improvement, and improper marketing activities.

BEST PROSPECTS

The best sales prospects for U.S. franchises are as follows:

Fast food/restaurants
Non-Food Franchise:
- Specialty retail shops
- Hotel Chains
- Automotive Aftermarket Services
- Cleaning and Maintenance Services
- Training Programs
- Delivery Services
- Entertainment services (Video rental and Music shops)
- Childcare

Following are highlights of some of the opportunities:

Food Franchises

Food franchises account for 30 percent of the total franchise market. Most of the major U.S. food franchises are already operating successfully in the Thai market. Well-known brand names include: Kentucky Fried Chicken (KFC), McDonalds, A&W, Pizza Hut, Burger King, Big Boy, Starbucks, Swensen's, Dairy Queen, Baskin Robbins, Sizzler, Mister Donut, Au Bon Pain, Mrs. Fields and Auntie Anne's, to name a few. There are 93 McDonald's, 270 Kentucky Fried Chickens, 76 Swenson's, 75 Pizza Huts 78 Chester's and 25 Starbucks. As of the end of 2000, Thailand had 1,500 fast food and family restaurant outlets with the number expected to increase to 2,000 by the end of 2001. Brand, quality, standards and acceptance by consumers were keys to the success of food franchises.

Just three years after the economic crash, the fast food industry was back to pre-crisis levels in 2000, with growth at 20 percent and a market value of US$211 million. The frequency rate of visits has returned to normal. During the economic crisis, customers made an average of eight visits per every three months. Now, the rate has increased to ten visits per every 3 months. Customers' average expenditures per visit also have increased from US$ 2.2/visit to US$3.3/visit. Horizontal growth in the pizza subsector is expected due to fierce competition between Pizza Hut chain and The Pizza Comany to expand operating units. Accordingly, traditional outlets, such as shopping centers and department stores will be saturated. As a result, new locations such as gas stations, discount stores and commercial buildings will gain new types of commercial tenants and larger profits.

The plans of many franchises in Thailand are growth-oriented since they account for only 4 percent of the whole food industry, This figure is comparatively small compared to neighboring countries like Malaysia (9 percent), the Philippines (20 percent) and Singapore (20 percent). McDonalds plans to add 15 more outlets every year increasing the number to 101 in 2000. Tricon plans to have more than 300 KFC outlets and 100 Pizza Hut outlets by the end of 2001. Starbucks currently has 25 units in Thailand and plans to have 500 outlets in Asia with in 3-4 years.

For additional analytical, business and investment opportunities information,
please contact Global Investment & Business Center, USA
at (202) 546-2103. Fax: (202) 546-3275. E-mail: rusric@erols.com

Thai people view fast food as unhealthy and expensive; therefore, most fast food restaurants have developed strategies to improve the quality, service and variety of their products. For sample, McDonald's offers more varieties on their menu and gets it to you faster, using a timer to measure the servers' speed. Fast food delivery is also a huge business and one can receive an order with in 30 minutes.

Although food franchises are quite popular, competition is very stiff because the market is nearly saturated. Fast food and restaurant opportunities are limited for newcomers unless a unique idea comes along or a failed franchise concept is revived.

Retail and Convenience Stores

Retail and convenience store franchises account for 50 percent of all franchise operations in Thailand. Drug and healthcare franchises have done well in the Thai market, particularly G.N.C. (USA), Body Shop, Boots (U.K.) and Watson's of Hong Kong. The Thai convenience store market has been dominated by 7-Eleven (U.S.) which has 1,400 outlets as of 2000, and is expected to grow to 2,000 units by 2003. The other major competitors, AM/PM (300 in 1999) and Family Mart of Japan (100 in 1999) pale in comparison. At the end of 2000, there were about 5,700 retail and convenience stores with total sales of US$ 849 million. Boots expects Thailand to be a showcase for their business. They plan to have 150 shops opened by 2002, controlling 25 percent of health/beauty market. Retail and convenience stores are also the fastest growing sector among local franchises.

Hotel Chains

Tourism has been increasing dramatically over the past few years due to government promotional activities. According to the Tourism Authority of Thailand, Thailand earns approximately US$11 billion per year from its tourist industry. Tourism has created opportunities for U.S. chain hotels to find local partners who are interested in instituting better management or marketing structures. Currently, five star hotels such as the Holiday Inn, Marriott, Hilton, Radisson and Sheraton chains are already in the Thai market. There is also potential for small and medium U.S. hotel chains such as Days Inn, Best Western, Hotel 6, or Clarion if they consider offering financial and management support.

Automotive Aftermarket Services

Thailand has approximately eight million vehicles in use that are serviced by three groups of after-market service providers; authorized service centers (50 percent), family-owned service providers (40 percent), and chain service centers (10 percent). The size of the market is estimated about US$25 million. The market for automotive after-market service is strong, and there are many opportunities for US franchises.

Current franchises concentrate mainly on express maintenance service and light repairs such servicing, tires, brakes, and suspension systems. They are Max AutoExpress, B-Quik, Cockpit Car Service Center, Borneo Auto Care and Check Point Auto Center.

Most of the new car sales in Thailand have automatic transmission and sophisticated, computerized features, which require special maintenance or equipment. Servicing newer cars is beyond the capability of local service stations and car owners are also dissatisfied with the quality and fees of local garage services. Thus, the market is open to U.S. franchises supplying organized, standardized systems.

Aside from traditional autmotive aftermarket services and repair facilities, most modern gas stations will soon be equipped with convenience stores, car washes, and restaurants to cater Thai and international travelers on the roads.

Cleaning and Maintenance Services

The Thai real estate industry was hurt by the economic crisis and many buildings have been left empty. As the economy recovers, the owners of many of these high-rise buildings will benefit from a return to pre-crisis occupancy levels. Given the possibility of a near-term recovery in the real estate market, opportunities exist for new management and maintenance services including cleaning, gardening and hospitality services. These services are new to Thailand, so there are few competitors. Furthermore, local competitors have yet to provide an adequate serrange of services or enough personnel to serve the market.

Education Centers

Education franchises show bright prospects not only for students but also for workers who need to develop their skills. Education opportunities can be divided in two parts.

English and Training Centers

Globalization and the technological revolution have increased the demand for English. An increase in the number of multi-national corporations demanding language or management training will continue in the future. In the short term, English language schools are encouraged to set up corporate-run operations to train staff in their unique methodologies and better assess the students' needs and teaching skills of the limited number of native speakers available before franchising their programs.

Children's' Play and Learning Centers

As the number of households with two parents working expands, the need for child centers rises. Children's' play and learning centers have become available in many locations in Thailand. The leading franchises from Japan and Britain are major players in this sector. The leading brands are Fun Language, Future Kids, Kumon, Computer Tot, etc.

Video and Music Shops

Local and international video and music stores are thriving with a market value of $22 million. Leading brands in the market are Blockbuster (US), Tsutaya (Japan), VDO EZY form Australia, CD Warehouse, Mang Pong, and Showtime. Mang Pong and Show Time are local franchises.

Mailing and delivery services

The rapidly growing internet industries and e-commerce industries will not only create demand for computer sales and computer maintenance services but they will also generate demand for related delivery and shipping services.

The U.S. has a firm grasp on the shipping industry. Most leading American brands have already been introduced to the market. EMS, DHL, UPS, FEDEX, US Mail Box are all currently operating here.

For additional analytical, business and investment opportunities information, please contact Global Investment & Business Center, USA at (202) 546-2103. Fax: (202) 546-3275. E-mail: rusric@erols.com

COMPETITIVE ANALYSIS

Domestic Production

Thai franchises represent only 30 percent of total sales, but they are found in every subsector of the franchise market. There are many major local franchises including M.K restaurant, The Pizza Company, Narai Pizza, Black Canyon, Smart Brain, NEQ, EZ's, ECC, Siam Computer, Showtime, Fit-flex, Ti-Noi, V Shop, Check Point Auto Center, Laundry Quick, Lemon Green, and Fun Language. However, local franchises still lack experience and know-how. The Franchise Association reported that an average of 20 local franchises join the market each year and about the same number leave.

According to a recent published report, an established leader in the restaurant business, the Charoen Pokphand Group (CP), is planning to re-enter the market for fried chicken with a new entrant, Deli Chick. The first unit will open soon. The CP Group dropped its Kentucky Fried Chicken franchise last year and also has created the Chester's Grill franchise, which specializes in grilled chicken. Franchise and delivery sales for Chester's are expected to grow by 20 percent. The CP also forecasts a 17% increase in franchise sales and hopes to increase the number of operating units by 15 more outlets to 93 in 2002. The CP Group also plans to target regional markets, including China in the near future. The Charoen Pokphand Group plans to compete aggressively for market share against major American chains including A&W, Chicken Treat, KFC and McDonald's.

Aside from CP's plans, the number of local food franchises should increase further due to the government's support of successful local restaurants seeking to franchise through investors in other countries,

Future growth in franchising local concepts is expected due to the fact that the Thai government believes SME (Small Medium Enterprises) are going to help the Thai economy recover from the crisis. Therefore, the government has started to promote SME development. According to the Thai Franchise Association, franchise systems have supported the government policy to promote SME's.

Total franchise sales in 2000 were estimated at US$1,697 million, of which US$1,188 million was generated by international franchises. The U.S. is the leader among international franchises and controls 80 percent of the entire international market of US$ 950 million. The rest are followed by franchises from Japan (8 percent), France (4 percent), Britain (4 percent), the Netherlands (2 percent) and others (2 percent). It is expected that the growth of proven, reliable U.S. franchises will continue for the next few years even though the dollar is stronger than the Baht and the local economy is still in recovery. However, U.S. franchisers should be aware that there are differences among countries in values, taste, lifestyles and perceptions. What is work in the U.S. may not work in Thailand. There are many U.S. companies that have successfully adapted to local conditions and are successfully operating in Thailand. Therefore, U.S. companies have the potential to maintain their leadership position.

The following are U.S. franchises that successfully operate in Thailand: McDonald's, Burger King, Kentucky Fried Chicken, Pizza Hut, A&W, Dunkin Donuts, Cinnabon, Jpopeye's, Tony Roma's, TGI Friday, Hard Rock Café, Starbucks, Sizzler, Swensen, Baskin Robbins, Haagen-Dax, TCBY, Seven Eleven, Am Pm, Hertz, Avis, Budget, Midas, Mail Boxes, Guess, Levi's, Holiday Inn, Best Western, Quality Inn, California Fitness, Berlitz, ELS, and Radio Shack.

For additional analytical, business and investment opportunities information,
please contact Global Investment & Business Center, USA
at (202) 546-2103. Fax: (202) 546-3275. E-mail: rusric@erols.com

Local investors are very receptive to franchises from the United States. Quality, name recognition, standards and innovation all play a big part of their success with Thai investors; however, they are also know for the large capital investments required. Approximately 20 percent of all local and international franchises fail each year; it is important that U.S. franchisers choose the best franchisee. Know-how and dedication to adapting the franchise concepts, proven operational and marketing methods and the financial resources to launch the franchise over the long term all aid in a franchise's success.

END-USER ANALYSIS

In 2000, Thailand had about 220 franchise systems, which comprised one fourth of all retail spending. Retail and convenience store franchises are more popular than food franchises. Thai consumers love to shop at modern and conveniences store. Even during economic crisis, they remained loyal to their favorite foreign brands. This is a significant reason why franchise outlets can succeed when independent retail operations may fail.

Franchisee

Franchises are usually open to all candidates but some franchisor organizations may show preference based on age, experience, financial capability, sex, and marital status. For example, auto repair centers tend to seek male investors as operators and cosmetic franchises will generally recruit women.
Trade sources reported that most of the franchisees operating in Thailand are women, with an average age of 30-40 years old. Of all franchisees, sixty one percent have finished undergraduate school and twenty two percent have finished graduate school. Forty five percent of franchisees have prior experience in operating some type of business before and thirty five percent were employees who were laid off or took early retirement when the economic crisis hit the country three years ago. Sixty seven percent of franchisees also operate other businesses. Most investors start up franchises with capital of between US$ 20,000-65,000.

The key element for the successful development of the franchise system is the master franchisees. Good master franchisees need to know and understand clearly a franchise's concepts such as: product standardization, international thinking, systematizing operations, strict adherence to operating manuals, training, etc. Many franchisees in Thailand that fail have operators who do not fully grasp the intricacies of the franchise system.

MARKET ACCESS

Import Climate

There are no trade barriers for foreign franchises in Thailand; however, American franchisers should be aware that what worked in the US may not work in Thailand. For example, franchise fees, which are normally high in the U.S., should be flexible. Even though, the Thai economy has improved since the crisis in 1997, it is still in recovery.

Distribution/Business Practices

Bangkok, a capital city which is home to over 12 million people, is a prime area that all franchises should target. The next locations should be major cities such as Pattaya, Phuket, Hadyai, Chiengmai, Nakorn Ratchasrima, and Khon Khen. The largest cost for franchise operators in Thailand are rental fees, which are relatively high. Another major cost is the royalty fee which franchisees have to pay to franchisers. Commonly, royalty fees in Thailand are paid as a

For additional analytical, business and investment opportunities information, please contact Global Investment & Business Center, USA at (202) 546-2103. Fax: (202) 546-3275. E-mail: rusric@erols.com

percentage of total sales, with fees ranging from 3-5 percent. Some will pay an initial fee for each outlet.

From a legal perspective, the franchising industry does not fall under any special legislation and legal franchising issues are dealt with under civil and commercial laws. The law is neutral about dispute settlement procedures, leaving agreement for the parties to decide, preferably in writing, at the time of signing the contract.

Financing

The financial crisis that began in 1997 severely affected the availability of credit. At the time, 74 out of 107 financial institutions were shut down, taken over by the state as insolvent, or merged with others. Non-performing debt climbed to 48 percent of the total financial system's assets. Local banks and other financial institutions have since been more cautious on new lending due to the fear of creating new non-performing loans. According to interviews with all major local banks, credit growth for this year is targeted at 1.5 percent and credit will be tight. Most franchisees have to use their own personal capital to get started.

Additionally, banks are reluctant to finance the purchasing of new franchises. However, for well-established franchises like a McDonald's or KFC, local banks can finance local investors with guarantees from the U.S. franchisors. For import and export of capital goods, commodities, and services, local banks can provide full banking services such as standby letters of credit, letters of guarantee, bills of collection, etc.

KEY CONTACTS:

Trade Promotion Opportunities

Name:	Inter Shop Asia 2002
Location:	Queen Sirikit National Convention Center
Dates:	April 25-27, 2002
Organizer:	N.C.C. Management and Development Co.,Ltd.
	60 New Ratchdapisek Road, Klongtoey
	Bangkok 10110
Tel:	662-229-3000
Fax:	662-229-3191

Name:	Global Franchising 2002
Location:	Singapore International Convention & Exhibition Center
Dates:	September 18-20, 2002
Organizer:	Singapore Exhibition Services Pte Ltd.
	47 Scotts Road, 11th Floor Goldbelt Towers
	Singapore 228233
Tel:	(65) 738-6776
Fax:	(65) 732-6776
Website: www.sesmontnet	

WATER RESOURCES AND EQUIPMENT

The development and management of water resources is a priority being pursued by the Thai Government. The market in Thailand offers good prospects for the sale of American water resources equipment and services. The market has an estimated size of 550 million USD and an average annual growth rate of 3-5%. Key opportunities exist in providing engineering design and construction services as well as equipment. Strong market potential exists for hardware and software for flood forecasting and warning systems. Good prospects also exist for engineering consultancy services required for the development of large-scale water resources projects, particularly technologies for Roller Compacted Concrete Dams, Rock Filled Dams, Tunneling Drainage Systems and Pipe Irrigation.

The water resources equipment and services market in Thailand is highly competitive with an increasing number of international suppliers vying to win projects. Japanese suppliers lead the engineering consultant services market with a 40% share, followed by suppliers from the European union countries. Japan, Korea and the People's Republic of China dominate the machinery and equipment market. Local companies control the construction services market.

This report provides an overview and recommendations to access the market for water resources equipment and services in Thailand. It explains overall market subsectors: Consultant Services, Construction Services, and Machinery and Equipment. This report also analyzes the competitive strengths of successful players in each market subsector.

MARKET HIGH LIGHTS AND BEST PROSPECTS

STATISTICAL DATA

There is no published statistical data available for the market size of the Water Resources Equipment and Services market in Thailand. Therefore, the following statistics were estimated based on interviews with consultant companies and with officers at the Royal Irrigation Department.

Statistical Data (US$ million)
Water Resources Equipment and Services

	1999	2000	2001(e)	Avg. Annual Growth Rate For next 2 Years
A. Total market	500	525	551	+5%
B. Local production	371	390	410	+5%
C. Exports	-	-	-	-
D. Imports	129	135	141	+5%
E. Imports from U.S.	19	20	21	+4%
Exchange rate US$1=Baht	45	45	45	
Inflation	3.5	2.5	2.0	

Note: The above statistics are unofficial estimates and (e) represents estimate

MARKET ASSESSMENT

Thailand has an estimated annual rainfall of 800,000 million cubic meters, of which 600,000 million cubic meters is run-off and only 200,000 million cubic meters can be utilized. At present, only 20% of the 200,000 million cubic meters can be harnessed using irrigation and dams. The government has goal to utilize as much as 50% of the estimated 200,000 million cubic meters. Therefore, an additional 60,000 million cubic meters will still be unharnessed.

It is estimated from Royal Irrigation Department (RID) that the water demand for Thailand in 2002 should be 65,539 million cubic meters with average growth rate of 3%. Of the total demand, 88 percent will be used for irrigation, 3 percent for industrial facilties and 9 percent for public consumption. Because the demand for water is increasing due to population growth and expansion of industrial and services sectors, all agencies involved in water resource development are preparing plans to construct more projects.

The government budget for water resource development is allocated primarily to the Royal Irrigation Department (RID), which is reports to the Ministry of Agriculture and Cooperatives. In principle, most of the budget at the RID is used in the development and maintenance of dams to support the agricultural sector. The Thai Government annually invests massive budget outlays for irrigation projects to ensure adequate water supply for the country. An additional budget of over $100 million, using funds borrowed from Asian Development Bank and Japanese Bank of Investment Cooperative (JBIC), was recently allocated for five water resources maintenance and development projects (Mae Laos, Haey Luang, Kra-Sie, Thun Samrit and Lower Mae Ping). This is resulting in a growing demand for engineering services and equipment required in water resources development.

Flooding has long been a recurrent problem in the major river basin. It has worsened over the last two decades due to global climate changes and urbanization along the rivers. The most recent significant flooding occurred in 1995 and 2001 as a result of heavy rains. The losses and damages affecting lives and properties has been high due to the lack of appropriate flood management and administration in the basin. Thai government has consequently stipulated a plan for flood forecasting and the development of an early warning system in the nation's important river basins.

The water resources equipment and services market is estimated at approximately $556 million in 2002, with an annual average growth rate of 3-5 percent. Engineering services required are for feasibility studies, environment studies, detailed design, project management and construction supervision. There is also for imported equipment using advanced technologies.

The number of water resources projects are increasing but at a slower rate due to conflicts between the RID and local communities on land compensation and the efforts of conservationist groups to re-examine the potential negative impact of certain projects on the environment and livelihood of the population in different parts of the country.

BEST PROSPECTS

Engineering Service companies with expertise in the following areas:
> Roller Compacted Concrete Dam
> Rock Filled Dam
> Tunneling Drainage System
> Pipe Irrigation

Equipment:
> Earth Moving Equipment

Weeds Removal Equipment
Dredger

Others:
Flood Forecasting and warning Technique
Telemetering network
Real-time Communications Network
Remote Sensing

COMPETITIVE ANALYSIS

Domestic Production

Consultant Services: Local engineering companies have half of the market for engineering consultant services in water resources development in Thailand. They are most competitive in the standard engineering segment of the engineering services market. They dominate the market for detail design and feasibility studies for small and medium water resources projects. They have significant cost advantages over their foreign counterparts. However, they are unable to compete with the foreign engineering consulting services utilizing newly advanced technologies which are a high value-added component of all the major irrigation projects in Thailand.

Construction Services: The market for construction services is driven by price and hence is dominated by the lowest cost supplier. Local construction contractors dominate the market but are challenged by construction contractors from the People's Republic of China. Since price is the most important factor in this market, technology and superior quality have little significance in the competition.

Machinery and Equipment: Domestic production of irrigation equipment/machinery is extremely limited. Thailand does not have its own manufacturing capability for industrial or construction machinery. Local capability is limited to assembling imported parts and manufacturing of simple parts, based on imported original designs.

Third Country Imports

International engineering consultants dominate the detail design market of large-scale water resources projects in Thailand because local engineering consultants lack the know-how to compete in the market. Japan has a 40% market share; Germany, the Netherlands and France account for a combined total of 40%. However, Thai sources indicate that the cost of European and Japanese consulting services are about 6 times higher than local services. By comparison, the US has approximately a 15% share of the market. Australia and Canada each have a smaller presence.

The Japanese share of the market will expand significantly over the next few years, as a result of a recent loan package conceived under the Miyazawa plan presented by the Japanese Government to Thailand. Part of these loans is used to fund a number of vital irrigation projects. Japanese suppliers of services and equipment have significant advantages to compete in these projects due to loan conditions.

Generally, foreign governments' loan and aid programs provide major competitive advantages to companies from the lending/donor countries. Aid that comes in a form of a grant and technical assistance is normally given for feasibility study of potential development projects. In some cases, a donor government sponsors a study team for preparation of the feasibility study. Grants

For additional analytical, business and investment opportunities information,
please contact Global Investment & Business Center, USA
at (202) 546-2103. Fax: (202) 546-3275. E-mail: rusric@erols.com

are also given with a condition that the contract funded by the grant money is awarded to short-listed companies from the donor countries. Similarly, the loan agreement usually requires that the short-listed companies and their term of reference be approved by the lending agency. Moreover, companies conducting the feasibility studies have technical advantages over their competitors in bidding for the detail design contract since they have better information on the project. Japan and the European countries have been major donors/creditors for development of Thailand's water resources. Consequently, Japanese and European companies have better market access that enable them to succeed in the market.

As of 2001, there were 7 water resources development projects and one flood forecasting project funded by grants and loan from foreign government agencies summarized as follows:

Organizations	Number of Projects
Overseas Economic Cooperation Fund (OECF)	3
Japan International Cooperation Agency (JICA)	1
Kreditanstalt fur Wiederaufbau (KfW)	1
Asian Development Bank (ADB)	1
Spain Government	1
US Trade Development Agency	1

Machinery and Equipment: Imports account for more than 90% of the construction machinery, pumps and other related equipment used in Thailand. Japan and Korea dominate the market for construction equipment, while Korea, China and India have captured larg shares of the water pump market with their lowest prices and standards that meet the general specifications of the bid. However, for high quality pumps of over 85% efficiency, companies from Germany, Japan, the UK and the U.S. are qualify for bidding. Suppliers of products and equipment for new irrigation projects sell their products to the government agencies via construction contractors. When entering the bid, bidders for the construction contracts are required to propose a complete package including equipment and machinery specified in the detail design.   High-quality products are unlikely to win in this market if prices are considerably higher since specifications of equipment and machinery required in the projects tend to focus on the basic functions with little emphasis on technology and quality.

U.S. Market Position & Share

American products and engineering services have a good reputation for their quality and advanced technology in the field of water resources and flood forecasting system in Thailand. In fact, U.S. technologies in water resources were among the first introduced in the Thai market in the 19060's. The prominent U.S. presence in the Thai water resources market can be attributed to the active role of the International Bank for Reconstruction and Development (IBRD) which was among the few major lenders funding water resources projects in this country at the time. Manuals and standards used in water resources projects by the Thai Government agency were prepared based on Bureau of Reclamation standards.

However, the U.S. position and market share has declined dramatically in the past two decades as a result of aid programs and lending activities started by Japan and European countries. U.S. companies have had less success in this market as prices of their products and services are usually higher than that of their competitors. A local source said that the cost of US consulting service is about 10 times higher than local consulting companies and is nearly two times more than the cost of European consulting companies. That said, however, local consultants are keen to work with U.S. consultants because of American expertise in the sector.

In the field of flood forecasting and warning systems, American is the leader in both hardware and software especially in telemetering networks, real-time communication networks, remote sensing, planning and management, image processing, Geographic Information Systems (GIS) application development and data analysis, and flood forecasting techniques.

END-USER ANALYSIS

The Royal Irrigation Department, Ministry of Agriculture and Cooperatives is the principal public authority responsible for the country's water resources development, flood control, and water conservation. The Department develops more than 90% of irrigation projects in Thailand, and hence is the major user for related equipment and services. The Office of Accelerated Rural Development at the Ministry of Interior and the Department of Energy Development and Promotion under the Ministry of Science manage other water resources development activities. Each has an annual budget of about 13 million USD to purchase equipment for water resource development but both offices develop only small-scale irrigation projects. Local sources report that the bidding standards for the Office of Accelerated Rural Development and the Department of Energy Development and Promotion are lower than the Royal Irrigation Department. Suppliers of low price/low quality products can compete well for projects tendered by these entities. Equipment from Korea, China and India are frequently selected for projects by decision makers in these two departments.

Bidding is the purchasing procedure in Government organizations, making price the final deciding factor for most cases. However, products and services must be of a certain quality and technology to allow the supplier to be invited to bid. Bidders must first submit a technical proposal and then pass the technical evaluation to be a qualified bidder. International Competitive Bidding is called for as specified in the loan agreements with international lending agencies. Furthermore, agencies use International Competitive Bidding in sophisticated large-scale projects requiring imported technology.

The Royal Irrigation Department's Water Resources Development Master Plan (1997-2001)

The Master Plan for water resources development emphasizes two basic objectives: 1) finding more sources of raw water, and 2) improving the efficiency of irrigation projects. The plan identifies the following priorities:

1)   Pipe irrigation for the Northeast, East, and lower Central area;
2)   Large-scale projects: In general, a large scale project shall be a project implemented for multipurpose benefits including agriculture, domestic consumption, industrial use, electricity generation, inland navigation, fish culture, recreation, etc. To achieve such purposes, the project can be constructed in various forms, such as a storage dam; diversion dam or weir; pumping, distribution or drainage systems, and on-farm irrigation systems. In brief, a storage dam shall be determined as a large-scale project if it is characterized by:1) a reservoir of over 100 million cubic meter; 2) the impounded water surface of over 15 square kilometers, or 3) covering an area of at least 12,800 hectares. There are 8 on-going projects and 10-11 new projects planned a year;
3)   Medium-scale Projects: There are 44 existing projects and 70 new projects planned per year. These projects have a maximum storage capacity of 100 million cubic meters or cover a maximum irrigate acreage of 12,800 hectares; and
4)   Small-scale Projects: Small projects are projects that are completed within a year. A total of 1,650 projects are planned for five year, with 330 new projects planned each year.

Information and updates on developments of any project managed by the Royal Irrigation Department are available at the Office of Budget Programming and Project Planning. The Office is the key agency within the Department that provides necessary market information for companies interested in developments related to water resources projects in Thailand. The Office is the first and most important Thai government agency any interested companies should contact.

MARKET ACCESS

Import Climate

Thailand has no barriers against entry of foreign services or equipment used in flood forecasting system and water resources development projects. Neither import restrictions nor specific technical standard requirements exist to regulate importation of water resources equipment. However, aggressive existing international suppliers have presented stiff competition and the market's sensitivity to price can make it difficult for new entrants to penetrate the market.

Distribution/Business Practices

Most international engineering consultants services companies establish themselves in Thailand by forming a partnership with local consulting firms. They rely on the market expertise of their local partners and the low-cost local services content provided by the local partner. Meanwhile, they offer the high value-added content to the project, based on their reputation, past references and expertise. The strategy results in a successful synergistic relationship for companies seeking to compete in the market with minimal time and investment.

However, in practice, the current government has circulated instructions to all government agencies that they prefer to work with local engineering consultants companies. If the project needs technical know-how, the government prefers a joint venture in which foreign partners' share should not exceed 30 percent of the company.

Local engineering consultants companies are keen to work with their international counterparts. They often have to seek international expertise on the subject, when working on large-scale projects. Companies interested in the Thai market should promote their expertise to potential local engineering services companies. Organizing a seminar for the local engineering consultant community or conducting personal visits to prospective companies are two common practices in the market.

Appointing local agent/distributors is the market entry approach used by the majority of international suppliers of equipment and machinery in Thailand. Through their local representatives, suppliers can market their products with minimal time and financial investment. Marketing support is the only major investment required from foreign suppliers. Local representatives assume full responsibility in marketing the products. Thus, selecting a competent agent/distributor is the key to successful market penetration. The U.S. Commercial Service in Bangkok offers the International Partner Search and Gold Key Service to American exporters seeking to establish local agent/distributor relationships in Thailand and many other countries.

Financing

A financing plan for any project is completed before the bidding process. Contractors to supply services or products for irrigation projects can not influence the bidding decision based on any

For additional analytical, business and investment opportunities information,
please contact Global Investment & Business Center, USA
at (202) 546-2103. Fax: (202) 546-3275. E-mail: rusric@erols.com

favorable financing term for the products or services they plan to offer. All bidders compete based on one set of regulations with payment terms defined by the buying agency.

Trade Shows

Event: ENTECH '02   International Exhibition and Conference on Engineering and Technology
Date: November 2002
Venue: To be announced
Frequency: Annual
Organizer: Engineering Institute of Thailand
              Nuclear Technology Bldg.
              Faculty of Engineering, Chulalongkorn University
              Henry Dunan Road, Wangmai
              Bangkok 10330
              Tel: (662) 218-6794/9
              Fax: (662) 251-2506
              Attn: Associate Professor Dr. Narong Yoothanom, President

Event: Entech Pollutech Asia 2002
Date: May 8-12, 2002
Venue: Bangkok International Trade & Exhibition Center
Frequency: Annual
Organizer: CMP Media (Thailand) Co., Ltd.
              41 Lertpanya Building, Suite 801, 8th Floor, Soi Lertpanya, Sir Ayuthaya Rd,
              Thanon Phyathai, Rajathewee
              Bangkok 10400 Thailand
              Tel:66-2642-6911
              Fax: 66-2642-6919/20
              Email: patcharin@cmpthailand.com
              Website: www.thai-exhibition.com/entech/index.html

Event: Aquatech 2003
Date: March 10-13, 2003 (tentative)
Venue: Bangkok International Trade & Exhibition Center
Frequency: Annual
Organizer: RAI Exhibitions (Thailand) Co., Ltd.
              226/36-37 Bond Street, Riviera Tower 1
              Muang Thong Thani, Bangpood
              Pakkred, Nonthaburi 11120 THAILAND
              Tel: 66-02960-0141
              Fax: 66-02960-0140
              E-mail: mail@bkkrai.com
              Website: www.bkkrai.com

AIRPORT AND GROUND SUPPORT EQUIPMENT

Airport and Ground Support Equipment is in service at 28 local and international airports located throughout the country. In the year 2000, the size of the market was estimated at around US$ 30 million. A small contraction occurred in 2001 as a result of the completion of expansion and improvement projects at some provincial airports. However, market growth expected in the local in 2002 as manufacturers and suppliers of APG equipment explore opportunities resulting from the construction of the New Bangkok International Airport (Suvarnabhumi Airport) and its Passenger Terminal Complex (PTC). The project will continue for four years and procurement of airport and ground support equipment is expected to start in early 2002. Budget for the PTC alone is about US$ 1 billion while the total budget for the whole project is estimated at US$ 2.6 billion. The second most important airport improvement project is the Bangkok International Airport (BIA) site and facility improvement project. The budget set for the project is US$ 96 million and will help absorb the increasing number of passengers prior to the completion of Suvanabhumi Airport. Following the year 2002, future growth of the total APG market in Thailand is estimated to be at around 5 percent.

From our analysis, the country's demand encompasses almost all APG product lines: Air Side Equipment, Land Side Equipment, Passenger and Hangar Service Equipment. The best sales prospects include but are not limited to: airport lighting equipment; crash and rescue equipment; navigation aids; electrical systems; baggage handling and checking equipment; metal detectors, and X-ray and access control systems. Because Thailand sources most APG equipment abroad, there is a high volume of foreign products in the market. American suppliers hold the largest market share at about 55%, followed by European nations including Belgium, Italy and Norway. Japan is also a major competitor. As in other countries, a large procurement project requires international bidding practices which are considered transparently fair by all parties. However, there are some products which could be ordered directly from specific suppliers including spare parts and supplies and special equipment.

Locating users of APG products in Thailand is not complicated, as there are only a handful of well-known users/buyers in the country. Most of them are state-owned airports authorities under the Ministry of Transportation and Communication (MOTC). The Airport Authority of Thailand (AAT) and the Department of Aviation (DOA) both operate airports in the country. The Aeronautical Radio of Thailand (Aerothai) provides air traffic control services and Thai Airways International Public Company is the national flag carrier for passengers and cargo. There are two additional two major ground support service companies; Thai Airport Ground Service (TAGS) and Bangkok Aviation Fuel Services (BAFS). TAGS, and its subsidiaries, handles all ground related services ranging from cargo handling to aircraft washing while BAFS is a private firm authorized by the government to install aviation fuel storage facilities and to operate fuel services at the Bangkok International Airport (BIA).

A. MARKET HIGHLIGHTS AND BEST PROSPECTS

Industry Structure

In Thailand there are a total of 28 commercial airports serving passengers at present. Out of the total, 7 are international airports and 21 are domestic. The Ministry of Transport and Communication (MOTC) designated policy and indirectly managed and control these airports thru two state enterprises, the Airport Authority of Thailand (AAT) and the Department of Aviation (DOA). AAT administrates 5 major international airports located in major cities: Bangkok, Chiang Mai, Hat Yai, Phuket and Chiang Rai. The remaining 23 airports are under the administration of the DOA and are geographically disbursed covering different part of the country, as follows:

§ NORTH : Phrae , Nan , Mae Hong Son , Lampang , Tak , Mae Sot , Phetchabun
§ CENTRAL : Phitsanulok , Hua Hin
§ NORTHEAST : Ubon Ratchathani International Airport , Udon Thani , Khon Kaen (unofficial) , Sakon Nakhon , Leoi , Nakhon Phanom , Buriram , Nakhon Ratchasima , Roi-Et
§ SOUTH : Surat Thani , Nakhon Si Thammarat , Trang , Pattani , Narathiwat , Ranong , Chumphon , Krabi

Thailand's Major Airports

1. Bangkok International Airport (BIA)

BIA is the country's busiest airport. Located in the capital city, it can accommodate up to 34 million passengers annually. The airport consists of two international passenger terminals, one domestic terminal and four cargo terminals. The four cargo terminals cover 114,048 sq. m. and have a combined freight capacity of one million tons. Currently BIA serves more than 80 airlines, over 25,000,000 passengers, 160,000 flights and 700,000 tons of cargo. The number of passengers at BIA is forecasted to increase to 50 MAP in 2006, therefore BIA is now undergoing an expansion program to accommodate the projected volume. The budget for BIA expansion is set at US$ 96 million for equipment and site and facility improvement of runways and parking areas, road and transport system construction and building construction. A civil works construction contract was awarded to CKAE Consortium in September 2000 for a construction period that started in September 2000 and is expected to be completed in March 2003.

2. Chiang Mai International Airport (CNX)

Chiang Mai is Thailand's major province in the north and a tourist hub for Thailand northern provinces. Currently CNX handles more than 2,000,000 passengers, 15,000 flights served by 9 airlines, and facilitates about 16,000 tons of cargo. The runway of CNX is 3,100 meters long and 45 meters wide and can accommodate up to 24 flights/hour. The apron area is 85,996 sq. m. and equipped with 16 aircraft parking, 2 with contact gate and 14 remote parking bays.

3. Chiang Rai International Airport (CEI)

CEI is another distinguished international airport in the northern of Thailand which plays a vital role for Thailand's tourism industry. The passenger terminal covers 22,960 square meters of usable area and the airport serves more than 500,000 passengers arriving and departing on over 3,900 flights provided by two air carriers. The airport also handles 2,700 tons of cargo. The runway at CEI airport is 3,000 meters long, 45 meters wide and can accommodate up to 20 flights/hour. The apron area is 28,800 sq.m. with 4 parking stands, 2 with contact gates and 2 remote parking bays.

4. Had Yai International Airport (HDY)

Located in Songkhla Province, southern Thailand, Had Yai International Airport is widely recognized as a gateway to the trading center of the South linking businesses between Thailand and Malaysia. The airport also plays a key role in serving Thai-Muslims passengers making the pilgrimage to Mecca each year. The airport runway is 3,050 meters long and 45 meters wide with a capacity of 30 flights/hour. There are 7 taxiways with 56,461 sq. m. of apron area. Three airlines have more than 9,500 flights a year arriving at and departing from Had Yai. Over 800,000 passengers and 12,000 tons of cargo pass through this airport.

5. Phuket International Airport (HKT)

Phuket province is Thailand's famous tourist destination and the Phuket International Airport is the second busiest nationwide in terms of passenger and cargo volume. Most passengers visiting Phuket are tourists coming from countries all over the world. Ten airlines provide 20,000 flights a year and transport more than 2,900,000 passengers. In addition, 12,000 tons of cargo are handled at this airport. The runway is 3,000 meters long and 45 meters wide and can accommodate 10 flights/hour. The airport also equipped with 94,800 sq. m. apron area and 25 parking stands.

6. Ubon Rachathani International Airport

Located in the northeastern part of Thailand, Ubon Rachathani has potential as a gateway to Indochina. The Cabinet approved a budget of THB541,689,673.00 in 1989 to establish an international airport here. The terminal can handle 250 arriving and 250 departing passengers per hour. The area of the passenger terminal is 17,380 sq. m. and can accommodate up to 1,500 passengers per hour. There are 3 aprons One is for international, commercial, civil, and government aircraft. The other two aprons are for the Royal Thai Airforce.

7. U-Tapao International Airport (Naval Air Division, the Royal Thai Navy)

Owned and operated by the Royal Thai Navy's Directorate of Royal Thai Naval Air Division, U-Tapao airport is a regional airport located 25 minutes from Pattaya and Rayong, which are among the best beach resorts in Thailand. Rayong is also a major industrial area. U-Tapao currently serves both Royal Thai Navy and general passengers. Three airlines use the facility: Thai Airways International, Bangkok Airways and Thai Flying Services. These airlines mainly link U-Tapao with neighboring countries and tourist destinations in Thailand, i.e. Samui-Utapao as well as Phnom Penh, Cambodia. The passenger terminal has a capacity of 300 seats, and offers other support ground service facilities include aircraft fueling, customs/Immigration, Health & Agricultural quarantine and medical facilities. In 1998, U-Tapao airport was to be developed into a Global Transpark positioning it to be an air transport and global business hub. The United States Trade and Development Agency (USTDA) funded a feasibility study of the project. However, due to budget constraints, the project was delayed until June 5, 2001. At that time, the Industrial Estate Authority of Thailand (IEAT) and Thai Airways International Plc. signed an agreement to continue the project and established Asia Transpark Co., Ltd. to run the project. The Baht 1.2 billion (approximately US$ 26.67 million) investment fund for this project will turn U-Tapao into a commercial airport with 200,000 sq. m. of warehouses. It is expected that the Global Transpark

For additional analytical, business and investment opportunities information, please contact Global Investment & Business Center, USA at (202) 546-2103. Fax: (202) 546-3275. E-mail: rusric@erols.com

will be open sometime in 2002. U.S. firms should monitor the situation closely as there will be a continued demand for several types of airport and ground support equipment for capacity expansion of terminal facilities, warehouses and main infrastructure, i.e. aircraft and cargo handling facilities, air field improvements, communication center, aircraft rescue and fire fighting (ARFF), etc.

8. Suvarnabhumi Airport (Nong Ngu Hao)

Suvarnabhumi Airport or the New Bangkok International Airport (NBIA) at Nong Ngu Hao is now under construction and is expected to be completed by 2005. Budgeted at US$ 2.6 billion, the new airport will handle 100 million of passengers and 6.40 million tons of cargo annually, as well as 122 aircraft movements per hour. Currently the construction of the Passenger Terminal Complex (PTC) is underway. A consortium, ITO join venture, led by Italian Thai Construction Public Company Limited was chosen as a general contractor. There will be several opportunities for airport and ground support equipment providers especially in the following categories: Construction materials for the PTC, Site Utilities Facilities, Security and Support Facilitieduring the next 4 years construction period.

9. Provincial Airports

More than 75 percent of the Department of Aviation (DOA) budget has been utilized to improve and expand the capacity of domestic airports in major provinces, including Khorn Kaen, Hua Hin, Phetchabun and Phitsanulok. Most of the expansion and improvements projects have been delayed due to economic problems faced by contractors. Upgrades at these airports will focus on passenger terminal improvements, taxi ways extensions, installation of air bridges, construction of ATC towers and aircraft parking aprons, procurement and installation of communication and navigation aids, installation of airport lighting, procurement of airport safety and security equipment.

Airport & Ground Support Equipment Market Size

In the year of 2000, about US$ 30 million worth of airport equipment has been imported, of which US$ 16.6 million or 55% was made in the United States. Local production is insignificant and accounted for less than 1% of the total market. Local sales activity results from procurement of ground-based communication equipment, automatic switching systems and air traffic control services.

STATISTICAL DATA

Market Size (Unit: US$ Millions)

Inflation Rate
1.7 1.9

Best Sales Prospects

In light of the increasing number of passengers to Thailand's major destinations there are mainly two group of prospects for airport and ground support equipment in Thailand. The first group includes the development of the US$ 2.6 billion new Suvarnabhumi airport and the development of US$ 26.67 million U-Tapao Global Transpark. The second group is the expansions and improvements of existing airports, the largest of which is the US$ 96 million Bangkok International Airport expansion project. Both group will create opportunities for products in the following categories:

· Air Side Equipment
- Runway lighting systems
- Power distribution and duct bank
- Runway sweeping trucks
- Crash and rescue equipment

· Land Side Equipment
- Main transformer
- Water treatment plant and other equipment
- Lighting equipment
- Taxiway guidance sign
- Airport Information Management Systems
- Navigation Aids: DVOR/DME, ILS
- Meteorological devices
- Radar
- Aeronautical and telecommunication equipment
- Preconditioned (PC) Air
- 400 Hertz Ground power unit
- Air conditioning system
- Electrical systems
- Aircraft towing tractor
- Air conditioning system

· Passenger Services Equipment
- Passengers boarding bridges
- Baggage handling equipment
- Conveyors
- Metal detector
- Access control systems
- Luggage weight measurement
- X-ray and baggage checking equipment
- Escalators and moving sidewalks
- Signboards and various sign

· Aircraft Hangar Service Equipment
- Docking Guidance System
- Fuel Hydrant
- Aircraft fueling rolling stocks

B. COMPETITIVE ANALYSIS

· Major Industry Players

Almost all airport and ground support equipment used in Thailand is of foreign origin. The amount and variety of locally produced equipment is very limited. Only the Aeronautical Radio of Thailand (Aerothai), a local designer and manufacturer, is capable of producing air traffic control and telecommunication systems and associated equipment. Aerothai also provides ATS services. Products are predominantly sourced from the United States, Europe and Japan. Most of the imports are safety and security systems, cargo handling equipment and passenger services equipment (X-ray machines, alarm systems, conveyors, lighting and air conditioning systems). Major US products sold in Thailand are: X-ray machines (Perkin Elmer), fire alarm systems (Simplex), conveyors (Rapistan Demag), air conditioning (York and Carrier), and Air Bridges supplied by Jetway and Rampway. European products have captured a considerable share of the market, such as: lighting and electrical equipment (ADB of Belgium), CCTV monitors and sound systems (Philips of Italy), 12KV. highVoltage switchgear (ABB of Norway), and safe gates manufactured by Besam of Sweden.

· Import Product Market Share

Airport and ground support equipment imported from U.S. accounts for 55.58% of the Thai market. Suppliers from these other countries have also captured a share of the market: Belgium --12.50%; Italy -- 8.47%; Norway – 7.62%, and Japan – 6.42%.

· Competitive Environment

The airport and ground support industry in Thailand relies mostly on imported products especially for those high technology and state of the art instruments and equipment such as airport safety and security equipment and navigation aids. Competition is fierce whenever there is a large procurement for new equipment. For example, foreign manufacturers and local suppliers are competing to supply the passenger services and cargo handling equipment at the existing Bangkok International Airport. Opening up the bidding to international competition is a common practice in this market though purchases of some types of replacement parts can be made directly through local suppliers.

· Synergy through partnerships between local and foreign firms

Even though airport authorities sometimes procure major airport equipment directly from a foreign manufacturer, there is an advantage to having established local contacts with local airport equipment suppliers or distributors. Local suppliers can add a competitive edge in terms of offering better after- sales services to existing and potential clients. Because they known, and operate, locally, they can find out about potentially lucrative procurement projects more quickly.

END-USER ANALYSIS

The end users for airport equipment in Thailand can be classified into two major groups, airport equipment users and ground support equipment users. Detailed information regarding these end users is described in the following sections.

Airport Equipment
- Airport Authority of Thailand (AAT)
- New Bangkok International Airport Co., Ltd. (NBIA)
- Department of Aviation (DOA)

- Aeronautical Radio of Thailand (AEROTHAI)

Ground Support Equipment
- Airport Authority of Thailand (AAT)
- Thai Airways International Plc. (THAI)
- Thai Airport Ground Service Co., Ltd. (TAGS)
- Bangkok Aviation Fuel Service Co., Ltd. (BAFS)

1. Airport Authority of Thailand (AAT)

AAT is a state enterprise under the Ministry of Transport and Communication (MOTC). This organization administers five international airports in major provinces and in Bangkok. The organization is to be privatized in the future to bring in strategic partners and increase public participation in AAT. AAT is a major user of both airport and ground support equipment. Equipment used by AAT at its airports has been purchased from both European and American suppliers. The majority of the equipment is from the U.S. Some of the major equipment used at AAT-administered airports includes: X-ray machine from Perkin Elmer (U.S.); fire alarms systems from Simplex (U.S.); CCTV from American Dynamics (U.S.); conveyors from Rapistan (U.S.); air conditioners from York and Carrier (U.S.); air bridges from Jetway and Rampway (U.S.); airport lighting from ADB (Belgium); CCTV and airport sound systems from Philips (Italy); safe gates from Besam (Sweden); high voltage switchgear from ABB, and elevators and escalators from Hitachi (Japan).

2. New Bangkok International Airport Co., Ltd. (NBIA)

The NBIA is a private company which was established in 1995 to oversee the development of the New Bangkok International Airport (NBIA) or Suvanabhumi airport. Shareholders in NBIA are government agencies, 91.49% by the Airport Authority of Thailand and 8.51% by the Ministry of Finance. Although the NBIA is not a current user of airport and ground support equipment, there will be large procurements for a full range of airport ground and ground support equipment once the construction of the Suvanabhumi airport is underway. The new international airport will need aircraft maintenance facilities, passenger terminal facilities and equipment, ground support facilities and equipment, cargo handling equipment, a main transformer station, a water supply system, a waste water treatment system, state-of-the-art telecommunication systems, and airport/personal security and safety systems.

3. Department of Aviation (DOA)

The DOA is a government agency under the Ministry of Transport and Communication (MOTC). The DOA is responsible for the administration of 23 provincial airports. Its main responsibilities are as follows.

i.) Airport Transport Administration and Support
- Issuing license for commercial air navigation business
- Aircraft registration and personnel licensing
- Controlling Thai airline companies to work in compliance with license conditions
- Controlling foreign airlines operating to Thailand to comply with international laws and agreements
- Air negotiating and air transport development planning

- Co-operating with international organizations and concerned government administrations

ii.) Air Transport Services
- Providing construction, maintenance and management services to airports
- Furnishing air navigation aids, communication equipment and air traffic services
- Providing technical training in civil aviation, aircraft accident investigation
- Rendering search and rescue services to aircraft in distress

As a user of airport equipment, especially for the maintenance and expansion of new airports, DOA has continually been upgrading its provincial airports by improving passenger terminals, extending and improving runways, installing navigation aids, and building new airports and aprons where demand is high. Currently, the DOA is in the process of procuring various equipment, namely, Simple&CAT.I Approach Lighting System, COSPAS-SARSAT's search and rescue instruments, X-ray scanners, walkthrough scanners, handheld Scanners and airfield lighting. The total budget needed for the above equipment is estimated at Baht 624 million (approx. US$ 13.87 million). The DOA allocated Baht 578 million (approx. US$ 12.84 million) for Lighting Systems and COSPAS-SARSAT's Search and Rescue Instruments during fiscal year 2001. The procurement contract was signed in October 2001 and implementation will occur during fiscal year 2002.

4. Aeronautical Radio of Thailand (Aerothai)

Aerothai is mainly responsible for providing air traffic control services, including operating communication centers, throughout Thailand as part of the Aeronautical Fixed Telecommunications Network (AFTN). Aerothai is also a Thai state enterprise under the Ministry of Transport and Communication (MOTC). Ninety-one percent of its shares are held by the MOTC, the remaining nine percent are held by 63 member airlines who have scheduled flights to Thailand. In the 2000 fiscal year, Aerothai had spent Baht 393 million (approx. US$8.73 million) to acquire the following systems: AERONET Satellite Communication, ILS (Instrument Landing System), FDP (Flight Data Processing System), and DVOR/DME Navigation Aids. From 2001 onwards, Aerothai will install more ILS, FDP and DVOR/DME. There will be a special emphasis on the NBIA's requirements for Aerothai to assist in tasking for the procurement and installation of Air Traffic Control (ATC) Complex, Navigation Aids and Radar. It is estimated that, as of 2001, Aerothai will have begun spending more than Baht 350 million (approx. US$7.78 million) annually for air traffic control and navigation equipment.

In addition to air traffic services, Aerothai also utilizes its engineering capabilities to manufacture a comprehensive range of ground-based aviation equipment, serving specific customers' requirements by design. Aerothai also installs and maintains various communication devices for its clients. Aerothai products are sold to aviation agencies in Thailand and to 15 countries in the Asia Pacific region. International customers include Nepal (Remote Control Unit), Mongolia (ATC Training Package), Bangladesh (Mini Automatic Switching System) and Malaysia (Satellite Communication Service). In percentage of the total revenues, the value of products and services sold overseas is 37.5%, compared to 62.5% for local sales.

For additional analytical, business and investment opportunities information, please contact Global Investment & Business Center, USA at (202) 546-2103. Fax: (202) 546-3275. E-mail: rusric@erols.com

5. Thai Airways International Plc. (THAI)

As the national flag carrier established in 1960, THAI not only provides air transportation services for passengers. It also offers aircraft maintenance and cargo services for its own fleet, as well as other airlines. Major shareholders of THAI are the Ministry of Finance (79.46%) and the Government Saving Bank (13.39%). Airport and ground support equipment currently used by THAI includes the following:

Equipment Group Brands Units

A/C Towing Tractors Pay Mover 4
Schopf 21
Shinko 1
Douglas 1

Air Condition Unit ACE 19
Air-A-Plane 18
Daikin 3
Trietron 2
Lear Siegl 1

Air Starter Unit Aerzen 4
Airsearch 2
Devtec 2
Stewart&Stevenson 21
Auto Die 3
Houchin 1
Atlas Corp. 1
Ace 5

Cargo Towing Tractor Clark 35
Stewart&Stevenson 30
Tiger 26
Harlan 19
Mulag 3
Wollard 1
Flanklin 2
TM 12
Toyota 4

Container Pellet Loaders FMC 31
Shinko 9
Trepel 4

Container Pellet Wide-Bridge FMC 16
Trepel 1
Air Marrel 2

Conveyor Belt Loader Nordco 6
Wiedemann 3

Tug 4
Shinko 11
Wallard 33

Ground Power Units Hobart 47
Stewart&Stevenson 14
ACE 5
Auto Die 3
Arvco 5

Main Deck Loaders FMC 3
Trepel 3
Air Marrel 1

Main Deck Capability Trepel 1

Passenger Step Vehicle DAHMS 4
Hino 2
Loxco 29
Shinko 14
Universal 7
Wallard 1
Nordco 3
Hasting D. 1
Nordkok 1

Transporters FMC 30
Shinko 7
Trepel 2
Lantis 1

Toilet Service Units Auto Die. 2
Loxco 1
Devtec 13
Nordco 1

Water Supply Units Auto Die. 2
Devtec 14
Loxco 2
Nordco 1

At present, according to THAI, a total budget of approximately US$ 26 million has been allocated to procure a total of 123 units of airport and ground support equipment which are classified into four major categories.

Million Baht Million US$

Passenger Service Equipment 258 5.74

Cargo Handling Equipment 554 12.30

Cargo Handling Facilities 114 2.53

Aircraft Service Equipment 261 5.80

For additional analytical, business and investment opportunities information, please contact Global Investment & Business Center, USA at (202) 546-2103. Fax: (202) 546-3275. E-mail: rusric@erols.com

6. Thai Airport Ground Services Co., Ltd. (TAGS)

The Thai Airport Ground Services Co., Ltd. (TAGS) was founded in 1990 by ground support operators at the Bangkok International Airport (BIA) as a non-state enterprise under the Ministry of Transport and Communication (MOTC). TAGS' main activities are the handling of airport ground services, namely cargo handling, ramp and passenger handling, and contracted services. The quality of service provided by TAGS is up to international standard and it was awarded the Airport Handling (AHS) Standard by the IATA (International Air Transport Association) in 1999 and 2000. In order to properly manage the services and provide complete coverage of airport ground services, TAGS has subcontracted works to the following subsidiaries:

Subsidiaries Joint Venture Partners Operation and Equipment

Bangkok ULD Repair Co., Ltd. (BUR)
Driessen Aircraft Interior Systems (Netherlands)
Repair and maintenance of in-flight catering and air cargo equipment, i.e. Unit Load Devices (ULD) and pallets

Thai Airports Technical Services Co., Ltd. (TATS)
Suwatana Supply and Services Co., Ltd. and INET Airport System
Operation and maintenance of 400 Hz ground power and preconditioned air systems

Eximnet Co., Ltd.
Thai Airfreight Forwarder Association (TAFA), Computer enterprises, EDI users, Customs brokers
Support for all customs and ground handling EDI systems (Electronic Data Interchange)

Thai Aero Services Co., Ltd. (TAS)
Nordic (Thailand) Co., Ltd.
Offer exterior aircraft washing and waxing services using a sophisticated technology from "The Nordic Dino", a computerized mobile aircraft-washing robot.

7. Bangkok Aviation Fuel Service Co., Ltd. (BAFS)

BAFS is a privately owned organization which obtained rights from Thai government to install aviation fuel storage facilities and to operate the fueling services at the Bangkok International Airport. The major shareholders of BAFS are private oil companies: Shell, Caltex, Esso and Elf which have a combined shares of 38.40%. The remaining shares belong to Thai Airways International (30.72%), CPB Equity Co., Ltd. (10.56%), the Petroleum Authority of Thailand (PTT) (9.60), the Airport Authority of Thailand (6.72%), and others (4.00%). Ninety percent of the Baht 860 million (approx. Baht 20 million) revenue generated by BAFS in 2000 came from service charges. Currently, BAFS operates five storage tanks with a total capacity of approximately 42 million liters. All of the tanks are cylindrical cone-roof type, fully epoxy coated and equipped with floating suctions for fuel delivery. There are 11 main hydrant pumps operated by BAFS. Each has a pumping flow rate of 270,000 liters per hour and can deliver jet fuel up to 2,970,000 liters per hour. For fueling aircraft, BAFS has 30 hydrant dispensers and 10 refuellers – dispensers are used where hydrant fueling system is available. By using both dispensers and refuellers, BAFS can serve more than 20 flights at the same time.

BAFS expects to generate new sources of revenue since the firm was authorized in 1996 by the New Bangkok International Airport (NBIA) to operate the hydrant system at the Suvarnabhumi Airport. BAFS subsequently established a new company, Thai Aviation Refueling Co., Ltd. (TARCO), jointly with NBIA and the Industrial Finance Corporation of Thailand (IFCT) to operate the system.

MARKET ACCESS

· Procurement methods

The procurement methods for airport and ground equipment vary by the nature of the end users. If the end user is a government authority such as the Airport Authority of Thailand or Thai Airways International, an international bidding method is normally used. In some occasions when there is an urgent need for products or to procure small orders for routine maintenance and spare part replacements, a direct order to local suppliers would be placed. Local non-government users normally buy directly from suppliers or dealers of foreign products by asking them to provide quotations. As far as payment of goods is concerned, an internationally accepted Letter of Credit (L/C) is commonly used in Thailand. Terms of payment under an L/C are normally 80% after 30 days from the date of the bill of lading (B/L) and 20% after the product is cleared for use by the organization's receiving committee.

· Market perception toward imported foreign equipment

Even though Aerothai, a Thai State enterprise, is capable of producing locally made communication devices, switching systems and services for local and oversea clients, more sophisticated equipment needs to be imported. Pricing is not always the most important issue. Other factors influencing the purchasing decision include the product's acceptance in other international markets, whether it has appropriate certifications, as well as its inter-operability with other types of equipment. Products from the US. have captured the highest market share, especially safety and security equipment such as X-ray and fire alarms systems. In addition, local end users prefer that manufacturers stand behind their products in terms of training, after- sales support and services. It is recommended that firms appoint a local representative or agent to coordinate customer service activities for equipment which needs periodical maintenance and spare parts replacement. Local agents also serve to maintain long term relationships and continued product support to Thai clients.

· Approach to reach the end-users and opportunities for U.S. firms

Interested airport and ground support equipment manufacturers, suppliers or local agents/suppliers should contact each airport authority directly or periodically check with the U.S. Department of Commerce web-sites. The U.S. Commercial Service in Bangkok's website is www.csbangkok.or.th (now, www.buyusa.gov/thailand/en). Visit these sites for updates on the current procurement projects and airport expansion plans, including immediate parts and services requirements. The U.S. Commercial Service of the American Embassy can also provide insight market information, make an introduction to airport authorities and other airport operators, as well as arrange introductions for American manufacturers with qualified Thai candidates through the Gold Key

Service program.

· Regulations, Tax & Custom Duties

Airport and ground support equipment falls under normal import tariffs imposed by Thai Customs Department. Tariffs range from 3% to 50% of CIF price, depending on the type of equipment imported. Import tariff rates are established, maintained and updated by the Customs Department. The department has established an Internet web-site offering customs related information to the general public, overseas exporters and local importers. The site can be used as a preliminary source of information for Thailand customs and tariff rates. Information is available in both Thai and English language and can be access at http://www.customs.go.th.

· Method of Financing

Procurement of airport and equipment is normally done through an outright purchase by end-users with a budget supplied by airport authorities. The budget of the state-owned airport authorities is allocated by the Thai government on an annual basis, in accordance with equipment procurement plans and requests from each airport authorities. For other mega-projects such as the construction of the New Bangkok International Airport (NBIA) or Suvarnabhumi Airport, where the government budget alone is not sufficient, private funds from international financing institutions are being mobilized. For the NBIA in particular, shareholders equity and loans will be used to finance the construction of the airport and its passenger terminal complex, with a target project debt to equity ratio of around 5:1.

ELECTRICAL POWER SYSTEMS EQUIPMENT

Historically, Thailand has offered a solid mid-sized market for U.S. manufacturers of electric power equipment with an open market for imported products. Since 1997 and the impact of the Asian financial crisis, growth in Thailand's national demand for electric power has slowed, which in turn has restricted demand for new generation equipment. However, demand for repair and replacement parts still constitutes a $1.8 billion market annually, with imports from U.S. firms representing 8 percent of the market, against stiff competition from Japanese and European manufacturers.

Thailand is currently deregulating its power generation and distribution industry, and given the aging of existing installed base of equipment, as well as prospects for stronger economic growth, we anticipate some growth in market opportunities for U.S. firms in the near to medium term. In addition, as a rise in electricity demand will likely stimulate some construction of new generation facilities, prospects for sales to both government and new private sector producers should increase. Best sales potential in Thailand is for generators and parts; transmission lines and systems; equipment for substations and terminal stations; power poles and high voltage distribution lines; connectors, switches and control components.

MARKET HIGHLIGHTS AND BEST PROSPECTS

Overview of Thailand's Power Services

The power services sector in Thailand is semi-regulated by the Thai government. Electricity is provided to consumers by the public sector, through three Thai Government owned state enterprises: the Electricity Generating Authority of Thailand (EGAT), the Metropolitan Electricity Authority (MEA), the Provincial Electricity Authority (PEA), and other independent and small private power producers (IPPs and SPPs). These enterprises have been the only energy operators and their roles are divided into four main parts: generation, transmission, distribution and retail systems.

Generation and Transmission: EGAT controls the energy generation and transmission systems. It is also a power producer and supplier selling electricity via high-voltage transmission lines to the MEA and PEA for further distribution to consumers. EGAT also purchases electricity generated by private operators who are allowed by the Thai government to participate in the generation business. These private operators are power producers who generate electricity and sell to EGAT under the Independent Power Producers (IPPs) and Small Power Producers (SPPs) programs (see End User Analysis section for details). EGAT will then re-sell the electricity purchased from those IPPs and SPPs to MEA and PEA.

Distribution and Retail: MEA is responsible for the distribution of electricity to consumers in the Bangkok metropolitan area and vicinity, including Nonthaburi and Samutprakarn provinces. PEA is responsible for distributing electricity to consumers in other provinces throughout the country. Currently there is no competition in the distribution and retail systems. Almost all consumers have to depend on the electricity supplied by either by MEA or PEA.

Most power plants in Thailand are steam turbine power plants, followed by combined cycle power plants and hydro power plants, respectively. The EGAT operates more than 70% of the country's power plants. The source of energy used in power generation in Thailand varies, depend on the cost of the fuel and its impact on the environment. However, because of its domestic abundance natural gas is used to produce more than 70% of the country's installed energy capacity. Other sources of fuel for power generation in Thailand are coal, hydro, alternative energy and heavy fuel oil. Listed below are fuel sources and their percentages of contribution to Thailand's power generation industry in 2001.

Deregulation of Thai power sector

Given the rapid increase in energy demand when Thailand's economy took off in the early 1980s, the government recognized the need for deregulation and private sector participation in power industry. In 1992 the National Energy Policy Council (NEPC) approved the establishment of the Electricity Generating Company (EGCO), which operates power plants spun-off from EGAT, and approved regulations governing power purchase from Small Power Producers (SPPs).

One chief reason for deregulation of the Thai power industry was insufficient financial availability. Government-owned power operators have been unable to increase power generation capacity to cope with rising power demand. The three state enterprises--EGAT, MEA and PEA--formerly had utilized both internal revenues and loans to finance capacity expansion, with foreign loans the chief source of funding for expansion. These loans proved to be a major liability, even though internal revenues were sufficient to service interest payments. Although these entities' status as state agencies entitled them to loan guarantees from the government, this in fact passed on risk to the general public. In addition to financial problems, other operational problems such as lack of organizational efficiency and poor human resources management also had a deleterious impact on the operation and management of each organization.

In 1994, to encourage private sector participation in electricity generation, EGAT issued the first solicitation for power purchase from Independent Power Producers (IPPs). EGAT signed Power Purchase Agreements (PPAs) with seven power producers under the IPP program, for a total capacity of 5,944 MW. The generating capacity of these IPPs ranges between 340 MW and 1,400 MW. Currently two IPP projects have commercially supplied electricity into the system; Tri Energy Co., Ltd. and Independent Power (Thailand) Co., Ltd. Both are using natural gas as fuel and having generating capacity of 700 MW each.

On the supply side, in October 2000 the Thai Cabinet had approved a proposal for the Electricity Supply Industry Reform (ESI) submitted by the National Energy Policy Office (NEPO). The ESI includes guidelines and market rules for establishing a national power pool. Under the power pool concept, competition in the power supply industry will be enhanced. Electricity generating companies will compete to supply electricity to the power pool at competitive prices. An Independent System Operator (ISO) will be set up to choose power producers who can offer the most attractive electricity prices from the power pool. Currently, NEPO and the two power distributors, MEA and PEA have reviewed the Grid Code and Distribution Code drafted by an independent consultant, KEMA Consulting. MEA has also completed an organization restructuring plan and will be privatized in late 2003 through public offering of shares. Planned privatization of the PEA has been delayed due to opposition on the privatization from employees. However, an independent consultant was selected to draft an organization restructuring plan for PEA.

Installed Capacity

The country's total installed power generation capacity is currently at 22,830 megawatts. EGAT and its affiliates are capable of generating up to 18,000 megawatts, or 79% of the overall installed electricity generating capacity. EGAT operates major power plants in key strategic locations countrywide, including all hydro power plants attached to dams in the upcountry areas. Independent Power Producers (IPPs) and Small Power Producers (SPPs) offer 21% at the total installed capacity, totaling 4,800 megawatts to EGAT. However, the largest portion of electricity supply by private power producers is provided by SPPs, primarily from twenty-one SPP natural gas fired power plants. Please see the following table for details.
Power Plants in Thailand

Transmission Systems

Thailand's electricity transmission systems of EGAT connecting with the national grid consist of a transmission lines running a length of 27,069 circuit-kilometers, 194 substations and transmission capacity of 57,997 M.V.A. Statistics for the transmission systems categorized by voltage level are listed as follows.

Supply and Demand Situations

The total installed capacity from local operators within the country currently totals 22,835 megawatts (MW), supplemented by a power purchase agreement from the Lao PDR of 340 megawatts. Altogether Thailand has an available installed generation capacity of 23,175 megawatts. Thailand's electricity supply had increased during the economic boom time when the government predicted double digit economic growth, and had invited several private operators to participate in supplying electricity to EGAT under the IPP and SPP programs. The available installed capacity of 22, 835 MW is currently far higher than the country's generation requirement as estimated by EGAT. In the fiscal 2001 the peak generation in

16,126 MW in April, the summer of Thailand, while the maximum demand in the same month was only 15,190 MW. This current oversupply situation has given Thailand a 30% energy reserve, which is expecting to last for quite some time before the Thai economic recovers from the crisis and stimulates the demand for electricity, from both industrial and residential uses.

Market Trends

Shown below, are comparisons between EGAT's Generation Requirement and its total sales of electricity to transmission and distribution agencies (MEA/PEA). The electricity generation as required by EGAT to serve local users in 2001 was highest at 16,126 MW where the maximum demand in MW for the sales of electricity was only at 15,190 MW, this was 6% under the peak generation and sufficient to meet demand. However, there is a forecast that in the event that economic recovery is strong in 2002, the maximum demand could rise to 18,194 MW where EGAT would need to increase its peak generation to 18,678 MW or 3% over the maximum demand.

In next 5 years (2002-2006), under the load forecast of EGAT, the peak generation of energy is estimated to increase at around 6 percent each year, mainly to support future overall economic growth of the country. Under this scenario the current installed capacity would be sufficient for at least 5 years and thereafter would need to be increased if the same growth rate is continue.

Electric Power Systems Equipment Market Size

In the year of 2001, about US$ 1.854 billion worth of electric power system-equipment was imported into Thailand, of which US$ 152 million or 8% was imported from the United States. Local production is significantly high at about US$ 1.5 billion mainly generated from sales of transformers, static converters, inductors, switching apparatus and rectifiers.

Market Size (Unit: US$ Millions)

The scope of the market size includes the following product classifications under the Harmonization System (HS) Codes - Commodity Classification.

8502 Electric generating sets and rotary converters
8503 Parts for electric motors, generators(including sets), rotary converters
8504 Electric transformers, static converters & inductors; parts thereof rectifiers
8533 Electrical resistors, (not heating resistors); parts thereof rheostats, potentiometers
8535 Electrical apparatus for switching or protecting electrical circuits, for electrical connection over 1000 volts switches, fuses, lightening arresters, surge suppressors, plugs, junction boxes

8536 Electrical apparatus for switching or protecting electrical circuits, for electrical connection not over 1000 volts switches, relays, fuses, surge suppressors, plugs, junction boxes, lamp-holders
8537 Boards, panels, consoles, desks, cabinets, etc with electrical switching apparatus etc. of 8536 or 8536
8538 Parts for electrical switching apparatus of 8535,8536,8537

Inflation Rate (%)	1.5	1.5	2.5

Sources: Customs Department's Import & Export Statistics

Compiled by: U.S. Commercial Service, U.S. Embassy, Bangkok, Thailand

Best Sales Prospects

Under the government plan to privatize the country's power generation activities through its State Enterprise Reform, as well as enhancing private sector's role in the Electricity Supply Industry (ESI) using the power pool concept, there should be several procurement opportunities for electric power equipment from both government's owned and private power producers, including the retail power distributors. In light of the high energy reserve margin, the government had delayed some IPPs projects while encouraging the use of existing capacity of the power producers who had already commenced commercial operation. However, some active power producers who have signed a power purchase agreement with EGAT, are progressing on their plans in selling electricity to EGAT. Listed below are projects with potential to generate demand for U.S. products.

Under the current maintenance and expansion plans of the Electricity Generating Authority (EGAT) the following projects are underway: supply of transmission line conductor and communication equipment, reconstruction of conveyor line for ash and gypsum disposal system, fuel oil receiving and transferring systems, construction of water treatment plant, and telecommunication network renovation. In the future, under the 9th Power Development Plan (2002-2006), projects to be implemented by EGAT are as followed.

The Metropolitan Electricity Authority (MEA) is undergoing an improvement and expansion of power distribution systems in Bangkok metropolitan and vicinity which includes; development of terminal stations and substations system, substitution of Aluminum Partial Insulated Conductors (APC) for the Aluminum Spaced Aerial Conductor (ASC), reinforcement of power poles and relocation of high voltage distribution lines. These activities generate needs for the following equipment: numerical 3-phases over-current and earth-fault relay, overhead connectors, 24 kV gas insulated switch-gear, distribution board, battery, battery charger and capacitor, ring main unit, zinc coated steel wire, lightning arrester, connectors, fuses & switches, electrolytic cathode copper, porcelain insulators, and aluminum ingot.

In regard to the Provincial Electricity Authority (PEA), responsible of installation and maintenance of power distribution networks in provincial areas, the electric power equipment that is frequently utilized are those concerned with power distribution systems, namely: connectors, hot line clamps, preformed fittings, disconnecting switches, H.T. surge arresters 20-21 kV. 10kA., bypass cables 22kV., cable spacers and fuse cutouts 22kV. 100 A. 8kA. Equipment currently needed to be procured by PEA in the near future are as follows: 0-100 V. adjustable 3 phases power supply, clamp-on leakage current tester, special tool for on-load tap-changer (OLTC), connector (or lug) size 95 sq.mm./185 sq.mm., and large number of transformer repair kits.

In addition, according to the procurement plan for the affiliates of Thai Oil Co., Ltd.; Independent Power (Thailand) Co., Ltd. or "IPT", and Thaioil Power, another plant under SPP program. IPT is currently operating 700 MW combined cycle power plant, will procure in the next three years the following parts: Generator Spare Parts (carbon brushes, brush holder and renewal part, generator bearing gland seal), Automatic Regulator Part (regulator relay, PSS I/O module, firing circuits mod 60 Hz 10uf, AC isolation transducer, voltage build-up module, GRD detector), Control components (starter kit, high voltage part). IPT has estimated the value in US$ for the procurement of the aforementioned spare parts at 344,037 U.S. dollars. As for Thaioil Power, operating co-generation 3-on-1 combined cycle with a total capacity of 115 MW, is planning to procure spare parts in preparation for a major plant inspection as follows: Turbine Bucket, Turbine Nozzle, and Shroud Set. Thaioil Power has allocated a budget of US$ 2.8 million for the equipment.

COMPETITIVE ANALYSIS

Foreign Competition

The electric power equipment market in Thailand attracts products from different parts of the world: Europe, Asia, and the United States. In 2001, Electric Power Systems equipment imported from Japan dominated the market at 30% market share, followed by products from China (10.35%), Singapore (8.65%), U.S.A. (8.14%), Germany (5.44%), and Taiwan (4.39%). Competition from the market leader, Japan, is relatively high especially from well-known brands such as Toshiba, Mitsubishi, and Hitachi. Products from China mostly are electrical apparatus for switching or protecting electrical circuits including connections and parts. U.S. companies which have established a strong market position, especially in the generation business, are: General Electric (for turbine generators), Siemens Westinghouse and Cutler-Hammer (for generator's parts and control components). Market reception toward products from Europe is also strong in Thailand. Among the major European manufacturers, the following are those exported to Thailand: Alstom (France) for generators, ABB (Sweden) for circuit breakers and switching gears, and Coelme (Italy) for switching gears.

Local Competition

Competition from the local Thai electric power equipment industry is relatively strong especially among local distributors or agents of imported equipment due to the high number of companies. Most of these distributors or agents also provide after sales maintenance services to endusers. Regarding local manufacturing capability, Thai manufacturers have received know-how from foreign manufacturers and are literally able to manufacture products that conform to the international standards such as International IEC, Japan's JIS, Germany's VDE and DIN, and the USA's ANSI. Most of local manufacturers also export their products overseas, especially those making transformer, ballast, wire and cable. Competition among local manufacturers is quite intense, both local and export markets.

Listed below are some the well-known electric power equipment manufacturers in Thailand.

Company	Products Manufactured
Ekarat Engineering Public Company Limited	Transformers and Components: Single Phase, Hermetically Sealed, Conservator type Oil Immersed Transformer, CSP type, Conservator Transformer, Dry type Cast Resin
Thai Maxwell Co., Ltd.	Transformers: Oil Immersed type, Hermetically Sealed, Dry type, Cast Resin. Non-Flammable, Instrument Transformer, Special Designed Transformer
Thai Energy Conservation Co., Ltd.	Various kind of magnetic ballast, Electronics control gear in energy saving lighting system
Charoong Thai Wire and Cable Public Company Limited	Electric Wire Cable and Telephone Cable: aluminum cable , copper wire cable, and insulated high voltage cable
Piller (Thailand) Co., Ltd.	Piller Uniblock Plus Dynamic UPS Systems:

| | Generating Set, Unit substation, Static (ATS), Harmonics filter, and Power supply 50/60, 400 Hz. |
| Energy Maintenance Service Co., Ltd. | Develop and supply "Enertic 200" Peak Demand controller |

Synergy through partnerships between local and foreign firms

Even though electricity authorities sometimes procure major equipment directly from foreign manufacturers, there is a definite advantage of establishing contacts with local equipment suppliers or distributors. Local suppliers can add a competitive edge in terms of better after sales service to existing and potential clients. In addition, as they have people on the ground who know the market movements and can alert U.S. companies whenever an opportunity arises. Most of them maintain a good relationship with the government's electricity authorities and can be a good outpost for maintaining relationships with existing clients.

END-USER ANALYSIS

The end users for electric power equipment in Thailand can be classified into three major groups; 1)generation, 2) transmission and 3)distribution. Information on each user is described below.

Generation

1.   Electricity Generating Authority of Thailand (EGAT)

EGAT is state owned utility company involves in construction, operation and maintenance of power plants and transmission network. Aside from EGAT's facilities, it also purchases power from Independent Power Producers (IPPs), Small Power Producers (SPP) and small power plants in Laos. At present the EGAT generation system includes fifteen thermal power plants and twenty hydro power plants nationwide. EGAT's transmission system (grid) consists of long-distance high voltage transmission lines and substations that transmit power from both EGAT's and privately owned power plants to distributing authorities: Metropolitan Electricity Authority (MEA) and Provincial Electricity Authority (PEA) for distribution to industrial and residential clients.

EGAT is restructuring its organization under the Thai government policy toward electricity supply industry reform.   Currently EGAT consists of six business units and five operating units; business units are transmission, generation1, generation 2, engineering, maintenance and fuel; and operating units are policy and planning, account and finance, administration, construction, and hydropower plant.   In the future these units will be transformed into five business groups: Hydropower, Thermal Power Plant, Transmission, Central Administration, and Power Trade.

2.   Independent Power Producers (IPPs)

IPP are privately owned and relatively sizeable power producers with installed capacity of more than 150 MW. IPPs use commercially available fuel sources such as natural gas, coal (both indigenous an imported) and oil-emulsion, but excluding nuclear power.
Since the IPPs concept was introduced in 1994, the government has approved seven IPPs. Two who have already transmitted electricity to the national (EGAT) grid are Tri-Energy Co.,

Ltd. and Independent Power (Thailand) Co., Ltd. The total combined capacity if all seven IPPs were operating would be 5,943 megawatts.

Independent Power, owned 24% by Unocal and 20% by Westinghouse, operates a 700 MW gas-fired power plant in Chonburi province. In 2001 the firms purchased US$ 97.5 million worth of generators' spare parts from the U.S.A. In 2002 it plans to purchase an automatic regulator for generator, and within the next 4 years Independent Power had budgeted a US$ 344,037 to purchase automatic regulator and generator parts, control components and high voltage parts.

Tri-Energy commenced operation in late 1997. It is 37% owned by Texaco Inc. and 25% by Edison Mission Co. Ltd. of the U.S.A. Tri Energy operates a 1,400 MW gas-fired generator in Ratchburi province. There are two sets of 224 MW frame 9FA+e gas turbines and a set of 252 MW steam turbines at the plant. General Electric (GE) is the major equipment supplier for Tri Energy.

Other IPPs will soon, on differing timeframes, begin transmitting electricity to the national grid. The next IPP to start commercial operation is Eastern Power & Electric Co., Ltd. (Bang Bo), in July 2002. The last one is BLCP Power Co., Ltd., in early 2007.

3.   Small Power Producers (SPPs)

SPP are privately owned small power producers using renewable energy sources. Types of fuel used among SPPs are bagasse, paddy husk, wood chips, natural gas, coal, oil, black liquor, municipal waste, and waste gas from production process. Bagasse and natural gas are the most common types of fuel used among SPPs. Installed capacity of an SPP ranges between 120-150 MW. As of January 2002, 50 power plants under SPP program had already dispatched electricity to EGAT. The combined generating capacity of SPPs is 3,468 megawatts, of which sales made to EGAT are 1,961 MW.

Listed below are major SPPs using non-conventional fuel sources. (Source: National Energy Policy Office; NEPO)

-    Sun Hua Seng Group, the group operates seven SPP projects under several subsidiaries: Thai Power Supply (1) Co., Ltd. (47.4 MW from paddy husk and wood chips), Thai Power Supply (2) Co., Ltd. (10.4 MW from paddy husk and wood chips), Advance Agro Plc. (74 MW from bark, wood chips and black liquor), Thai Power Supply (3) Co., Ltd. (3 MW from paddy husk, wood chips and eucalyptus), National Power Supply (1) Co., Ltd. (164 MW from coal and eucalyptus bark), National Power Supply (2) Co., Ltd. (164 MW from coal and eucalyptus bark), A.A. Pulp Mill 2 Co., Ltd. (32.9 MW from black liquor).

-    Saraburi Sugar Co., Ltd. This SPP operates a sugar factory in Saraburi province and is using bagasse to produce electricity. The generating capacity is 29.5 MW.

-    Thai Rungruang Co., Ltd. This SPP operates a sugar factory in Petchboon province using bagasse to produce electricity. The generating capacity is 29.5 MW.

Transmission and Distribution

1.   Metropolitan Electricity Authority of Thailand (MEA)

MEA is a state enterprise established since 1958 and now under the Ministry of Interior. The organization is responsible for selling and distribution of electricity to users in Bangkok metropolitan and vicinity includes Nonthaburi and Samutprakarn provinces. Distribution areas of MEA cover 3,192 square meters which is divided into 14 districts.

Currently MEA is modernizing its services and internal operations. The organization is implementing several automated systems to enhance power distribution and customer services. Major projects under development at the MEA are listed as follows.

- Implementation of Geographic Information System (GIS): - MEA has been implementing a GIS system and now in its 3rd phase covering 1,100 square kilometers. Information from the GIS system is utilized in planning for the power distribution systems.

- Improvement of Supervisory Control and Data Acquisition (SCADA) and Energy Management System (EMS):- MEA is improving its SCADA/EMS to efficiently control the power distribution system and to create interoperability with other systems such as GIS and Customer Service System

- Upgrade of the existing computer and peripheral

- Development of the Customer Service System (CSS) to enhance customer services for MEA's district offices.

2. Provincial Electricity Authority of Thailand (PEA)

Similar to MEA, PEA is another state owned utility company under the Ministry of interior selling and distributing electricity. The difference is the coverage areas, PEA covers all other parts except those already served by MEA. The total area served by PEA is 510,000 square kilometers. Established in 1960, PEA provides electricity to residential and industrial users in 73 provinces excluding Bangkok, Samutprakarn and Nonthaburi. PEA operates from its head office in Bangkok, which controls other four regional offices. The head office is responsible for policy, plan, and procurement of equipment for other regional offices. Each regional office oversees three district offices, therefore altogether there are twelve district offices controlled by PEA.

MARKET ACCESS

Access Strategies

Thai users of electric power systems equipment normally purchase equipment from original equipment manufacturers. International brands such as GE (Turbines), Hitachi(Generators), ABB (Switching gears), Alstom (generators), and Siemens, are among the major electric power systems equipment widely used in Thailand. Selling of electric power products can be done directly to the end users, however, having a local agent or distributors present locally is highly recommended. A qualified local representative can add benefit to foreign manufacturers and suppliers in gathering market information and alert them on the upcoming market opportunities.

To participate in large procurement project, such as construction of new power plant or development of transmission systems, etc., it is advisable to be in touch with users early in design specification phase. This approach increases the chance of winning bids as well as protecting from being excluded by "lock-out-spec.", a practice whereby a manufacturer manages to have Terms of Reference written in favor to a particular manufacturer. In addition, after the economic crisis in 1997, locally made products are gaining popularity among government buyers. However, locally made products are those less sophisticated equipment such as transformers, ballast, wire and cable, circuit breakers and control panel. Thailand still relies on import products for high-tech equipment like generator and spare parts.

Market perception toward imported foreign equipment

Pricing is not always the most important issue but internationally accepted, certified, and inter-operability of the equipment are all important factors that users consider when making purchasing decision. In addition, local end users prefer that manufacturers stand behind their products in terms of training, after sales support and services. It is recommended that for those equipment needed periodical maintenance and spare parts replacement to appoint a local representative or agent to coordinate customer service activities as to maintain long term relationship and continued product supports to overseas clients.

Procurement practices

The procurement methods for electric power systems equipment vary by end users. The Electricity Generating Authority (EGAT) normally invites bids from local and foreign suppliers for wide range of equipment needed. EGAT use international open bid method for large procurement project such as the supply and construction of power generation plant. For smaller procurement of equipment valued lower than 100,000 Baht (approx. US$ 2,300) EGAT purchasing agent can negotiate prices and purchase directly from suppliers. MEA and PEA also follows the same path as EGAT in procurement practice. All three organizations announce bids invitations to general public via its public relations departments. They also distribute an invitation letter to embassies for disseminating to interested foreign suppliers. Interested bidders can purchase details Terms of Reference from each organization directly.

Products distribution and opportunities for U.S. firms

Interested Electric Power Systems Equipment manufacturers, suppliers or local agents/suppliers should contact each power generating companies or power distributors directly, or they may periodically check with the U.S. Department of Commerce web-site, www.usatrade.gov, to update the current procurement projects, invitation for bids, and immediate parts and services requirements. The Commercial Service of the American Embassy can also provide insight market information, make an introduction to electricity related authorities, as well as be able to propose qualified candidates who are interested in developing partnerships with American manufacturers and suppliers.

Regulations, Tax & Custom Duties

Electric Power Systems Equipment falls under normal import tariff imposed by Thai Customs Department, with import tariff ranging from 3% to 35% of CIF value, depending on type of equipment imported. Import tariff rates are established, maintained and updated by the Customs Department. The department has established an Internet web-site offering customs related information to general public, overseas exporter and local importers. The site can be used as a preliminary source of information for Thailand customs and tariff rates. Information is available in both Thai and English language and can be access at http://www.customs.go.th.

For additional analytical, business and investment opportunities information,
please contact Global Investment & Business Center, USA
at (202) 546-2103. Fax: (202) 546-3275. E-mail: rusric@erols.com

AUTOMOTIVE AFTERMARKET ACCESSORIES

The continuing expansion of Thailand's vehicle market, at a projected growth rate of 20% per annum over the next few years, offers potential for American exporters of automotive accessories. One-ton pickups, compact passenger cars and sport utility vehicles are the three most promising segments here because of market size, growth potential and market propensity for accessories.

Annual vehicle sales in Thailand are expected to surpass the pre-crisis peak of 600,000 units by 2005, based on 2001 sales of 297,056 units, and an annual growth rate of 20%. Locally assembled Japanese makes have captured more than 90% of the market. In fact, the five major players in the market, Toyota, Isuzu, Honda, Nissan, and Mitsubishi have a combined 85% market share. Mazda is also active, to a lesser degree. One-ton pickups are the largest segment (55%), followed by passenger cars (35%) and sport utility vehicles (3.83%).

Best prospects for U.S exports of automotive accessories in Thailand can be found in the following categories: accessories for sport utility vehicles, racing and performance products, suspension systems, and tinted film.

This report attempts to provide an overview of Thailand's vehicle market by focusing on essential facts about organization, production and market characteristics of the Thai market so that U.S. exporters can best evaluate the potential for their products in this market.

Note: Due to the widely dispersed nature of the accessories market and the lack of official statistics , all numbers on market values are estimates gathered from interviews with industry experts.

Market Overview

Vehicle Market: The majority of vehicles operating in Thailand are locally assembled by Japanese manufacturers. One-ton pickups are the most popular vehicles among Thai consumers. Based on 2001 sales, pickup trucks account for 55% of the market (163,638 units), passenger cars 35.7% (104, 502 units) and sport utility vehicles 3.83% (11,371 units).

Overall Market

Japanese makes have dominated the Thai market for the past 30 years, despite competition from nearly all global automakers. Toyota, Isuzu, Honda, Nissan, and Mitsubishi are the five best selling vehicles with a combined market share of 85%. As noted above, Mazda has a lesser share. Toyota is the overall market leader in passenger car sales, with Honda trying to make inroads in this segment. Isuzu has been the most popular producer of pickup trucks in Thailand but Toyota is aggressively competing for market dominance in that segment as well.

2001 Vehicle Market (by Makes)

	Unit Sales	Market Share	% Change from 2000
Toyota	83,440	28.1	17
Isuzu	70,484	23.7	22.3
Honda	38,820	13	29
Nissan	34,993	11.8	12

Mitsubishi	24,870	8.4	-17.8
Mazda	5,920	2	-18.3
Hyundai	345	0.1	-51
Kia	1,591	0.5	363.8
Daewoo	0	0	-100
FORD	17,432	6	5.2
Mercedes-Benz	4,476	1.5	58.2
BMW	3,226	1.1	33.6
Volvo	1,823	0.6	14.50
CHEVROLET	2,316	0.8	58.3
Volkswagen	1,325	0	13.90
Chrysler	448	0	-55.6
PEUGEOT	555	0.2	0.9
Seat	338	0.1	26.6
Citroen	297	0.1	N/A
Skoda	193	0.1	124.4
Land Rover	162	0.1	N/A
Saab	93	0	132.5
Lexus	74	0	12.1
Jaguar	61	0	-31.5
Porsche	47	0	N/A
Subaru	33	0	-25
Hino	2,658	0.9	-15.2
Audi	385	0	-4
TOTAL	297,056	100	13.3

Automotive Accessories Market: Thailand's automotive accessories market consists of a large number of small companies and hence none of them has a significant share of the market. They supply wide varieties of products ranging from genuine new & used genuine products to imitation or counterfeit goods. The sales distribution networks are comprised of wholly owned subsidiaries of global automotive manufacturers, authorized agents, brokers, non-exclusive wholesale importers, as well as importers and manufacturers of imitative or counterfeit products. Some imitative and fake products are made locally while others are imported from China and Taiwan. They are widely available and popular among car owners and enthusiasts in the lower end segment of the market which cannot afford the more expensive, genuine products.

Ease of market entry and exit is one key contributor to the highly dispersed nature of the automotive accessories market in Thailand. Many car enthusiasts set up small stores to retail automotive accessories in an attempt to turn their hobby into a business. It is common for some of these operators to bypass local authorized wholesalers by purchasing foreign products and importing them through non-conventional channels so that they can pay lower duties or avoid paying any duty at all. This allows them to undercut prices set by authorized distributors. Market acceptance of such practices implies that price is viewed as more important than distributor credibility. In fact, distributors' credibility and product popularity in this market are built on word of mouth, and recommendations from mechanics and automotive columnists. Hence, distributorship rights are of secondary importance to local importers since such rights do not provide a significant marketing advantage to the rights holders.

By comparison, established authorized importers have usually sought volume discounts from U.S. and other parts exporters to maintain a competitive edge against such non-conventional business operators. However, only a few succeed in doing so since their purchases are too small to warrant the discounts requested. Instead, importers have opted to coordinate with regional counterparts to combine orders up to the volume required to gain volume discounts.

VEHICLE MARKET TRENDS

Thailand's vehicles market is expected to grow at 20% annually for the next few years and surpass its pre-crisis salespeak of 600,000 units by 2005. Industry experts expect little change in market shares for key vehicle categories. One-ton pickups will maintain its 55% share of the market with the double cab models having the strongest sales prospects. The passenger car market share is expected to solidify at 35%, while Sport Utility Vehicles are gaining in popularity. In 2002, the Thai vehicle market is expected to grow 8% to a total of 320,000 units, with sales of pickups forecasted at 179,000, passenger cars - 108,000, sport utility vehicles - 14,000, and other types of vehicles totaling 19,000.

Pickup Truck Market: Pickup Trucks are the most popular vehicle in Thailand, with a 55% share of the market. Pickups appeal to a broad range of consumers because of price and versatility. They are much more affordable to the mass market because of the excise tax advantages they have over passenger cars (3% VS 35%). Moreover, pickups perform dual functions as both goods and people carriers. Models such as double cab, four-doors are made in response to market preference for dual functionality. In fact, the design of new pickup models including improved
suspension systems tend toward increasing passenger comforts over the transport of goods. Manufacturers also focus design and marketing efforts to create a perception in the market of fuel efficiency and powerful performance for their products. As a result, nearly 90% of all one-ton pickups sold in Thailand have diesel engines and more than half of them have turbo chargers. The number of pickups with gasoline engines has already begun to decline and some manufacturers no longer offer pickup models with gasoline engines.

Five Leading Makes (2001)

Make	Model	Units	% Market Share
Isuzu	Diesel: 2.5 - 3.0 Litre (Turbo) Gasoline: 3.0 Litre	65,029	39.74
Toyota	Diesel: 2.4 - 3.0 Litre Gasoline: None	39,477	24.12

For additional analytical, business and investment opportunities information, please contact Global Investment & Business Center, USA at (202) 546-2103. Fax: (202) 546-3275. E-mail: rusric@erols.com

Nissan	Diesel: 2.5 & 2.7 Litre Gasoline: 1.6 Litre	19,421	11.87
Mitsubishi	Diesel: 2.5 & 2.8 Litre 2.8 Litre (Turbo) Gasoline: 3.0 & 3.5 Litre	18,118	11.07
Ford	Diesel: 2.5 & 2.9 Litre 2.5 & 2.9 Litre (Turbo) Gasoline: None	16,735	10.23
Other		4,858	2.97
TOTAL		163,638	100.00

Industry experts expect pickups, especially Japanese makes, to maintain a dominant share of the vehicle market in Thailand. All pickups sold in Thailand are locally assembled base on Japanese designs and model platforms. Ford began to compete in 1996 when it launched its "Ranger" model in Thailand. Just last year, Ford became the fifth best selling pickup with a 10% share of the market. Like all other makes, Ford also assembles its pickup products in Thailand, and bases its design on a Japanese platform.

Because of its size and market potential, competition in the pickup market is intense as all makers attempt to increase their share. Isuzu has long been the market leader, particularly upcountry. Toyota has made a strong effort to overtake Isuzu. Based on last year's figures, Isuzu has close to 40% of the market, followed by Toyota 24%, Nissan 12%, Mitsubishi 11%, and Ford 10%.

Passenger Car Market: Passenger cars with engine sizes ranging from 1.5 Litres up to 1.8 Litres account for 74% of all such vehicles sold in 2001. The small passenger car segment can be divided into two basic sub-categories; the budget models and the worldwide models. They account for 26% and 48% of the small passenger car market, respectively. Cars with engine size of 2.0 Litres and above comprise the other 26% of the passenger car market.

Budget Small Passenger Car Market (2001)

Make	Model	Units	% Market Share
Toyota Soluna	1.5 Litre	12,173	44.11
Honda City	1.5 Litre	15,416	55.86
TOTAL		27,589	99.97

Honda City and Toyota Soluna are the two basic players in this market. Both are designed and manufactured as entry-level passenger car principally for the ASEAN market. However, Industry experts expect significant changes
in this particular segment with both Honda and Toyota shifting towards using platforms of their worldwide models. Honda's new City will be based on its Fit model (known as Jazz in Europe or Mobilo in Japan). Meanwhile, Toyota is believed to be replacing its Soluna model with the Platz.

For additional analytical, business and investment opportunities information, please contact Global Investment & Business Center, USA at (202) 546-2103. Fax: (202) 546-3275. E-mail: rusric@erols.com

The newer model will have some modifications with special appeal in the Thai market. Toyota is expected to also launch the Verso, along with the Platz. In addition, Suzuki is expected to enter this segment with the Aerio, which also known as Liana in Europe. All these models would be available in both sedan and hatchback versions.

Small Passenger Car Market (2001)

Make	Model	Units	% Market Share
Toyota Corolla	1.6 & 1.8 Litre	19,009	37.89
Honda Civic	1.6 - 1.8 Litre	16,205	32.30
Nissan Sunny	1.6 Litre	8,216	16.38
Mitsubishi Lancer	1.5 - 1.8 Litre	4,762	9.49
Mazda 323	1.6 Litre	1,046	2.08
Ford Laser	1.6 & 1.8 Litre	695	1.39
Other Isuzu Vertex Audi Seat Cordoba	 1.6 Litre 1.8 Litre 1.9 Litre	240	0.47
TOTAL		50,173	100.00

Toyota Corolla and Honda Civic have a combined 70% share of the small passenger car market. Nissan Sunny and Mitsubishi Lancer hold distant third and fourth places in the category, respectively. In 2002, principal models available in the Thai market include the Nissan Sunny NEO, Honda Civic, Toyota Corolla Altis, Mitsubishi Lancer Cedia, Mazda 323 Protégé, and Ford Tierra.

Competition in Thailand's small passenger car market is intense and manufacturers employ varied strategies to increase sales. Some of the oft-used strategies include minor exterior design changes, special financing packages and additional accessories. In fact, provision of accessories becomes an essential tool in increasing the vehicle's value. The strategy, to some extent, decreases potential sales of aftermarket accessories. For example, a decline in the audio system market is viewed as a result of such strategy. The increase in vehicles having manufacturer-installed audio systems reduces overall sales of audio systems sold through aftermarket dealers. Hence, potential aftermarket audio system sales are limited to high-end products for a small segment of upper end market buyers. Industry experts
expect vehicle manufacturers to provide an increasing number of accessories that will further impact upon sales of aftermarket accessories, particularly those of appearance parts.

Mid-Size Passenger Car & Luxury Car Market

Sales of mid-size passenger cars and luxury cars totaled 26,740 units last year. Key makes and models in this segment are the Toyota Camry, Nissan Cefiro and Honda Accord. Based on last year's figures, these three models accounted for the majority of sales of mid-size cars. Unit sales

For additional analytical, business and investment opportunities information,
please contact Global Investment & Business Center, USA
at (202) 546-2103. Fax: (202) 546-3275. E-mail: rusric@erols.com

reached 10,823 units (Camry - 4,081units, Cefiro - 3,787 units, and Accord 2955 units). [Note: Please refer to the overview market table for other makes in this segment]

Mercedes-Benz and BMW are two key makes in Thailand's luxury car market. Last year, Mercedes-Benz sales totaled 4,500 units, a 55% increase over 2000 figures. By comparison, BMW sold 3,226 units, a 34% increase over the previous year. Both German makes compete intensely in the Thai market and are optimistic about their potential growth. This year, Mercedes-Benz set its sales target at 5,000 units, while BMW is aiming for sales of 3,400 units. Both makers have local assembling facilities and plan to assemble their mainstream models in Thailand.

Sport Utilitiy Vehicle Market (2001)

Make	Model	Units	% Market Share
BMW	X5 4.4I, 3.0 D & 3.0 I Litre	87	1.4
Chrysler	Cherokee 2.5 & 4.0 Litre Wrangler 4.0 Litre Grand Cherokee 4.0&4.7 Litre	421	6.6
Honda	CRV 2.0 Litre	4,009	63.1
Hyundai	Santa 2.4 & 2.7 Litre Terios 1.3 Litre	75	1.2
Isuzu	Trooper 3.2 Litre New Trooper 3.0 Litre New Vega 3.0 Litre Vega 2.8 & 3.0 Litre	643	10.1
KIA	Grand Aportage 2.0 Litre Sportage 2.0 Litre	45	0.7
Land Rover	Defender Discover 2.0-4.0 Litre	150	2.4
Mercedes-Benz	G 2.3 - 3.0 Litre ML 2.7 & 3.2 Litre	72	1.1
Mitsubishi	Pajero 2.8 -3.5 Litre	129	2
Suzuki	Caribean 1.3 Litre Vitara 1.6 Litre	647	10.2
Toyota	L'Crusier Prado 3.4 Litre Land Crusier 2.5 & 4.5 Lexus 4.7 Litre RAV 2.0 Litre	76	1.2
Other			

-Ford	Explorer 4.0 Litre	3	0.0
-Nissan	Petrol 3.0 Litre (Turbo)		
Total		6,357	100.0

Small Sport Utility Vehicles have a much larger share of the Thai market than traditional, larger SUVs. This is because smaller SUV are more affordable and appeal to a larger group of buyers. The price of a small SUV falls into the same range as those of passenger cars and their targeted markets tend to overlap. Leading small SUVs in 2001 are Honda's CRV with 63% market share and Suzuki with a 10% market share.

Unlike the small SUV market, the majority of large Sport Utility Vehicle owners can afford to buy a number of cars and most likely own more than one vehicle. In fact, Sport Utility Vehicles are often classified as luxury vehicles. Sales of SUVs of traditional large size have declined quite severely in the past few years due to the economic downturn and competition from less expensive locally assembled SUVs, that are a modified version of a 4-Wheel pickup and have similar size and appeal of the large traditional SUVs. The excise tax advantage gives the local SUV a great price advantage while its size and design appeals to potential buyers of largeSUVs. However, industry experts believe the decline in the large SUV market will be reversed because the excise tax advantage gap between locally modified 4-Wheels pickups and large SUV has narrowed as a result of changes in regulations. The locally modified vehicle market is expected to decline accordingly. Meanwhile, global manufacturers are introducing new SUV models to compete for market share. New models in the market include Ford Escape, Land Rover Free Lander, Jeep Liberty and Toyota's Land Cruiser Prado.

Imports and Competition

The automotive accessories market in Thailand is as much a market of global competition as the vehicle market itself. All leading global makers of accessories have a presence in the Thai market, and consumers are knowledgeable about global trends. As a result, internationally known products especially those popular in automotive trend-setting countries like Japan, Germany and the U.S are more readily accepted in the Thai market.

Local Production: Thailand is host to a large number of automotive accessories manufacturers. They are both locally owned operations and subsidiaries of internationally known suppliers. Subsidiary operations of global parts manufacturers are in Thailand to primarily serve vehicle assemblers. They are considered accessories manufacturers because they also manufacture after-market parts such as tire and wheels that are viewed as accessories buy certain group of buyers.

Most locally owned companies concentrate in manufacturing of appearance parts both for local market and export markets. Manufacturing for the local market tends to focus on producing parts for large volume vehicles such as aero parts for popular small passenger cars like the Toyota Corolla, wooden interior trim, pickup canopies, pickup bed liners, bumpers, side skis, roll bars, bug guards, grille guards and spoilers. The quality of these parts varies, depending on the manufacturers' capital investment and know-how. Many products are low-quality imitations of foreign-designs and/or imported products. Others are made for exports such as wooden interior trim and truck bed liners.

Wheel & Tires: Major manufacturers of wheels and tires in Thailand are global manufacturers set up as Original Equipment Manufacturers to primarily serve vehicle assemblers. However, they also manufacture after-market parts that are marketed as replacements and accessories. Because of local manufacturing capacity, U.S. export potential for wheels and tires is extremely limited.

Global makes of alloy wheels with manufacturing operations in Thailand are Enkai, Lemerz, Kosei, Yashiyoda, and Asahi. Last year, production of alloy wheels as Original Equipment Manufacturer parts for local assemblers was estimated at 1.38 million units. Production for the accessories market was estimated at less than 60,000 units. Imports are estimated at less than 3,500 units per year. The majority of importers are small businesses bringing in products via non-conventional channels. Most imports are from Japan, Germany and the U.S.A. The potential market for imported alloy wheels is extremely small and limited to the high-end, higher priced segment.

Global tire manufacturers with local production facilities in Thailand are Michelin, Goodyear, and Bridgestone. They manufacture 100% of OEM tires required by local assemblers and approximately 95% of the replacement market's need. Leading imported makes are Yokohama, Falken, and Dunlop. Each of these makes are imported and distributed by their exclusive distributors. Sales of imported tires, as accessories, have small market potential and are limited to only world famous brands.

Appearance Parts: Industry experts estimate the annual market for appearance parts of automotive accessories to be around USD 2 Million. The term, Appearance parts, refers to a wide range of products that are installed to improve vehicle appearance according to the vehicle owner's preference. Typically, appearance parts are interior and exterior trim, specialty waxes, and chemicals, audio systems and car-theft prevention devices.

German imports dominate the accessories market for luxury cars where consumers tend to focus on appearance, comfort and safety. Therefore, the majority of German accessories imported into Thailand are appearance parts and suspension systems. Appearance parts imported from Germany are mainly performance body kits and alloy wheels. Since Mercedes Benz and BMW are the two major makes in the segment, accessories made for both makes have the best competitive advantage. Popular German makes in the accessories market are M Technic, AMG, Lorinser, AC SCHNITZER, HAMANN, AMG, Zender, Carlsson, Al Pina, Hartge, Breyton, and BRABUS.

Similar to the popularity enjoyed by German aftermarket accessories makers that resulted from the success of German vehicles, American-made Sport Utility Vehicle / Off-road accessories are also the market leader in the latter category. The success of Jeep in pioneering Thailand's SUV/Off-road market has made American accessories the trendsetters here. Well-known U.S. makes in this market include PROCOMP, WARN, Sway-A-Way, and MICKEY THOMSON.

In addition, U.S. makes have a leading share in the automotive tinted film market. U.S. imports account for an estimated share of 40-50 % share of the tinted film market. The key competitive strength of U.S. imports of tinted film is their high-quality images that enable them to maintain their share at the high-quality, high-price market. Products at lower price positions are from Taiwan, Korea, Israel, and India. Taiwan imports account for 30% share of the market, while Korean imports account for 20%. Korean imports have had the fastest growth in the market despite getting a late start because they are perceived to have good quality at reasonable prices. Wide varieties of tinted film makes are in the market, including 3M, KOOLPLUS, VCOOL, INFRATEC, Super-Kool, Hi-Kool, Merridium Solar Control Film, KEEP KOOL, Xtra-Cole, Johnson Window Films, Lamina, and Hanita.

Racing and Performance Parts: Experts estimate the racing and performance market at USD 12 million. Used parts imports from Japan account for 70% of the overall sales. Imports of new parts account for another 30%, with U.S. makes and Japanese makes having almost equal market shares. Japanese makes have a competitive advantage because Japanese small to mid-size passenger cars and pickups account for most of the modified vehicles in Thailand. In addition, a wide range of both new and used performance accessories imported from Japan are available at prices to suit low to high end buyers. Well-known Japanese makes accessories in the Thai market include TRD, NISMO, Rally Art, HKS, GREEDY, BLITZ, SARD, PIVOT, OMORI, DEFI (Japanese), IHI, TOMEI, and BOMEX.

American-made racing and performance accessories, such as turbo chargers, filters and gauges, are well known in Thailand and sell well in the mid-market range. Popular U.S. makes that have been in the Thai market for many years include Garrett, Auto Meter and K&N. Due to the lack of American model vehicles in Thailand, the prerequisite for U.S. makes accessories to succeed in this market is their compatibility with the different types of non-U.S. model vehicles in the market. In addition, quality is another factor inn the sales of U.S. accessories in Thai market.

Suspension System: American makes dominate the imported shock absorbers market because of price and quality. U.S. makes have 70% of the imported shock absorbers after-market for pickups and 20% share of the after-market for passenger cars. Well-known U.S. brands include Gabriel, Trail Master, Monroe, and Rancho. Imported shock absorbers account for 30% share of the total market in Thailand. Locally, a Japanese manufacturer produces the "Kayaba" brand, which accounts for the other 70% of the market for shock absorbers. Cumulatively, the annual replacement market for shock absorbers is estimated at USD 24 million.

In the luxury car market, German brands of shock absorbers by SACHS, KONI, and BILSTEIN have the largest combined share though well-designed imports from Australia have increased markedly in recent years. Australian products are especially sought by owners of pickups and off-road vehicles. Product designs are the key competitive strength of Australian shock absorbers. Their attractive designs and colors are well regarded by pickup and SUV owners favoring accessories that enhance their vehicle's appearance.

Sales Prospects

Generally vehicle owners tend to purchase the largest number of accessories items during their initial ownership of the vehicles regardless of whether the vehicle is brand new or used. Their level of spending and selection of accessories varies according to personal preference.

Tinted Film: This is the most common item selected by nearly every vehicle owner. Accordingly tinted film has tremendous market potential and a promising growth rate of 15%, in line with expansion of the country's vehicle market. Because of Thailand's tropical climate, tinted film is purchased for its functional purpose as an accessory that reduces heat and the impact of the sun's rays.

Racing & Performance Products: Unlike tinted film, racing and performance products appeal to a specific niche market of car enthusiasts. Most buyers of racing and performance products are between 20 to 35 years old. They are usually university students or among the newly employed graduates. Many of them are from well-to-do families and often acquire financial assistance from their parents to support this hobby. They learn of new products from friends, importers and/or specialized mechanics at the shops or garages they frequent. They keep updated on trends and are keen to accept new products. For these reasons, U.S. racing and performance products that are adaptable to local models and are popular in the U.S. have strong potential to succeed in the

Thai market. The racing and performance market in Thailand is expected to expand 10% per year.

Suspension System: Similarly, experts expect the market for suspension systems to increase at a similar rate and U.S. makes have an advantage, especially in sales of shock absorbers. U.S. makes have had a solid reputation for having good quality which is a key buying factor among a substantial number of vehicle owners. These potential buyers view a suspension system as an after-market replacement part and place strong emphasis on the product's durability and performance. They are mostly owners of goods-carrying pickups, used mid-size passenger cars, luxury cars, and SUV/Off-road.

Accessories for Sport Utility Vehicles / Off-road: In addition to growth prospects in the suspension system market, sales of SUV/ Off-road accessories also offers considerable potential for U.S. suppliers. SUV/Off road vehicle owners are growing in number and the vehicle by design offers its owners extensive possibilities to install or modify a variety of accessories. Some of these accessories include lift kits, winches, head lamps, torsion bars, tires, wheels, wheel covers, side steps, roof racks, mud terrain, grille guards, bumpers, as well as headlight and tail light protectors. For many SUV/Off-road owners, enhancements are made for the trendy appearance of a fully-equipped off-road vehicle - even if the vehicle is only operated in urban areas. Consequently, famous makes and flashy items that are in fashion are highly likely to succeed in this market.

MARKET ACCESS

Thailand is an open market with no barrier especially developed to deter imports of after market accessories. Limited regulations exist in term of standards and safety requirement to deter imports of accessories. Moreover, local distributors do not consider duty rates of 20-40% on accessories barrier to their marketing success. Accessories with the right quality and design that appeal to the local market at the right price are likely to success in the market, despite intense competition. Meanwhile, qualified local distributors would lessen the cost disadvantages caused by unconventional import channels. Moreover, qualified local distributors would also be instrumental in providing effective market penetration, despite the highly disperse nature of the market.

The majority of local importers have good knowledge and experience in handling customs procedures. It is in their best interest to advise foreign manufactures on customs issues that may affect the sales of their products in Thailand. However, more information on Thai customs can be obtained at www.customs.go.th, or by contacting:

The Customs Department
Suthornkosa Road, Khlong Toey,
Bangkok 10110, Thailand
Tel: (662) 249-0431 thru 40
Fax: (662) 249-4199)

Financing

Thai commercial banks provide financing to importers based on the financial situation and credit standing of each company. Payment to the U.S. supplier is, in general, made by Letter of Credit. Therefore, the exporter receives final payment from the transaction bank after the shipment is completed. For small sample orders, payment by cash remittance through a bank transfer is usually preferred.

Trade Promotion

U.S. exporters often meet potential Thai distributors at international automobile and accessories trade exhibitions. At the fairs, importers survey new products to import from suppliers in Japan, Germany, and the U.S. Additionally, through the International Buyer Program, the U.S. Commercial Service organizes buyer delegations to attend major events like the Automotive After Market Industry Week in Las Vegas. In addition to making contacts made at such fairs overseas, U.S. automotive accessories suppliers should select a local distributor to facilitate their market entry into the Thai market. The U.S. Commercial Service provides a wide range of services to determine the market potential for products and identify qualified local distributors and importers. Exporters can also benefit from listings on BuyUSA.com which reaches an international buying audience of 20,000 and by advertising in Commercial News USA.

MUNICIPAL SOLID WASTE PROJECTS

Thailand spends an estimated US$41 million dollars a year on goods and services for municipal solid waste management. About a quarter of this is imported. While the solid waste industry now is characterized by unsafe practices (such as open dumping) and inefficient administration (such as heavy governmental subsidies), economic and regulatory pressures are slowly driving the market to adopt modern, efficient solid waste management techniques. In the next three to five years as the market matures, US environmental technology companies that can demonstrate technologies and services adapted to Thailand's tropical climate will find greater opportunities to sell in Thailand.

The Bangkok Metropolitan Authority (BMA) operates the biggest single solid waste management system in Thailand. In mid-2002, the BMA was drafting terms of reference to solicit quotations for three contracts to operate its transfer stations and solid waste disposal facilities. Requirements to upgrade the existing transfer stations into integrated waste handling stations are expected to be included in the TORs. However, the existing contract holders have an upper hand in the bidding for the new contracts. Provincial municipalities, which include large cities and resort areas, are largely underdeveloped and offer the best growth potential, especially as the market matures over the next few years. Rural areas account for a large portion of waste generation. However, they offer little or no commercial viability because of the dearth of infrastructure. A niche market with potential is the disposal of non-hazardous industrial waste. The planned privatization of collection and disposal of solid waste from commercial residential sites (hotels, apartment blocks and condominiums) also holds some potential.

As an indicator of the importance the government places on environmental issues, it announced a 16 percent increase in the fiscal year 2003 budget for the Ministry of Science, Technology and Environment (MOSTE). The ministry has earmarked 4.4 billion baht (about US$105 million) for solid waste and wastewater treatment programs. During the budget debate in parliament, the only objection the opposition raised to the proposed increase was that it was not enough.

Central and local government bodies are the most obvious end-users for this market. Less obvious end-users are environmental service and civil engineering companies already in Thailand. These already have contacts and market entry and are open to reviewing innovative services or specialty technologies that may have potential in the Thai market.

The following have been identified as best prospects in the Municipal Solid Waste market:
· collection and transportation management

- recycling and reprocessing systems
- composting systems
- waste separation and volume reduction technologies
- sanitary landfill design and maintenance
- small incinerators
- innovative sanitary landfill technologies (especially liners and coverings)
- rehabilitation of former open dumps
- sanitary landfill design and maintenance (adapted for tropical environment)
- presses or compactors
- bailers
- chemical or organic treatment of waste in landfills
- leachate pumps
- safe disposal of mobile phone batteries

During interviews for this ISA, specific requests were made for:
- technology to control smell and leakage during transfer (e.g., wrapping systems)
- specialized sorting/recycling technologies (e.g., for specialty plastics or refuse   paper)
- technologies to produce small quantities of alternative fuels
- efficient aerators

MARKET HIGHLIGHTS AND BEST PROSPECTS

Market Profile

Thailand produces around 46,000 tons of non-hazardous solid household waste per day. The Pollution Control Department (PCD) of the Ministry of Science, Technology and Environment, estimates municipal solid waste generation is growing about 4% per year. The Municipal Solid Waste Industry in Thailand has three sectors: the Bangkok metropolitan area, which is governed by the Bangkok Metropolitan Administration (BMA) and generates about 25% of the total waste; urban centers in the provinces, which produce about 35% of the total, and rural provincial areas, which produce the remaining 40%. The BMA is the best-organized market with the most developed infrastructure. Provincial urban centers are known as municipalities and number more than 1,100. Although largely underdeveloped, commercial potential is developing in this segment. Rural areas are unorganized and lack any meaningful infrastructure. Each subsector has a unique set of needs. Also of interest to US companies would be the 1,200 tons of non-hazardous waste generated per day by Thailand's industrial estates.

The Bangkok Metropolitan Authority (BMA): The BMA has made tremendous progress in recent years in the collection of household solid waste. More than 95% of the waste generated is properly collected, and around 30% of it is sorted for recycling. BMA personnel collect the waste and carry it to three transfer stations (On-nut, Nong-Khaem and Tha-Raeng). Two private companies have contracts with the BMA to operate the waste transfer sites and transport waste to sanitary landfills, one at Kamphaeng-Saen and the other at Lad-Krabang. The BMA requires that the landfills be approved by the PCD and by authorities in the locales in which the landfills are situated, and that they operate according to PCD standards. The current landfill sites should be useable for about another 10 years. The BMA is looking for ways to enhance the efficiency of its collection system and reduce the volume of waste it sends to landfills. Recycling is somewhat inefficient, because by informal agreement it is done by BMA collection personnel and street scavengers. The BMA has a program that teaches schools and community groups the benefits of recycling. A small composting plant operates at the On-nut transfer site. The BMA hopes to increase the efficiency and effectiveness of its recycling and composting projects. The authority also sees these areas as potential revenue generators.

The BMA's biggest challenges are fees and fee collection. Based on a rate set in the 1970s, Bangkok households now are assessed 4 baht (about 9 US cents) per month for garbage collection. But even at this rate, the percentage of fees actually collected is extremely low. In early 2002 the BMA drafted legislation to raise solid waste fees to 40 baht per household. The law won initial approval, but the City Council had yet to approve it before council elections in June 2002. Whether or when the new council will approve the law is not known. To increase fee collections, the BMA has moved fee collection responsibilities to the district level. In mid-2002 district officials were surveying their districts to determine who should be paying collection fees and who have not been paying.

Best Prospects: The BMA has expressed interest in technologies and services in the following areas: management of collection and transportation, recycling systems, composting and reprocessing systems, waste separation and volume reduction technologies, sanitary landfill design and maintenance, and incineration technologies. A specific request was made for technologies that reduce the smell of landfills. Public awareness has been growing about the need for safe disposal of mobile phone batteries. Domestic telecommunication service providers have established some collection points, but their efforts have been limited.

Future Prospects: In mid-2002, the BMA was in the early stages of three projects that together would reduce the volume of waste it sends to landfills by 5,000 tons per day.
·   *Renovation of the On-nut and Nong Kehm transfer stations:* According to the terms of reference (TOR) being drafted, the new contract holders will have to renovate and upgrade the transfer stations at On-nut and Nong Kehm to enable more efficient sorting. The BMA hopes to reduce the waste transferred to landfills by 1,000 tons per day per station through this project. The renovation specifications are to be included in the TOR. The current contracts, each worth about 780 million baht (US$18.5 million), have four-year tenures that expire in 2004.
·   *An integrated waste facility at On-nut:* Renovations at On-nut are to include a larger composting plant and an incinerator. At least 2,000 tons of waste per day is to be sorted with 600-700 tons per day being sent for composting and the remainder sent to an incinerator. The project has been initially approved with a budget of 7.9 billion baht, most covered by a loan from the Japan Bank for International Cooperation that has a concessional interest rate of 0.75%. The BMA central authorities and the JBIC were negotiating details before issuing the TOR for the project.
·   *A biogas plant at the Nong Khem transfer station to handle 1,000 tons/day of organic waste.* The BMA was drawing up the TOR for this project in mid-2002.

The BMA is also devising a plan for the privatization of commercial waste collection. This would involve the collection of solid waste from hotels and large residential buildings, hazardous waste from hospitals and clinics, and construction waste.

Municipalities: This segment includes the cities and towns outside the BMA area. The larger and better known areas would be, Chiang Mai in the north, Hat Yai in the south, and the resort areas of Pattaya and Phuket, as well as provincial capitals. To be designated a municipality, an area must meet criteria for area, population and population density. The 1,101 municipalities are further divided into cities (20 of these) with more than a hundred thousand residents, towns with tens of thousands of residents and townships with a few thousand residents.

Each municipality is responsible for its own solid waste management. However, municipalities are assisted logistically by the Public Works Department (PWD) of the Ministry of Interior and receive investment and operational budgets from the Office of Environmental Policy and Planning (OEPP) in the Ministry of Science, Technology and Environment (See note on government decentralization in the last section of this report). In addition, the Ministry of Interior's Department of Local Administration (DOLA) offers local governments support for environmental planning and recommends appropriate technology through its department of Natural Resource and Environmental Management.

In mid-2002, more than 100 landfills were in operation in Thailand and about 30 were under construction. About 75% of the landfills are registered with the PCD, the others are not. Few would come close to meeting US-EPA standards for sanitary landfills. Most municipalities use open dumps. Similar to the BMA, larger municipalities generally handle waste collection and private firms handle disposal and operate the landfills. According to the PCD, municipalities own 79 landfills nationwide.

In 1999, the PCD conducted a study (funded by the US-EPA and USTDA) of municipal solid waste. Preliminary recommendations suggested centralizing solid waste disposal by constructing one sanitary landfill for every three provinces. (Thailand has 76 provinces.). However, the final recommendation was one landfill for every province. PCD officials said the recommendation acknowledges that getting municipalities working together across provinces is unrealistic. They said getting municipalities within the same province to work together is extremely difficult.

Three incinerator projects for non-hazardous solid waste are operating in Thailand: a 250-ton-per-day unit on the resort island of Phuket, a 140-ton-per-day plant (2 units) on the resort island of Samui, and a 20–ton-per-day unit for the municipality of Lamphun. The incinerators have proven to be much more expensive to operate and maintain than had been projected. Other large municipalities that have investigated the use of incinerators have abandoned these plans because of prohibitively high investment and operating costs.

Phitsanulok: A Case Study in Solid Waste Management: One of Thailand's newest designated cities, Phitsanulok, about 200 miles north of Bangkok, is an interesting case study in solid waste management. Since 1999, it has been the site of a solid waste demonstration program funded by the German development agency Deutsch Besellschaft fur Technische Zusammenarbeit (GTZ, or German agency for technical cooperation). This city has an area of 18.26 sq. km. and a population of 87,535 people living in 27,888 registered households (2000 census figures). An estimated 30,000 to 40,000 people live in the city in non-registered households. Before the program began, Phitsanulok's 27 trash trucks were collecting about 127 tons of solid waste a day and depositing it in an open dump. About half the waste collected was recyclable materials, 30% organic waste and 20% non-organic.

Building an acceptable sanitary landfill was the first activity the GTZ program undertook. Then through aggressive public education programs and community organizing, it established effective waste separation and recycling programs (selling some materials and composting organic waste). This enabled the city to reduce the waste it collects to 84 tons a day and cut its fleet to 15 trucks, affecting significant cost savings. When the program began, collection fees (about 20 baht per household per month) paid only about 10% of the total cost of solid waste management. An unexpected benefit of the community organizing was a greater willingness of people to pay their fees. By 2002, the program claimed to be collecting 80% of fees owed and reportedly the public did not balk when monthly fees increased to 30 baht per household per month. Organizers admit, however, that the true cost of solid waste management in Phitsanulok is between 80 baht and 100 baht per household per month.

The program has expended considerable effort in building the capacity of local government officials, launching programs in: improving service mentality; planning, monitoring and evaluation; human resources management; and computerizing information systems. The program also worked closely with local entrepreneurs to develop a commercially viable program for selling and buying recyclable materials. Spurred by the Phitsanulok program, a recycling company, Wongpanit Group, has begun to expand its operations throughout Thailand and is even selling franchises.

With the expertise it has gained, the municipality was able to win service contracts to manage solid waste at four nearby military bases. Similar approaches to smaller, neighboring municipalities were not successful.

Best Prospects: The untapped potential in municipalities makes them attractive for US firms that exercise caution. The watchwords in this segment are "small" and "appropriate". Given municipalities' stubborn reluctance to consolidate efforts, waste volumes are small. Furthermore, municipalities generally lack staff qualified to operate and maintain the equipment and administration of a modern solid waste management system.
Specific requests have been made for recycling and composting technologies; innovative landfill technologies (especially liners and coverings); chemical or organic treatment of waste in landfills; rehabilitation of former open dumps; sanitary landfill design and maintenance; presses or compactors; bailers; and technology to control smell and leakage during transfer, such as wrapping systems.

Future Prospects: This market segment is on the verge of significant change. Despite the municipalities' reluctance to embrace regionalization and consolidation of solid waste management, that is exactly where this market segment is headed. The main drivers are economic and regulatory. Small landfills and small collection and transportation operations are not economically sustainable, and municipalities have limited capacity to continue to absorb expensive subsidies. The larger cities and towns are already looking for ways to trim costs; this will only intensify. The OEPP plans to push municipalities to greater cooperation by reducing funding for single municipality projects and increasing founding for joint projects. Furthermore, public pressure continues to mount in support of enforcing Thailand's environmental regulations. Private sector experts and public sector officials expect to see significant changes in the municipal solid waste management systems in the next five years.

Given this trend, private sector players and government officials believe that the best commercial potential in the medium-term (three to five years) will exist for privately owned transfer stations and transfer operators. After five years, there may be potential for large, privately owned sanitary landfills that could handle upwards of 200 tons of solid waste per day. The best sites would be in the north and in the south. (See more in the end-users section below)

Rural Provincial Areas: In Thailand, areas outside of municipalities are organized in tambon (subdistrict) administration organizations (TAOs), which are sometimes called sanitary districts. There are about 6,750 of these. Because of the lack of infrastructure, this segment has little or no commercial interest to US companies.

Non-Hazardous Industrial Waste: Because of government regulations, various tax and non-tax incentives, and superior infrastructure, the most prominent manufacturers in Thailand -- including local units of multinational corporations -- build their factories in industrial estates. Nationwide, industrial estates generate about 1,200 tons of non-hazardous waste per day. Each industrial estate provides solid waste disposal as a service to clients. Most industrial estates now use incineration, but fuel costs make this expensive. This market segment should be of interest to US companies because of the segment's unique set of drivers, which are:
· laws that require industrial estates (and clients within) to dispose of waste properly;

·   factories' need to prove compliance with multinational corporate environmental guidelines (either as a local unit of a multinational or as a supplier or vendor to a multinational);

·   factories' need to prove compliance with environmental regulations of importing countries; and

·   the desire to cut costs.

Best Prospects: Suppliers for this segment should think small and specialty. End users would be industrial estate operators and individual factories. Specific requests include: small bailers, leachate pumps, efficient aerators, specialized sorting/recycling technologies (for example, for specialty plastics or refuse paper), and small quantities of alternative fuels.

Market Trends

Market Size
Industry observers believe that the municipal solid waste market in Thailand could be worth as much as US$205 million if collection, transfer, recycling and land filling were handled properly. In fact, the market is a mere fraction of this. Best estimates put the actual value of the market at US$41 million and a growth rate of about 4% per annum for the next few years.

Estimated Market Value*

Unit: millions US$	2002	2003	2004	2005	Growth (%)
Total Market Value **	41.096	42.763	44.499	46.305	4.0
Local Production	30.822	32.072	33.374	34.729	4.0
Exports	n.a.	n.a.	n.a.	n.a.	n.a.
Imports	10.274	10.691	11.125	11.576	4.0
US Imports	n.a.	n.a.	n.a.	n.a.	n.a.

*Based on industry projections of value, July 2002. **Includes equipment, operations, and maintenance, excludes construction costs.*

Potential Market Value*

Unit: millions US$	2002	2003	2004	2005	Growth (%)
Total Market Value**	205.483	213.819	222.496	231.3958	4.0
Local Production	154.112	160.364	166.872	173.547	4.0
Exports	n.a.	n.a.	n.a.	n.a.	n.a.
Imports	51.371	53.455	55.624	57.849	4.0
US Imports	n.a.	n.a.	n.a.	n.a.	n.a.

*Based on industry projections of value, July 2002. **Includes equipment, operations, and maintenance, excludes construction costs.*

COMPETITIVE ANALYSIS

The bulk of products and equipment sold in the Thailand market are produced in Thailand, which is a reflection of the low level of technology generally used in the market. It also reflects the fact that many international firms selling to this market are manufacturing products domestically already. For example, the US firm Heil makes garbage truck bodies in Thailand and another US company, GSE (Thailand) Co., Ltd. makes liners for landfills.

For services and products at the higher end of the technology spectrum, the main third party competitors for US companies are Japanese and European companies; their technologies are generally very expensive, but some of them receive support from their governments. Australian firms are also well respected, and their technologies are not as expensive.

US firms that can provide specialty consultancy services in this market provide good entry point opportunities for US equipment and product manufacturers, according to industry experts interviewed for this report.

END-USER ANALYSIS

The most obvious end-users are governmental bodies, specifically the BMA and municipal governments and by extension the Ministry of Interior (DOLA and Public Works Department). Other stakeholders in the government sector are the PCD, which sets standards and gives technical assistance to municipalities, and the OEPP, which allocates budgets for spending on solid waste disposal and treatment.

Some less obvious end users would be large service-providing companies already established in Thailand, such as Black & Veatch, CH2M Hill and ERM-Siam. Such companies, which already have contacts and market entry, are open to reviewing innovative services or specialty technologies that may have potential in the Thai market.

Industry people suggest that the subsector in this market with the best growth potential is building and operating transfer stations. Economic pressures and PCD plans to implement regional or provincial landfills are driving the market to adopt more professional transfer services to feed into the regional/provincial landfills. Industry experts say this market subsector will open up within five years.

One company tackling this segment now is Modern Asia Environmental Ltd., a joint venture between American investors and the Global Environmental Fund. The company's sanitary landfill has a 2,000-ton-per-day capacity and meets US-EPA and European Union standards. The facility opened in 2001 and in mid-2002 was operating at about 10% of capacity. Located in the Chonburi Industrial Estate, this landfill is ideally suited to cover industries and municipalities in Thailand's Eastern Seaboard.

Another company looking at this segment is Professional Waste Technology (1999) Co., Ltd., which plans to build a sanitary landfill in Sa Kaew Province (far eastern Thailand). The company has plans for a 1,000-ton-per-day capacity (non-hazardous waste), and in early 2002 was securing necessary permits and licenses.

MARKET ACCESS

Import Climate
The tariff on equipment classified as "environmental technologies" is 5% or less on assembled imports. Importers generally experience relatively few problems bringing their goods into Thailand. Some equipment importers, however, have reported that sometimes the Customs Department will classify partially disassembled machinery as "spare parts", which carry import duties as high as 35%.

For additional analytical, business and investment opportunities information,
please contact Global Investment & Business Center, USA
at (202) 546-2103. Fax: (202) 546-3275. E-mail: rusric@erols.com

Distribution and business practices

Find a Thai Partner: Having a reliable Thai partner is essential. First of all, many bidding projects require that a Thai company be the main contractor. Also, significantly, a Thai partner will provide invaluable "local knowledge". The right partner will have ongoing relationships with the organizations supervising projects, will often receive a "heads-up" about upcoming projects, and can explain both the specifics of the project and the machinations of the bidding process, which is often more complicated than in the US. In addition, having a Thai partner can, to a large degree, smooth the language barrier and prevent problems that might arise with staff, suppliers, and logistics.

Finding the right Thai partner is essentially an investment of time. Begin by talking with members of the American Chamber of Commerce in Thailand (AmCham) and meeting with senior government officials at agencies such as the Board of Investment, who have much experience dealing with foreign investors and can provide names of companies they have confidence in. Many good consultants in Bangkok can help with the task, but only you can determine which potential partner shares your vision.

Intellectual Property Rights Concerns: American and European firms in Thailand have reported some dangers over intellectual property rights issues. For example, there have been reports of Thai subcontractors hired to install environmental technology systems attempting to reverse engineer designs and technologies. This reinforces the advice from American businessmen that finding the right Thai partner is essential to doing business in Thailand. The right Thai partner will protect the American firm's interests by ensuring the safety of design and technologies.

Financing
Companies that install or upgrade equipment that provides environmental protection or preservation can receive low-interest loans from the Green Fund administered by the Industrial Finance Corporation of Thailand.

Thailand's Board of Investment offers tax incentives and tariff exemptions and reductions to investors installing environmental protection and preservation equipment. It also gives tax incentives and duty exemptions to firms establishing manufacturing facilities for environmental protection and preservation equipment or service companies in Thailand.

KEY CONTACTS

Mr. Satit Sanonghpan
Deputy Director
US-Asia Environmental Partnership
American Embassy
Diethelm Tower A, Suite 303
93/1 Wireless Road
Bangkok 10330
Tel: 662-205-5301
Fax: 662-254-2838

Trade Promotion Opportunities
Entech Pollutec Asia -- Annually (usually in May or June)
CMP Media (Thailand) Co., Ltd.
41 Lertpanya Building, 8th Floor Suite 801
Soi Lertpanya, Sri Ayuthaya Road

For additional analytical, business and investment opportunities information,
please contact Global Investment & Business Center, USA
at (202) 546-2103. Fax: (202) 546-3275. E-mail: rusric@erols.com

Kwaeng Thanon Phayathai
Rajathewi, Bangkok 10400 Thailand
tel: (66 2) 642-6911-8; fax: (66 2) 642-6919-20
email: patcharin@cmpthailand.com   website: www.cmpthailand.com

World of Manufacturing Technology -- Annually (usually in June)
Reed Tradex Company
100/68-69, 32nd Fl., Sathorn Nakorn Tower,
North Sathorn Rd., Bangrak,
Bangkok 10500
telephone : (66 2) 636 7272, fax: (66 2) 636 7282
e-mail: ask@reedtradex.co.th   website : www.reedtradex.co.th

Special Notes

Enforcement of Regulations
For the most part, Thailand's environmental laws are rather stringent and meet most international standards for the country's level of development. The existence of tough environmental laws, however, does not translate directly into business opportunities, because the enforcement of these laws and regulations has been lax. Often, agencies and officers have insufficient power to act on their mandate because of Thailand's cumbersome legal system. Culture and tradition also mitigate against legal proceedings, with negotiation or third-party influence often used to settle disputes rather than formal proceedings.

Thailand also lacks an overriding enforcement agency. Jurisdictions overlap with little coordination between ministries, divisions and departments. It is not unusual for government entities to work at cross purposes and private companies can get caught in the crossfire. Furthermore, ministries mandated to promote economic growth and ministries mandated to enforce regulations can come into conflict. Similar conflicts can arise within ministries between promotion divisions and enforcement divisions.

Finally, low income levels within the civil service make employment in the private sector attractive, which leaves enforcement agencies critically short of staff competent to inspect and monitor industry. Low pay also increases a lax attitude toward corruption.

In recent years, environmental nongovernmental organizations and the media have increased environmental awareness of the public, which has brought some pressure on government agencies to enforce environmental regulations. Moreover, the PCD has recently seconded personnel to the Attorney General's office to aid investigating and prosecuting court cases related to environmental regulations.

In Thailand, like elsewhere, private companies adapt measures that help the environment for reasons not linked to laws and regulations. These include: reducing operating expenses, tax breaks, the need to meet international or corporate standards, or to boost corporate images.

The BOI and Environmental Protection
Thailand's Board of Investment has added to its list of "priority activities" projects that aim at preserving or protecting the environment. The BOI grants maximum promotional privileges to these projects, regardless of the investment zone in which they locate. These incentives include exemption from corporate income taxes and exemption or reduction in import duties for capital equipment. Besides benefiting US firms that want to manufacture environmental equipment,

For additional analytical, business and investment opportunities information,
please contact Global Investment & Business Center, USA
at (202) 546-2103. Fax: (202) 546-3275. E-mail: rusric@erols.com

these promotion incentives can also open opportunities for projects of US environmental service companies, which in turn would open opportunities for US technologies and equipment.

As of June 2002, the BOI had approved 12 projects in this category. Most focus on industrial and/or hazardous waste (9 projects), particularly recovery of slag (2 projects) and oil or chemicals (2 projects). Three projects deal with non-hazardous waste disposal and recycling that would include municipal solid waste.

Besides projects that receive BOI promotional incentives because they protect or preserve the environment, any project with BOI privileges can import duty free pollution control or environmental protection equipment.

To enhance environmental protection and preservation, the BOI's current policy (effective from August 1, 2000), encourages investors to locate within industrial estates, which already have such adequate infrastructure and environmental support as wastewater treatment, proper drainage and sewerage, and appropriate methods of solid waste disposal. Projects that locate in industrial estates receive greater levels of incentives than projects locating outside estates in the same zone.

Government Reform and Decentralization
The Thai government has embarked on massive reformation and reorganization programs with the main objective to decentralize power and responsibility. This is happening at two levels and will have short-term and a long-term impacts.

October 1, 2002 is the target date for a complete restructuring of the central government ministerial organizations. Ministries are being split and merged and generally shaken up. Departments are being stripped from some ministries and relocated to new ministries. Some departments are being dissolved and new departments are being created. A new ministry for the environment and natural resources is to be created from former MOSTE and forestry departments, but in mid-2002 details about the new structure (chains of command, specific areas of responsibility, even office arrangements) were not known. In the short term, confusion and some chaos is assured. Eventually things will be sorted out.

Of more consequence is the ongoing drive to relocate the focus of power and authority away from the central government to local governments. A major plank in this plan is the disbursement of public moneys to local governmental organizations. Currently, the central government controls how nearly all the revenue it collects is spent. This is changing. Since FY2001, 20% of central government revenues have been sent to local governments to administer. This percentage will increase to 35% in FY2006 and 80% by FY2010. Local governments are also – likely – to receive the power to levy taxes to support their own projects. Beyond the power of the budget, local governments are also to develop mature administrative organizations. For example, each local government body from subdistrict level to provincial level is to have an environmental committee to plan and oversee environmental projects in their locales.

Decentralization, which is enshrined in Thailand's 1997 Constitution, is changing the way the country governs itself and will affect the way US companies do business in Thailand.

Packaging Waste Reduction Legislation
Thai officials are preparing legislation that aims at reducing the volume of packaging materials in consumer goods. The legislation, which is probably at least four years away from enactment, will most likely include an excise tax on producers and importers of consumer goods. In mid-2002,

the PCD was consulting with business groups, including the Thai Federation of Industries, and drafting guidelines that will be used to draft the legislation.

ENERGY AUDITING AND CONSULTING SERVICES IN INDUSTRIES

Thailand implemented energy conservation legislation in 1992 but there appears to have been relatively little energy efficiency equipment investment over the past 10 years. The relatively low investment levels can be partially attributed to the after-effects of the 1997 financial crisis, as many firms are still not strong enough to fund new investments. Another factor contributing to the relatively low levels of investment is that the market for energy efficiency equipment is still in the early stages of development with industry players focusing on cultivating demand by educating the market and demonstrating the benefits of various types of energy efficient equipment.

Relevant government agencies seem committed to improving energy efficiency levels and are adopting new tactics to more effectively promote investments in energy efficient technology. Two pilot programs, consisting of a revolving fund and a subsidy program, will be launched in September 2002 and are expected to stimulate market demand for energy efficient investments.

The anticipated demand growth for energy efficient equipment is also expected to increase the demand for imported technology. Although some energy efficient technology is manufactured locally, the market is expected to rely on imports for the next several years, particularly for highly efficient or specialized equipment. Japanese imports appear to dominate the market, although U.S. suppliers do have a market presence and are considered to be leaders in gas turbine engines and chiller air conditioning systems. U.S. firms have the potential to increase their market share by demonstrating their commitment to the Thai market, providing after sales service and showing flexibility for Thai business practices.

The best energy efficient equipment sales prospects appear to be the 11 standard measures that are being promoted in conjunction with the investment subsidy program. The 11 measures are also the focus of the government's educational and promotional efforts, so it is likely that Thai facilities may be more inclined to invest in these measures as opposed to other types of equipment. The 11 standard measures consist of high frequency electronic ballasts, variable speed drives for air compressors and pumps, insulation, heat recovery equipment, controller of air supply for combustion, air-to-heat exchanger, high efficiency electric motors, luminaire reflectors and high efficiency fluorescent luminaries, power control for lighting and voltage regulators. Additionally, industry sources have indicated market potential for other types of equipment including gas turbines, inlet air cooling systems and high efficiency coal boilers.

The end-user segments with the strongest potential are financially stable firms in industrial sectors with relatively high energy consumption, or firms in commercial sectors that have long operating hours, such as hotels and department stores. Industry sources indicate that the food processing, textile, ceramics, metal manufacturing and power generation sectors seem to offer relatively good potential for energy efficient equipment. In the commercial sector, international retailers appear to offer particularly strong prospects.

Although considerable time and effort may be required to enter the market at this relatively early stage, industry sources agree that the best opportunity to gain market share is to enter the market and help to educate the market and create demand. Sources also recommend that new suppliers consider entering the market through a venture with a local company, as a local partner would have in-depth market knowledge, and an advantage in developing relationships with Thai customers and in understanding their needs and business practices.

For additional analytical, business and investment opportunities information, please contact Global Investment & Business Center, USA at (202) 546-2103. Fax: (202) 546-3275. E-mail: rusric@erols.com

MARKET HIGHLIGHTS AND BEST PROSPECTS

Market Profile

Thailand enacted energy conservation legislation in 1992 in the form of the Energy Conservation Promotion Act, together with a current $348.8 billion Energy Conservation Fund, to provide financial incentives to encourage energy efficient investment. Energy efficient investment and disbursements from the Fund have been extremely low, and concerned parties including Department of Energy Development and Promotion officials (DEDP), energy consultants and financial executives agree that attempts to encourage and promote energy efficiency have been largely unsuccessful.

Industry sources concur that the programs to date have failed to overcome the key barriers to energy efficient investment. The barriers hindering investment include a lack of confidence among facility owners in energy efficient technology, low business priority given to energy efficiency, lack of qualified energy consultants, financially weak companies that lack investment capital and excessively bureaucratic procedures involved in compliance with the Energy Conservation Promotion Act.

The DEDP is the government agency responsible for stimulating improvements in the energy efficiency of large factories and commercial buildings.   Facilities that meet the following criteria are considered to be "designated" facilities and fall under the supervision of the DEDP:

§   Peak electricity demand of 1,000 KW, or
§   1,175 KVA of total transformer, or
§   20 MMJ/yr. of energy

The designated facilities are required by the Energy Conservation Promotion Act to comply with the following regulations:

§   Appoint a person to be responsible for energy management
§   Maintain monthly records on energy consumption
§   Submit information on energy production, consumption and conservation
§   Set targets and plans for implementation of energy conservation
§   Implement the energy conservation measures according to the approved targets and plans
§   Assess and monitor the results of the energy conservation activities to ensure   that the energy conservation targets have been achieved

According to the Act, the energy conservation plans for designated buildings and factories must pertain to the measures specified in the following table.

Energy Conservation Measures in Designated Factories	Energy Conservation Measures in Designated Buildings
1. The use of energy-efficient machinery or equipment as well as the use of operational control systems and materials that contribute to energy conservation. 2. More efficient use of electricity through improvements in power factors,	1. Use and installation of machinery, equipment and materials that contribute to energy conservation in the building. 2. Efficient air-conditioning 3. Efficient lighting 4. Use of energy efficient construction

reduction of maximum power demand, use of appropriate equipment and other measures. 3. Prevention of energy loss. 4. Improvement in combustion efficiency of fuels. 5. Recycling of energy wastes. 6. Substitution of one type of energy for another. 7. Other means of energy conservation.	materials. 5. Use of operational control systems for machinery and equipment. 6. Reduction of heat from sunlight that enters the building. 7. Other means of energy conservation.

Although the implementation of energy efficient measures in the approximate 4,000 designated facilities is below industry expectations, a survey conducted by IIEC among selected designated facilities found that some basic improvements have been implemented. The most frequently implemented energy efficiency measures in the commercial sector tended to pertain to very basic improvements in lighting and air conditioning. The most common lighting improvements include installation of compact fluorescent lamps and low loss and electronic ballasts, as well as reducing the time that lights are used and reducing the number of lamps that are used. The most common air conditioning improvements consist of upgrading to a high efficiency chiller in addition to performing cleaning and maintenance and reducing the operating time. The industrial sector also implemented lighting improvements similar to that of the commercial sector, in addition to upgrading to high efficiency chillers, improving the combustion efficiency of boilers/furnaces, recovering condensate and reducing leakage from steam systems and reducing compressed air leakage.

Despite the current low levels of energy efficient investment, the IIEC estimated that the overall potential for energy efficient investment within designated facilities is between US $163 - $698 million over an approximate five to seven year period. The DEDP, the Energy Efficiency Association and local financial institutions are trying to adopt new strategies to effectively convert this market potential into actual energy efficient investments. Two major pilot programs, based on support from the Energy Conservation Fund, are being launched and will provide a revolving fund and subsidy schemes for energy efficient investments. The programs aim to reduce bureaucratic procedures and expedite the implementation of energy efficiency projects in designated facilities.

Statistical Data

MARKET SIZE (*US DOLLARS MILLIONS*)

	LAST Year 2001	CURRENT Year 2002	NEXT Year 2003	Projected Avg. Annual Growth Rate for following 2 Yrs.
Import Market	24.25	38.22	69.65	15%
Local Production	0.75	0.79	0.85	
Exports	0	0	0	
Total Market	25.0	39.0	70.5	
Imports from US	1.15	1.21	1.33	

SOURCES: Customs statistics and industry interviews.

Exchange Rates:
US $1 = 43 baht

Estimated Future Inflation Rate: 2%

Last Year's Import Market Share (Percent for US and Major Competitors):

> US: 4.60%,   Japan: 22.46% Germany: 5.86%

NOTES to Table:

1.   Market size estimates are based on interviews with industry sources and import statistics for electric motors, steam turbines, ballasts, boilers, air conditioners, burners, fluorescent lights, other automatic regulating or controlling instruments and apparatus with the following harmonized codes: 8501.100, 8501.200-005, 8501.310, 8501.340, 8501.400, 8501.320, 8501.330, 8501.510, 8501.610, 8501.620, 8501.520, 8501.530, 8406, 8402, 8403, 8404, 8505.100-100, 8415.810-005, 8416.100-17, 8539.310.003, 9032.890-003. This approach most likely results in an under-estimated market size.

2.   The above harmonized codes were used as they seem to most closely represent the equipment that is considered to be among the best prospects for the market. Please note that the codes are very broad and are NOT specific for energy efficient versions of the technology. After calculating the total import statistics for the above-mentioned products, the market for energy efficient technology was estimated to be 5% of the total import volume, based on industry sources that claim a 5% sales rate for energy efficient technology.

3.   Exports of energy efficient technology were assumed to be zero.

4.   Some energy efficient equipment can be manufactured or assembled locally, but production volumes and values were assumed to be very low.

5.   Import volume for the US was calculated as 5% of the actual import volume under the assumption that 5% would reflect imports of energy efficient equipment within the above-mentioned products and associated harmonized codes. US import growth was assumed to increase in tandem with market growth.

Market Size

It is extremely difficult to calculate the market size for energy efficient technology because statistics related to actual demand for energy efficient technology are not available. Industry experts are hesitant to offer estimates because they have been proven wrong in the past, when very optimistic market growth projections did not materialize. Some environmental experts, such as IIEC, have estimated overall market potential for energy efficient investments to be between $163 - $698 million between 2000 and 2007.   It is uncertain whether this will be achieved given the relatively low priority facility owners' give to energy efficient technology and the financial difficulties that many firms are facing.

The market size estimates show substantial increases in 2002 and 2003, mainly attributed to the DEDP's revolving fund and 30% subsidy programs that are described in the section on "Factors Influencing Demand." It was assumed that 25% of the $46.5 million revolving fund ($11.63 million) will be utilized in 2002, with the balance of approximately $35 million utilized to fund energy efficient equipment purchases in 2003.

Additionally, it was assumed that the 30% promotion subsidy targeted to designated facilities would generate investments of $7.6 million over the next two years. It was assumed that $3.8 million worth of investments would be made in 2003, with the balance made in 2004. It was also assumed that the potential 30% subsidy program targeted to SMEs would be approved, and would generate a total of $7 million worth of investment split equally between 2003 and 2004.

**For additional analytical, business and investment opportunities information,
please contact Global Investment & Business Center, USA
at (202) 546-2103. Fax: (202) 546-3275. E-mail: rusric@erols.com**

Besides the investment growth attributed to the revolving fund and the subsidy programs, it was assumed that non-promotional related investment would grow by approximately 5% in 2002, as industry sources indicate that the market seems to be showing a slight improvement over 2001. It is assumed that non-promotional investment growth will be 10% in 2003 as market awareness and understanding of energy efficient equipment improves.

The market growth rates for beyond 2003 will depend upon whether the government will continue to offer special investment funding and subsidy programs. If the current loan and subsidy programs are successful, it seems somewhat likely that the government would consider initiating other programs.

Factors Influencing Demand

Positive factors influencing demand for energy efficient technology

The most promising factors that may positively influence the demand for energy efficient technology are new government financial support programs that have been designed to make it quicker and easier for facilities to obtain funding than in the past. The funds are targeted to designated facilities and consist of a low interest revolving fund geared to major energy efficiency investments and a 30% investment subsidy program primarily for specific general efficiency measures.

By providing support and encouragement particularly for the standard measures investments, the DEDP hopes to achieve a critical mass of awareness, satisfaction and understanding that will stimulate overall market demand. It is expected that as more facilities invest in even basic types of energy efficient equipment, management may realize the benefits of these investments and may be inclined to make additional investments, perhaps in larger, more comprehensive projects. As more and more facilities invest in energy efficient technology, there may be a ripple effect as "word-of-mouth" advice encourages even more facilities to consider energy efficient investments.

It appears that the DEDP's technical promotional activities may be starting to exert a positive influence on the market, at least for certain types of energy efficient equipment. A major international equipment manufacturer was surprised that this year customers are actually coming to them to ask about energy efficient equipment. The manufacturer attributes this new interest to DEDP's educational and promotional campaigns.

Revolving Fund

A US $46.5 million revolving fund targeted to energy efficient investments in designated facilities is expected to be launched in September 2002. The Energy Conservation Fund released the money to the DEDP as a zero interest loan payable in 7 years. Private sector banks are participating in the program and will lend money from the revolving fund in support of energy efficient investments at a maximum interest rate of 4%. The credit limit is approximately US $1.1 million. The establishment of the energy efficient revolving fund is related to previous World Bank initiatives to support the development of an Energy Service Company (ESCO) industry in Thailand. There is also a possibility of obtaining a loan guarantee facility through the World Bank from the Global Energy Fund.

The Industrial Finance Corporation of Thailand (IFCT), together with selected commercial banks will manage the funds. The banks will be responsible for administering all aspects of the loan including marketing, technical/economic assessment, credit approval and loan repayment. The following financial institutions will be participating in the program: IFCT, Bank Thai, Bangkok

Bank, Bank of Ayudhya, Siam Commercial Bank, Krung Thai Bank, Thai Military Bank and Siam City Bank.

Although the DEDP has out-sourced almost all of the program, the banks will be supported by DEDP consultants and DANIDA. A consulting team consisting of professors and researchers from the Energy Research Institute of Chulalongkorn University will review the applications for compliance with the Energy Conservation Promotion Act. The consultants will act as a point of reference and will provide assistance to banks and facility owners as needed.

Involvement of the commercial banking sector is an important factor that can contribute to the future sustainability of energy efficient investments. Through participation in this pilot revolving fund program, local banks will gain understanding and experience in energy efficient projects and develop important contacts with key players such as ESCOs. It is expected that when the pilot program is over, the banks will continue lending to other energy efficient investment projects.

30% subsidy scheme

A two-year, US $2.33 million standard measures and individual project subsidy program is expected to be launched in September 2002. The program is being funded by the Energy Conservation Fund and aims to jump-start energy efficient investment among designated facilities. Under the program, designated firms will receive up to a 30% subsidy of total investment costs, up to a maximum of approximately US $46 thousand per facility. Facilities will have an option to either invest in 11 pre-approved, standard efficiency measures or they may propose their own individual energy efficient investment program. The 11 standard measures that have been selected by the DEDP are listed in the "Best Sales Prospects" section of the report.

It is hoped that by encouraging investment in the relatively small general measures, the subsidy program may help to increase awareness and confidence in energy efficient equipment, to ultimately ignite market demand for other energy efficient investments outside of the program.

Potential Subsidy Program for Small and Medium Sized Enterprises
(non-designated facilities)

The National Energy Policy Office (NEPO), which oversees energy efficiency in non-designated, small and medium enterprises, is considering a two-year US $2.1 million subsidy proposal to support investment in the 11 general measures among these smaller facilities. The initial proposal would cap the subsidy at 30% of investment costs with a preliminary average subsidy of approximately US $2,300 per facility. It is not known when, or if, this program may be approved.

Factors hindering the demand for energy efficient technology

Perhaps one of the main factors hindering demand is the fact that despite enacting energy conservation legislation in 1992, the concepts of energy conservation and efficiency are still quite new and not well-understood. One industry source explained that market is currently at the developmental level of demonstrating the various energy efficient technologies to educate the market about the benefits. He explained that overall there is almost no demand for energy efficient equipment, and that the various market players including bankers, the DEDP, equipment manufacturers, industry associations, energy consultants and ESCOs are promoting the energy efficiency concept in an effort to create demand.

**For additional analytical, business and investment opportunities information,
please contact Global Investment & Business Center, USA
at (202) 546-2103. Fax: (202) 546-3275. E-mail: rusric@erols.com**

Since the market is so new, several hindrances seem to stem from a lack of trust and confidence in the equipment and a perceived low priority for energy efficient equipment. Additionally, many firms are still suffering from the economic crisis and are not financially strong enough to make major investments. The most common hindrances encountered by industry players, along with some potential solutions, are presented below.

Market Hindrances	Potential Solutions
Customer not confident the equipment will perform as expected, do not believe the equipment will save as much energy as expected	§ Demonstrate the equipment to the customer and measure the difference in energy consumption when using the energy efficient equipment § Provide customer with equipment warranty, contract or other means of guaranteeing equipment performance
Low priority given to energy efficient equipment vis-à-vis daily operation, marketing and sales	§ Organize training seminars to demonstrate equipment and explain the potential benefits. Top management should be included in educational efforts because in most cases, the senior executive ultimately makes the purchase decision, not the engineer. § Show that equipment can pay for itself within a relatively short time period (i.e., 3-4 years) § Target facilities in sectors that generally have high energy usage. For example, a potentially strong commercial sector may be hotels because they operate 24 hrs. a day, 7 days a week.
Period of relatively slow economic growth characterized by excess capacity levels and very few expansion projects	§ Some industry players try to convince companies to make energy efficient investments this year to be prepared for next year when the economy is expected to be stronger and they may be working at full capacity. § Some consultants promote energy efficiency as a good investment that may generate energy savings of approximately 10-15%, compared to extremely low bank deposit rates
Many companies are still in a somewhat weak financial situation as a result of the economic crisis and nay have difficulty buying the equipment or obtaining financing	§ Offer flexible payment terms such as installments or an ESCO-type plan § Provide technical assistance to support the customer in preparing loan applications and bid proposals § Specifically target firms that are in relatively good financial condition, such as

For additional analytical, business and investment opportunities information, please contact Global Investment & Business Center, USA at (202) 546-2103. Fax: (202) 546-3275. E-mail: rusric@erols.com

	strong, export-oriented firms

Best Sales Prospects

Included among the best sales prospects in the Thai energy efficient equipment market are the 11 standard measures that have been identified by the DEDP for promotion to approximately 4,000 designated facilities over the next 2 years. Although in certain instances, locally manufactured products are beginning to supplement imports and competition may be relatively strong in some categories, these 11 measures are considered to be among the best sales prospects for two key reasons. First, these products have the endorsement of the DEDP and are the focus of DEDP promotional and educational campaigns. In this respect, the DEDP is helping to create and develop market demand for these products. Secondly, these 11 measures qualify for financial subsidies to encourage investment and to potentially make it possible for firms to invest in equipment that might not otherwise have been affordable.

In addition to the 11 standard measures, a number of other types of energy efficient technology have been identified as potentially strong sales prospects based on interviews with industry experts.

11 Pre-Approved Standard Measures Promoted under the 30% Subsidy Scheme

1. **High frequency electronic ballasts**
2. It may become increasingly difficult for international suppliers to compete in the electronic ballast market due to increasing local competition. According to industry sources there are some local suppliers who sell their electronic ballasts for 250 baht compared to an approximate price of 1,000 baht for imported brands. The locally-made ballasts are covered by a 5 year warranty. Due to the generally high cost of electronic ballasts, particularly the imported brands, the best sales opportunities may be found in factories that operate 24 hours a day and require a lot of lighting, such as electronics factories. Commercial buildings with long hours of operation may also offer sales potential. A retail sales option that is used by Philips is to sell imported electronic ballasts at modern international retail outlets such as Tesco Lotus and Carrefour.

3. **Variable speed drive on air compressors**
4. Although most industries, including chemical, electronic, ceramic and metal, use compressed air, the market for variable speed drives on air compressors is only just starting to develop. Factors that have hindered the market development include the perception that this is very new and advanced technology and that it is more complicated to apply VSDs on air compressors than it is on pumps.

5. **Variable speed drive on pumps**
6. The use of VSDs on pumps is more prevalent in Thailand than the application on air compressors. Almost all engineering processes use pumps, providing many potential applications for VSDs. The application of VSDs on pumps is relatively well-proven and less expensive and easier to apply compared to VSDs on air compressors. Air conditioning systems in Thailand are generally not designed to include VSDs, so theoretically there is large market potential for this application.

7. **Insulation of pipes and surfaces**

For additional analytical, business and investment opportunities information, please contact Global Investment & Business Center, USA at (202) 546-2103. Fax: (202) 546-3275. E-mail: rusric@erols.com

8. The DEDP is specifically promoting the following types of materials for heating / cooling surface insulation: glass wool, polyurethane foam, polyethylene foam, cellulose fiber, closed cell elastomeric thermal insulation. For heating reflective insulation, the DEDP is focusing on ceramic coating and aluminum foil.

9. Heat recovery equipment
10. Heat recovery equipment can be important in improving the efficiency of thermal systems. It can be applied to a variety of media such as steam, hot oil, and water, from which heat can be recovered for use in production processes. Boilers and hot oil systems may have strong potential for heat recovery equipment, particularly in food processing, chemical and textile sectors. Thai companies can manufacture heat recovery equipment for applications in normal systems such as with water, but specialized applications such as for certain chemicals, will require imported equipment.

11. Controller of air supply for combustion
12. A controller of air supply for combustion is used to measure oxygen content in exhaust gas to then control the input between fuel input and oxygen levels to assure optimum combustion for boilers and furnaces.

13. Air-to-air heat exchanger
14. Air-to-air heat exchangers can be applied anywhere that there is a difference in the temperature of two air streams. The most common applications of air-to-air heat exchangers are in air conditioning systems in which cool exhaust air can be used to pre-cool incoming air streams. Some local companies are assembling this equipment in Thailand using imported steel plates.

15. High efficiency electric motors
16. High efficiency electric motors have applications in almost all industrial sectors. The market is supplied by imports, as high efficiency electric motors are not manufactured locally.

17. Luminaire reflectors and high efficiency fluorescent luminaries
18. These are fixtures that generate more reflected fluorescent light than standard luminaries, and can provide an equal amount of light with fewer fluorescent tubes. Luminaries are manufactured locally, although the top-end luminaries are imported.

19. Power control for lighting
20. Power control for lighting uses electronic ballasts and sensors to control lighting systems. These systems use sensors to monitor light levels in a room, such as the amount of sunlight, and can adjust the levels of fluorescent light by dimming or increasing the brightness as appropriate.

21. Voltage regulator
Voltage regulators adjust incoming voltage as appropriate and control voltage fluctuations. They are particularly applicable for facilities that are either very close or very far from electricity sub-stations, as these facilities tend to receive voltage that is either too high or too low. Voltage regulators can also be used to adjust lighting levels. The main applications for voltage regulators tend to be in the commercial sector, particularly those with extended hours of operation such as hotels and department stores. The main market consists of businesses that operate 24 hours a day on a daily basis.

Additional energy efficient equipment opportunities

Discussions with industry experts from among ESCOs, equipment manufacturers and energy consultants indicate a potential local market need for additional energy efficient technology besides the 11 standard efficiency measures targeted by the DEDP. In some cases, the industry experts have recommended complex, comprehensive systems such as co-generation, while in other cases they have suggested specialized equipment that may be very new to the market but which, based on their industry experience, they feel represents a potential opportunity for US manufacturers.

Co-generation including gas turbine and gas engines
Industry sources indicate a potentially strong market for co-generation, as a co-generation system has the ability to dramatically improve a plant's operational efficiency. Potential end-users would include private sector industry as well as public sector power plants. The gas turbine market is also expected to expand, in part due to the growth potential of co-generation systems. The demand for gas engines may also grow in factories that have relatively low steam consumption.

Inlet air cooling system
The demand for inlet air cooling systems would be related to demand for gas turbine engines, as this system improves the efficiency of gas turbine engines. Thailand has a very hot climate and since hot air is light, this reduces the efficiency of the turbines. The inlet air cooling system cools the air and increases air density to improve turbine efficiency. This technology is very new to Thailand and is being used in approximately three private sector factories. An energy consultant explained that the current users are very secretive about this technology because they consider it to be a very important business advantage.

Efficient chillers and chiller management technology
Although the market for energy efficient chillers is expected to be strong, it is already dominated by Trane, Carrier and York, and it may be quite difficult for new entrants to compete against these entrenched players. On the other hand, there appears to be a potentially strong market for good quality, reasonably priced, chiller management technology. The major chiller manufacturers do offer chiller management technology but an industry source claims that nobody uses it because it is too expensive. There is no local production of chiller management technology. The industry source estimated the potential market size for good quality, reasonably priced chiller management technology to be approximately 60% of designated facilities.

High efficiency coal boilers
Fuel oil boilers are commonly used in Thailand, but as the price of fuel oil has doubled in the past few years, this is now an expensive option and factories are starting to consider coal-fired boilers. The most popular size is 10 tons. Although coal-fired boilers can be made locally and are also imported from India, China and Germany, industry sources believe that a US manufacturer has an opportunity to differentiate itself by supplying a high efficiency coal boiler.

Burners
Industry sources indicate that there is a potentially strong market for burners for use with existing boilers and furnaces. Burners would be particularly important for industries that have relatively high energy costs, such as glass and ceramics industries.

Motor optimization

For additional analytical, business and investment opportunities information, please contact Global Investment & Business Center, USA at (202) 546-2103. Fax: (202) 546-3275. E-mail: rusric@erols.com

The motor optimization market is relatively new, as it was just launched in 2001 when Powerboss entered the market. The main applications are for motors that turn on and off quickly, such as those used in plastic injection molding and ice making.

Ozone laundry system

Large hospitals and large five star hotels represent potential markets for ozone laundry systems. This represents a potential opportunity to save energy and other costs as it eliminates the need use hot water and cleaning chemicals in the laundry process, and requires only one rinse cycle.

Process Improvements

In addition to the potential market opportunities previously described, industry sources concur that there is a market for energy efficiency process improvements. Sources say that this represents an unmet market need.

COMPETITIVE ANALYSIS

Domestic Production

Local manufacturers are producing energy efficient equipment, mainly lighting supplies, insulation and non-specialized varieties of other equipment. It appears that domestic production is strongest in the areas of lighting improvements, particularly regarding the production of electronic ballasts, and it may be difficult to compete with the locally produced electronic ballasts that are considerably less expensive than the imported variety. The production of other types of energy efficient equipment would mainly involve relatively basic applications.

Major Local Suppliers and Brands of Selected Energy Efficient Equipment
Available in the Thai Market

Insulation Products: Aeroflex, ECI, Lamtex, Home Insulation, Cool or Cosy, Miccell, Micro Fiber, SFG, Cera Cote

Voltage Regulators: Silicon Power Supply, Advance Electric

Lighting Improvements: Luso, Delight, Metrolight, Babcock-Hunsa, Jatabac, Schneider, X-tra Lux, Silverbell, X-tra Brite, TEI, PC-Lux, Linear, BEC, VS, Advanced Electric

Steam boilers / burners: Babcock-Hunsa, Jatabac, Schneider,

3rd – Country Imports

It is expected that imports will continue to be an important source of energy efficient equipment for the next several years, particularly regarding high efficiency and specialized equipment.

Although Thailand sources supplies from a variety of nations, including Europe, the U.S. and Japan, Japanese equipment seems to dominate the overall import market. It appears that Japanese suppliers may have an edge over European and American firms in the area of customer relations. Industry sources explain that Japanese firms, being Asians, seem to have a relatively better understanding of doing business with other Asians, such as Thais. The Japanese advantage seems to be that they generally understand Thai business practices regarding issues such as contract negotiation and pricing. Thais may also feel more comfortable doing business with fellow Asians as compared to Europeans or Americans.

For additional analytical, business and investment opportunities information,
please contact Global Investment & Business Center, USA
at (202) 546-2103. Fax: (202) 546-3275. E-mail: rusric@erols.com

Another strong Japanese advantage, particularly over American firms, is that Thais perceive Japanese companies to be very serious and committed about doing business in Thailand. Sources mention that Japanese firms will assist their Thai customers with developing project proposals and bid documents, something that American firms usually do not do.

Another factor contributing to the strength of Japanese imports is the relatively large number of Japanese-owned factories in Thailand that purchase their equipment from Japanese suppliers.

Major Competitive Suppliers and Brands of Selected Energy Efficient Equipment
Available in the Thai Market

Insulation Products: CPAC (Australia)

Voltage Regulators: Mutsumi (Japan)

Lighting Improvements: Osram (Germany); Philips (Netherlands); Matsusita, National (Japan); Sumtobel, Atco,(Australia)

Steam boilers / burners: Wanson, Wiefhaept, Zanker,(Germany); Baltur, Naval, Riello (Italy); Prime Life (Singapore); Oilon (Finland); Nuway (U.K.); Ever Hot (Australia)

Motor Optimization: Powerboss (U.K.)

Variable Speed Drives: Danfoss (Denmark), Siemens (Germany)

Controller of Air Supply for Combustion: Yokogawa (Japan)

High Efficiency Electric Motors: Mitsubishi, Hitachi (Japan); Siemens (Germany); ABB

Gas Turbine (30MW+): Mitsubishi (Japan), Rolls Royce (U.K.)

US Market Position

Despite a reputation for leading-edge technology in certain cases, the general impression of American firms is that they are not serious enough about doing business in Thailand and that Thailand seems to be a relatively low priority for many American firms. Although U.S. suppliers are market leaders for certain energy efficient equipment such as chiller air conditioning systems, co-generation and gas turbine engines, Thai perceptions about a low commitment to the local market may be hindering overall sales potential for U.S energy efficient technology.

Thai industry sources generally feel that many American manufacturers do not want to expend effort to gain sales and market share, instead the impression seems to be that American firms just want to sit back and take orders. In comparison, sources explain that Japanese firms are known to work with local players to help market their products and even help to prepare bid proposals.

Some Thais also seem to have doubts about American firms' market commitment, particularly related to after-sales service and the ability to obtain spare parts. Thais seem to have more confidence in some European brands that either have factories in Thailand or have dealers who provide after-sales service and maintain a stock of spare parts.

For additional analytical, business and investment opportunities information,
please contact Global Investment & Business Center, USA
at (202) 546-2103. Fax: (202) 546-3275. E-mail: rusric@erols.com

To improve their image and sales potential in Thailand, industry sources recommend that American firms consider the following options for gaining the trust of the Thai market:

§   Be more proactive in sales efforts, such as providing support to energy consultants, for example, who are bidding on potential projects
§   Show concern and commitment for after-sales service and provide spare parts stock
§   Introduce advanced technology or improvements over current technology levels at competitive prices
§   Be more flexible about contract terms and negotiations

Major U.S. Suppliers and Brands of Selected Energy Efficient Equipment Available in the Thai Market

Insulation Products: Token, Tarsec, Cell Pro

Voltage Regulators: Superior Electric

Lighting Improvements: GE, Sylvania

Steam boilers / burners: Kewanee, Hurst, Cleaver-Brooks, Fulton, Maxon

Chiller Systems: Carrier, Trane, York

Variable Speed Drives: Reliance

Controller of Air Supply for Combustion: Honeywell

High Efficiency Electric Motors: GE

Gas Turbine (1-10 MW): Solar Turbine

Gas Turbine (30 MW+): GE, Pratt & Whitney

END-USER ANALYSIS

The main challenge facing suppliers of energy efficient equipment is to find financially strong sectors that have either the investment funds on hand or the ability to secure financing to fund the investments. Another consideration in targeting end-users is whether a firm is in an energy-intensive sector, in which case it may be favorably inclined to invest in energy efficient equipment as this could represent substantial energy savings. In the commercial sector, the facilities that operate 24 hours a day, 7 days a week, such as hotels, hospitals and some shopping centers / department stores seem to represent potentially strong prospects for energy efficient equipment.

This section presents the opinions and experiences of several industry experts including energy consultants, ESCOs, and equipment distributors and suppliers regarding the industry sectors that seem to offer the most potential in the Thai market. These are either the sectors and equipment types that the industry experts are currently targeting, or the sectors that have been showing interest in various types of energy efficient technology. Following this current compilation of industry players' opinions are tables that present investment potential in designated facilities for main types of energy efficient equipment according to industry sector. These charts are from an IIEC study conducted in 2000 regarding ESCO development in Thailand.

Industry Experts' Opinions About Important End-User Sectors

Food processing
§   Factories in the food processing sector that require electricity and steam represent potential markets for co-generation and heat recovery equipment.
§   The frozen food sector may also be a potential market for refrigeration improvements.
§   The most promising firms within the food processing sector would be those with strong export sales, as they may have relatively strong finances.

Textiles
§   The large, high quality textile factories seem to offer the best investment potential as they may be in relatively stable financial condition.
§   Equipment with the best market potential includes variable speed drives for motors.
§   Co-generation with steam may be used for wet processes, mainly for drying and spinning the cloth, as this is a main energy consumption area.
§   Older factories may be ready to replace their old air conditioning systems with efficient chiller systems.
§   The DEDP is specifically targeting this sector for promotions and seminars related to energy efficient technology.

Ceramics
§   Ceramics factories tend to have high energy costs relative to total production costs, with most of the energy costs attributed to the furnace. Sources say that the Thai ceramics industry has higher costs compared to some other countries, and that the sector needs to trim costs to stay competitive. Investments in energy efficient technology would be one way to reduce production costs to maintain competitiveness.
§   Potential energy efficient equipment needs include burners for existing boilers and furnaces, co-generation, heat recovery equipment, high efficiency motors and chillers for the cooling processes.

Aluminum
§   Factories in the aluminum sector have potential needs for a variety of energy efficient equipment including co-generation in which the exhaust heat can be used to heat the raw material, motor optimization equipment, variable speed drives, and motor control devices to match the energy input with the workload.

Electricity Generating Authority of Thailand
§   Industry sources claim that power plants owned by the State-run Electricity Generating Authority of Thailand (EGAT) may have opportunities for energy efficiency improvements, but that it does not seem likely that EGAT will consider efficiency improvements at this time.
§   Sources state that the plants generally operate at under 40% efficiency, and that the plants could use combined cycle to recover the waste heat to produce additional electricity and improve the efficiency to about 45%. Inlet air cooling systems may also be applicable to improve the efficiency of gas turbine engines.

Independent Power Producers and Small Power Producers
§   Potentially more promising alternatives to EGAT are the Independent Power Producers and Small Power Producers. These are private firms, under EGAT regulatory supervision, from which EGAT buys power to supplement its supply. These firms tend to have foreign partners and sources say they may be receptive to efficiency improvements, such as inlet air cooling systems.

For additional analytical, business and investment opportunities information,
please contact Global Investment & Business Center, USA
at (202) 546-2103. Fax: (202) 546-3275. E-mail: rusric@erols.com

Hotels
§   Four-and-five-star hotels, and other businesses that operate 24 hours a day, seem to offer potential for voltage regulators. It seems like hotels prefer to test the equipment at one property, and if it works well, they consider expanding to other properties.
§   Air conditioning and lighting system improvements may also offer strong potential.
§   Demand control systems are popular among relatively large hotels such as the Pan Pacific, Regency Park, Novotel Siam Square, Amari Atrium.
§   Ozone laundry systems may have potential at large hotels.

Hospitals
§   Hospitals may be potentially good candidates for air conditioning system improvements and lighting improvements including electronic ballasts, reflectors and energy efficient bulbs.
§   Large hospitals may also offer potential for ozone laundry systems.

International Retailers
§   The international retail sector, including Tesco Lotus, Carrefour, Makro and Big C may offer strong potential for a variety of energy efficient equipment. These retailers have foreign partners and tend to be in relatively good financial condition. Additionally, the foreign partners may also have a general understanding of the benefits of energy efficient equipment.

IIEC Energy Efficient Market Potential Estimates for Designated Facilities
by Industry Sector

Industrial Sector / technology type	Total # Designated Factories	Estimated Achievable Facilities *	Energy Efficient Technology Investment Potential (US $)
Chemical	378	76	
A/C cleaning & maintenance			95,071
Absorption chiller			42,355,702
Air pressure leak reduction			1,450,465
Combustion efficiency improvement			447,754
Condensate tank retrofit			527,442
Economizer for boiler			4,219,535
Electronic thermostat			182,672
Luminaire and reflector retrofit			2,999,618
Steam leakage reduction			1,142,791
Steam trap retrofit			140,651
Production process improvement			9,135,117
Total			62,696,819

* Assumes 20% of total designated factories will potentially invest in energy efficient technology
Source: IIEC Thailand ESCO Development Project, 2000

Industrial Sector / technology type	Total # Designated Factories	Estimated Achievable Facilities *	Energy Efficient Technology Investment Potential (US $)
Fabricated Metal	527	105	
Energy-efficient air compressor			25,737,209
Combustion efficiency improvement			404,442
Electronic thermostat			236,326
Luminaire and reflector retrofit			2,885,141
Steam trap retrofit			46,572
Transformer capacity matching			68,633
Ventilation fan retrofit			73,535
Production process improvement			19,503,864
Total			48,955,722

* Assumes 20% of total designated factories will potentially invest in energy efficient technology
Source: IIEC Thailand ESCO Development Project, 2000

Industrial Sector / technology type	Total # Designated Factories	Estimated Achievable Facilities *	Energy Efficient Technology Investment Potential (US $)
Food & Beverage	517	103	
Building insulation			1,934,782
Combustion efficiency improvement			1,435,432
Compact fluorescent lamp			216,462
Condensate recycling system retrofit			28,855,814
Cooling system control improvement			25,489,302
Economizer for boiler			12,023,256

Electronic thermostat			238,301
Luminaire and reflector retrofit			2,302,699
Steam piping insulation			672,869
Production process improvement			8,574,445
Total			81,743,363

* Assumes 20% of total designated factories will potentially invest in energy efficient technology
Source: IIEC Thailand ESCO Development Project, 2000

Industrial Sector / technology type	Total # Designated Factories	Estimated Achievable Facilities *	Energy Efficient Technology Investment Potential (US $)
Non-Metallic	119	24	
A/c cleaning & maintenance			4,871
A/c package retrofit			464,199
Air compressor retrofit			1,549,767
Combustion efficiency improvement			38,744
Electronic ballast			108,177
Electronic thermostat			87,983
High efficiency motor			1,046,348
Low-loss ballast			256,758
Luminaire and reflector retrofit			240,232
Motor speed controller (inverter)			959,071
Production process improvement			4,626,189
Total			9,382,340

* Assumes 20% of total designated factories will potentially invest in energy efficient technology
Source: IIEC Thailand ESCO Development Project, 2000

Industrial Sector / technology type	Total # Designated Factories	Estimated Achievable Facilities *	Energy Efficient Technology Investment Potential

For additional analytical, business and investment opportunities information,
please contact Global Investment & Business Center, USA
at (202) 546-2103. Fax: (202) 546-3275. E-mail: rusric@erols.com

			(US $)
Textile	**316**	**63**	
A/c cleaning and maintenance			74,738
Blow down system retrofit			1,014,140
Combustion efficiency improvement			52,912
Compact fluorescent lamp			72,753
Electronic ballast			2,994,563
Electronic thermostat			145,262
Fluorescent tube lamp (high efficiency)			826,083
High efficiency motor			2,726,618
Low loss ballast			660,078
Luminaire and reflector retrofit			2,186,667
Steam trap retrofit			414,107
Production process improvement			31,591,688
Total			**42,759,609**

* Assumes 20% of total designated factories will potentially invest in energy efficient technology
Source: IIEC Thailand ESCO Development Project, 2000

Industrial Sector / technology type	Total # Designated Factories	Estimated Achievable Facilities *	Energy Efficient Technology Investment Potential (US $)
Paper	80	16	
A/c cleaning & maintenance			7,070
Boiler retrofit			2,306,977
Combustion efficiency improvement			35,349
Compact fluorescent lamp			26,566
Electronic thermostat			105,674
Low-loss ballast			31,039
Luminaire and reflector retrofit			215,381
Production process improvement			2,270,277
Total			4,998,333

For additional analytical, business and investment opportunities information,
please contact Global Investment & Business Center, USA
at (202) 546-2103. Fax: (202) 546-3275. E-mail: rusric@erols.com

*Assumes 20% of total designated factories will potentially invest in energy efficient technology

Source: IIEC Thailand ESCO Development Project, 2000

Commercial Sector / technology type	Total # Designated Buildings	Estimated Achievable Facilities *	Energy Efficient Technology Investment Potential (US $)
Office	574	114	
A/c package retrofit			1,216,036
Building insulation			4,024,205
Compact fluorescent lamp			70,816
Electronic ballast			3,087,105
Low-loss ballast			1,628,278
Luminaire and reflector retrofit			13,393,583
Window film			1,861,223
Office total			25,281,245
Shopping Center	201	40	
Chiller system retrofit			12,564,837
Compact fluorescent lamp			69,287
Electronic ballast			6,874,331
Low-loss ballast			692,260
Luminaire and reflector retrofit			1,080,679
Room key switches			7,011,628
Shopping Center total			28,293,022
Hotel	256	51	
Building insulation			3,091,769
Chiller system retrofit			4,762,791
Compact fluorescent lamp			1,417,755
Electronic ballast			2,124,217
Low-loss ballast			120,934
Luminaire and reflector retrofit			1,307,100

Room key switches			2,027,520
Hotel total			14,852,086
Hospital	207	41	
A/c cleaning & maintenance			111,275
A/c package retrofit			69,802
Building insulation			1,944,115
Compact fluorescent lamp			174,671
Electronic ballast			1,487,627
Low-loss ballast			918,479
Hospital total			4,705,970
Commercial Sector Total			73,132,323

*Assumes 20% of total designated factories will potentially invest in energy efficient technology
Source: IIEC Thailand ESCO Development Project, 2000

MARKET ACCESS

Import Climate

The Energy Conservation Promotion Act permits an import duty reduction down to 5% for machinery and equipment that meets the following criteria:

§ Enhances or replaces existing machinery / processes with energy efficient equipment
§ Recycles industrial waste or exhausted energy
§ Uses alternative sources of energy other than electricity or petroleum products

The person eligible to appeal for duty reduction must meet one of the following criteria:

1. Importer of subject items for use in own operations
2. Distributor / importing distributor of subject items
3. Buyers for own use

An application for duty reduction must be obtained from the Technology Promotion Division of the Ministry of Science, Technology and Environment. Applications will be reviewed on a case-by-case basis by the Department of Energy Development and Promotion.

An appeal for duty reduction must be made prior to importing the subject item(s), so that the importer can use the official letter in seeking duty reduction with the Customs Department at point of entry.

Documents required for the duty reduction Appeal include the following:

1. Appeal letter
2. 13 copies of application form
3. 13 copies of invoice
4. 13 copies of catalog and specifications of subject item(s)
5. 3 copies of Company Registration issued by Ministry of Commerce
6. 3 copies of license to operate industrial plant
7. In case the license to operate industrial plant is expired, 3 copies of
   a. petition for license to operate industrial plant must be submitted
8. 3 copies of floor plan where subject item(s) will be installed
9. Other documents such as Packing List and Bill of Lading
10. The importing distributor who is importing the product for sale to end-
    a. users must also submit the following:

-    Purchase contract between importer and buyer
-    Certified letter for every purchase transaction between importer and final end-user
-    Company registration for the end-user company

An initial duty reduction assessment can be made by submitting the product and specifications to the Technology Promotion Division of the Ministry of Science, Technology and Environment. A handbook, in the Thai language, outlining the complete regulations for the duty reduction is available from the Technology Promotion Division of the Ministry of Science, Technology and Environment.

This appears to be a long process and the duty reduction is not granted until the equipment has been installed and tested to be sure that it meets energy efficient standards. The duty reduction program has not been well publicized and many equipment importers and industry sources are not aware of it. In 2001, duty reduction applications were submitted and are pending for the eight items listed below.

Duty-reduction applications submitted in 2001

Equipment Type	Country of Origin	Brand	Size	Quantity
Voltage regulator	Japan	Mutsumi	1500 KVA	2
			1750 KVA	1
Diesel engine with generator set	USA	Caterpillar	70kW	2
VRM ID Fan, Retrofit Modification	Japan	Hamada Blower	14,100 m3 / min	1
Steam turbine generator	Japan	Shinko	6,000 kW	2

The process for import tax reduction may be simplified and the approval process may be changed from a case-by-case basis to a type approval basis. Under a type approval process, minimum energy efficiency standards would be established and all products of the same type that pass the performance criteria would automatically be approved for the duty tax reduction. This kind of revised system will reduce the time for necessary for the request and approval of the duty reduction. It is not known when the program modifications may go into effect.

Distribution

Distribution Structure

The main players in the energy efficiency market seem to be energy consultants, equipment suppliers / manufacturers and ESCOs. The local Energy Conservation Entrepreneurs Association is trying to encourage a separation in the market between consulting services and equipment suppliers to prevent potential conflicts of interest. The association encourages consultants to be unbiased in their proposals and equipment recommendations. The market structure can be described as follows:

§   Firms that sell the whole solution, that is, firms which have a consulting / design division as well as an equipment supply division within the same company.

§   Equipment manufacturers / suppliers who enter into contracts with energy and engineering consultants to provide consulting, design and installation services.

§   Equipment manufacturers / suppliers that have internal sales consulting divisions to educate potential customers about the benefits and applications of their equipment.

§   ESCO / energy consultants that provide performance guarantee contracts, but that have no relationship with equipment suppliers.

§   ESCO / suppliers and manufacturers that provide performance guarantee contracts for their own equipment.

§   ESCO / construction contractors that serve as the main contractor for a project but have no relationship with equipment suppliers.

New Market Entrants

Sources recommend that a new supplier should consider entering the market through some type of venture with a local company. The benefits that a local partner would bring include in-depth knowledge of local industrial and commercial sectors, and the ability to develop relationships with local customers and understand their needs and requirements regarding contract terms and negotiations.

US equipment manufacturers that are interested in considering a local business partner can contact the Energy Conservation Entrepreneurs Association for assistance in reaching potential energy efficient equipment distributors.

New entrants should be prepared to spend considerable time and effort in promotional and sales activities. Industry sources concur that the sales success rate averages about 5%, and it generally takes about one year to negotiate a contract and 1.5 years for implementation, depending upon the project type. Although entering the market at such an early stage can be

For additional analytical, business and investment opportunities information,
please contact Global Investment & Business Center, USA
at (202) 546-2103. Fax: (202) 546-3275. E-mail: rusric@erols.com

relatively difficult, industry sources agree that the best opportunity to gain market share is to come in with the initial group of firms that are educating the market and creating demand.

Finance

As many firms in various industrial sectors are still suffering financially from the economic crisis, the availability of financing is a critical factor affecting the ability to invest in energy efficient technology. There seem to be 3 financing options that are employed in energy efficient technology investments.

1.   100% up-front cash payment. This may be viable for very small projects, but it is generally not feasible for medium or large investments.

2.   Medium-term credit / installment option. Most companies require some type of credit terms. One manufacturer offers a 6 month installment plan as a middle-of-the-road option between the extremes of no credit, and a longer ESCO-style repayment plan.

3.   ESCO program. ESCO activity began in Thailand with a pilot program in which the World Bank provided a grant for engineering consulting work related to the first 5 pilot ESCO projects. The pilot projects are in the frozen chicken, textile, ceramic, aluminum and hospital sectors. The customers are required to obtain a bank loan to cover the equipment cost, with loan interest rates subsidized by the government. After equipment installation, the customer uses his energy cost savings to fund the loan payments.

> Aside from the ESCO pilot program, it seems that the ESCO concept is becoming an important financing method for encouraging customers to invest in energy efficient technology. One example of an ESCO operation is that the ESCO will typically approach a potential customer and prepare an energy efficiency proposal outlining proposed energy efficient equipment. An important component of the program is the ability to accurately monitor the effectiveness of the energy efficient equipment to determine the energy cost savings. The ESCO will prepare a contract guaranteeing the equipment's energy efficient performance and cost savings. It is generally the customer's responsibility to obtain a bank loan to pay for the equipment, but sometimes the ESCO may provide the financing. The contract will also stipulate the percentage of energy savings that will be used to pay off the bank loan, a percentage that will go to the ESCO as a service fee, and a percentage that the customer may keep. The contract will guarantee a certain level of monthly energy savings, and, if under normal circumstances, the savings level falls short of the guaranteed amount, the ESCO may be required to fund the difference.

> Some companies may also offer various ESCO options related to the percentage of energy savings that the customer may keep and the length of the financing period. For example, one firm provides financing for its customers and offers an ESCO plan in which the energy cost savings is shared by the customer and the ESCO in a 25% : 75% ratio, with a repayment period of three years. At the end of the three year period, the customer owns the equipment.

> Another option represents a 50% : 50% energy cost savings ratio with a payback period of 5-6 years. At the end of the payback period, the customer has the option to either purchase the equipment for a fee to cover interest, renew the contract or end the contract at which point the ESCO will remove the energy efficient equipment.

To facilitate bank financing for environmentally friendly investment projects, the Industrial Finance Corporation of Thailand established the Environment and Energy Development Center in 2001 to manage and promote lending for energy efficient and environmental projects. The center, combined with the commercial banks' upcoming participation in the new environmental revolving fund, may make it easier than before for firms to obtain financing for environmental projects.

Trade Promotion Opportunities

The following organizations periodically organize energy efficient training seminars. Energy efficient equipment manufacturers may contact these organizations to discuss the possibility of participating in the seminars.

Mr. Sitichoak Watcharasemakul
Training Director
Training Division
Department of Energy Development and Promotion
Bangkruay – Sainoi Rd.
Bangkruay, Nonthaburi 11130
Thailand
Tel: 662-446-7050
Fax: 662-446-7055
Web site: www.teenet-dedp.com

Mr. Arthit Vechakij
Secretary
Energy Conservation Entrepreneurs Association
1179/21-25 Rimtangrodfaisaipaknam Rd.
Klongtan, Klongtoey
Bangkok 10110
Tel: 662-249-3976
Fax: 662-672-7041
e-mail: arthit@thai-ecea.com

Mr. Jakkanit Kananurak
Alliance to Save Energy
No. 1 Fortune Town Office Bldg., 30 fl.
Ratchadapisek Rd.
Dindaeng, Bangkok 10320
Tel: 662-641-1866
Fax: 662-642-1165
e-mail: jakkanit@ase.org

Ms. Elaine Blatt
Cleaner Production for Industrial Efficiency in Samut Prakarn
947/69 Bangna Complex Office Tower B, 14 fl.
Bangna-Trad Rd. Km. 3
Bangna, Bangkok 10260
Tel: 662-744-3045
Fax: 662-744-3049
e-mail: elaine@cpiesp.com

CARDIOVASCULAR DEVICES

Thailand's market for cardiovascular devices and accessories grew by an estimated 4 percent in 2001 and is expected to maintain steady growth of 5 percent between 2002-03. Thailand imports 100 percent of its cardiovascular device requirement. Products from the United States are very well received and account for 32 percent of total imports (total market share). Most international manufacturers of cardiovascular devices are represented in Thailand. Major competitors are firms from Japan, Germany, United Kingdom and other European countries. The Food and Drug Administration, Ministry of Public Health, Royal Thai Government controls importation of these devices, prior approval of imports is required.

U.S. products that have strong sales potential in Thailand include: heart valves, pacemakers, stents, catheters, minimum cardiovascular surgical devices, and artificial blood vessels.

The use of agents and/or distributors to market the cardiovascular devices in Thailand is highly recommended. The agent or distributor generally will handle any regulatory requirements for imports, as well as performing the usual market development functions.

MARKET OVERVIEW

Thailand completely relies on imports to meet its needs for cardiovascular and heart related devices. Currently, local production of these devices does not exist. The potential of local production is still remote as there is not any investment on research and development for products in this sector in Thailand by either the government or the private enterprise. Imports will continue to dominate this market for many years to come.

Currently, there are 392 cardiologists registered with the Medical Council, Ministry of Public Health. In total, they perform an average of 5,500 open-heart surgeries annually. They treated 5.4 million patients (both in and out patients) with heart or cardiovascular related diseases in 1999 (the latest year reported by the Ministry of Public Health).

Heart valves and pacemakers are covered in the Royal Thai Government's new universal healthcare "30 Baht Per Visit" scheme, the social security insurance plan for workers, and the civil servant health care plan. Private healthcare insurance does not cover the heart valves and pacemakers. Patients covered by private healthcare insurance pay these expenses out of their own pocket.

Although the demand for cardiovascular and other heart related products is very high, the high price of these products limits the volume of sales in Thailand. The average retail price for a heart valve in Thailand is $1,400 USD, a pacemaker is $1,100 USD, and a stent is $3,800 USD. This does not include the costs of the operation. The decision of the Thai government to include the cost of the heart valves and pacemakers in the universal health care scheme makes these devices accessible to all patients in Thailand. This recent decision should stimulate demand and we should expect a major increase in the market size and import in the near future.

Market Trends and Marketing Techniques

Cardiovascular disease was the third leading cause of death among Thais as reported by the Ministry of Public Health in 2000. The death rate was 52.3 per 100,000 population. Cardiovascular diseases used to be the leading cause of death in 1999 with the rate of 68.7 per 100,000 population. The Ministry of Public Health also reported that there were 5.4 millions Thai who were treated for the cardiovascular and blood circulatory related diseases in Thailand in

For additional analytical, business and investment opportunities information,
please contact Global Investment & Business Center, USA
at (202) 546-2103. Fax: (202) 546-3275. E-mail: rusric@erols.com

1999, representing 18 percent increase from a year before. Industry sources indicated that this is a good trend for the industry as there are more patients that require treatment, representing an increase demand. The reduced rate of death indicated that an increasing use of cardiovascular device occurred.

In 2001, Thailand's import of heart valves, pacemakers and defibrillators increased by 20 percent to the total amount of approximately 2.4 million U.S. Dollars as compared to 2 million U.S. Dollars in 2000. On the other hand, Thailand's import of electronic cardiovascular analysis and bed side monitors reduced heavily in 2001 to 26 million U.S. Dollars from 34 million U.S. Dollars in 2000, representing a 31 percent decrease. The reduction in the imports of the electronic cardiovascular analysis and monitors might stem from the limited budget each hospital has.

The 20 percent increase of the consumable cardiovascular devices indicated the increasing demands for such devices as heart valves, blood vessels, and pacemakers. The higher the heart and cardiovascular patients the higher the need. The recent decision of the Thai government, in early 2002, to include heart valves and pacemakers in the 30 Bath universal health care scheme should also result in greater demands for these devices in Thailand in the future. In the past, it was very difficult for majority of cardiovascular related patients to access to these high price devices.

The Universal Health Care Program - "30 Baht Scheme"

The Royal Thai Government, through the Ministry of Public Health has implemented the universal health care program since April 2001. Under this program, a patient, who does not have any type of healthcare insurance coverage, is eligible to visit a hospital (mainly public) within their neighborhood for a treatment of sickness at a fixed fee of Baht 30.- ($0.70) per visit. There are approximately 20 million Thai, who are not covered by any type of healthcare insurance, eligible under this program. This universal healthcare program does not cover cosmetic surgery, dialysis, and HIV treatment. The hospitals under this program will receive an annual capitation funding from the Ministry of Public Health of Baht1,200.- (approximately $29) per one registered patient. As a result of this program, most public hospitals face a budget management crisis, as the government almost completely cut its budgeting support and let the hospitals run on the fixed fee, and the capitation received from the Ministry of Public Health. This also results in the very limited investment of new medical devices and equipment, especially those requiring major capital investment. On the other hand, the inclusion of the cardiovascular devices into the universal healthcare program allows the accessibility of the cardiovascular related disease patients to these expensive devices.

Importers and distributors of cardiovascular devices in Thailand normally market and sell their products through cardiologists. Regular sale calls to the cardiologists create personal relationships and the great potential for the cardiologist to recommend the products. The cardiologist's recommendation to the patients is strictly followed and very well observed. The recent economic crisis in 1997 has created a new selling and marketing approach for the cardiovascular devices, especially heart valves, stents and pacemakers, which are normally expensive. Most hospitals, public and private, use the consignment technique in marketing these devices. The hospitals will allow the distributors to display their devices, and pay for the devices only when the sales are made with. This approach, the hospitals do not have to invest and purchase the devices. They do not need to carry inventory either.

Import Market

	Average Growth %	2001	2002	2003	
A.	Total Imports: 5	82	85	90	
B.	Total Local Production: 0	0	0	0	0
C.	Total Exports: 0	0	0	0	
D.	Total Market Size: 5	82	85	90	
E.	Total Imports from U.S.:	26	27	29	5

(Million U.S. Dollars)

The exchange rate is 1 U.S. Dollar/Baht41.00.

Sources: The Customs Department of Thailand.

2001 Import Market Share (% for U.S.A. and Major Competitors):

USA 32%; Japan 15%; Germany 11%; Denmark 4%; United Kingdom 4%; Italy 2%; Belgium 2%; France 2%; Switzerland 2% and others 26%.

Overall, U.S.' import of cardiovascular devices led the total market with 32 percent share. The U.S.' import of heart valves, pacemakers, stents and other cardiovascular products dominated the Thai market with approximately 56 percent share ($1.4 millions). The heart valves and pacemakers from Germany had the second leading share with approximately 13 percent ($0.4 million). Electronic cardiovascular analysis devices and monitors from the U.S. also led the market with approximately 38 percent share ($9.8 millions). Products in this subsector from Japan came second with 21 percent share ($5.3 millions), Germany third with 14 percent ($3.4 millions).

COMPETITION

Heart Valves: competition in this subsector is limited to only some countries, namely U.S., Germany, United Kingdom, Switzerland, Japan and Canada. Valves from the U.S. dominate the market with 58 percent share. All of the major producers of heart valves from the U.S. are represented here in Thailand. Baxter, Medtronic and St. Jude Medical are three leading suppliers in Thailand. Combined, they have approximately 60% market share. Germany, Japan, the Netherlands and Canada also export heart valves to Thailand.

Pacemakers: Pacemakers from U.S. also dominate the Thai market with 54 percent share. Products from Medtronic, St. Jude Medical, and Guidant Corporation lead the market and are well accepted in Thailand. Pacemakers are also imported from Sweden, Denmark, and Canada.

Cardiovascular Analysis and Monitors: competition among this subsector also limited to only a few countries including U.S., Germany, and Japan. These three countries command approximately 72 percent of the total cardiovascular related analysis and monitors. The U.S. alone has 38 percent share ($9.8 millions). Hewlett Packard and General Electric from the U.S. are the two leading suppliers. Siemens from Germany is also very strong in this subsector the same as Mitsubishi from Japan.

Some of the major international manufacturers of cardiovascular devices have successfully established their own branch office in Thailand to promote and market their products. These companies include; Guidant, Boston Scientific, Medtronic, Johnson & Johnson, GE, Hewlett Packard (all from the U.S.) and Siemens from Germany. Some of them do not market their products directly to the cardiologists even though they have their office locally, instead they use local distributor to market the products for them. These companies include; Medtronics, GE, and Hewlett Packard. This is simply because the local distributor has an established relationship with the cardiologists, FDA and customs official, and other players in the field, operates its own branch office in Bangkok and markets the products directly to the hospitals.

Local production does not exist, as the devices in this sector require extensive investment in research and development, which is very limited in Thailand.

END-USERS

The Ministry of Public Health's statistics in 2000 indicated that heart disease was the third major causes of death in Thailand, at a rate of 52.3 per 100,000 population. Accidents led the table at a rate of 66.4, followed by cancer at a rate of 63.9.

The number of patients that received treatment on the heart and cardiovascular related diseases as reported by the Ministry of Public Health are as follow:

	1997	1998	1999
Number of outpatients			
- diseases of the circulatory system	3,762,738	4,384,670	5,163,214
Number of in-patients			
- chronic rheumatic heart diseases		7,232	9,802	10,745
- hypertensive diseases		86,700	94,160	120,280
- ischaemic heart disease		26,886	33,269	45,488
- other heart diseases and diseases of pulmonary circulation	59,400	63,510	82,686
- other diseases of the circulatory system	22,642	24,240	29,100
Total number of heart and blood circulatory system patients	3,965,598	4,609,651	5,422,413
% Change		16%	18%

There are 244 registered cardiologists, 103 cardiology surgeons, and 45 pediatric cardiologists in Thailand in 2001. In all, they performed an average of 5,500 open-heart operations annually. They also implant approximately 1,000 pacemakers annually.

Eighty percent of the patients of heart related diseases in Thailand received treatment in public hospitals, especially medical schools, for two major reasons; lower expenses and higher expertise. Most cardiologists work at a public hospital in a medical school, where they can give lectures at the same time. There are five public medical schools in Bangkok, Mahidol, Chulalongkorn, Siriraj, Srinakarinvirote, and Thammasat. Siriraj, Mahidol, and Chulalongkorn are the three well-known medical schools/hospitals in Thailand for most major treatment of sickness, including cardiovascular diseases and surgery. There is one medical school in each of the following provinces; Chiangmai (north), Khon Kaen (northeast), and Songkhla (south). There are also 12 regional medical centers around the country that have cardiologists, who are capable of performing the heart operations. Open-heart operation at a private hospital is expensive. There are only a few private hospitals in Bangkok that are known to have cardiology specialists working part-time. They include Bangkok General Hospital, Bumroongraj Hospital, and Thonburi Hospital. Open-heart surgery in a private hospital outside of Bangkok is rare.

Sales Prospects

Best Prospects for cardiovascular devices from the U.S.:

products from the U.S. that have good prospect are:
- Heart valves, stents, and artificial blood vessels.
- Guide wires.
- Pacemakers
- Endoscope and other minimal invasive surgical devices

MARKET ACCESS

Importation of Medical Devices into Thailand:

The Medical Devices Control Division, Food and Drug Administration, Ministry of Public Health, controls importation of medical devices into Thailand. Prior approval of importation and device registration through this office is required. Any devices that are not allowed to be marketed or sold in the manufacturing country will not receive permission to be registered in, or imported into Thailand. The Thai Government does not allow importation of used or refurbished medical equipment.

The Thai FDA classifies medical devices into three classes:

Class 1, devices that need a license authorization from the Thai FDA to be manufactured, imported, and marketed. This class includes condoms, surgical gloves, syringes, and HIV test kits for diagnostic purposes.

Class 2, devices that do not need a license, but need to be registered, with a declaration of the details of their physical properties, contents, production process, quality, packaging, labeling, storing, and other required information. A Certificate of Free Sale issued by authorized agencies is required from, e.g. the U.S. Food and Drug Administration, authorized State office, or local Chamber of Commerce. Products in this class include rehabilitation devices, blood alcohol level measuring kits, silicone implants, and HIV test kits other than for diagnostic purposes.

Class 3, into which most devices fall, are general medical devices that can be imported if such devices are freely marketed and sold in the manufacturing country. A Certificate of Free Sale is required to register the product before import.

The Thai FDA will accept medical devices that pass the following standards; USFDA (U.S. Food and Drug Administration - United States), CE Mark (European), PAB (Pharmaceutical Affair Bureau - Japan), TGA (Therapeutic Good Administration - Australia), and SPAC (State Bureau of Pharmaceutical Administration of China - China).

To register the medical device with the Thai FDA, either a notarized Certificate to Foreign Government (issued by the U.S. FDA) or a notarized Certificate of Free Sale (issued by the State office or local Chamber of Commerce) is required. The authenticity of this certificate must be attested to by either the Thai Consulate in the U.S. (in Washington, DC), or the Commercial Service of the U.S. Embassy in Bangkok, Thailand.

It generally takes three months to complete the registration process. The product registration is valid for 2 years and the registration right belongs to the applicant, who normally is the agent or distributor for the foreign manufacturer. Should a foreign manufacturer change the Thai agent/distributor within this two-year period, the new Thai representative needs to re-register the product.

Official contacts for import authorization and registration of medical devices are:

Food and Drug Administration
Ministry of Public Health
Royal Thai Government
Tivanont Road
Muang, Nonthaburi 11000
Thailand
Phone: 662-590-7273/9
Fax: 662-591-8480
Dr. Vichai Chokevivat - Secretary General

Medical Device Control Division
Food and Drug Administration
Ministry of Public Health
Tivanont Road
Muang, Nonthaburi 11000
Thailand
Phone: 662-591-8479, 590-7245
Fax: 662-591-8480
Mr. Watana Akaraeaktalin - Director

Import duty rate for medical devices:

HS Code	Descriptions	Rate %
9006	Cameras specially designed for medical or surgical examination of internal organs	3
9018	Medical, Surgical, and Dental Instruments, Monitors, and Appliances	1
9021	Heart, Pacemakers and othe r Cardiovascular Devices	Exempted

DENTAL EQUIPMENT AND SUPPLIES

U.S. made dental equipment and accessories are well accepted in Thailand and lead the import market share. There is a strong potential to increase the U.S. share in this sector, which is a small but growing market. The total market in 1999 grew 12 percent from 1998 (from 25 million

U.S. Dollars to 28 million U.S. Dollars), future growth is estimated at 16 percent annually in 2000 and 2001. The growth rates for total import, and the U.S. share are expected to be in a 15 percent range per year over the next two year (2000-2001). The two best sales prospects for U.S. manufacturers of dental equipment include dental hand tools/hand pieces, and dental chair units.

In 1999, the Institute of Dentistry reports a total of 6,300 registered dentists and 1,973 registered private dental clinics (outside a hospital) in Thailand. Thailand produces approximately 350 dentists annually. In 2000, the institute expects the growth rate of privately run dental clinic at two percent over 1999.

The cost of dental care is paid for by two major sources: 1) Social Security Funds; and 2) out of pocket payments by patients. Thailand's economic recovery will increase patients' ability to afford dental care, increasing demand for services.

MARKET OVERVIEW

The dental equipment and accessories market is a small but growing market in Thailand. During the regional economic crisis in 1997-8, there was a sharp drop in imports of dental equipment and accessories. Since Thailand relies largely on imported dental equipment and accessories, the market is expected to do better as Thailand comes out of the crisis with a 4.2% economic growth rate in 1999 and a similar rate expected this year, recovery prospects are good.

The dental equipment and accessories market in Thailand is generally divided into four major sub sectors: 1) dental fillings; 2) dentifrice/toothpaste; 3) hand tools/hand pieces; and 4) dental chair units. U.S. made dental equipment and accessories lead the import market in every sub sectors. Overall, dental equipment and accessories from the U.S. lead the total import market with a 34 percent share. U.S. products are well accepted as having good quality and competitive prices. Receptivity for dental equipment from the U.S. is high. The level of receptivity of U.S. products should go up in the future as more and more dentists receive their specialized training in the U.S. In Thailand, the country where dentists received their training has a great influence on the selection of their source of supply for their equipment. Competition from third countries, except Germany, is very limited as dentists are familiar with U.S. dental equipment and can differentiate the quality of the product.

Local production of dental equipment is heavily concentrated on metal hand tools. The quality is still low as compared to imported products. Many of those tools manufactured locally end up at rural clinics or are exported to neighboring countries. A few local manufacturers are starting to produce dental chair units and offer them to the local market, priced in the range of 4,000 U.S. Dollars, while imported dental chair prices are in the range of 12,000 U.S. Dollars.

The Ministry of Public Health reports a total of 6,300 registered dentists in Thailand in 1999, and expects to add approximately 350 new dental graduates each year. All of them work in either public or private hospitals around the country. In 1999, the Institute of Dentistry reports a total of 1,973 registered private dental clinics (outside a hospital) in Thailand, five more clinics than in 1998. The institute claims that the economic crisis greatly reduced the number of new registered private dental clinics. The institute estimates that more dentists are expected to open their own clinic in the year 2000 after Thailand has recovered from the crisis. The potential growth rate of new registered private dental clinics in 2000 is expected to be at not more than two percent over 1999. Dental patients tend to use private dental clinics instead of going to public or private hospitals, for their dental care. Four main reasons behind this tendency: 1) private dental clinics charge lower fees, with comparable quality of service and equipment to a private hospital; 2) patients have to wait a much longer time to get poor dental care at public hospital; 3) private dental clinics are conveniently located; and 4) service charges for some of the services from private dental clinics can be reimbursed from the Social Security Office.

The cost of dental care is paid for by two major sources:
1. Social Security Funds: only the cost of dental extracting, filling, and scaling are covered by the Social Security Office, the Ministry of Labour and Social Welfare. Costs of other dental services will be paid on the patient's own account.
2.   By the patient, generally health care insurance does not cover dental services.

Market Trends

The demand growth for dental equipment in Thailand depends on three major factors: 1) the growth of the number of registered dentists; 2) the growth in the number of dental clinics; and 3) the general economic situation. Statistics from the Institute of Dentistry, Ministry of Public Health shows that approximately 325 dentists graduate from colleges annually. In 1999, approximately 6,300 dentists registered with the Institute of Dentistry, Ministry of Public Health, a growth rate of approximately 5 percent from 1998 (5,950 dentists). Industry sources state that 93 general public hospital centers located in every province around Thailand have an average of ten, fully equipped, dental units in each hospital. There are approximately 1,000 small and medium size public hospitals and healthcare centers that have an average of one fully equipped dental unit per center. 78 private hospitals located in Bangkok metropolitan have an average of five dental units per hospital. Approximately 300 private hospitals located outside Bangkok metropolitan area have an average of 2 dental units in each of them.

The Medical Registration Division, Ministry of Public Health reports that, in 1999, there were 1,973 private dental clinics (operating independently outside a hospital) in Thailand registered with the division. In 1998 there were 1,968 registered private dental clinic around the country. These privately owned clinics have an average of two dental units per clinic. In general, independent privately run dental clinics charge lower fee than dental clinic in the hospital.

Import Market

Statistical Data

	1999	2000 Est.	2001 Est.	Est. Ave. Annual Real Growth in Next 3 yrs
	USD Millions			
Imports*	21.00	24.00	27.00	13%
Local Production#	27.00	35.00	45.00	29%
Exports*	20.00	26.00	34.00	30%
Total Market	28.00	33.00	38.00	16%
Import From U.S.A.*	7.50	8.50	10.00	15%

Exchange rate of Baht38.-/1 USD.
Expected inflation rate of 5 percent.

1999 Import Market Share: United States 34%, Germany 15%, Japan 12%, Australia 9%, Switzerland 5%, Italy 4%, Denmark 4%, Sweden 2%, Others 15% (United Kingdom, Ireland, Canada, Singapore, and South Korea).

For additional analytical, business and investment opportunities information, please contact Global Investment & Business Center, USA at (202) 546-2103. Fax: (202) 546-3275. E-mail: rusric@erols.com

Receptivity Score for U.S. products (5 is high, 1 is low): 5 (very high).

Sources of Information:
·   * data received from the Customs Department, Ministry of Finance.
·   # estimated data derived from discussion with local manufacturers and distributor of
dental equipment.

Dental equipment and accessories from the U.S. dominate the market in Thailand in every sub
sectors. Imports from the U.S. are expected to grow at an annual average rate of 15 percent over
the next three-year period in line with the expected growth in imports and the total market. Two
main reasons support this expectation: 1) the five percent growth of the number of new dental
graduates each year; and 2) the expected national economic growth rate of approximately five
percent. The projected thirteen percent growth rate for total imports is based on the expected
bounce back in purchases following Thailand's recovery from the economic crisis. We should be
able to see a bigger growth rate in 2001 and beyond if Thailand's economy progresses at its
current pace. The growing tendency to import high-priced dental equipment from Germany and
Japan will definitely allow more room for dental equipment from the U.S.

COMPETITION

Dental drills and hand pieces constitute 35 percent (7.5 million U.S. Dollars) of the total import
market in 1999. Products from the U.S. dominated the market with 37 percent share (2.8 million
U.S. Dollars) and Germany came second with 24 percent share (1.8 million U.S. Dollars).
Leading brands from companies in the U.S. include Kerr Corp., Dentsply, A-Dec, Inc., and Hu-
Friedy. Industry sources indicate that products from the U.S. are generally considered as good
quality at a good price. Their price is generally cheaper than products from Germany, the primary
competitor. Although the price is higher than products from Japan and locally produced hand
pieces, good quality seems to offset these shortcomings. Products from Germany, Kovo,
considered to be high quality with a high price, dominate the market and are well accepted by
dentists. These products from Kovo have been well established in the Thai market.

The country where dentists receive their training is a strong influence on purchasing preference.
In the past, most dentists received their training in Germany. At present, training centers have
turned to many medical/dental schools in the U.S., resulting in growing popularity of hand pieces
and other dental equipment from the U.S.

Dentifrice and toothpaste constitute 17 percent of the total import market (3.6 million U.S.
Dollars). Products from the U.S. dominate the market with approximately 85 percent share (3
million U.S. Dollars). Leading companies in this sub sector include 3M, Procter & Gamble, Kerr,
and Dentsply. Imports from other country are not significant.

Dental chair units constitute 7 percent of the total import market (1.5 million U.S. Dollars). Dental
chairs from the U.S. are first with approximately a 42 percent share (0.70 million U.S. Dollars).
Leading dental chairs from the U.S. include products from Midmark Corp., Belmont Equipment, A-
Dec, Inc., and Marus. Dental chairs from Germany come second with 23 percent share (0.40
million U.S. Dollar). Kovo is a leading brand from Germany. Yoshida and Y Seiko from Japan
have approximately a 4 percent share (0.10 million U.S. Dollars). Again, Kovo from Germany is
the leading brand and is regarded as high quality but also very high price. It has been in this
market for a long time and before most its competitors including those from the U.S. Industry
sources indicated that dental chair units from Germany offer more features than dental chairs
from other countries. They also indicated that dental chairs from the U.S. last longer with a

For additional analytical, business and investment opportunities information,
please contact Global Investment & Business Center, USA
at (202) 546-2103. Fax: (202) 546-3275. E-mail: rusric@erols.com

cheaper price as compared to chairs from Germany and other countries. Yoshida's dental chair from Japan is also regarded as a good quality product, but it is also very expensive. Y Seiko is a cheaper version of the dental chair manufactured by Yoshida. There are also dental chair units from Italy (Sirona) and Brazil (Amadeous) competing in the market.

Industry sources stated that the price and features of the dental chair seem to be the two most important competitive factors. Good, reliable after sales and spare part services is also another deciding buying factor used by dentists. Good personal relationships between local distributor and dentists also counts as a factor influencing buying decisions. Most local distributors of dental chair units use pricing, credit and installment policies as their marketing strategies to win sales.

List of U.S. Dental Equipment used in Thailand:

Dental Chair Unit	A-Dec, Inc., Belmont Equipment Corp., Midmark Corp.
Dental Hand pieces	A-Dec, Inc., Dentsply, Kerr Corp., Hu-Friedy
Sterilizer	Midmark Corp.

Major producers of dental equipment from the U.S. are well represented here in Thailand.

Sales Prospects

List of two sub sectors that have the best sales prospects for products from the U.S.:

- HS9402-Dental Chair Units
- HS9018-Dental Hand Tools

Thailand's recovery from the economic crisis should allow more dentists to start their own clinics and to open the opportunity for the sale of dental chairs and hand tool sets made from the U.S. to supply their offices. Dental chair units from the U.S. have plenty of room to expand in this market for the following reasons: 1) Industry sources interviewed stated that dental chairs from the U.S. are the best buy comparing quality and price; 2) U.S. made dental chairs are durable and offer complete features sufficient for good dental practice satisfying both the dentist and patient; and 3) Dental chairs from Germany, which dominate the market at the moment, are considerably more expensive, and limited in number of offices that can afford them.

MARKET ACCESS

Most dental equipment manufacturers appoint a local company as their distributor to market their products in Thailand. Working with a local agent or distributor is the best way to enter the dental equipment market in Thailand. Local distributors will also facilitate the certification process for imported dental equipment with the Food and Drug Administration, Ministry of Public Health.

Import Duties:

3006	Dental Filling	15%
3306	Dentifrice, Toothpaste	20%
9018	Dental Drills, Hand pieces	1%

9402	Dental Chairs	20%

The importation of dental equipment is controlled by the Medical Device Control Division, Food and Drug Administration, Ministry of Public Health, Royal Thai Government. In order to import dental equipment into Thailand, the importer needs to apply for or to receive an import authorization/registration permit from the Thai FDA prior to the actual shipment. The permit has to be renewed every three years. The Thai FDA requires that the manufacturer or its representative register in person. The Thai FDA will accept medical devices that pass the following standards; USFDA (U.S. Food and Drug Administration - United States), CE Mark (European), PAB (Pharmaceutical Affair Bureau - Japan), TGA (Therapeutic Good Administration - Australia), and SPAC (State Bureau of Pharmaceutical Administration of China - China). The government of Thailand does not allow the importation of used or refurbished medical devices into the country. The Thai FDA requires the notarized Certificate to Foreign Government issued by either U.S. Food and Drug Administration, Health Department of State office, or Chamber of Commerce in the U.S. A copy of the Certification to Foreign Government should also be attached if notarized copy of the Certificate to Foreign Government is used. All the documents need to be legalized by either the Thai Consulate in the U.S. or the U.S. Embassy in Thailand. The Thai FDA official will grant import authorization and notify the Thai Customs Office to clear the devices when they enter the port.

KEY CONTACTS

Local Government Contacts:

Food and Drug Administration
Ministry of Public Health
Royal Thai Government
Tivanont Road
Muang, Nonthaburi 11000
Thailand
Phone: 662-590-7273/9
Fax: 662-591-8480
Dr. Narong Chayakul - Secretary General

Medical Device Control Division
Food and Drug Administration
Ministry of Public Health
Tivanont Road
Muang, Nonthaburi 11000
Thailand
Phone: 662-591-8479, 590-7245
Fax: 662-591-8480
Mr. Boonlert Kongkamee - Director

Institute of Dentistry
Department of Medical Services
Ministry of Public Health
Tivanont Road
Muang, Nonthaburi 11000
Phone: 662-951-0420/2
Fax: 662-588-4004
Mr. Piyaphongh Niklodha, M.D. - Director

For additional analytical, business and investment opportunities information,
please contact Global Investment & Business Center, USA
at (202) 546-2103. Fax: (202) 546-3275. E-mail: rusric@erols.com

Associations:

Thai Medical Device Suppliers Association
6th Fl., Dr. Gerhard Link Bldg.
33 Soi Lertnava, Krungthepkreetha Road
Huamark, Bangkapi
Bangkok 10240
Phone: 662-379-4296
Fax: 662-379-4297
Mr. Bernd R. Dombrowe - President

Major Importers of Dental products in Thailand:

Accord Corp., Ltd.
33/2-5 Rongmuang Soi 4 Road
Pathumwan, Bangkok 10330
Phone: 662-214-5290, 662-214-4002
Fax: 662-216-3235
Ms. Suchada Charnsethikul, Managing Director

Anton (Bangkok) Co., Ltd.
178/3 Sukhumvit Soi 16 Road
Phrakanong, Bangkok 10110
Phone: 662-258-1531
Fax: 662-259-3488
Mr. Surin Seneewong Na Ayudhya, Managing Director

Bangkok Dental Supply Co., Ltd.
27 Ramkhamhaeang Road
Bangkapi, Bangkok 10240
Phone: 662-717-2057/9
Fax: 662-717-2060
Mr. Tri Isarabhakdi, Manager

Bangkok Hospital Supply (Thailand) Co., Ltd.
415/36 Arunamarin Road
Bangkoknoi, Bangkok 10700
Phone: 662-424-1393, 662-424-1398
Fax: 662-433-8703
Mr. Somsak Jiradirek, Managing Director

Endurable Surgical Supply Co., Ltd.
2044/19 New Petchburi Road
Bangkok 10310
Phone: 662-319-9500, 662-314-1421
Fax: 662-319-9499
Mr. Vorapong Suriyamonkol, President

General Hospital Products Public Co., Ltd.
75/1 Rama 6 Road
Bangkok 10400

**For additional analytical, business and investment opportunities information,
please contact Global Investment & Business Center, USA
at (202) 546-2103. Fax: (202) 546-3275. E-mail: rusric@erols.com**

Phone: 662-245-5550
Fax: 662-246-7305
Mr. Thumrong Chaisumrej, Dental Product Manager

Geomed Co., Ltd.
52/1 Sukhumvit Soi 23 Road
Phrakanong, Bangkok 10110
Phone: 662-235-5937/8, 258-4107
Fax: 662-236-5798
Mr. Chanintorn Bulpakdi, Managing Director

K.V Science Co., Ltd.
136 Nares Road
Bangrak, Bangkok 10500
Phone: 662-233-0151, 662-233-9460
Fax: 662-238-1264
Mr. Karn Thamchaipenet, Managing Director

Meditop Co., Ltd.
334 Ladphrao Soi 71 Road
Bangkapi, Bangkok 10320
Phone: 662-933-1133
Fax: 662-933-0811/2
Mr. Chanin Sangkatumvong, President

Pioneer Inter Supply Co., Ltd.
40/15 Moo 2, Bangmodland Industry
Putthabucha 36 Road
Bangmod, Thungkhru
Bangkok 10140
Phone: 662-426-3304
Fax: 662-426-3327
Mr. Boonchuay Sakdapisut, Manager

Sky Lab Co., Ltd.
93/90 Soi Prachanukul 2
Ratchadapisek Road
Bangsue, Bangkok 10800
Phone: 662-910-0950/68
Fax: 662-587-7168
Mr. Charnchai Udomlarptham, President

Thanes Development Co., Ltd.
18 Ramkhamhaeng Soi 52 Road
Bangkapi, Bangkok 10240
Phone: 662-374-8781/4
Fax: 662-374-8780
Mr. Vaivudhi Thanesvorakul, MD, Managing Director

Local contact for U.S. companies:

The Commercial Service

American Embassy
3rd Fl., Diethelm Towers A, Room 304
93/1 Wireless Road
Pathumwan, Bangkok 10330
Phone: 662-205-5090
Fax: 662-255-2915
Mr. David L. Gossack - Commercial Attache
E-Mail: david.gossack@mail.doc.gov
Mr. Nalin Phupoksakul - Commercial Specialist
E-Mail: nalin.phupoksakul@mail.doc.gov

Trade Show:

Name: Meditech Asia & Dental Asia 2000
Date: March 1-4, 2000
Venue: Bangkok International Trade & Exhibition Centre
      (BITEC), Bangkok, Thailand
Organizer: Bangkok International Trade & Exhibition Centre
      (BITEC)
      8 Bangna-Trade Road, KM 1
      Bangna, Bangkok 10260
      Thailand
    Phone: 662-749-3939, ext. 2161, 2164
      Fax: 662-749-3959
      E-mail: info@bitec.net
      Website: www.bitec.net
      Ms. Praneejit Lopinich-Project Director

LEASING

The leasing sector in Thailand is showing signs of recovery in the wake of the economic downturn of 1997-99. Financing companies provide leasing options and there are also firms which strictly lease. Lease-purchase arrangements have led the leasing sector in terms of level of activity. Auto lease-purchase arrangements have showed particularly strong growth, concomitant with the 51.5% increase in domestic automobile sales in 1999. However, the slow down in capital investment by local manufacturers has led leasing companies to de-emphasize equipment/machinery leasing, despite the government's relaxation of tight leasing regulations.

Leasing companies have become selective in extending loans to corporate clients seeking to purchase equipment from suppliers as a result of the financial crisis of 1997, which forced many corporations into bankruptcy. Increasingly, individuals with good credit standing would be prime candidates for leasing firms. Leasing firms can offer larger down payments with shorter financing terms at low interest rates to these individuals.

As Thailand's auto lease-purchasing industry becomes more attractive, there are new foreign players entering the market and generating their main source of revenue from auto lease-purchasing. They are forcing most local firms to be more competitive. Competition will intensify after commercial banks are allowed to engage in leasing operations under the new Financial Institutions Law. American firms looking for opportunities in Thailand's growing leasing market should target auto lease-purchases (hire purchase) rather than equipment/machinery leasing.

In the future, the leasing industry will be more standardized, with open competition from all type of operators. However, access to cheap funding source will be a common problem for locally-owned leasing firms. Success will come as a result of well-planned marketing strategies, good relationships with dealers and clients, as well as a thorough understanding of the local market and Thailand's regulatory environment.

A. MARKET OVERVIEW

The leasing industry in Thailand was greatly affected by the Thai economic crisis in 1997. The annual business volume peaked at 54 billion baht (US$ 1.44 billion) in 1996, but dropped drastically to only 28 billion baht (US$ 758 million) in 1997. The onset of the financial crisis in 1997 led to a radical change in the structure of local financial institutions. The number of finance firms listed on the Stock Exchange of Thailand dropped from 91 in 1996 to only 22 in August 1999 after the Bank of Thailand ordered a close-down of these firms due to their severe financial standings. Prior to the closure, each of these firms had been experiencing liquidity problem, exacerbated by high funding costs and high ratios of non-performing loans (NPLS).

However, in 1999 the leasing industry began to recover due to the expansion in sales of commercial vehicles, leased at attractively low interest charges. The local interest rate is expecting to remain low level as the Bank of Thailand tries to stimulate more economic growth. Local leasing firms benefit from low interest rates since consumers would perceive this as a good time to lease.

The top three players in the industry are GE Capital Auto Lease (GECAL), Toyota Leasing, and Siam Panich Leasing (SPL). Their combined loan portfolio totals over 30 billion baht (approximately US$790 million), representing about 40% of the total market size. Each player approaches the market with a different strategy. GECAL uses its lower funding cost and quick, high quality service as its competitive advantages. SPL changed its focus in the past year, to concentrate more on the used car market with careful risk management in place. Toyota leasing remains focused on financing sales of Toyota automobiles, a captive market which it needs to retain its market share.

The leasing industry features distinctive segments where different but closely related means of financing are being used. Described below are the two main segments--hire purchase and pure leasing, including both financial leases and operating leases.

Business Factors Hire Purchase Lease

Type of assets Consumer credits Capital assets; mainly for commercial and industrial uses, i.e. machinery, automobile for commercial use

Objective Ownership Use or of asset ownership

Ownership of asset Belongs to lessor Lessee has a right to nd will be purchase the asset at transferred to a pre-determined price essee at the end at the end of the of the contract contract

Normal Contract 1-3 years 3-5 years

Term

Maintenance cost Lessee's expense Lessee's expense for financial lease, and

Lessor expenses for operating lease

Thailand's hire purchase market is directly tied to the fortunes of the automobile industry, which slumped during the crisis in 1997 and 1998. During that period, overall sales decreased by 61%. Many automobile manufacturers at that time faced a major slowdown. Poor sales compounded problems with low liquidity and high foreign debts caused by the devaluation of the baht. Total domestic automobile sales in 1998 were 140,000 units, 61% lower than a year earlier, while export sales in 1998 were 50,000 units or 48.54% higher than the previous year. These statistics reflect a decrease in Thai citizens' purchasing power at that time. However, the 51.5% increase in domestic automobile sales in 1999 resulted in 218,330 unit sales for the manufacturers. The government's stimulus package and other factors including combining lower interest rates and higher liquidity in the money market contributed to the surge in auto sales.

Other clear evidence of the recent change in the industry was the entry of new foreign players such as GE Capital and Ford Leasing. GE Capital acquired distressed assets from auctions arranged by the Financial Restructuring Agency (FRA) in late 1998 and early 1999. Ford Leasing focused on supporting sales by its local automobile manufacturer (Auto Alliance Thailand, a joint venture between Ford & Mazda). These two new players quickly accumulated assets and customer bases, and established a strong presence in the local hire purchase market.

Demand for leasing machinery and equipment has gone up, in sharp contract to demand for purchase. This is because many companies are continue to have financial difficulties and financial institutions --including leasing companies--are more careful than ever in granting new loans. They prefer to concentrate on existing performing loans rather than taking on the risk of new ones. Given Thailand's current economic conditions, machinery and equipment are still difficult to resell in the event of foreclosure. By contrast, automobiles are much easier to resell in order to recover money quickly if a loan goes bad.

For the above reasons, leasing companies have de-emphasized corporate clients and machinery/equipment leasing, and turned their interest to the automobile hire purchase market, where growth is more rapid and profit potential is higher.

Three major regulatory changes governing the leasing industry has given the sector a great boost. There have been three main changes in the regulations. The first, governing down payments, allows buyers to set the minimum down payment and installment payment period by themselves, whereas previously a minimum 25% down payment and maximum 48 installment payments were required. Secondly, the definition of whether a loan is in default has been changed from 2 to 3 consecutive missed payments, before the finance firm can repossess the vehicle. Thirdly, the ceiling for passenger car leasing is expanded to more than 5 percent of the total credit extension of commercial banks and finance companies. Previously, credit extension was restricted to no more than 5 percent of total capital. Thus, available credit for leasing business is expected to rise sharply.

STATISTICAL DATA

MARKET SIZE (LOANS PORTFOLIO) (in US$ MILLIONS)

Projected Avg. Annual Growth Rate for the following 3 years

1998 1999

Total Market 2,087 2,427 16%

Total - Local Firms 1,077 1,252 16%
Total - U.S. Based Firms 432 563 16%
Total – Other Foreign Firms 578 612 16%
Exchange Rate (Thai Baht/US Dollars): 38
Inflation Rate: 1.2% (Bank of Thailand's figure, as of Apr'00)

Source: Industry sources and Company Interviews

MARKET TRENDS

Demand Growth

The leasing market is driven by the need of business firms to procure capital assets (i.e. tools, machinery), utilizing mostly operating leases. As a result of the economic crisis, industries such as construction and steel have ceased new investment, and demand from this sector for financing through leasing is not expected to recover in the near term. On the consumer side, demand for automobiles continues to rise, increasing 51.5% in 1999 and 50.85% during the first half of 2000.

From the leasing company's perspective, hire purchase arrangements remain attractive, since this minimizes their risk. Statistics from the Bank of Thailand show that non-performing loans (NPLs) in the hire-purchase sector were the lowest of all sectors with NPLs. Out of total NPLs outstanding as of February 2000 of 2,052,380 million baht (approximately US$ 54 billion), only 0.01% or 241 million baht (US$ 6.34 million) are from hire-purchase businesses. Perhaps typical of the sector, one leading leasing company, GE Capital Auto Lease Public Company Limited (GECAL), reports that hire purchase income its main source of revenue. This focus on hire purchase is expected to continue, in line with trends in the nation's economic recovery and anticipated further increases in domestic car sales.

Changes in Market Structure

In recent years, the entry of new foreign leasing companies into Thailand's leasing market has increased competition. Foreign giants such as GE Capital Auto Leasing, Ford Leasing, and Benz Leasing are expanding their presence in Thailand. The new entrants are forcing most local firms to revise their operational and financial plans to survive in the increasingly competitive environment.

Among the new foreign players, GE Capital Auto Lease Public Company Limited (GECAL), is considered to be the largest automobile finance company in Thailand, with over 65,000 automobile hire purchase customer accounts and nationwide coverage featuring 13 full-service branches and 2 sub-branches. GECAL is wholly owned by General Electric Capital Corporation (GECC), a AAA rated global diversified financial service company. The company bought most of its hire-purchase assets in 1998 from the Financial Restructuring Agency (FRA), which seized assets of the troubled 56 finance companies closed by the government during the crisis.

In addition, under the new Financial Institutions Law, the scope of financial services that can be offered by local banks under a universal banking concept will be expanded to include leasing and hire purchase operations. Banks and foreign competitors have an advantage over smaller local leasing firms in that their funding costs are lower. However, according a report by the Thai Farmers Bank Research Center (TFRC), commercial banks may actually be reluctant to enter the leasing business because of greater requirements for exclusive specialization and experience in this field. Some banks are expected to address this by having their own subsidiaries run the leasing business in the market. Once the subsidiaries perform well, there would be no need for

For additional analytical, business and investment opportunities information,
please contact Global Investment & Business Center, USA
at (202) 546-2103. Fax: (202) 546-3275. E-mail: rusric@erols.com

commercial banks to run the business by themselves. Besides, leasing companies do not rely on branch networks, but rather just stay in touch with major dealers in Bangkok. This approach enables them to maintain about 80% of the total market share.

Other Leasing Instruments in Demand

There are other areas in which leasing and hire purchase arrangements can be utilized. Floor-plan or inventory financing, used-car financing, and fleet financing are non-conventional leasing applications that leasing companies are promoting to expand their service coverage. By using floor-plan schemes, car dealers can get financing from the leasing company for demonstration cars and inventory, and if the cars cannot be sold during the financing period, the dealer can sell the car back to the manufacturer at a pre-determined price. This method allows the leasing company to serve both individuals consumers and auto dealers. The collateral value pledged in form of cash or bank guarantees is required for the floor-plan arrangement, normally at 35%-50% of loan value, with average credit terms of 60 to 120 days. GECAL first introduced floor-plan services to Nissan, Mitsubishi, and BMW car dealers in 1998.

Used-car financing is gaining in popularity among leasing companies. In the past it was primarily the

focus of car manufacturers' related leasing companies, but the combmination of consumers lower purchasing power, higher new car prices, and attractively low interest rates have stimulated new sales in Thailand's used car market. One company actively engaged in used car financing is Siam Panich Leasing (SPL), which is shifting emphasis to the used car market where effective rates are still around 18%-20% (flat rates of 5%-6%). Its hire purchase portfolio has shifted from 5% used car financing before 1997 to 20% in 1999.

Another way of expanding leasing activities in Thailand is to provide what the industry calls fleet financing, where leasing companies add value to their services. Fleet financing takes the onus of maintenance, insurance, and annual registration renewal off of end-users. In addition, this type of leasing provides convenience for corporate users when dealing with a large number of corporate cars. The leasing company will assist its clients from the beginning, starting with the selection of the appropriate type of automobile to the resale of the car back to the leasing company or another buyer.

COMPETITION

Major Players

Three large companies hold the lion's share of the leasing market in Thailand; GE Capital Auto Lease Plc.(GECAL), Siam Panich Leasing Public Company Limited (SPL), and Toyota Leasing Co., Ltd. Among these three companies, only SPL is a Thai firm; it is listed on the Stock Exchange of Thailand and is majority held by Siam Commercial Bank Plc. Toyota Leasing is considered a captive leasing company supporting Toyota Motor Sales in Thailand. GECAL is a subsidiary the U.S.-based financial services company, General Electric Capital Corporation (GECC).

Total assets of each company at the end of 1998 were as follows; Toyota Leasing was the highest at 13.108 billion baht (US$ 345 million), followed by GECAL at 9.768 billion baht (US$ 257 million), and SPL at 9.223 billion baht (US$ 243 million). In 1999 GECAL added more hire purchase loans to its portfolio, such that its total assets reached 12.944 billion baht (US$ 341 million) at year end, almost equal to those of Toyota Leasing in 1998. The total asset figure for

Toyota Leasing for 1999 was not available in order to draw a comparison. In the same period (1999) SPL's total assets closed at 9.190 billion baht (US$ 242 million), a little lower than the previous year because the number of new loan accounts taken on was lower than those retired.

Identifiable Difference in the Competition

Each of the top players has their own differences in how they compete. As a new comer, GECAL entered the market with lower interest charges to its auto-loan clients, combined with a speedy loan application service whereby customers can get response within one day. Other marketing strategies that GECAL is utilizing are: loan applications via the Internet using the www.thailifestyle.com website; joint ventures (JV) with automobile manufacturers like Mitsubishi, Nissan, and BMW in providing leasing campaigns under the name of each JV (Nissan Vehicle Leasing, Mitsubishi Leasing, and BMW Leasing Program.

While newcomers are utilizing innovative ways of competing, SPL had concentrated its efforts on portfolio risk management and on maintaining good relationships with multiple makes and dealers. By not being specifically tied to any particular group of manufacturers/dealers, SPL had an open opportunity to cultivate relationships with a larger client base. Moreover, SPL had also shifted its focus to the used car market where effective rates are still around 18%-20% (and or flat rates are 5%-6%). SPL's hire-purchase portfolio has shifted from roughly 5% used cars in 1997 to 20% in 1999.

Toyota Leasing continues to focus its marketing efforts on servicing existing Toyota clients. The company has also prepared for intense competition in the future by adding 2.6 billion baht (US$ 68 million) to its previous 400 million baht capital. This strengthens Toyota Leasing's ability to lower its funding cost and allows the company to compete by providing lower interest charges to its customers.

Key Competitive Factors

Successful leasing companies need to consider several competitive factors in this sector. First, they must have access to a large capital base, have the capability to lower the funding cost and must have nationwide service coverage. To be able to secure the required capital at low cost, a leasing company has to demonstrate the quality of its loan portfolio (i.e. low non-accrual loans balance and provisions to doubtful accounts), and must show that it has a careful and transparent credit approval process, adheres to strict collections procedures and has conservative bad debt reserve policies. GECAL was able to dominate the market for new car loans quicker than expected due to its cost of funds advantage. GECAL itself is rated A by Thai Rating and Information Services (TRIS). Its parent company GECC is rated AAA by Standard & Poor's and Aaa by Moody's. The rates on new car loans have been driven down to a flat rate of 5.5%-6.5%, which translates approximately into an effective rate of 11%-13%.

In fact, foreign leasing companies or local ones who have strong parent companies' backup are in a better position when it comes to financing. GECAL and leasing companies such as SPL, which have the support of commercial banks (SPL's comes from Siam Commercial Bank) can be more flexible in dealing with volatility in the money and capital markets, compared to other local independent leasing companies. Leasing companies with greater territorial coverage and a higher number of branches nationwide have an advantage over those that do not. Branches can be newly established, or acquired through a merger or direct buy-out of a distressed financial institution.

Marketing strategies & techniques

For additional analytical, business and investment opportunities information,
please contact Global Investment & Business Center, USA
at (202) 546-2103. Fax: (202) 546-3275. E-mail: rusric@erols.com

There are several key marketing strategies and techniques that successful leasing companies have been using effectively.

1. Continuous Improvement in Service Quality: Focusing on service quality and continuously maintaining and improving service at all times will prepare a leasing company for future competition. Some of the former finance companies clearly took advantage of their customers, who were unable to re-claim their car registration books once the finance company was closed, even though they had already paid all loans outstanding. Customers are now quality-conscious, prefer higher services of a more reliable leasing company even if the price is a little higher.

2. Expand Branch Network: Having service available in the right place at the right time is the key to success for leasing and hire purchase businesses. Leading leasing companies like GECAL and SPL provide the same services at their branches in provincial areas where demand is high, especially on pick up trucks, allowing customers easy access to such services. Leasing companies need to continuously monitor demand to estimate where additional branch offices may be required, and whether such expansion is worth the investment.

3. Cultivate Relationships with Manufacturers/Dealers: new customers can be either walk-ins or those referred by dealers or manufacturers. In the hire-purchase business, referrals account for a much higher volume of business than do direct walk-in clients. As such, keeping close ties and maintaining good relationships with manufacturers will help business grow in a stable fashion.

4. Provide Value Added Services: A good strategy is to combine services such as Fleet Leasing with value-added services such as maintenance, annual registration renewal, insurance service, down-time replacement service, and resale service. Most large international firms such as Shell, Esso, and Caltex have used fleet leasing services, as reported by a leading leasing company.

5. Use Technology Innovatively: Internet has become an effective tool to reach wide range of customers. Leasing companies who enable their clients to access their services through this channel will have direct contact with potential clients for other services as well, including personal loans, insurance services, and electronic-shopping. The advantage of Internet credit application is the speed of service where customers' credit information can be obtained quickly on-line, thus speeding up the credit approval process and reducing clerical work at the leasing company.

How can U.S. companies adapt their products for the local market?

In Thailand, the words leasing or hire purchase are used interchangeably in the market, especially when the underlying asset is an automobile. In Thai culture, people value ownership of the asset when they buy big-ticket items, e.g. a car. Most consumers prefer hire-purchase arrangements, since the objective is to gain ownership of the asset, rather than pursuing a true lease-type transaction.

From our discussion with the Thailand Leasing Association, currently hire-purchase auto leases account for 75% of the total leasing business, with the remaining 25% accounted for by machinery and equipment leases, mainly for industrial and corporate usage. Given this, any US company looking for opportunities in Thailand's leasing market might consider focusing on consumer market financial products rather than leasing capital assets for industrial use. It may take quite some time before the industrial sector recovers from the economic downturn. When it does, it is expected that demand for machinery and equipment leasing will rebound.

END-USER ANALYSIS

The economic crisis left in its wake only strong corporate and industrial users which are capable of controlling costs and making marginal profits to survive. Demand for capital assets remains sluggish, which in turn means leasing services required by these two end-user groups are minimal and designed chiefly for the purpose of replacing old machinery. Leasing companies' focus, therefore, has switched to consumers, especially given the upswing in domestic vehicle sales in 1999. Other supporting factors are the low interest rate environment in both borrowing and saving rates (MLR @ 8.5% p.a., Saving @ 3.5% p.a.), which has encouraged consumers who have extra money to spend rather than save at such a low rate. Accordingly, an automoile purchase is an attractive choice.

Car buyers in Thailand can be divided into two major groups; new car buyers and used car buyers. The used car market has become popular again after the crisis, since consumers' purchasing power is lower and the price of new cars is rising. More people have decided to buy used cars in order to save money for other emergency uses and the potential threat of lay-offs.

However, people with enough wealth are taking the opportunity to borrow at low rates to buy new or imported cars. As mentioned by a foreign based leasing company in Bangkok, this high-end group of consumers are of better credit standing, and thus many leasing companies offer them special rates. They are also considered to be low-risk customers, since they can make high down payments, and borrow the rest at short term (less than the normal 3-4 years hire purchase terms).

Another emerging group of customers are Internet surfers, as currently pursued by GECAL (www.thailifestyle.com) and Ford Leasing Thailand (www.fordleasingthai.com). Even though there is no clear evidence yet that customers were attracted from the Internet, since this is a new way to reach customers, this channel is expected to play a growing role in reaching target customer groups, not just regarding their leasing needs but to meet other personal financial service needs, as well.

BEST SALES PROSPECTS

The best sales prospects identified in the leasing business come to three categories of hire-purchase related products: joint ventures with local manufacturers (so-called OEMs), Fleet Leasing Program, Floor Plan, and Leasing Service via Internet.

OEM or the Original Equipment Manufacturer's concept stems from OEM practices in the manufacturing environment. OEM-type leasing allows non-captive leasing companies (leasing companies without any connection with the manufacturer of the underlying assets) to have access to clients of manufacturers (i.e. car manufacturer) under a JV names. GECAL for example, has joint ventures with several automobile manufacturers and has set up OEM leasing programs called Nissan Vehicle Leasing, Mitsubishi Leasing, and BMW Leasing Program. Ford Credit's leasing firm, Primus Leasing, also provides leasing services under the name of their respective automobile makes: Ford Leasing, Volvo Leasing, and Mazda Leasing. Both manufacturer and leasing company having mutual benefits over this type of arrangement. Leasing companies can get more business volume from clients referred by the manufacturer. Manufacturers, in return, will be able to offer full sales support service such as financing plans to their clients. This is considered a win-win situation for both parties.

Fleet leasing programs are another option for attracting corporate clients, who value the convenience of this type of scheme. Under a fleet leasing arrangement, the lessee is able to utilize assets to their fullest without having to worry about maintenance or other administrative work involved. Moreover, fleet leasing is suitable for a corporation, which needs a large fleet of automobiles. A leasing company can provide a total solution ranging from consulting on appropriate make, type, and price of automobile, to maintenance services, to resale at the end of the vehicle's economic useful life.

To foster a close relationship with automobile dealers, leasing companies can also provide value-added service like Floor Plan financing. This type of product helps dealers who lack capital funding to operate their businesses. Financing to procure inventory or demonstration cars in the dealer's showroom can be obtained under the Floor Plan. In some situations, leasing companies may consider providing Floor Plan arrangements as a complimentary service to reputable automobile dealers with good credit standing which have already established hire purchase business relationships.

Almost all new leasing companies in Bangkok are using the Internet as part of their strategy to access and establish a firm foothold in the Thai leasing industry. Leasing via Internet is one of the best prospects for the future and cannot be overlooked as a strategy without risking being left behind. The ease of use and prompt response to consumer financing needs are the key strengths of this approach.

MARKET ACCESS

Leasing companies in Thailand fall under the Thai Civil and Commercial Codes and are treated as limited companies, as distinct from commercial banks and finance & securities firms that are governed by the Bank of Thailand and the Ministry of Finance. In order to set up a limited company to operate a leasing business in Thailand, a party must register with the Department of Commercial Registration; apply for permission to use the company name; make a Memorandum of Association; and apply for company registration with the Department.

Currently there are efforts initiated by several government bodies to develop and improve laws governing leasing businesses. The Office of the Consumer Protection Board (OCPB) within the Office of the Prime Minister is drafting a Standard Leasing Contract that aims at protecting consumers from unfair treatment by leasing companies. For instance, it will set a maximum penalty fee for late payment and establish an advance notice requirement for contract termination. Currently both OCPB and existing local leasing companies are reviewing this Standard Leasing Contract. This standard contract is expected to come into use sometime in 2000.

In addition, a new Leasing Business Law was drafted by the Financial Suppression Policy Division of the Fiscal Policy Office, Ministry of Finance, and was submitted in spring, 2000 to the Ministry of Commerce for approval. The new law will spell out roles and responsibilities of both lessor and lessee. It will promote systematic registration of leasing companies, together with defining clearer duties for all parties involved.

Listed below is contact information for certifying local authorities and leasing companies:

Governmental Agencies:
Foreign Affairs and Business Services
The Department of Commercial Registration, Ministry of Commerce
Ratchadamnoen Klang Ave.,
Bangkok 10200, Thailand
Tel: 662-547-4419
Fax: 662-547-4420

Financial Suppression Policy Division
Fiscal Policy Office, Ministry of Finance

Rama VI Road,
Bangkok 10400, Thailand
Tel: 662-273-9020
Fax: 662-618-3368

The Office of Consumer Protection Board (OCPB),
Office of the Prime Minister
Red Building 3, The Government House,
Rajadamnern-Nok, Dusit,
Bangkok 10300, Thailand
Tel: 662-280-1661, 282-4579
Fax: 662-282-7786

Leasing Companies:

Organization: A.C.L. Leasing Co., Ltd.
Mailing Address: Asia Sermitr Tower, 49 Soi Pipat, Silom
Bangkok 10500, Thailand
Contacts: Jirawat Lewprasert (Director)
Tel: 231-5234
Fax: 231-5767

Organization: ABN Amro Asia Securities Plc.
Mailing Address: 3rd. Flr., Sathorn City Tower, 175 South
Sathorn Rd. Silom, Bangkok 10120,
Thailand
Contacts: Bhongbhichai Bhitakburi (Managing Director)
Tel: 231-5611
Fax: 285-1832

Organization: AIG Finance (Thailand) Company Limited
Mailing Address: 102 Soi Aree, Sukhumvit 26 Rd.
Bangkok 10110, Thailand
Contacts: Zati Sangkhawanich
Head of Hire Purchase Product
Tel: 259-0063-72
Fax: 259-7390

Organization: Ayudhya Development Leasing Co., Ltd.
Mailing Address: 22nd Flr. Chamnan Phenjati Tower A,
65/182-185 Rama IX Rd.,
Bangkok 10310, Thailand
Contacts: Somchai Boonnamsiri (President)
Tel: 643-1977/86
Fax: 643-1059/60

Organization: Ayudhya International Factors Co., Ltd.
Mailing Address: 20th Flr. Lumpini Tower 1168/55 Rama IV
Rd., Bangkok 10120, Thailand
Contacts: Pakinai Na Chiengmai (President)
Tel: 285-6326; 679-9140/4
Fax: 285-6335

Organization: Bangkok Central Leasing Co., Ltd.
Mailing Address: 16th Flr. Sethiwan Tower, 139 Pan Rd.,
Bangkok 10500, Thailand
Contacts: Murota Masamitsu (Managing Director)
Tel: 266-6040

Fax: 266-6190, 237-4492

Organization: Bangkok Grand Pacific Lease PCL
Mailing Address: 24th Flr. Sathorn City Tower, 175 South
Sathorn Rd., Thoongmahamek, Sathorn,
Sathorn, Bangkok 10120, Thailand
Contacts: Lo Jun-Long (Managing Director)
Tel: 679-6226, 679-6262
Fax: 679-6241/2

Organization: Bangkok Leasing Co., Ltd.
Mailing Address: 8/14 Soi Intamara 49, Suthisarnvinijchai
Dingdaeng, Dindaeng,
Bangkok 10320, Thailand
Contacts: Sornthep Gomutputra (Managing Director)
Tel: 259-8636
Fax: 256-8692

Organization: Bangkok Sakura Leasing Co., Ltd.
Mailing Address: 19th Flr. Sathorn City Tower, 175 South
Sathorn Road, Bangkok 10120, Thailand
Contacts: Thongchai Ananthothai (Managing Director) Tel: 679-6161
Fax: 679-6160

Organization: Bara Sumi-Thai Leasing Co., Ltd.
Mailing Address: 10th Flr. U-Chu Liang Bldg., 968 Rama IV
Rd., Silom, Bangrak,
Bangkok 10500, Thailand
Contacts: Somchai Limpattanasin (General Manager)
Tel: 637-5445/51
Fax: n/a

Organization: BTM Leasing (Thailand) Co., Ltd.
Mailing Address: 4th Flr. Harindhorn Tower, 54 North
Sathorn Road, Bangkok 10500, Thailand
Contacts: Pichet Nuansirikosol (Director)
Tel: 266-3060
Fax: 266-3067

Organization: CMIC Leasing Co., Ltd.
Mailing Address: 8th Flr. CMIC Tower, 209 Sukhumvit 21
Rd., Bangkok 10110, Thailand
Contacts: Sobhon Dhammapalo (Managing Director)
Tel: 664-1366, 664-1360/2
Fax: 664-1365

Organization: CTI Assets Leasing Co., Ltd.
Mailing Address: 191/89 CTI Tower, M. Floor, Ratchadapisek
Road, Bangkok, Thailand
Contacts: Peansook Manrakrean
(Deputy Managing Director)
Tel: 662-661-8800-5
Fax: 662-261-1050

Organization: DKB Leasing (Thailand) Co., Ltd.
Mailing Address: 10th Flr. Bubhajit Bldg., 20 North
Sathorn Rd.,Bangkok 10500, Thailand
Contacts: Hisao Nishida (President)

For additional analytical, business and investment opportunities information,
please contact Global Investment & Business Center, USA
at (202) 546-2103. Fax: (202) 546-3275. E-mail: rusric@erols.com

Tel: 266-6431/6
Fax: 266-6440

Organization: Global Leasing Co., Ltd.
Mailing Address: 9th Flr. Maneeya Center Bldg.,
518/5 Ploenchit Rd.,
Bangkok 10330, Thailand
Contacts: Kittisak Bencharit
(Acting Managing Director)
Tel: 652-0814/16
Fax: 652-0821/2

Organization: Krung Thai IBJ Leasing Co., Ltd.
Mailing Address: 18th Flr. Thai Obayashi Bldg.,
161 Rajadamri Rd., Pathumwan,
Bangkok 10330, Thailand
Contacts: Phinyavat Chantrakantanond (President)
Tel: 651-8120, 252-9620
Fax: 254-6119

Organization: KTT Leasing Co., Ltd.
Mailing Address: 11th Flr. Sermmitr Tower 159 Soi Asoke,
Sukhumvit Rd., Bangkok 10110, Thailand
Contacts: Napaporn Ownwijitwat (Managing Director)
Tel: 661-6373 ext. 7500/4
Fax: 661-6388

Organization: Mercedes-Benz Leasing(Thailand) Co., Ltd.
Mailing Address: Rajjanakarn Building, 20th Floor
183 Sathorn Tai Road, Yannawa,
Bangkok 10120, Thailand
Contacts: Parithat Kieatbumphen
Tel: 277-0572
Fax: 690-0943

Organization: Nava Leasing Plc.
Mailing Address: 16-16/1 Soi Kasemsant 1, Payathai,
Bangkok 10330, Thailand
Contacts: Phornchit Piyawattanametha
(Managing Director)
Tel: 612-6233
Fax: 612-3255, 612-3291

Organization: Phatra Leasing Public Co., Ltd.
Mailing Address: 29th Flr. Muang Thai Phatra Complex,
252/6 Rachadapisek Rd.,Huaykwang,
Bangkok 10310, Thailand
Contacts: KrikchaiK Siribhakdi (President)
Tel: 693-2288
Fax: 693-2299

Organization: President Holding Co., Ltd.
Mailing Address: 278 Sri Nakarin Rd., Huamark,
Bangkok 10240, Thailand
Contacts: Kamthorn Tatiyakavee (President)
Tel: 374-4730
Fax: 374-7971

Organization: Primus Leasing Co., Ltd.
Mailing Address: 193/106-110 Ratchadapisek Rd.,Klongtoey,

For additional analytical, business and investment opportunities information,
please contact Global Investment & Business Center, USA
at (202) 546-2103. Fax: (202) 546-3275. E-mail: rusric@erols.com

Bangkok 10110, Thailand
Contacts: Wan Arkasalerks (Sales Manager)
Tel: 661-8822 ext.2699
Fax: 661-8470

Organization: S-One Capital Co., Ltd.
Mailing Address: 19th Flr. United Tower, 323 Silom Rd.,
Bangrak, Bangkok 10500, Thailand
Contacts: Sawad Jiarathanakul
(Managing Director)
Tel: 631-2853/7
Fax: 631-2850

Organization: SB Leasing (Thailand) Co., Ltd.
Mailing Address: 19th Flr. Ramaland Bldg.,
952 Rama IV Rd.,
Bangkok 10500, Thailand
Contacts: Takafumi Morotomi
(Managing Director)
Tel: 632-9250
Fax: 632-9258

Organization: Scandinavian Leasing PCL
Mailing Address: 20th Flr. Two Pacific Place,
142 Sukhumvit Rd.,
Bangkok 10110, Thailand
Contacts: Vinit Samritpricha
(Managing Director)
Tel: 653-2533-49
Fax: 653-2532, 653-2531

Organization: Siam City Showa Leasing Co., Ltd.
Mailing Address: 1091/179-181 New Petchburi Rd., Rajthevi,
Bangkok 10400, Thailand
Contacts: Tanabodee Kusinkert (Managing Director)
Tel: 254-1573
Fax: 253-5371

Organization: Siam Panich Leasing Publich Co., Ltd.
Mailing Address: 3rd - 5th Flr. Sino-Thai Tower,
32/24-26, 53 Sukhumvit 21 Rd., Klongtoey, Wattana,
Bangkok 10110, Thailand
Contacts: Shatchawan Kiatgraigangwan
(President)
Tel: 260-1200/7
Fax: 260-1209

Organization: Siam Samaggi Leasing Co., Ltd.
Mailing Address: 27th Flr. Sindhorn Tower,
3130-132 Wittayu Rd.,
Patumwan, Bangkok 10330, Thailand
Contacts: Thaweesin Devahastin Na Ayudhaya
(Managing Director)
Tel: 263-2990; 263-2995
Fax: 263-2991

Organization: Siam Sanwa Trilease Co., Ltd.
Mailing Address: 23rd Flr. Thaiwah Tower II, 21/145-146
South Sathorn Rd., Tungmahamek
Sathorn, Bangkok 10120, Thailand

Contacts: Pravidhya Suvaruchiphorn
(Managing Driector)
Tel: 246-9783/7
Fax: 246-9791

Organization: Sin Bualuang Leasing Co., Ltd.
Mailing Address: 9/1 Suepa Rd., Pomprab,
Bangkok 10100, Thailand
Contacts: Viboon Suchinai (Senior Vice President)
Tel: 623-1400/14
Fax: 221-5898

Organization: Thai Orix Leasing Co., Ltd.
Mailing Address: 24th Flr. C.P. Tower, 313 Silom Road,
Bangrak, Bangkok 10500, Thailand
Contacts: Suwit Arunanondchai (President)
Tel: 231-0589/99
Fax: 231-0661, 231-0936

Organization: Thaimex Leasing Co., Ltd.
Mailing Address: 24th Flr. Thai Life Insurance Bldg.,
123 Ratchadapisek Road,
Bangkok 10320, Thailand
Contacts: Smaijit Vephula (General Manager)
Tel: 246-9783/7
Fax: 246-9791

Organization: TISCO Leasing Co., Ltd.
Mailing Address: 48/5 North Sathorn Road,
Bangkok 10500, Thailand
Contacts: Rungroj Jarasvijitkul (General Manager)
Tel: 633-7799
Fax: 6337900

Organization: Toyota Leasing (Thailand) Co., Ltd.
Mailing Address: 18th -19th Flr. Abdullahim Place,
990 Rama IV Rd., Silom,
Bangrak, Bangkok 10500, Thailand
Contacts: Montri Nimkanond (Managing Director)
Tel: 636-1313, 636-1333
Fax: 636-1410/2

For additional analytical, business and investment opportunities information, please contact Global Investment & Business Center, USA at (202) 546-2103. Fax: (202) 546-3275. E-mail: rusric@erols.com

TRAVEL TO THAILAND

US STATE DEPARTMENT SUGGESTIONS

COUNTRY DESCRIPTION: Thailand is a constitutional monarchy. It is a popular travel destination, and tourist facilities and services are available throughout the country.

ENTRY/EXIT REQUIREMENTS: U.S. citizen tourists staying for less than 30 days do not require a visa, but must possess a passport and onward/return ticket. A departure tax must be paid in Thai Baht to Thai Immigration Authorities at any point of exit. Thailand's Entry/Exit information is subject to change without notice. For further information on Thailand's entry/exit requirements, please contact the Royal Thai Embassy, 1024 Wisconsin Avenue, N.W., Washington, D.C. 20007, telephone (202) 944-3600 or their Internet web site http://www.thaiembdc.org, or one of the Thai consulates in Chicago, Los Angeles, or New York City.

SAFETY AND SECURITY: Tourists should exercise caution in all border areas. They may wish to obtain information from Thai authorities about whether official border crossing points are open, and should cross into neighboring countries only at designated crossing points. In 2003, some Western tourists who strayed across the border into Burma were held in custody by the Burmese military for several days. Upon returning to Thailand, they also faced immigration violations for departing Thailand outside of a designated border crossing point. Licensed guides can help ensure that trekkers do not cross inadvertently into a neighboring country.

Pirates, bandits, and drug traffickers operate in the border areas. In February 2000, two Australians camping near the Burma border in Ang Kang Park, in the Fang District, were attacked by robbers. One of the campers was shot and killed. In April 1999, a dozen Thai villagers and tribesmen were killed in separate incidents near Thailand's northern border with Burma. In January 2000, 10 gunmen from two fringe groups in Burma crossed into Thailand and took several hundred people hostage at a provincial hospital in Ratchaburi Province. All ten gunmen were killed when Thai authorities stormed the hospital to end the crisis.

Travelers should be aware that there are occasional incidents of violence on Thailand's northern border with Laos in connection with the attempts of ethnic Hmong insurgents to cross into Laos. In July 2000, five people were killed and several fled to Thailand during a skirmish between Lao insurgents and government forces in Laos near the Chong Mek border crossing. Additionally, two U.S. citizens in 1999 and one in early 2000 were reported missing after attempting to cross into Laos at the Lao-Thai border.

Although tourists have not been targeted specifically by this occasional violence, due caution remains advisable. It is recommended that persons wishing to travel to border areas check with the Thai tourist police and the U.S. Consulate General in Chiang Mai or the U.S. Embassy in Bangkok.

CRIME INFORMATION: Pickpocketing, purse snatching, and other petty crimes are common in areas where tourists gather. Many tourists fall victim to gem scams, in which a friendly stranger offers to show the tourist an exceptional place to buy gems. The gems turn out to be greatly overpriced, and money-back guarantees are not honored. If you have fallen victim to a gem scam, please contact the local branch of the Thai Tourist Police or the Tourist Assistance Center at their local toll free phone number of 1155.

For additional analytical, business and investment opportunities information,
please contact Global Investment & Business Center, USA
at (202) 546-2103. Fax: (202) 546-3275. E-mail: rusric@erols.com

When attempting to catch a taxi at the airport, travelers should avoid unlicensed taxis and only enter taxis from the airport's official taxi stand or go to the airport limousine counter and hire a car and driver there. All major hotels in Bangkok can arrange to have a car and driver meet incoming flights. Also, it is not common for Thai taxis to pick up additional passengers, and travelers should be wary of drivers seeking to do so. In March 2000, a U.S. citizen was attacked and robbed by a taxi driver and his accomplice whom the driver picked up en route.

A growing number of travelers report being robbed after consuming drugged food or drink offered them by a friendly stranger, sometimes posing as a fellow traveler. Americans have also reported being drugged by casual acquaintances they have met in a bar or on the street. In recent years, the death of one U.S. citizen was allegedly the result of a drugging incident. Some trekking tour companies, particularly in northern Thailand, have been known to make drugs available to trekkers. Travelers should avoid accepting drugs of any kind, as the drugs may be altered or harmful, and the use or sale of drugs by trekking tour companies is illegal.

Credit card fraud has also been increasing. Travelers may wish to protect their credit cards and use them only in known or established businesses.

The loss or theft abroad of a U.S. passport should be reported immediately to the local police and the nearest U.S. embassy or consulate. U.S. citizens may refer to the Department of State's pamphlet, *A Safe Trip Abroad*, for ways to promote a more trouble-free journey. The pamphlet is available by mail from the Superintendent of Documents, U.S. Government Printing Office, Washington, D.C. 20402, via the Internet at http://www.access.gpo.gov/su_docs, or via the Bureau of Consular Affairs home page at http://travel.state.gov.

MEDICAL FACILITIES: Medical treatment, especially in Bangkok, is good. Thailand has been experiencing an epidemic of HIV infection and AIDS. Heterosexual transmission accounts for most HIV infections, and HIV is common among prostitutes of both sexes. Additionally, alcoholic beverages, medications and drugs may be more potent and of a different composition than similar ones in the United States. Several U.S. citizen tourists die each year of apparent premature heart attacks after drinking in public places or using drugs.

MEDICAL INSURANCE: U.S. medical insurance is not always valid outside the United States. U.S. Medicare and Medicaid programs do not provide payment for medical services outside the United States. Doctors and hospitals often expect immediate cash payment for health services. Uninsured travelers who require medical care overseas may face extreme difficulties.

Please check with your own insurance company to confirm whether your policy applies overseas, including provision for medical evacuation, and for adequacy of coverage. Serious medical problems requiring hospitalization and/or medical evacuation to the United States can cost tens of thousands of dollars or more. Please ascertain whether payment will be made to the overseas hospital or doctor or whether you will be reimbursed later for expenses that you incur. Some insurance policies also include coverage for psychiatric treatment and for disposition of remains in the event of death.

Persons with serious medical conditions who travel to Thailand may wish to consider insurance that specifically covers medical evacuation, because the cost for medical evacuation from Thailand can be extremely expensive.

Useful information on medical emergencies abroad, including overseas insurance programs, is provided in the Department of State's Bureau of Consular Affairs brochure, *Medical Information for Americans Traveling Abroad*, available via the Bureau of Consular Affairs home page or autofax: (202) 647-3000.

OTHER HEALTH INFORMATION: Information on vaccinations and other health precautions may be obtained from the Centers for Disease Control and Prevention's hotline for international travelers at 1-877-FYI-TRIP (1-877-394-8747); fax 1-888-CDC-FAXX (1-888-232-3299), or via the CDC's Internet site at http://www.cdc.gov.

TRAFFIC SAFETY AND ROAD CONDITIONS: While in a foreign country, U.S. citizens may encounter road conditions that differ significantly from those in the United States. The information below concerning Thailand is provided for general reference only, and may not be totally accurate in a particular location or circumstance.
Safety of Public Transportation: Good
Urban Road Conditions/Maintenance: Good
Rural Road Conditions/Maintenance: Good
Availability of Roadside Assistance: Poor

Traffic moves on the left in Thailand. The city of Bangkok has heavy traffic composed of motorcycles, cars, trucks, and three wheeled "tuk-tuks." Accidents are common. In 1999, five Americans were killed in traffic accidents in Thailand. Two of these Americans were killed while riding motorcycles. Use of motorcycle helmets is mandatory, but this law is rarely enforced. Congested roads and a scarcity of ambulances can make it difficult for accident victims to receive timely medical attention. Paved roads connect Thailand's major cities, but most have only two lanes. Slow-moving trucks limit speed and visibility. Speeding and reckless passing in all regions is common. Consumption of alcohol, amphetamines and other stimulants by commercial drivers is also common. In February 1999, there were two serious bus crashes involving foreign passengers on overnight bus trips; one of these crashes resulted in fatalities. Motorists may wish to obtain accident insurance that covers medical and liability costs. The more affluent driver, even if not at fault, is frequently compelled to cover the expenses of the other party in an accident in Thailand.

Travelers may wish to use Bangkok's recently unveiled skytrain to travel about the city. The multi-million dollar project was completed in late 1999. The system offers a cheap and fast alternative to maneuvering Bangkok's congested city streets. The skytrain operates everyday from 6:00am to 12:00 midnight.

For specific information concerning Thai driver's permits, vehicle inspection, road tax and mandatory insurance, please contact the Thai National Tourist Organization offices in New York via the Internet at http://www.tat.or.th/index-shock.htm.

AVIATION SAFETY OVERSIGHT: The U.S. Federal Aviation Administration (FAA) has assessed the Government of Thailand's civil aviation authority as Category 1 - in compliance with international aviation safety standards for oversight of Thailand's air carrier operations.

For further information, travelers may contact the Department of Transportation within the U.S. at telephone 1-800-322-7873, or visit the FAA's Internet web site at http://www.faa.gov/avr/iasa/. The U.S. Department of Defense (DOD) separately assesses some foreign air carriers for suitability as official providers of air services. For information regarding the DOD policy on specific carriers, travelers may contact the DOD at telephone (618) 229-4801.

For additional analytical, business and investment opportunities information, please contact Global Investment & Business Center, USA at (202) 546-2103. Fax: (202) 546-3275. E-mail: rusric@erols.com

CUSTOMS REGULATIONS: Thai customs authorities may enforce strict regulations concerning temporary importation into or export from Thailand of items such as firearms, explosives, narcotics and drugs, radio equipment, books or other printed material and video or audio recordings which might be considered subversive to national security, obscene, or in any way harmful to the public interest and cultural property. It is advisable to contact the Embassy of Thailand in Washington, D.C. or one of the Thai consulates in the United States for specific information regarding customs requirements.

Thai customs authorities encourage the use of an ATA (Admission Temporaire/Temporary Admission) Carnet for the temporary admission of professional equipment, commercial samples, and/or goods for exhibitions and fair purposes. ATA Carnet Headquarters, located at the U.S. Council for International Business, 1212 Avenue of the Americas, New York, NY 10036, issues and guarantees the ATA Carnet in the United States. For additional information, please call telephone (212) 354-4480, or send an e-mail to atacarnet@uscib.org, or visit http://www.uscib.org for details.

CRIMINAL PENALTIES: While in a foreign country, a U.S. citizen is subject to that country's laws and regulations, which sometimes differ significantly from those in the United States and may not afford the protections available to the individual under U.S. law. Penalties for breaking the law can be more severe than in the United States for similar offenses. Persons violating Thai laws, even unknowingly, may be expelled, arrested or imprisoned.

In this connection, it is inappropriate to make negative comments about the King or other members of the Royal Family. Thais hold the King in the highest regard, and it is a serious crime to make critical or defamatory comments about him. This particular crime, dubbed "lese majeste," is punishable by a prison sentence of 3 to 15 years. Purposefully tearing or destroying Thai bank notes, which carry an image of the King, may be considered such an offense.

Penalties for possession, use, or trafficking in illegal drugs in Thailand are strict, and convicted offenders can expect jail sentences and heavy fines. Thailand strictly enforces its drug laws, including those prohibiting possession of small quantities of marijuana. The U.S. Embassy frequently does not learn of the arrest of U.S. citizens for minor drug offenses, particularly in Southern Thailand, until several days after the incident. Prison conditions in Thailand are harsh, and Thailand has a death sentence for serious drug offenses. Americans convicted of drug trafficking have received long sentences, often in excess of forty years. There are more than thirty Americans serving long-term prison sentences in Thailand. A ruse sometimes used to get U.S. citizens to transport drugs out of the country involves offering the American a free vacation to Thailand, then requesting the American's assistance in transporting excess "luggage" or gifts back to the United States. The American's claim that he or she did not know that the package contained drugs has not been a successful legal defense in Thailand.

CHILDREN'S ISSUES: For information on international adoption of children and international parental child abduction, please refer to our Internet site at http://travel.state.gov/children's_issues.html or telephone (202) 736-7000.

REGISTRATION/EMBASSY AND CONSULATE LOCATIONS: Americans living in or visiting Thailand are encouraged to register at the Consular Section of the U.S. Embassy in Thailand and obtain updated information on travel and security within Thailand. The U.S. Embassy is located at 95 Wireless Road in Bangkok; the U.S. mailing address is APO AP 96546-0001. The telephone number is (66-2) 205-4000 and the fax number is (66-2) 205-4103. The web site for the U.S. Embassy in Bangkok is http://usa.or.th/embassy/index.htm. The U.S. Consulate General in Chiang Mai is located at 387 Wichayanond Road; the U.S. mailing address is Box C, APO AP 96546. The telephone number is (66-53) 252-629 and the fax number is (66-53) 252-633.

KING TAKSIN: WARFARE AND NATIONAL REVIVAL

KING TAKSIN : [1767-1782]

After the shattering defeat which had culminated in Ayutthaya's destruction, the death and capture of thousands of Thais by the victorious Burmese, and the dispersal of several potential Thai leaders, the situation seemed hopeless. It was a time of darkness and of troubles for the Thai nation. Members of the old royal family of Ayutthaya had died, escaped, or been captured by the Burmese and many rival claimants for the throne emerged, based in different areas of the country.

But out of this national catastrophe emerged yet another saviour of the Thai state : the half-Chinese general Phraya Taksin, former governor of Tak. Within a few years this determined warrior had defeated not only all his rivals but also the Burmese invaders and had set himself up as king,

Since Ayutthaya had been so completely devastated. King Taksin chose to establish his capital at Thon Buri [*across the river from Bangkok* .

Although a small town, Thon Buri was strategically situated near the mouth of the Chao Phraya River and therefore suitable as a seaport. The Thais needed weapons, and one way of acquiring them was through trade. Besides, foreign trade was also needed to bolster the Thai economy, which had suffered extensively during the war with Burma(now Myanmar). Chinese and Chinese-Thai traders helped revive the economy by engaging in maritime trade with neighbouring states, with China, and with some European nations.

King Taksin's prowess as a general and as an inspirational leader meant that all attempts by the Burmese to reconquer Siam failed. The rallying of the Thai nation during a time of crisis was King Taksin's greatest achievement. However, he was also interested in cultural revival, in literature and the arts. He was deeply religious and studied meditation to an advanced level. The stress and strain of such much fighting and the responsibility of rebuilding a centralized Thai state took their toll on the king. Following an internal political conflict in 1782. King Taksin's fellow general Chao Phraya Chakri was chosen king. King Taksin's achievements have caused posperity to bestow on him the epithet *"the Great".*,

BUSINESS TRAVEL

BUSINESS CUSTOMS

Business relationships in Thailand are not as formal as those found in Japan, China, Korea or the Middle East, but neither are they as relaxed and impersonal as is common in the West. Many business relationships have their foundations in personal relationships developed within the social circles of family, friends, classmates and office colleagues. Although Thailand is a relatively open and friendly society, it is advisable to approach potential business contacts with a prior introduction or personal reference. Thais will be more receptive if you arrive with an introduction or letter from a known government official or business contact. Using the Commercial Service's Gold Key Program is also an effective way to gain access.

The Thai cultural values of patience, respect for status (age, authority, etc.) and not losing face, are significant factors in business relationships as well. Thais feel great pride for their country and have deep respect for tradition. Sometimes, however, observance of traditional formalities may

For additional analytical, business and investment opportunities information, please contact Global Investment & Business Center, USA at (202) 546-2103. Fax: (202) 546-3275. E-mail: rusric@erols.com

seem inconsistent to the tolerant, relaxed nature of living in Thailand. This can be confusing or frustrating to Westerners who are more informal and more time conscious.

Respect for, and consideration of, one's elders, superiors and patrons is deeply rooted in the Thai cultural and social environments. Thais are very reluctant to hurt the feelings of others or to cause them any dissatisfaction. Losing one's composure is losing face and losing respect in Thailand. Therefore, it can be difficult for Westerners to be sure they have received accurate and complete answers to questions, or that they have solicited frank and open opinions. (Source: Thailand Business Basics, Standard Chartered Bank.)

The revelation of what Westerners regard as rampant graft, corruption, and favoritism as an integral part of Thai business and political practice, and the recognition of the great cost to society these actions have caused in the wake of the financial disaster, is causing many Thais to openly criticize, for the first time, the behavior of the privileged and powerful. Previously referred to euphemistically as "the Thai way", such favoritism was not necessarily tolerated, but not directly challenged. The new economic and social era in the making holds promise of also being fairer and more transparent.

U.S. business travelers are encouraged to obtain a copy of the "Key Officers of Foreign Service Posts: Guide for Business Representatives" available for sale by the Superintendent of Documents, U.S. Government Printing Office, Washington, D.C. 20402; Tel. (202) 512-1800; Fax (202) 512-2250. Business travelers to Thailand seeking appointments with US Embassy Bangkok Officials should contact the Commercial Section in advance. The Commercial Section can be reached by telephone at (662) 205-5090, Fax at (662) 255-2915, or email at obangkok@mail.doc.gov.

ETIQUETTE

"Khun" is the Thai form of address for Mr., Mrs. and Ms. - The "wai" is a traditional gesture of greeting and respect in Thailand. Practice by placing your palms together in a prayer- like position. - Business cards are an indispensable part of making business contacts in Thailand. Bring lots of your own as a general form of introduction.

- Remove shoes before entering a home or temple.
- Touching someone on the head or pointing your feet to anything
is considered by Thais to be very rude.
- Thais hold the Royal Family in the highest esteem and you are
also expected to do so.

TRAVEL ADVISORY AND VISAS

Americans who register at the U.S. Embassy or a U.S. Consulate can obtain updated information on travel and security within the country.

US citizens holding American passports and onward/return tickets do not need visas for stays of up to 1 month. However, without a visa, entry is permitted only when arriving at the international airports in Bangkok, Phuket, Hat Yai or Chiang Mai. For longer stays, or overland entry, travelers can obtain visas in advance from a Thai embassy or consulate. For stays of up to 90 days a tourist visa is required, the fee for which is $20. For more current information travelers may contact the Royal Thai Embassy,1024 Wisconsin Avenue, N.W. Washington D.C. 20007, Tel (202)944-3600, Fax (202)944-3611.

For additional analytical, business and investment opportunities information,
please contact Global Investment & Business Center, USA
at (202) 546-2103. Fax: (202) 546-3275. E-mail: rusric@erols.com

HOLIDAYS:

During the calendar year 2000, the following are the commercial holidays on which most business and government offices in Thailand will be closed.

January 1 New Year's Day
February 5 Chinese New Year
March* Maka Bucha Day
April 6 King Rama I Memorial & Chakri Day
April 13 Songkran Day
April 14 Songkran Day
April 15 Songkran Day
May 1 National Labor Day
May 5 Coronation Day
May 14 Ploughing Day
May* Visakha Bucha Day (Full Moon Day)
July 1 Bank Mid-Year Closing Day
July 17 Asalha Bucha Day (marks the beginning of
Buddhist Lent)
August 12 H.M. the Queen's Birthday
October 23 Chulalongkorn Day
December 5 H.M. the King's Birthday and National Day
December 10 Constitution Day
December 31 New Year's Eve

* Dates vary each year according to the lunar calendar.

In addition, the American Embassy and many other U.S. offices will observe the following holidays:

January 17 Martin Luther King, Jr. Birthday
February 21 President's Day
May 29 Memorial Day
July 4 Independence Day
September 4 Labor Day
October 9 Columbus Day
November 10 Veterans Day
November 23 Thanksgiving Day
December 25 Christmas Day

WORK WEEK:

The common professional workweek in Thailand is 40 hours per week consisting of five 8-hour days, Monday through Friday. Office hours in Bangkok vary to accommodate flex-time travel through the city's notorious traffic. Common office hours are 8:00am to 5:00pm. Most offices are closed on Saturday and Sunday.

BUSINESS INFRASTRUCTURE

TRANSPORTATION

The business traveler has access to a range of ground transportation in Bangkok and major cities. Metered taxis are common and most hotels offer limousine services. Chauffeured cars can be rented for extended stays. Public transportation in the form of inter-city air-conditioned buses, and minibuses serve the general population and vary in comfort and efficiency. Inter-city rail service ranges from comfortable and efficient to primitive. Inter-city air service is efficient.

Thailand's road system compares favorably with that of other developing countries in the region. Transport of goods and passenger services by rail, sea, air and road generally is good. Major inter-city links are being expanded into 4 or more lane highways. Rural roads are being improved. However, Bangkok metropolitan area traffic is legendary for its congestion -- vying for being the worst in the world.

Expressways, highways and mass transit infrastructure are all in the works, but during their construction period, they are actually making the situation worse in traffic, pollution and safety. Road transportation is considered Thailand's key transportation mode for goods and passengers. Thus the RTG plans to invest about 9 billion Baht (approximately US$229 million at an exchange rate of US$1 = Baht 40) for the construction of three inter-city motor ways which will be privatized and tolls charged. They are scheduled to be completed in 1999/2000.

Because of the cash shortfalls due to the economic crisis, several mass transit systems, including the Hopewell Red Line Rail (elevated train) project have been abandoned by their contractors. The contract was finally canceled by the government, which is now looking at restructuring options. The BMTA sky train will be in operation in the second half of 1999 and the subway will be completed in the next three years.

The State Railway of Thailand operates 3,800 kms of rail tracks with 623 destinations and four main routes: Bangkok-north to Chiang Mai; northeast to Nongkhai and Ubon Rajathani; east to Prachinburi; and, south to the Thai-Malaysian border. A rail route from Rayong to the Eastern Seaboard Development Project to Bangkok is being studied and designs evaluated. Because rail development is needed, the State Railway of Thailand, when RTG budget becomes available, will accelerate implementation of its planned 800 kilometers double-track construction project.

Thailand has coastlines on the Gulf of Thailand and on the Andaman Sea with 58 sea channels, 40 operational seaports and 90 fishing trawler piers. Out of 6,000 kilometers of navigable inland waterways, 1,750 kilometers can be used as transportation routes for bulk cargo. Thailand offers the advantages of low-priced handling, cheap labor and inexpensive storage costs.

Thailand currently has five international airports: Bangkok International Airport, Chiang Mai International Airport, Chiang Rai International Airport, Hat Yai International Airport, and Phuket International Airport. Thailand also has 27 airports that service domestic flights. Bangkok International Airport (BIA), which is located just north of Bangkok, serves as Thailand's main gateway for air transportation. Handling 27 million passengers per year, the Bangkok International Airport will reach its handling capacity by 2003.

The Royal Thai Government (RTG) has decided to return to the original plan of developing a Second Bangkok International Airport (SBIA) as Thailand's primary international airport and aviation hub with a passenger capacity of 30 million per year by 2003-4. In addition, four other domestic airports -- Nakhon Sri Thammarat; Roi-et; Petchabun, and Krabi -- are now under construction and expected to be completed and in operation by the year 1999/2000.

For additional analytical, business and investment opportunities information, please contact Global Investment & Business Center, USA at (202) 546-2103. Fax: (202) 546-3275. E-mail: rusric@erols.com

LANGUAGE

Thai is the national language. English is the next most commonly spoken language, especially among the business community. (There are four distinct language dialects in Thailand, with the Central Thai dialect being the first language of 75 percent of the population.) Many Sino-Thais also speak Chinese. Because of the large number of Japanese subsidiary companies in Thailand, Japanese is also common.

BANKING SERVICES

A good range of commercial banking services is available in Thailand for both business and retail customers. Deposit accounts, lending facilities, foreign exchange, import/export facilities and other products and services such as credit cards and automatic teller machines (ATM) are offered. Some limitations, such as on mortgage lending to foreigners, do exist, reflecting restrictions on foreign ownership of property. Foreign banks have applied to join the local ATM network. The Hong Kong Shanghai Bank was admitted in December 1996, and Citibank in May 1996. This enables their customers to use their overseas bank ATM card at any ATM within the domestic network. There are about 5,000 ATM's in Thailand and the number continues to grow.

COMMUNICATIONS

Communications for the business traveler in Bangkok and major cities is efficient, with worldwide access for voice, fax and data with international direct dialing. Cellular phones are very common and can be rented for short stays. A foreign cellular phone will not work in Thailand, although the appearance of the new global G.P.S. phones will change that. In rural or remote areas cell coverage is spotty and only first class hotels have reliable land coverage.

Thailand is a member of the International Telecommunications Satellite Consortium, and maintains 2 ground stations connected to satellites over the Pacific and Indian oceans to provide convenient radio communication services. On December 17, 1992, THAICOM, the first Thai national satellite, was launched into orbit followed by THAICOM 2 on October 8, 1994, and THAICOM 3 on April 16, 2002.

Thailand is served by the major international cable television channels including CNN, BBC, CNBC, ABN, Star TV, HBO etc. which are widely available in hotels, residences and other public places.

Thailand's economic plunge has caused a sharp decline in the demand for telecommunications services that include landline telephone, cellular phone, radio communications, paging, and VSAT services. Consequently, planned investments in the expansion of 6 million landline telephones and cellular phones in the radio frequency ranges of 1500 and 1900-megahertz have been deferred. However, the installation of rural public long distance telephone lines and the installation of submarine fiber optic cable are not affected by the present economic crisis.

For a landline telephone, the installation fee is US$103, the required deposit is $84, the monthly service fee is $2.80, and the flat rate for a local call is $0.08. For a cellular phone, handset prices range from US$300 to $1,000, the mandatory deposit is $84, the connection fee is $36, the monthly service fee is $14, and local cellular calls cost $0.08 per minute.

For electronic communications, Thailand provides 3 main solutions for temporary Internet access. First, purchasing an Internet package from a local ISP in prepaid amounts for anywhere from 10 to 50 hours. Second, cyber-cafés, which are located throughout Bangkok and in major provinces. Third, Internet access provided in high-end hotels catering to business travelers.

UTILITIES

Electrical current in Thailand is 220 volts. Business travelers should bring converters and surge protectors but they are also available on the local market.

Water quality ranges widely. Many Thai people drink bottled water which is inexpensive and readily available. In Bangkok and major cities, tap water is safe enough for bathing. Water is priced from $0.15 to $0.43 per cubic meter in accordance with the usage.

HEALTH

Excellent medical treatment is available in Bangkok, with good to adequate treatment available throughout the country. While the general level of health and nutrition is good, some tropical diseases are a problem. Hepatitis is endemic. The incidence of AIDS has plateaued due to educational awareness campaigns by the Royal Thai Government. However, Thailand is still considered a high-risk country, especially among prostitutes and intravenous drug users. Malaria is a problem in rural border areas, but not in Bangkok, major cities, or major tourist destinations. Dengue fever outbreaks occur periodically throughout the country.

Doctors and hospitals often expect immediate cash payment for services, and U.S. medical insurance is not always valid outside the United States. Many hospitals in Bangkok and other major cities will accept standard credit cards. For additional useful health information, contact the International Travelers' Hotline at the Center of Disease Control at 404-332-4559.

FOOD

Eating is an important part of the Thai group-oriented culture. Thai food has become internationally popular because of its sophistication and variety. The staples of this cuisine include rice, noodles, vegetables, meats, fish, spices and chilies. Thai food can be enjoyed in a wide variety of venues, from street-side kiosks to elegant world-class restaurants. In addition, all other international cuisines are available in the major cities and resort areas ranging from European fine dining, to other Oriental and ethnic restaurants, to American fast food.

ACCOMMODATION

All types of accommodations are available - from five star international hotels, to serviced apartments, to moderate, comfortable business hotels, to modest but safe, clean guesthouses. Establishments catering to business clientele usually offer full-service business centers with international communications. The economic downturn, and overbuilding of hotels means that Bangkok is offering some of the best accommodation bargains in the world, and Thailand is vying actively for business and leisure travel and convention business.

Ample western style residential apartments and houses are available for foreign residents. The construction of high-rise condominium projects in the past few years has increased available quality accommodation in the Bangkok metropolitan area and other major cities.

TEMPORARY ENTRY OF GOODS

Thai Customs Department policy and procedures on temporary entry of goods for business practices and exhibitions are described below. For further information, please contact Bangkok International Airport Customs House tel: (662) 535-1550, Public Relations Sub-Division, Customs Department tel: (662) 249-9017, 249-3298; Customs Department web site: www.customs.go.th or the Commercial Service Bangkok tel: (662) 205-5090.

GOODS FOR BUSINESS PRACTICE

Laptop Computers: The Thai Customs Department considers laptop computers as reasonable personal effects and not dutiable, restricted or prohibited goods. If travelers carry laptop computers for use while visiting Thailand, they should check the "Nothing to Declare" box on customs declaration form and submit the form at the Green channel.

Computer Software: Unwrapped computer diskettes for use while visiting Thailand are not dutiable. Check the "Nothing to Declare" box on customs declaration form and submit the form at the Green channel. However, significant volumes of wrapped software packages are considered dutiable and import duty payment may be requested.

EXHIBIT MATERIALS

There are 2 choices of Customs procedures for entering exhibit materials exempted from duty payment into Thailand.

1. Bonded Guarantee (A.T.A.Carnet): A.T.A. Carnet is an international system that provides bonded guarantees on goods imported temporarily. Its purpose is to facilitate customs procedures for temporary import-export of goods which are exempt from payment of duty without prohibited and restricted conditions. All member states accept and provide this service under their own laws and regulations.

The Thai Customs Department recommends exhibit materials enter into Thailand through a carnet as it cuts down the required Customs procedures. The guarantee issuer and guarantor must be approved by the Customs Department and be a member of the international guarantee issuer organization such as a U.S. Trade Association or Chamber of Commerce. The guarantee issuer organization can issue a letter of guarantee to exporters in which they agree to pay duty if carnet conditions are not followed.

An importer can use the letter of guarantee as a substitute to the import entry form and the payment guarantee. The importer must complete the carnet import/re-export document and submit it to Customs officers at Thailand's port of entry. The Customs officers will inspect the goods, keep a copy of the import entry form and return the carnet book to the importer. If the goods are not taken out within the period of time stated in the contract, the guarantor will have to pay duty, a 10 percent penalty, and any applicable fees. For further information, please contact the Privilege Goods and Investment Promotion Sub-Division tel: (662) 249-4150, fax: (662) 249-4212.

2. Imported goods for exhibition in Thailand: Exhibit materials apply to goods which are imported for public exhibition and goods on which the importer has placed a bonded guarantee and will be re-exported in the certain period of time. Goods used up in an exhibition such as printed documents, advertised articles, and distributed materials are not duty exempted items. The process for temporary importation of exhibit materials into Thailand is as follows:

* The importer must provide detailed information on the exhibition including the host, venue, period of time, reasons for importation, and goods category to the Customs Department for temporary import permission.

* The importer must submit a duty exempted application with certification of the exhibition, an import entry form with documents such as invoice, Airway bill, and packing list and a permission form for import of restricted goods. The importer signs for the materials, states the period of temporary entry (must be under 6 months), and places a cash deposit or Bank's guarantee for the following total (duty + 140 percent + VAT.)

* Customs officers will inspect the goods and return a copy of the special Import Entry Form to the controller of the goods to be presented on the way of taking the goods out of Thailand. The controller may appoint a local firm, as an importer, to deliver the material from the port of entry to the exhibition site.

* When taking the materials out of the country, the controller shall present a copy of the special Import Entry Form to the Customs officers and shall withdraw the guarantee contract. If the importer has shown intention of not taking the goods out of country within the period of time stated in the contract, the guarantee contract will be enforced.

* Regarding contract extensions, the importer can request an extension of 6 months from the date of entry. To receive this extension, the importer must submit an application to the Customs House or to the Laws and Regulations Division, Customs Department for approval.

SUPPLEMENTS

U.S. AND THAILAND CONTACTS

The U.S. & Foreign Commercial Service and the Economic Section at the U.S. Embassy in Bangkok maintain extensive files on key organizations in Thailand. Contact them for more information.

U.S. GOVERNMENT

U.S. EMBASSY, THAILAND
The Honorable Richard E. Hecklinger
Ambassador of the United States of America
to the Kingdom of Thailand
120 Wireless Road
Bangkok, Thailand 10330
or mail from U.S.
American Embassy - Bangkok
APO AP 96535
Tel: 662-205-4000
Fax: 662-205-4499

U.S. AND FOREIGN COMMERCIAL SERVICE
Senior Commercial Officer: Ms. Karen Ware
U.S. Embassy Bangkok
Diethelm Towers A, 3rd Floor
93/1 Wireless Road
Bangkok 10330
Tel: 662-205-5090
Fax: 662-255-2915
E-mail: obangkok@mail.doc.gov
or mail from U.S.
American Embassy - Bangkok
Box 51
APO AP 96546
Note: The U.S. and Foreign Commercial Service helps U.S. business to export to and develop their business in Thailand.

ECONOMIC SECTION
Economic Counselor: Mr. Robert Fitts
U.S. Embassy Bangkok
120 Wireless Road
Bangkok 10330
Tel: 662-205-4995
Fax: 662-254-2839
or mail from U.S.
American Embassy - Bangkok
APO AP 96546

U.S.D.A. FOREIGN AGRICULTURAL SERVICE
Agricultural Counselor: Mr. Maurice House
U.S. Embassy Bangkok

Diethelm Towers A, 4th Floor
93/1 Wireless Road
Bangkok 10330
Tel: 662-205-5106
Fax: 662-255-2907
or mail from U.S.
American Embassy - Bangkok
APO AP 96546
E-mail: agbangkok@fas.usda.gov

U.S.-ASIA ENVIRONMENTAL PARTNERSHIP (US-AEP)
Director of Technology Cooperation: Mr. Jack Kneeland
Diethelm Tower A, 3rd Floor
93/1 Wireless Road
Bangkok 10330
Tel: 662-651-5782, Central line: 205-4000 Ext. 2761, 2762
Fax: 662-254-2838
E-mail: usaepbkk@lox2.loxinfo.co.th
or mail from U.S.
Box 51
APO AP 96546
Note: US-AEP is managed by the U.S. and Foreign Commercial Service in Bangkok. It provides cost-share assistance grants to U.S. environmental companies and sponsors environmental business conferences and workshops.

ROYAL THAI GOVERNMENT

GENERAL

MINISTRY OF FOREIGN AFFAIRS

Department of Economic Affairs
Director: Mr. Kobsak Chutikul
Saranrom Palace, Sanam Chai Road, Bangkok 10200
Tel: 662-225-7382
Fax: 662-226-1841

Department of American and South Pacific Affairs
North America Division
Director: Mr. Isorn Pocmontri
Saranrom Palace, Sanam Chai Road, Bangkok 10200
Tel: 662-222-3813
Fax: 662-225-7388

Royal Thai Embassy in Washington
His Excellency Mr. Nitya Pibulsonggram
Ambassador Extraordinary and Plenipotentiary
1024 Wisconsin Avenue, N.W. Suite 401
Washington, DC 20007
Tel: 202-944-3600
Fax: 202-944-3611

OFFICE OF THE PRIME MINISTER

National Economic and Social Development Board (NESDB)
Secretary-General: Mr. Sansern Wongcha-un
962 Krung Kasem Road, Bangkok 10100
Tel: 662-282-5417, 281-0947
Fax: 662-280-0892

Board of Investment (BOI)
Secretary-General: Mr. Staporn Kavitanon
555 Vipavadee Rangsit Road
Bangkok 10900, Thailand
Tel: 662-537-8111, 537-8155
Fax: 662-537-8177

National Energy Policy Office (NEPO)
Secretary-General: Dr. Piyasvasti Amranand
78 Ratchadamnoen Nok Road
Bangkok 10300
Tel: 662-282-9027/31
Fax: 662-280-0292, 280-0281, 280-2035

MINISTRY OF INTERIOR

Office of the Board of the Control of
The Engineering and Architectural Profession Division
Director: Mr. Polwat Chayanuwat
Office of the Permanent Secretary for Interior
Atsadang Road, Bangkok 10200
Tel: 662-281-1567, 282-2161

MINISTRY OF COMMERCE

Department of Foreign Trade
Director-General: Mr. Pracha Charutrakulchai
Sanam Chai Road
Bangkok 10200
Tel: 662-224-4883/4
Fax: 662-224-7269

Department of Commercial Registration
Director-General: Mr. Somsak Yamasmit
Maharat Road
Bangkok 10200
Tel: 662-224-0031
Fax: 662-255-8493

MINISTRY OF FINANCE

The Customs Department
Director-General: Mr. Somchainuk Engtrakul
Soonthornkosa Road, Khlong Toey

For additional analytical, business and investment opportunities information,
please contact Global Investment & Business Center, USA
at (202) 546-2103. Fax: (202) 546-3275. E-mail: rusric@erols.com

Bangkok 10110
Tel: 662-249-0442, 249-0430/40
Fax: 662-249-2874

MINISTRY OF INDUSTRY

Department of Industrial Works
Environment Department
Director-General: Mr. Thien Mekanontchai
76/5 Rama VI Road
Bangkok 10400
Tel: 662-202-4100
Fax: 662-245-6715

Department of Industrial Promotion
Director-General: Mr. Manu Leopairote
Rama VI Road, Ratchathevi
Bangkok 10400
Tel: 662-245-6655, 202-4555
Fax: 662-246-1155

Thai Industrial Standards Institute
Secretary-General: Ms. Kanya Sinsakul
Rama VI Road, Ratchathevi
Bangkok 10400
Tel: 662-202-3400,202-3401/2
Fax: 662-246-4085

Industrial Estates Authority of Thailand
Governor: Mr. Somchet Thinapong
618 Nikhom Makkasan Road, Ratchathewi,
Bangkok 10400
Tel: 662-253-3398, 253-4085
Fax: 662-253-4086

MINISTRY OF SCIENCE, TEHNOLOGY AND ENVIRONMENT

Office of Environmental Policy and Planning
Secretary-General: Mr. Chatree Chueyprasit
60/1 Soi Pibulwatana 7
Rama VI Road, Bangkok 10400
Tel: 662-279-8086, 279-7180 ext. 300
Fax: 662-270-1661

Pollution Control Department
Director-General: Mr. Saksit Tridech
404 Phaholyothin Center Building
Samsen Nai, Phaya Thai,
Bangkok 10400
Tel: 662-619-2316, 619-2299 ext. 103
Fax: 662-619-2285

MINISTRY OF PUBLIC HEALTH

Food and Drug Administration
Secretary-General: Dr. Mongkol Na Songkhla
Tivanond Road, Muang
Nonthaburi 11000
Tel: 662-591-8441
Fax: 662-591-8452

OTHER INDEPENDENT GOVERNMENT AGENCIES

Bank of Thailand
Governor: Mr. Chatu-Mongkol Sonnakul
273 Sam Sen Road
Bangkok 10200
Tel: 662-283-5001, 283-5353
Fax: 662-280-0449

Bangkok Metropolitan Administration
Governor: Mr. Bhichit Rattakul
173 Dinso Road
Bangkok 10200
Tel: 662-621-0812/27
Fax: 662-21-0831

Trade Associations

AMERICAN CHAMBER OF COMMERCE IN THAILAND (AMCHAM)
Executive Director: Mr. Thomas A. Seale
7th Floor, Kian Gwan Bldg.
140 Wireless Road
Bangkok 10330
Tel: 662-651-9266/7, 651-4473
Fax: 662-651-4472, 651-4474
Note: AmCham is the premier U.S. business organization in Thailand with more than 600 U.S. member companies.

U.S.-ASEAN COUNCIL FOR BUSINESS AND TECHNOLOGY, INC.
President: Mr. Ernest Bower
1400 L Street, N.W. Suite 375
Washington, D.C. 20005-3509
Tel: 202-289-1911
Fax: 202-289-0519

THAILAND-U.S. BUSINESS COUNCIL
Chairman: Mr. Chatri Sophonpanitch
49 Asia Sermkij Tower
Soi Pipat, Silom Road
Bangrak, Bangkok 10500
Tel: 662-231-5934/8
Fax: 662-231-5919

For additional analytical, business and investment opportunities information,
please contact Global Investment & Business Center, USA
at (202) 546-2103. Fax: (202) 546-3275. E-mail: rusric@erols.com

Note: These partner business councils are important for policy and senior executive business information exchange.

U.S. THAILAND BUSINESS COUNCIL
Co-Chairmen: Mr. Rubin Mark & Mr. Theodore Roosevelt
3050 K. Street, N.W. Suite 105
Washington, D.C. 20007
Tel: 202-337-5973
Fax: 202-337-0039
Note: This Council is at the forefront of U.S.-ASEAN affairs and sponsors senior interchanges including the annual U.S.-ASEAN Ambassador's Tour in the U.S. and senior executive visits to ASEAN.

BOARD OF TRADE OF THAILAND (BOT)
Chairman: Mr. Vichien Techapaibul
150 Rajbopit Road
Bangkok 10200
Tel: 662-221-0555, 221-1827, 221-9350, 221-1827, 222-9031, 223-2069
Fax: 662-225-3995, 226-5563

FEDERATION OF THAI INDUSTRIES (FTI)
Chairman: Mr. Tawee Butsoonthorn
Queen Sirikit National Convention Center
Zone C, 4th Floor, 60 New Rachadapisek Road
Klong Toey, Bangkok 10110
Tel: 662-229-4255
Fax: 662-229-4941/2
Note: The Federation of Thai Industries membership represents most of the major industry sectors and their industry associations.

THAI CHAMBER OF COMMERCE (TCC)
President: Mr. Vichien Techapaibul
150 Rajbopit Road
Bangkok 10200
Tel: 662-225-0086
Fax: 662-225-3372

COMMERCIAL BANK WITH U.S. AFFILIATIONS

BANK OF AMERICA BANGKOK BRANCH
Country Manager: Mr. Frederick Chin
2/2 Wireless Road, Bank of America Center
Bangkok 10330
Tel: 662-251-6333
Fax: 662-253-1905

BANK OF AYUDHYA PCL.
President: Mr. Krit Ratanarak
1222 Rama 3 Road, Bang Pongphang
Yannawa
Bangkok 10120

Tel: 662-296-3009
Fax: 662-253-8615

BANGKOK BANK PUBLIC CO., LTD.
President: Mr. Chartsiri Sophonpanich
333 Silom Road,
Bangkok 10500
Tel: 662-231-4333, 231-4665
Fax: 662-236-8288

CHASE MANHATTAN BANK
Managing Director: Mr. Raymond Chang
20 North Sathorn Road, Bubhajit Building
Bangkok 10500
Tel: 662-234-5992/5, 238-1720/4
Fax: 662-234-8386, 234-7853

CITIBANK NA
General Manager: Mr. Henry Ho
Citibank Tower, 82 North Sathorn Road
Bangrak, Bangkok 10500
Tel: 662-639-2000, 232-2000
Fax: 662-639-2560, 639-2550

KRUNG THAI BANK LTD.
President: Mr. Singh Tangtatswas
35 Sukhumvit Road
Bangkok 10110
Tel: 662-255-2222
Fax: 662-255-9391/7, 255-9378, 255-8436

SIAM CITY BANK PUBLIC CO., LTD.
President: Mr. Sompoch Intranukul
1101 New Petchburi Road
Phayathai, Bangkok 10400
Tel: 662-253-0200/43, 208-5000
Fax: 662-253-1240

SIAM COMMERCIAL BANK PUBLIC CO., LTD.
President: Ms. Jada Wattanasiritham
9 Rachadapisek Rd.
Ladyao, Jatujak
Bangkok 10900
Tel: 662-544-1111, 937-7777
Fax: 662-937-7687

THAI FARMERS BANK LTD.
President: Mr. Banthoon Lamsam
1 Moo 2, Soi Thai Farmer
Ratburana Road, Khet Ratburana
Bangkok 10140

**For additional analytical, business and investment opportunities information,
please contact Global Investment & Business Center, USA
at (202) 546-2103. Fax: (202) 546-3275. E-mail: rusric@erols.com**

Tel: 662-470-1122, 470-1199
Fax: 662-470-2748/9

THAI MILITARY BANK
President: Dr. Thanong Bidaya
3000 Phaholyothin Road
Chatuchak
Bangkok 10900
Tel: 662-273-7164
Fax: 662-273-7121

MARKET RESEARCH FIRMS

AGRISOURCE
Managing Director: Mr. Tim Welsh
Resources for Agribusiness
Ambassador's Court, 4th Fl., No. 416
76/1 Soi Lang Suan, Ploenchit Road
Bangkok 10330
Tel: 662-251-8655/6, 251-8669
Fax: 662-251-0390

ASIAN SOLUTIONS RESEARCH
Managing Director: Mr. Bill Condie
76/26 Lang Suan House
Soi Lang Suan, Ploenchit Road
Bangkok 10330
Tel: 662-652-0940/1
Fax: 662-652-1842
E-Mail: bcondie@pobox.com

THE BROOKER GROUP LTD.
Managing Director: Mr. George Hooker
2nd Floor, Zone D, Room #201/2
Queen Sirikit National Convention Center
60 New Rachadapisek Road
Klongtoey, Bangkok 10110
Tel: 662-229-3111
Fax: 662-229-3127

BUSINESS ADVISORY THAILAND
President: Mr. Jon Selby
6th Floor, Chrysler Building
1643/5 New Petchburi Road
Bangkok 10310
Tel: 662-253-6295, 255-8977/8
Fax: 662-254-4576

BUSINESS INTERNATIONAL DATACONSULT
ORIENT RESEARCH LTD.
Director for Indochina & Thailand: Mr. Christopher Bruton
54 Soi Santipharp, Nares Road

Bangkok 10500
Tel: 662-236-2780, 233-5606/7
Fax: 662-236-8143

COOPERS & LYBRAND
Executive Director: Ms. Waraporn Saynpatharn
8th Floor, Sathorn Thani Building I
90/14-16 North Sathorn Road, Bangkok 10500
Mail: GPO Box 788, Bangkok 10501
Tel: 662-236-5227/9, 236-7814/9
Fax: 662-236-5226, 237-1201

DEEMAR CO., LTD.
Managing Director: Mr. Chris J. Andrews
26th Floor, United Center
323 Silom Road
Bangkok 10500
Mail: PO Box 2732, Bangkok 10501
Tel: 662-231-1931, 236-7747
Fax: 662-231-1959

J.P. ROONEY & ASSOCIATES GROUP
Chairman: Mr. James P. Rooney
4th Floor, Panunee Building
518/3 Ploenchit Road
Bangkok 10330
Mail: PO Box 1238, Nana Post Office
Bangkok 10112
Tel: 662-251-9832, 254-7343, 251-2323
Fax: 662-652-0788

MIDAS AGRONOMICS CO., LTD.
President: Mr. Anthony M. Zola
Mekong International Development Associates
Technic Building, Room 403
48 Soi 12, Sri Ayudthaya Road,
Bangkok 10400
Tel: 662-246-1714
Fax: 662-246-5785
E-mail: zolaa@mozart.inet.co.th

PRICE WATERHOUSE MANAGEMENT CONSULTANTS
Chief Executive Officer: Mr. John P. Wheatley
10th Floor, Sathorn City Tower
175 South Sathorn Road
Bangkok 10120
Tel: 662-679-6444
Fax: 662-679-6493/5

THAI WEB SITES FOR AMERICAN INVESTORS AND EXPORTERS

US COMMERCIAL SERVICE - http://csbangkok.or.th
The U.S. Commercial Service helps U.S. businesses invest in and export to Thailand.

USIS - http://usa.or.th
Whatever your interests, the USIS Thailand homepage helps.

AMERICAN CHAMBER OF COMMERCE - http:/amcham-th.org
This site provides information on Chamber activities.

THE BOARD OF INVESTMENT OF THAILAND - http://www.boi.go.th
A wealth of valuable information on Thailand, for investors. Exporters will also find it useful.

THAI INDUSTRIAL STANDARDS INSTITUTE - http://www.tisi.go.th
This site provides information on standards for products to be sold in Thailand. The site also contains data on the certification mark activities and ministerial regulations.

English Language Newspapers in Thailand

BANGKOK POST - http://www.bangkokpost.net

THE NATION - http://www.nationmultimedia.com

BUSINESS AND ECONOMY

THE NATIONAL ELECTRONICS AND COMPUTER TECHNOLOGY CENTER (NECTEC) - http://www.nectec.or.th
A list of Internet servers (domestic and abroad) with information pertaining to Thailand.

THAI CABINET MINUTES - http://nectec.or.th/bureaux/opm/index.html

FINANCIAL SECTOR RESTRUCTURING AUTHORITY (FRA)
http://www.fra.or.th
The FRA was established to liquidate the assets of 56 finance companies closed by the government in 2002.

BANK OF THAILAND - http://www.bot.or.th/
Library has weekly list of interesting newspaper/periodical articles!!

ASIAN DEVELOPMENT BANK - http://www.asiandevbank.org
News, press releases, documents and information on business opportunities, conferences and seminars.

THREE OF THE LARGEST THAI BANKS

SIAM COMMERCIAL BANK - http://www.scb.co.th

THAI FARMERS BANK - http://www.tfb.co.th

BANGKOK BANK - http://www.bbl.co.th

MISCELLANEOUS

AMAZING THAILAND - http://www.amazingthailand.th
The objective of this site is to persuade people to visit and learn more about Thailand.

"THAILAND TALES" - http://www.mcb.co.uk/apmforum/columns/thai.htm
This column is useful for foreigners who come to do business in Thailand.

NATIONAL TRADE DATA BANK (NTDB) www.stat-usa.gov
Contains US & FCS reports on various developments in the Thai market throughout the year, as well as reports from embassies world-wide.

MARKET RESEARCH REPORTS

1. (Land-side Road System) For Bangkok Int'l Airport
2. ACE Energy Services
3. AGC Agro-Chemicals
4. AGM Agricultural Machinery 4
5. AIR Airport Equipment
6. APG Airport Groung Support Equipment
7. APG Instrument Landing System for
8. APG Pre-qualifications of Contracts
9. APS Asia Automotive
10. APS BMW Production Hub for ASEAN
11. APS Consolidation and Competition Emerge
12. APS Detroit of the East
13. APS Parts Makers to Upgrade Their Production
14. APS Thailand Vehicle Export on the Rise
15. APS Vehicles Market Update
16. AVS Airport Management and Consulting Services
17. Bangkok Int'l Airport
18. BLD Processed Wood-Bldg. Products
19. Complex Foundations for the Second
20. CON Bang Yai - Bang Pong Motorway
21. CON Elemental Construction Costs
22. CON Pre-qualification of Construction
23. CON Specialty Construction Equipment
24. Construction of Passenger Terminal
25. Contractor for Group Improvements
26. COS Cosmetics
27. CPT Computer Peripherals
28. CPT Establishment of a Data Processing Zone in Thailand
29. CPT ID Chip Card
30. CPT Information Technology Update
31. CPT New Internet Services
32. CSF Software for Enterprise Resource Planning
33. CSV Computer and Telecommunication
34. CSV Computer Maintenance Service
35. CSV Computer Services
36. CSV E-Commerce Update
37. CSV Internet Service Update
38. CSV Y2K Issues Update
39. EDS Education and Training Services

40. EDS English Language/Computer Training
41. ELC Electronics Industry Update
42. ELC Hard Disk Drive Production
43. ELP Egat's Budget in Fiscal Year
44. ELP Electric Conferences and Exhibitions Thailand
45. ELP Electric Generation Equipment
46. ELP Electric Power Generation and
47. ELP Energy Sector Update - Thailand
48. ELP Energy Services Sectors 3/99
49. ELP Experts Perspective on Energy Sector
50. ELP Legal Requirements for Independent Power Producers in Thailand
51. ELP Power Plants to be Rehabilitated
52. FOD Food Suppliments, Health Food
53. FPP Liquid Food Processing Equipment
54. FRA Franchising of Services
55. FRA Non-Food Franchising
56. FUR Office Furniture
57. GSV Distribution Channels
58. HTL Hotel & Restaurant Equipment
59. ICH Industrial Chemicals
60. in ASEAN's Auto Hub
61. Information Services Internet Access
62. LAB Chemical Analysis Instruments
63. MCS Management Services
64. MED Implantable Medical Devices
65. MED Medical Test Kits
66. OGM Oil/Gas Retailing Equipment
67. OMS Operations & Maintenance
68. PCI Programmable Controllers
69. PKG Packaging Equipment and Machinery
70. POL Air Pollution Control Measuring Equipment
71. POL Bioremediation Supply
72. POL Environmental engineering/consulting
73. POL Hazardous Waste Treatment
74. POL Soil Remediation
75. Privatization in Thailand
76. Provincial Airports
77. PRT Port Equipment
78. SEC Security Equipment
79. SPT Sporting Goods
80. Standard Factory Thailand
81. TEL Cable TV Equipment
82. TEL Telecommunication Equipment
83. TOY Educational and Electronic Toys
84. TRA Travel and Tourism
85. Transmission in Thailand
86. WRE Water Resources Equipment

SELECTED SUB-SECTOR ANALYSIS (ISA)

For additional analytical, business and investment opportunities information,
please contact Global Investment & Business Center, USA
at (202) 546-2103. Fax: (202) 546-3275. E-mail: rusric@erols.com

AIR Aircraft & Aircraft Parts 4/27/99
COS Cosmetics / Make-up and Skin 12/98
Care
CPT Computers and Peripherals 11/30/98
CSV Computer Services 3/31/99
FILM Movie / Theater Market in 12/1/98
Thailand
FOD Health Food 10/19/98
FPP Food Processing and 4/21/99
Packaging Equipment
PCI Programmable Logic Controller 11/30/98
TEL Telecommunications Industry 10/15/98
WRE Water Resources and 5/20/99
Equipment Services

AGRICULTURAL REPORTS:

The Foreign Agricultural Service (FAS) of the U.S. Department of Agriculture at the U.S. Embassy, Bangkok, prepares a number of agricultural reports according to the following schedule. They may be obtained from the FAS office or from the FAS Website: www.fas.usda.gov.

Grain & Feed Report 3/99
Sugar Report 4/99
Tobacco Report 5/99
Oilseeds and Products Report 6/99
Cotton Report 6/99
Poultry Report 6/99
Market Information Report 7/99
Forest Products Report 7/99
Livestock Report 8/99

THAI MISSIONS IN THE US

THAI EMBASSY

Chancery :
1024 Wisconsin Avenue, N.W., Suite 401
Washington, D.C. 20007
Tel : (202) 944-3600
Fax : (202) 944-3611
URL : http://www.thaiembdc.org
E-mail : thai.wsn@thaiembdc.org

Consular Office :
1024 Wisconsin Avenue, N.W., Suite 101
Washington, D.C. 20007
Tel : (202) 944-3608
Fax : (202) 944-3641
E-mail : consular@thaiembdc.org

Office of the Defense and Military Attache :

2440 Foxhall Road, N.W.
Washington, D.C. 20007
Tel : (202) 333-9381
Fax : (202) 333-9384
URL : http://dma.thaiembdc.org
E-mail : officedma@dma.thaiembdc.org

Office of the Naval Attache :

1024 Wisconsin Avenue, N.W., Suite 302
Washington, D.C. 20007
Tel : (202) 944-3628-9
Fax : (202) 944-3630
URL : http://navy.thaiembdc.org
E-mail : officedma@dma.thaiembdc.org

Office of the Air Attache :

1024 Wisconsin Avenue, N.W., Suite 303
Washington, D.C. 20007
Tel : (202) 338-9700
Fax : (202) 338-9702
http://www.rtaf-airattache.com
E-mail : rtafdc@aol.com

Office of Commercial Affairs :

1024 Wisconsin Avenue, N.W., Suite 202
Washington, D.C. 20007
Tel : (202) 467-6790-3
Fax : (202) 429-2949
URL : http://oca.thaiembdc.org
E-mail : inquiries@oca.thaiembdc.org

Office of Education Affairs (Students' Department) :

1906-23rd Street, N.W.
Washington, D.C. 20008
Tel : (202) 667-9111-3
Fax : (202) 265-7239
URL : http://www.thai-edu-in-us.org
E-mail : oea@thai-edu-in-us.org

Office of Economic and Financial Affairs :

1024 Wisconsin Avenue, N.W., Suite 201
Washington, D.C. 20007
Tel : (202) 944-2111
Fax : (202) 944-3313
URL : http://mof.thaiembdc.org
E-mail : mof@mof.thaiembdc.org

Office of Agricultural Affairs :

1024 Wisconsin Avenue, N.W., Suite 203
Washington, D.C. 20007
Tel : (202) 338-1543
Fax : (202) 338-1549
URL : http://www.erols.com/moacdc
E-mail : moacdc@erols.com

Office of Science and Technology :
1024 Wisconsin Avenue, N.W., Suite 104
Washington, D.C. 20007
Tel : (202) 944-5200
Fax : (202) 944-5203
URL : http://www.ostc-was.org
E-mail : ostc@ostc-was.org

Office of the Economic Counsellor (Investment) :
1 World Trade Center, Suite 3729
New York, NY 10048
Tel : (212) 466-1745-6
Fax : (212) 466-9548
E-mail : boiny@aol.com

Permanent Mission of Thailand to the United Nations :
351 East 52nd Street
New York, NY 10022
Tel : (212) 754-2230
Fax : (212) 754-2535
E-mail : thaun@undp.org

Royal Thai Consulate-General, Chicago :
700 North Rush Street
Chicago, IL 60611
Tel : (312) 664-3129
Fax : (312) 664-3230
E-mail : thaichicago@aol.com

Royal Thai Consulate-General, Los Angeles :
611 North Larchmont Boulevard, 2nd Floor
Los Angeles, CA 90004
Tel : (323) 962-9574-77
Fax : (323) 962-2128
URL : http://www.thai-la.net
E-mail : thai-la@mindspring.com

Royal Thai Consulate-General, New York :
351 East 52nd Street

New York, NY 10022
Tel : (212) 754-1770, 754-2536-8, 754-1896
Fax : (212) 754-1907
E-mail : thainycg@aol.com

Royal Thai Consulates-General, (Honorary Consuls-General) ALABAMA ROYAL THAI CONSULATE-GENERAL

P.O. BOX 4504
MONTGOMERY, AL 36103-4504
Tel : (334) 269-2518
Fax : (334) 269-2518
E-mail : henrytile@mindspring.com
**Honorary Consul-General, Mr. Robert F.
Henry, Jr.**

**COLORADO
ROYAL THAI CONSULATE-GENERAL**
1123 AURARIA PKWY, SUITE 200
DENVER, CO 80204
Tel : (303) 892-0118
Fax : (303) 892-0119
E-mail : snklfrtz23@aol.com
**Honorary Consul-General, Mr. Donald W.
Ringby**

**FLORIDA
ROYAL THAI CONSULATE-GENERAL**
2801 PONCE DE LEON BLVD., SUITE
1170
CORAL GABLES, FL 33134
Tel : (305) 445-7577
Fax : (305) 446-9944
**Honorary Consul-General, Mr. Frank D.
Hall**

**GEORGIA
ROYAL THAI CONSULATE-GENERAL**
3333 CUMBERLAND CIRCLE, SUITE 400
ATLANTA, GA 30339
Tel : (770) 988-3304
Fax : (770) 988-3301
**Honorary Consul-General, Mr. Robert M.
Holder, Jr.**

**HAWAII
ROYAL THAI CONSULATE-GENERAL**
1278 KALANI STREET, SUITE 103
HONOLULU, HI 96817
Tel : (808) 845-7332
Fax : (808) 848-0022
E-mail : cmiyabara@maiddrigade.com
**Honorary Consul-General, Mr. Colin
Miyabara**

**LOUISIANA
ROYAL THAI CONSULATE-GENERAL**
335 JULIA STREET
NEW ORLEANS, LA 70130
Tel : (504) 522-3400
Fax : (504) 522-3434
E-mail : aqd335@aol.com

**Honorary Consul-General, Mr. Arthur Q.
Davis**

**MASSACHUSETTS
ROYAL THAI CONSULATE-GENERAL**
20 PARK PLAZA, SUITE 1010
BOSTON, MA 02116
Tel : (617) 350-6200
Fax : (617) 350-6205
**Honorary Consul-General, Mr. Vernon R.
Alden**

**MISSOURI
ROYAL THAI CONSULATE-GENERAL**
8109 LEE BLVD.
LEAWOOD, KS 66206
Tel : (913) 385-5555
Fax : (913) 385-5556
**Honorary Consul, Ms. Mary Frances
Taylor**

**OKLAHOMA
ROYAL THAI CONSULATE-GENERAL**
25900 EAST 81ST STREET
BROKEN ARROW, OK 74014
Tel : (918) 357-2886
Fax : (918) 357-1334
**Honorary Consul-General, Mr. Richard H.
Hughes**

**OREGON
ROYAL THAI CONSULATE-GENERAL**
121 S.W. SALMON STREET, SUITE 1430
PORTLAND, OR 97204-2924
Tel : (503) 221-0440
Fax : (503) 221-0550
E-mail : thai@siaminc.com
Honorary Consul, Mr. Nicholas J. Stanley

**PUERTO RICO
ROYAL THAI CONSULATE-GENERAL**
COND. AVILA, SUITE 11-F, COSTA RICA
ST.
URB. PINERO, HATOREY, PR 00917
Tel : (787) 751-0151
Fax : (787) 753-7276
E-mail : rkthai@tld.net
Mailing address :
P.O. Box 7386
SAN JUAN, PR 00916-7386
**Honorary Consul-General, Mr. Rolando J.
Piernes**

TEXAS (Dallas)

For additional analytical, business and investment opportunities information,
please contact Global Investment & Business Center, USA
at (202) 546-2103. Fax: (202) 546-3275. E-mail: rusric@erols.com

ROYAL THAI CONSULATE-GENERAL
3232 MCKINNEY AVENUE, SUITE 1400
DALLAS, TX 75204-2429
Tel : (214) 740-1498
Fax : (214) 740-1499
Honorary Consul-General, Mr. W. Forrest Smith

TEXAS (El-Paso)
ROYAL THAI CONSULATE-GENERAL
4487 N. MESA, SUITE 204
EL PASO, TX 79902
Tel : (915) 533-5757
Fax : (915) 532-0781
E-mail : landrulis@aol.com
Honorary Consul-General, Ms. Mary Lee Leavell Pinkerton

TEXAS (Houston)
ROYAL THAI CONSULATE-GENERAL
2800 TEXAS COMMERCE TOWER
HOUSTON, TX 77002-3094
Tel : (713) 229-8733
Fax : (713) 228-1303
Honorary Consul-General, Mr. Charles C. Foster

DOMINICAN REPUBLIC
ROYAL THAI CONSULATE-GENERAL
COND. AVILA, SUITE 11-F
COSTA RICA STREET
URB. PINERO, HATO REY, PR 00917
Tel : (809) 541-7445
Fax : (809) 567-8995
Mailing address :
EPS-A-571, P.O. BOX 02-5256 I
MIAMI, FL 33102-5256
Honorary Consul, Mr. Gustavo E. Turull

Thai Trade Center, Chicago :
401 N. Michigan Ave., Suite 544

Chicago, IL 60611
Tel : (312) 467-0044-5
Fax : (312) 467-1690
E-mail : ttcc@wwa.com

Thai Trade Center, Miami :
200 South Biscayne Blvd., Suite 4420

Miami, Florida 33131
Tel : (305) 379-5675
Fax : (305) 379-5677
E-Mail : ttcmiami@earthlink.net

Thai Trade Center, New York :
One World Trade Center, Suite 3729
New York, NY 10048
Tel : (212) 466-1777
Fax : (212) 524-0972
E-Mail : thtradny@ix.netcom.com

Thai Trade Center, Los Angeles :
611 N. Larchmont Blvd., 3rd Floor
Los Angeles, CA 90004-1321
Tel : (323) 466-9645 Fax : (323) 466-1559
E-mail : ttcla@earthlink.net

Tourism Authority of Thailand, New York :
5 World Trade Center, Suite 3443
New York, NY 10048
Tel : (212) 432-0433 Fax : (212) 912-0920
E-mail : ttny@aol.com

Tourism Authority of Thailand, Los Angeles
(*Regional Office of the Americas*) :
611 North Larchmont Blvd., 1st Floor
Los Angeles, CA 90004
Tel : (213) 461-9814 Fax : (213) 461-9834

IMPORTANT ADDRESSES FOR THAILAND

IMPORTANT GOVERNMENT AND BUSINESS CONTACTS

The U.S. Commercial Service and the Economic Section at the U.S. Embassy in Bangkok maintain extensive files on key organizations in Thailand. Contact them for more information.

U.S. GOVERNMENT

U.S. EMBASSY, THAILAND

Ambassador of the U.S. to Thailand: The Honorable Kristie A. Kenney
Street Address: 120 Wireless Road, Pathumwan, Bangkok, Thailand 10330 Mailing Address:
American Embassy – Bangkok, APO AP 96535 Tel: 662-205-4000 Internet:
http://bangkok.usembassy.gov
U.S. COMMERCIAL SERVICE
Senior Commercial Officer: Ms. Cynthia A. Griffin
Street Address:
U.S. Embassy Bangkok GPF Witthayu Building, Tower A, 3rd Floor, 302 93/1 Wireless Road,
Pathumwan Bangkok 10330
Mailing Address: American Embassy - Bangkok FCS Box 51 APO AP 96546
Tel: 662-205-5090 Fax: 662-255-2915, 205-5914 E-mail: bangkok.office.box@trade.gov Internet:
http://www.buyusa.gov/thailand/en
Note: The U.S. Commercial Service helps U.S. firms to export to and develop their business in
Thailand.

ECONOMIC SECTION

Economic Counselor: Ms. Julie Chung
Street Address:
U.S. Embassy Bangkok 120 Wireless Road, Pathumwan Bangkok 10330
Mailing Address: American Embassy – Bangkok APO AP 96546
Tel: 662-205-4995, 205-4726 Fax: 662-254-2839
U.S.D.A. FOREIGN AGRICULTURAL SERVICE
Agricultural Counselor: Mr. John Wade
Street Address:
U.S. Embassy Bangkok GPF Witthayu Building, Tower A, 4th Floor, 404 93/1 Wireless Road,
Pathumwan Bangkok 10330
Mailing Address: American Embassy - Bangkok APO AP 96546
Tel: 662-205-5106 Fax: 662-255-2907 E-mail: agbangkok@fas.usda.gov

U.S. TRADE AND DEVELOPMENT AGENCY (USTDA)

Regional Manager for Asia: Mr. Mark J. Dunn

U.S. Embassy Bangkok GPF Witthayu Building, Tower A, 3rd Floor, 302 93/1 Wireless Road,
Pathumwan Bangkok 10330

Tel: 66-2-205-5600 Fax: 66-2-255-4366 Email: mdunn@ustda.gov Note: TDA promotes
economic development and trade in developing and middle-income countries by funding
feasibility studies, consultancies, training programs and other project planning services.

ROYAL THAI GOVERNMENT

MINISTRY OF FOREIGN AFFAIRS

443 Sri Ayudhya Road, Bangkok 10400 Tel. (622) 643-5000 Internet: http://www.mfa.go.th

• Department of American and South Pacific Affairs

Tel: 662-643-5128 Fax: 662-643-5127 North America Division 443 Sri Ayudhya Rd., Bangkok
10400 Tel: 662-643-5121/2 Fax: 662-643-5124 E-mail: american02@mfa.go.th

• Royal Thai Embassy in Washington

1024 Wisconsin Avenue, N.W. Suite 401 Washington, D.C. 20007 Tel: 202-944-3600 Fax: 202-944-3611 Internet: http://www.thaiembdc.org

OFFICE OF THE PRIME MINISTER

Internet: http://www.opm.go.th

• Office of the National Economic and Social Development Board (NESDB)

962 Krung Kasem Road, Wat Sommanut Pomprab, Bangkok 10100 Tel: 662-280-4085 Fax: 662-281-3938 Internet: http://www.nesdb.go.th

• Office of the Board of Investment (BOI)

555 Vibhavadi-Rangsit Road, Chatuchak Bangkok 10900 Tel: 662-553-8111 Fax: 662-553-8222 Internet: http://www.boi.go.th

• Energy Policy and Planning Office (EPPO)

121/1-2 Phetchaburi Road, Thungphayathai Ratchathewi, Bangkok 10400 Tel: 662-612-1555 Fax: 662-612-1364 Internet: http://www.eppo.go.th

MINISTRY OF INTERIOR

Internet: http://www.moi.go.th

MINISTRY OF COMMERCE

Internet: http://www.moc.go.th

• Department of Foreign Trade

44/100 Nonthaburi 1 Road (Sanambinnam) Bangkrasor, Muang, Nonthaburi 11000 Tel: 662-547-4771/86 Fax: 662-547-4791/2 Internet: http://www.dft.moc.go.th

• Department of Commercial Registration/Dept. of Business Development

Building 3rd Floor, 44/100 Nonthaburi 1 Road (Sanambinnam) Bangkrasor, Muang, Nonthaburi 11000 Tel: 662-547-5050 Fax: 662-547-4459 Internet: http://www.dbd.go.th

Registration of Public Companies, Group of Bank and Financial Institution, Insurance Companies, Storage and Warehousing

MINISTRY OF FINANCE

Internet: http://www.mof.go.th

• The Customs Department

1 Soonthornkosa Road, Khlongtoey

Bangkok 10110

Tel: 662-667-7880/4, 667-7100 Fax: 662-667-7885, 667-7767 Email: customs_clinic@customs.go.th Internet: http://www.customs.go.th

MINISTRY OF INDUSTRY

Internet: http://www.industry.go.th

• Department of Industrial Works

75/6 Rama VI Road, Ratchathewi Bangkok 10400 Tel: 662-202-4000, 202-4014 Fax: 662-354-3390 Email: pr@diw.mail.go.th Internet: http://www.diw.go.th

• Department of Industrial Promotion

Rama VI Road, Ratchathewi Bangkok 10400 Tel: 662-202-4414/8, 202-4511 Fax: 662-354-3299 Internet: http://www.dip.go.th

• Thai Industrial Standards Institute

Rama VI Road, Ratchathewi Bangkok 10400 Tel: 662-202-3505 Fax: 662-202-3041 Email: thaistan@tisi.go.th Internet: http://www.tisi.go.th

• Industrial Estate Authority of Thailand

618 Nikhom Makkasan Road, Makkasan Ratchathewi, Bangkok 10400 Tel: 662-253-0561 Fax: 662-253-4086 Email: ieat@ieat.go.th Internet: http://www.ieat.go.th

MINISTRY OF NATURAL RESOURCES AND ENVIRONMENT

Internet: http://www.mnre.go.th

• Office of Natural Resources and Environmental Policy and Planning

60/1 Soi Phibunwattana 7, Rama VI Road Samsennai, Phayathai Bangkok 10400 Tel: 662-265-6500 Fax: 662-265-6511 Internet: http://www.onep.go.th

• Pollution Control Department

92 Soi Phahonyothin 7, Phahonyothin Road Samsennai, Phayathai, Bangkok 10400 Tel: 662-298-2000 Fax: 662-298-2002 Internet: http://www.pcd.go.th

MINISTRY OF PUBLIC HEALTH
Internet: http://www.moph.go.th
• Food and Drug Administration

88/24 Tivanond Road, Muang Nonthaburi 11000 Tel: 662-590-7000/1 Fax: 662-591-8441 Internet: http://www.fda.moph.go.th

OTHER INDEPENDENT GOVERNMENT AGENCIES

Bank of Thailand

273 Samsen Road, Bangkhunprom Pranakhon, Bangkok 10200 Tel: 662-283-5353 Fax: 662-280-0449, 280-0626 Internet: http://www.bot.or.th

Bangkok Metropolitan Administration

173 Dinso Road, Saochingchar Pranakorn, Bangkok 10200 Tel: 662-221-2141/69 Fax: 662-621-0831, 221-2170 Internet: http://www.bangkok.go.th

TRADE ASSOCIATIONS

American Chamber Of Commerce In Thailand (AMCHAM)

Executive Director: Ms. Judy Benn 7th Floor, GPF Witthayu Building, Towers A 93/1 Wireless Road, Lumpini Pathumwan, Bangkok 10330 Tel: 662-254-1041 Fax: 662-251-1605 E-mail: service@amchamthailand.com Internet: http://www.amchamthailand.com

Note: AmCham is the premier U.S. business organization in Thailand with more than 600 U.S. member companies.

US-ASEAN Business Council **1101 17th Street, NW Suite 411 Washington, DC 20036 Tel: 202 289-1911 Fax: 202 289-0519 Email: mail@usasean.org Internet: http://www.us-asean.org**

Note: The US-ASEAN Business Council is the premier national private organization in the United States representing private sector interests in ASEAN, the Association of Southeast Asian Nations.

Bangkok Office:

Thailand Representative: Mr. Praab Pianskool

US-ASEAN Business Council 23rd Fl., Siam Tower 989 Rama 1 Road, Pathumwan Bangkok 10330, Thailand Tel: 662-649-1119 Fax: 662-658-0619 E-mail: praab@usasean.org

Thailand - U.S. Business Council

7th Floor, Asia Sermkij Tower 49 Soi Pipat, Silom Road Bangrak, Bangkok 10500 Tel: 662-636-9020-5 Fax: 662-636-9026 Internet: http://www.tusbc.org

Note: The business council is important for policy and senior executive business information exchanges.

U.S. - Thailand Business Council

3050 K. Street, N.W. Suite 205 Washington, D.C. 20007 Tel: 202-337-5973 Fax: 202-337-0039 E-mail: ustbc@ustbc.org Internet: http://www.ustbc.org

Note: This Council is at the forefront of U.S.-ASEAN affairs and sponsors senior interchanges including the annual U.S.-ASEAN Ambassador's Tour in the U.S. and senior executive visits to ASEAN.

Board Of Trade Of Thailand

150 Rajbopit Road, Pranakhon Bangkok 10200 Tel: 662-622-1860/76 Fax: 662-225-3372 E-mail: bot@thaichamber.com Website: http://www.thaichamber.com

Federation Of Thai Industries (FTI)

4th Fl., Zone C, Queen Sirikit National Convention Center 60 New Rachadapisek Road Klongtoey, Bangkok 10110 Tel: 662-345-1000 Fax: 662-345-1296/9 E-mail: information@off.fti.or.th Internet: http://www.fti.or.th

Note: The Federation of Thai Industries membership represents most of the major industry sectors and their industry associations.

The Thai Chamber Of Commerce (TCC)

150 Rajbopit Road, Pranakorn Bangkok 10200 Tel: 662-622-1860/76 Fax: 662-225-3372 E-mail: tcc@thaichamber.com Internet: http://www.thaichamber.com

MARKET RESEARCH FIRMS

Agrisource Co., LTD. **Ambassador's Court, 4th Fl., Room 416 76/1 Soi Langsuan, Ploenchit Road Bangkok 10330 Tel: 662-251-8655 Fax: 662-251-0390 Email: admin@agrisource.co.th Internet: http://www.agrisource.co.th**

The Brooker Group PLC. **26th Fl., The Trendy Office Building 10/190-193 Soi Sukhumvit 13 Sukhumvit Road, Klongtoey Nua Wattana, Bangkok 10110 Tel: 662-168-7100 Fax: 662-168-7111/2 Email: info@brookergroup.com Internet: http://www.brookergroup.com**

Business Advisory (Thailand) Ltd **15th Fl., Maneeya Center Building 518/5 Ploenchit Road, Lumpini Pathumwan, Bangkok 10330 Tel: 662-255-8977 Fax: 662-254-4576 Email: jon@bathailand.com Internet: http://www.bathailand.com**

The Nielsen Company (Thailand) Ltd. **26th Fl., United Center 323 Silom Road, Bangrak Bangkok 10500 Postal address: P.O. Box 2732, Bangkok 10501 Tel: 662-674-6000 Fax: 662-231-1959, 236-7747 Internet: http://www.th.nielsen.com**
J.P. Rooney & Associates Group
4th Fl., Panunee Building 518/3 Ploenchit Road, Pathumwan Bangkok 10330 Postal Address: P.O. Box 1238, Nana Post Office Bangkok 10112 Thailand Tel: 662-254-7343, 251-2323 Fax: 662-652-0788 Email: jprooney@jprooney.com Internet: http://www.jprooney.com

Pricewaterhousecoopers

15th Fl., Bangkok City Tower 179/74-80 South Sathorn Road Thungmahamek, Sathorn, Bangkok 10120 Postal Address:

P.O. Box 800, Bangkok 10501 Thailand Tel: 662-286-9999, 344-1000 Fax: 662-286-5050
Internet: http://www.pwc.com

WEB SITES FOR AMERICAN INVESTORS AND EXPORTERS

U.S. Commercial Service

The U.S. Commercial Service helps U.S. businesses export to and invest in Thailand. They also offer information in Thai to potential buyers of American exports and services in Thailand. http://www.buyusa.gov/thailand/en

U.S. Department of Commerce http://www.commerce.gov

National Trade Data Bank (NTDB)

The NTDB (National Trade Data Bank) provides access to Country Commercial Guides,

Market Research reports, Best Market reports and other programs. http://www.stat-usa.gov

U.S. Embassy In Thailand **http://bangkok.usembassy.gov**

US Export Import Bank (Ex-Im)

Assists U.S. exporters by providing loans, guarantees, and insurance to U.S. exporters http://www.exim.gov

U.S. Immigration And Customs Enforcement http://www.ice.gov/

TRADE ORGANIZATIONS IN THAILAND

American Chamber of Commerce **http://www.amchamthailand.com**

Thai Industrial Standards Institute

This site provides information on standards for products to be sold in Thailand. The site also contains data on the certification mark activities and ministerial regulations. http://www.tisi.go.th

ENGLISH LANGUAGE NEWSPAPERS IN THAILAND

Bangkok Post http://www.bangkokpost.com

The Nation http://www.nationmultimedia.com

BANKING AND FINANCE

Bank Of Thailand http://www.bot.or.th

Asian Development Bank http://www.adb.org

Siam Commercial Bank **http://www.scb.co.th**

Kasikorn Bank **http://www.kasikornbank.com**

Bangkok Bank **http://www.bangkokbank.com**

MISCELLANEOUS

Tourism Authority Of Thailand\

The objective of this site is to persuade people to visit, and learn more about, Thailand.
http://thai.tourismthailand.org

MARKET RESEARCH

To view market research reports produced by the U.S. Commercial Service please go to the following website: http://www.export.gov/mrktresearch/index.asp and click on Country and Industry Market Reports.

Please note that these reports are only available to U.S. citizens and U.S. companies. Registration to the site is required, but free of charge.

Trade Events http://www.export.gov/tradeevents/index.asp
http://www.buyusa.gov/thailand/en/upcoming_events.html

INTERNATIONAL ORGANIZATIONS

Asian Institute of Technology (AIT)
58 Moo 9, km 42, Phaholyothin Road, Klong Luang, Pathum Thani 12120. PO Tel: (662) 516-0110
Fax: (662) 516-2126

Economic and Social Commission for Asia and the Pacific (ESCAP)
United Nations Building, Ratchadamnern Nok Avenue, Bangkok 10200.
Tel: (662) 288-1234
Fax: (662) 288-1000

International Bank for Reconstruction and Development (IBRD)
The World Bank Regional Mission in Bangkok. 14th Floor, Diethelm Tower A, 93/1 Wireless Road, Bangkok 10330
Tel: (662) 252-2305-7, 256-7792-4
Fax: (662) 256-7795

International Labor Organization (ILO)
10th-11th Floors, United Nations Building, Ratchadamnern Nok Avenue,
Bangkok 10200.
Tel: (662) 288-1234
Fax: (662) 280-1735
International Monetary Fund (IMF)
Resident Representative Office
3rd Floor, Bank of Thailand, 273 Samsen Road, Bangkhunprom, Bangkok 10200
Tel: (662) 283-6128-30 Fax: (662) 283-6131

United Nations Development Programme (UNDP)
12th Fl, UN Building, Ratchadamnern Nok Ave., Bangkok, 10200
Tel: (662) 288-2138 Fax: (662) 280-0556

European Commission
Kian Gwan House, 19th Floor,
140 Wireless Rd., Bangkok 10330
Tel: (662) 255-9100 Fax: (662) 255-9113-4

PUBLIC SECTOR INSTITUTIONS

Government

Government House
Government House, Thanon Nakhon
Pathom, Bangkok 10300
Tel: (662) 282-6543, 282-6877
Fax: (662) 282-8587, 282-8631
Home Page : www.thaigov.go.th
Ministry of Foreign Affairs
Si Ayutthaya Road
Bangkok 10400
Tel: (662) 643-5000
Fax: (662) 643-5180
Home Page: www.mfa.go.th

Investment

Office of the National Economic and Social
Development
962 Krung Kasem, Bangkok, 10100
Tel: (662) 282-8434
Fax: (662) 282-0891
Home Page: www.nesdb.go.th

Office of the Board of Investment
555 Vibhavadi-Rangsit Road
Chatuchak, Bangkok, 10900
Tel: (662) 537-8111, 537-8155
Fax: (662) 537-8177
Home Page: www.boi.go.th

Industry

Ministry of Industry (MOI)
Rama VI Road, Ratchathewi,
Bangkok, 10400
Tel: (662) 202-3000
Fax: (662) 202-3048
Home Page: www.moi.go.th

Department of Industrial Promotion
(Under the MOI)
Thanon Rama VI, Ratchathewi,
Bangkok 10400
Tel: (662) 202-4415-6
Fax: (662) 246-0031
Home Page: www.dip.go.th

Industrial Estate Authority of Thailand
(Under the MOI)
618 Thanon Nikhom Makkasan
Ratchathewi, Bangkok 10400

Tel: (662) 253-0561, 253-5758
Fax: (662) 253-4086
Home Page: www.ieat.go.th

Thai Industrial Standards Institute
(Under the MOI)
Thanon Rama VI, Ratchathewi
Bangkok 10400
Tel: (662) 202-3300
Fax: (662) 202-3415
Home Page: www.tisi.go.th

Trade

Ministry of Commerce (MOC)
Thanon Samamchai, Pranakorn
Bangkok 10200
Tel: (662) 282-6171-9
Fax: (662) 280-0775
Home Page: www.moc.go.th

Department of Foreign Trade
(Under the MOC)
Samamchai Road, Pranakorn,
Bangkok 10110
Tel: (662) 225-1315-29, 662--16
Fax: (662) 224-7269, 225-4763
Home Page: www.thaitrade.com

Department of Export Promotion
(Under the MOC)
22/77 Rachadapisek Road,
Bangkok 10900
Tel: (662) 513-1909-15, 511-5066-77
Fax: (662) 512-1079, 513-1917
Home Page: www.thaitrade.com

One Stop Service Center for Visas and
Work Permits
Krisda Plaza, 3-5 Floors, 207 Rachadapisek
Road, Din Daeng,
Bangkok, 10310
Tel: (662) 693-3333
Fax: (662) 693-9340

Tourism

The Tourism Authority of Thailand
Le Concorde Building, 202 Rachadapisek
Rd., Huai Khwang, Bangkok 10320
Tel: (662) 694-1222

**For additional analytical, business and investment opportunities information,
please contact Global Investment & Business Center, USA
at (202) 546-2103. Fax: (202) 546-3275. E-mail: rusric@erols.com**

Fax: (662) 694-1329
Home Page: www.tat.or.th

Immigration Division
The Royal Thai Police Department
Suan Plu Road, Thung Mahamek, Bangkok,
10120
Tel: (662) 287-3101-10
Fax: (662) 289-1516

Finance

Ministry of Finance (MOF)
Thanon Rama VI, Samsen-Nai,
Phayathai, Bangkok 10400
Tel: (662) 273-9021
Fax: (662) 293-9408
Home Page: www.mof.go.th

The Customs Department
(Under the MOF)
Atnarong Road, Klongtoey,
Bangkok, 10110
Tel: (662) 249-0431, 671-7555-7
Home Page: www.customs.go.th

The Industrial Finance Corporation
1770 New Petchburi Road,
Bangkok, 10500
Tel: (662) 253-7111, 253-9666
Fax: (662) 253-9677, 254-8098

Bank of Thailand
273 Samsen Road, Bangkhumprom,
Bangkok, 10200
Tel: (662) 283-5353
Fax: (662) 280-0449, 280-0626
Home Page: www.bot.or.th

Export-Import Bank of Thailand
Boon Pong Tower, 1193 Thanon
Phahonyothin, Bangkok 10400
Tel: (662) 271-3700, 278-0047
Fax: (662) 271-3204
Home Page: www.exim.go.th

Communications

The Communications Authority of Thailand
99 Chaeng Watthana Road,
Bangkok, 10002

Tel: (662) 573-0099
Home Page: www.cat.ot.th

Telephone Organization of Thailand
89/2 Moo 3 Chaeng Watthana
Don Muang, Bangkok 10002
Tel: (662) 505-1000
Fax: (662) 574-9533
Home Page: www.tot.or.th

Ministry of Transport and Communications
38 Thanon Ratchadanoen Nok,
Pomprab Sattruphai, Bangkok 10100
Tel: (662) 283-3000
Fax: (662) 281-3959
Home Page: www.motc.go.th

Utilities

Metropolitan Electrical Authority
30 Soi Chidlom, Thanon Ploenchit
Pathumwan, Bangkok 10330
Tel: (662) 254-9550
Fax: (662) 253-1424, 254-1355
Home Page: www.mea.or.th

Metropolitan Waterworks Authority
400 Thanon Prachachuen, Laksi
Bangkok 10210
Tel: (662) 504-0123
Fax: (662) 503-9490

Provincial Electrical Authority
200 Thanon Ngam Wongwan
Chatuchak, Bangkok, 10900
Tel: (662) 589-0100-1 Fax: (662) 589-4850-1
Home Page: www.pea.or.th

Provincial Waterworks Authority
72 Thanon Chaeng Watthana, Don Muang,
Bangkok 10210
Tel: (662) 551-1020 Fax: (662) 551-1239,
552-1547

PRIVATE SECTOR INSTITUTIONS

Chambers of Commerce

Board of Trade of Thailand
150/2 Ratchabophit Road, Bangkok 10200
Tel: (662) 221-0555, 221-1827,

221-9350
Fax: (662) 225-3995

Chambre de Franco-Thai
75/20 Soi 26, Sukhumvit Road,
Bangkok 10110
Tel: (662) 261-8276-7
Fax: (662) 261-8278

American Chamber of Commerce
7th Floor, Kian Gwan Building,
140 Wireless Road, Bangkok, 10330
Tel: (662) 251-9266-7, 251-1605
Fax: (662) 651-4474-2

German-Thai Chamber of Commerce
699 Silom Road, GPO Box 1728,
Bangkok 10330
Tel: (662) 236-2396

Australia-Thai Chamber of Commerce
20th Floor, Unit 202, Thai CC Tower, 889
South Sathorn Rd., Yannawa,
Bangkok, 10120
Tel: (662) 210-0216-7
Fax: (662) 210-0218

Indian-Thai Chamber of Commerce
13 Soi Attakanprasit, South Sathorn Road,
Bangkok, 10330
Tel: (662) 286-1961, 286-1506

British Chamber of Commerce
208, 7th Floor, Wireless Rd., Bangkok
Tel: (662) 651-5350-3
Fax: (662) 651-5354

Italian-Thai Chamber of Commerce
12th Floor, Vamit Bld., Room 1208
1126/1 New Petchburi Rd.,
Bangkok 10400
Tel: (662) 253-9904 Fax: (662) 253-9896

Chinese Chamber of Commerce
233 South Sathorn Road, Bangkok
Tel: (662) 211-8531, 211-8531
Fax: (662) 211-8531

Japanese Chamber of Commerce
13th Floor Amarin Tower,
500 Ploenchit Rd., Bangkok 10330

Tel: (662) 256-9170-3
Fax: (662) 256-9621

Philippine-Thai Chamber of Commerce
21st Floor, Sethiwan Tower, 139 Pan Rd.,
Silom, Bangkok 10300
Tel/Fax: (662) 266-6298

The Thai Chamber of Commerce
150 Ratchabophit Road, Bangkok 10200
Tel: (662) 225-0086, 225-4913-4

Thai-Canadian Chamber of Commerce
9th Floor, Sethiwan Building
139 Pan Road, Silom,
Bangrak, Bangkok 10500
Tel: (662) 266-6085-6
Fax: (662) 266-6087
Website: www.thai-canadian-chamber.org

Thai-Korea Chamber of Commerce
8th Floor, Kong Bunma Building
699 Silom Road, Bangkok 10500
Tel: (662) 233-1322-3

Associations

Federation of Thai Industries
60 Queen Sirikit National Convention
Centre, New Petchaburi Road, Bangkok
Tel: (662) 229-4255-83
Fax: (662) 229-4941-2

The Lawyers' Association
26 Ratchadamnern Avenue,
Bangkok, 10220
Tel: (662) 224-1873

The Thai Bankers' Association
4th Floor, Lake Rachada Office Complex,
Bldg II, 195/5 Rachadapisek Road, Bangkok
10110
Tel: (662) 264-0883-7
Fax: (662) 264-0888

The Foreign Bankers' Association
Sathorn Thani Bld. 2, 19th Floor, 92/55
North Sathorn Rd., Silom Bangrak, Bangkok
10500
Tel: (662) 236-4730, 236-7224
Fax: (662) 236-4731

**For additional analytical, business and investment opportunities information,
please contact Global Investment & Business Center, USA
at (202) 546-2103. Fax: (202) 546-3275. E-mail: rusric@erols.com**

Commercial Banks
Bangkok Bank PCL
333 Silom Road, Bangkok, 10500
Tel: (662) 231-433
Fax: (662) 236-8281-2

Chase Manhattan Bank
Siam Shopping Centre, 965 Rama I Road,
Bangkok 10330
Tel: (662) 252-1141

Bank of America NT & SA
2/2 Wireless Road, Bangkok, 10500
Tel: (662) 251-6333
Fax: (662) 253-1905

Siam Commercial Bank
9 Rachadapisek Road, Ladyao, Chatuchak
Bangkok, 10900
Tel: (662) 344-1111, 344-5000
Fax: (662) 937-7454

Bank of Asia PCL
191 South Sathorn Road, Bangkok, 10120
Tel: (662) 287-2211-3
Fax: (662) 287-2973-4

Hong Kong & Shanghai
Banking Corporation
Hong Kong Bank Building
64 Silom Road, Bangkok 10500
Tel: (662) 267-3000 Fax: (662) 236-7687

Import-Export Bank of Japan
138 Silom Road, Bangkok, 10500
Tel: (662) 235-7373

Standard Chartered Bank
990 Rama IV Road, Bangkok, 10500
Tel: (662) 636-1000 Fax: (662) 636-1198-9

Krung Thai Bank
35 Sukhumvit Road, Klong Toey,
Bangkok 10110
Tel: (662) 255-2222 Fax: (662) 255-9391-6

Thai Farmers Bank
1 Thai Farmers Lane, Rat Burana Road,
Bangkok, 10140
Tel: (662) 470-1122, 470-1199
Fax: (662) 470-1571

REGIONAL EXPORT PROMOTION CENTERS IN THAILAND

Export Promotion Centre, Chiang Mai
29/19 Singharaj Road, Chiang Mai 50200
Tel: (66 053) 216-350-1, 221-376
Fax: (66 053) 215-307

Export Promotion Centre, Khon Kaen
68/4 Kiang Muang Road,
Khon Kaen, 40000
Tel: (66 043) 221-472
Fax: (66 043) 221-476

Export Promotion Centre, Surat Thani
148/59 Surat-Nakornsri Road, Bang Kung
Surat Thani, Bangkok 84000
Tel: (66 077) 286-916, 287-108
Fax: (66 077) 288-632

Export Promotion Centre, Hat Yai
7-15 Jootee-Uthit 1 Road, Hat Yai, Songkla
90110
Tel: (66 074) 234-349, 231-744
Fax: (66 074) 234-329

Export Promotion Centre, Chanthaburi
30/31-32 Trirat Road, Chanthaburi, 22000
Tel: (66 039) 325-962-3
Fax: (66 039) 325-962

THAI TRADE REPRESENTATIVE OFFICES ABROAD

Thai Trade Representative Office, Boston
420 Boylston Street, Suite 403
Boston, MA, USA 02116
Tel: 617-536-0930 Fax: 617-536-7927

Thai Trade Representative Office,
Minneapolis
551 Eleventh Avenue South, Suite 340
Minneapolis, MN, USA 55415
Tel: 612-672-0872 Fax: 612-672-0933

Thai Trade Representative Office, Hawaii
Pan Am Building, 1600 Kapiolani Blvd.
Suite 1306, Honolulu, HI, USA 96814
Tel: 808-944-1747
Fax: 808-944-1739

For additional analytical, business and investment opportunities information,
please contact Global Investment & Business Center, USA
at (202) 546-2103. Fax: (202) 546-3275. E-mail: rusric@erols.com

Thai Trade Representative Office, Toronto
401 Bay Street, Suite 1400, Toronto,
Ontario, Canada, M5H 2Y4
Tel: 416-368-5747
Fax: 416-361-3459

Thai Trade Representative Office, Hiroshima
5th Floor, Hiroshima Prefecture Information
Plaza, 3-4-47 Sendamachi, Naka-Ku,
Hiroshima, Japan
Tel: 82-249-9911
Fax: 82-249-9921

BASIC TITLES FOR THILAND

title	ISBN
Thailand A ""Spy" Guide - Strategic Information and Developments	1433049120
Thailand A "Spy" Guide - Strategic Information and Developments	1438747802
Thailand Air Force Handbook	1438747810
Thailand Air Force Handbook	1433049139
Thailand Army Weapon Systems Handbook	1433061961
Thailand Army Weapon Systems Handbook	1433061961
Thailand Army Weapon Systems Handbook	1433061961
Thailand Banking & Financial Market Handbook	1438747829
Thailand Banking & Financial Market Handbook	1433049147
Thailand Business and Investment Opportunities Yearbook	1438747837
Thailand Business and Investment Opportunities Yearbook	1433049155
Thailand Business and Investment Opportunities Yearbook Volume 1 Strategic Information and Opportunities	1438778074
Thailand Business Intelligence Report	1438747845
Thailand Business Intelligence Report	1433049163
Thailand Business Law Handbook - Strategic Informtion and Basic Laws	1438747853
Thailand Business Law Handbook - Strategic Informtion and Basic Laws	1438771193
Thailand Business Law Handbook - Strategic Informtion and Basic Laws	1438771193
Thailand Business Law Handbook - Strategic Informtion and Basic Laws	1433049171
Thailand Clothing & Textile Industry Handbook	1438747861
Thailand Clothing & Textile Industry Handbook	143304918X
Thailand Company Laws and Regulations Handbook	1433070723
Thailand Constitution and Citizenship Laws Handbook - Strategic Information and Basic Laws	1438780001
Thailand Constitution and Citizenship Laws Handbook - Strategic Information and Basic Laws	1438780001
Thailand Country Study Guide - Strategic Information and Developments	143874787X
Thailand Country Study Guide - Strategic Information and Developments	1433049198
Thailand Country Study Guide - Strategic Information and Developments Volume 1 Strategic Information and Developments	1438775733
Thailand Country Study Guide - Strategic Information and Developments Volume 1 Strategic Information and Developments	1438775733
Thailand Customs, Trade Regulations and Procedures Handbook Volume 1	1438747888
Thailand Customs, Trade Regulations and Procedures Handbook Volume 2	1433049201
Thailand Diplomatic Handbook - Strategic Information and Developments	1438747896
Thailand Diplomatic Handbook - Strategic Information and Developments	143304921X

For additional analytical, business and investment opportunities information, please contact Global Investment & Business Center, USA at (202) 546-2103. Fax: (202) 546-3275. E-mail: rusric@erols.com

title	ISBN
Thailand Ecology & Nature Protection Handbook	143874790X
Thailand Ecology & Nature Protection Handbook	1433049228
Thailand Ecology & Nature Protection Laws and Regulation Handbook	1433075091
Thailand Economic & Development Strategy Handbook	1438747918
Thailand Economic & Development Strategy Handbook	1433049236
Thailand Education System and Policy Handbook	1433068486
Thailand Energy Policy, Laws and Regulation Handbook	1433072858
Thailand Export-Import Trade and Business Directory	1438747926
Thailand Export-Import Trade and Business Directory	1433049244
Thailand Foreign Policy and Government Guide	1438747934
Thailand Foreign Policy and Government Guide	1433049252
Thailand Immigration Laws and Regulations Handbook - Strategic Information and Basic Laws	1438783604
Thailand Immigration Laws and Regulations Handbook - Strategic Information and Basic Laws	1438783604
Thailand Industrial and Business Directory	1433049260
Thailand Internet and E-Commerce Investment and Business Guide - Strategic and Practical Information: Regulations and Opportunities	1438747942
Thailand Internet and E-Commerce Investment and Business Guide - Strategic and Practical Information: Regulations and Opportunities	1433049279
Thailand Investment and Business Guide - Strategic and Practical Information	1438747950
Thailand Investment and Business Guide - Strategic and Practical Information	1438768915
Thailand Investment and Business Guide - Strategic and Practical Information	1438768915
Thailand Investment and Business Guide - Strategic and Practical Information	1433049287
Thailand Investment, Trade Laws and Regulations Handbook	143307673X
Thailand Justice System and National Police Handbook	1438747969
Thailand Justice System and National Police Handbook	1433049295
Thailand King, Political System and Reforms Handbook	1433049309
Thailand Labor Laws and Regulations Handbook - Strategic Information and Basic Laws	1438781806
Thailand Labor Laws and Regulations Handbook - Strategic Information and Basic Laws	1438781806
Thailand Land Ownership and Agriculture Laws Handbook	1438760108
Thailand Land Ownership and Agriculture Laws Handbook	1438760108
Thailand Land Ownership and Agriculture Laws Handbook	1438760108
Thailand Medical & Pharmaceutical Industry Handbook	1438747985
Thailand Medical & Pharmaceutical Industry Handbook	1433049317
Thailand Mineral & Mining Sector Investment and Business Guide - Strategic and Practical Information	1438747993
Thailand Mineral & Mining Sector Investment and Business Guide - Strategic and Practical Information	1433049325
Thailand Mining Laws and Regulations Handbook	1433078333

title	ISBN
Thailand Parliament Guide	1438748000
Thailand Parliament Guide	1433049333
Thailand Political System and Developments Handbook	1438747977
Thailand Privatization Programs and Regulations Handbook	1438748019
Thailand Privatization Programs and Regulations Handbook	1433049341
Thailand Recent Economic and Political Developments Yearbook	1433062712
Thailand Recent Economic and Political Developments Yearbook	1433062712
Thailand Recent Economic and Political Developments Yearbook	1433062712
Thailand Research & Development Policy Handbook	1433062860
Thailand Research & Development Policy Handbook	1433062860
Thailand Research & Development Policy Handbook	1433062860
Thailand Royal Army, National Security and Defense Policy Handbook	1438748027
Thailand Royal Army, National Security and Defense Policy Handbook	143304935X
Thailand Royal Police Handbook	1438748035
Thailand Royal Police Handbook	1433049368
Thailand Starting Business (Incorporating) in Thailand Guide	1433047187
Thailand Starting Business (Incorporating) in....Guide	1433068494
Thailand Tax Guide	1438748043
Thailand Tax Guide	1433049376
Thailand Taxation Laws and Regulations Handbook	143308113X
Thailand Telecom Laws and Regulations Handbook	1433082551
Thailand Telecommunication Industry Business Opportunities Handbook	1438748051
Thailand Telecommunication Industry Business Opportunities Handbook	1433049384
Thailand Transportation Policy and Regulations Handbook	1433068508

For additional analytical, business and investment opportunities information,
please contact Global Investment & Business Center, USA
at (202) 546-2103. Fax: (202) 546-3275. E-mail: rusric@erols.com

WORLD INVESTMENT AND BUSINESS GUIDE LIBRARY

Ultimate guides for business and investment operations in the country.
Price: $149 each

1.	Afghanistan Investment and Business Guide
2.	Aland Investment and Business Guide
3.	Albania Investment and Business Guide
4.	Algeria Investment and Business Guide
5.	Andorra Investment and Business Guide
6.	Angola Investment and Business Guide
7.	Anguilla Investment and Business Guide
8.	Antigua and Barbuda Investment and Business Guide
9.	Antilles (Netherlands) Investment and Business Guide
10.	Argentina Investment and Business Guide
11.	Armenia Investment and Business Guide
12.	Aruba Investment and Business Guide
13.	Australia Investment and Business Guide
14.	Austria Investment and Business Guide
15.	Azerbaijan Investment and Business Guide
16.	Bahamas Investment and Business Guide
17.	Bahrain Investment and Business Guide
18.	Bangladesh Investment and Business Guide
19.	Barbados Investment and Business Guide
20.	Belarus Investment and Business Guide
21.	Belgium Investment and Business Guide
22.	Belize Investment and Business Guide
23.	Benin Investment and Business Guide
24.	Bermuda Investment and Business Guide
25.	Bhutan Investment and Business Guide
26.	Bolivia Investment and Business Guide
27.	Bosnia and Herzegovina Investment and Business Guide
28.	Botswana Investment and Business Guide
29.	Brazil Investment and Business Guide
30.	Brunei Investment and Business Guide
31.	Bulgaria Investment and Business Guide
32.	Burkina Faso Investment and Business Guide
33.	Burundi Investment and Business Guide
34.	Cambodia Investment and Business Guide
35.	Cameroon Investment and Business Guide
36.	Canada Investment and Business Guide
37.	Cape Verde Investment and Business Guide

38.	Cayman Islands Investment and Business Guide
39.	Central African Republic Investment and Business Guide
40.	Chad Investment and Business Guide
41.	Chile Investment and Business Guide
42.	China Investment and Business Guide
43.	Colombia Investment and Business Guide
44.	Comoros Investment and Business Guide
45.	Congo Investment and Business Guide
46.	Congo, Democratic Republic Investment and Business Guide
47.	Cook Islands Investment and Business Guide
48.	Costa Rica Investment and Business Guide
49.	Cote d'Ivoire Investment and Business Guide
50.	Croatia Investment and Business Guide
51.	Cuba Investment and Business Guide
52.	Cyprus Investment and Business Guide
53.	Czech Republic Investment and Business Guide
54.	Denmark Investment and Business Guide
55.	Djibouti Investment and Business Guide
56.	Dominica Investment and Business Guide
57.	Dominican Republic Investment and Business Guide
58.	Ecuador Investment and Business Guide
59.	Egypt Investment and Business Guide
60.	El Salvador Investment and Business Guide
61.	Equatorial Guinea Investment and Business Guide
62.	Eritrea Investment and Business Guide
63.	Estonia Investment and Business Guide
64.	Ethiopia Investment and Business Guide
65.	Falkland Islands Investment and Business Guide
66.	Faroes Islands Investment and Business Guide
67.	Fiji Investment and Business Guide
68.	Finland Investment and Business Guide
69.	France Investment and Business Guide
70.	Gabon Investment and Business Guide
71.	Gambia Investment and Business Guide
72.	Georgia Investment and Business Guide
73.	Germany Investment and Business Guide
74.	Ghana Investment and Business Guide
75.	Gibraltar Investment and Business Guide
76.	Greece Investment and Business Guide
77.	Greenland Investment and Business Guide
78.	Grenada Investment and Business Guide
79.	Guam Investment and Business Guide
80.	Guatemala Investment and Business Guide
81.	Guernsey Investment and Business Guide
82.	Guinea Investment and Business Guide
83.	Guinea-Bissau Investment and Business Guide
84.	Guyana Investment and Business Guide
85.	Haiti Investment and Business Guide
86.	Honduras Investment and Business Guide
87.	Hungary Investment and Business Guide
88.	Iceland Investment and Business Guide

89.	India Investment and Business Guide
90.	Indonesia Investment and Business Guide
91.	Iran Investment and Business Guide
92.	Iraq Investment and Business Guide
93.	Ireland Investment and Business Guide
94.	Israel Investment and Business Guide
95.	Italy Investment and Business Guide
96.	Jamaica Investment and Business Guide
97.	Japan Investment and Business Guide
98.	Jersey Investment and Business Guide
99.	Jordan Investment and Business Guide
100.	Kazakhstan Investment and Business Guide
101.	Kenya Investment and Business Guide
102.	Kiribati Investment and Business Guide
103.	Korea, North Investment and Business Guide
104.	Korea, South Investment and Business Guide
105.	Kosovo Investment and Business Guide
106.	Kurdistan Investment and Business Guide
107.	Kuwait Investment and Business Guide
108.	Kyrgyzstan Investment and Business Guide
109.	Laos Investment and Business Guide
110.	Latvia Investment and Business Guide
111.	Lebanon Investment and Business Guide
112.	Lesotho Investment and Business Guide
113.	Liberia Investment and Business Guide
114.	Libya Investment and Business Guide
115.	Liechtenstein Investment and Business Guide
116.	Lithuania Investment and Business Guide
117.	Luxembourg Investment and Business Guide
118.	Macao Investment and Business Guide
119.	Macedonia Investment and Business Guide
120.	Madagascar Investment and Business Guide
121.	Madeira Investment and Business Guide
122.	Malawi Investment and Business Guide
123.	Malaysia Investment and Business Guide
124.	Maldives Investment and Business Guide
125.	Mali Investment and Business Guide
126.	Malta Investment and Business Guide
127.	Man Investment and Business Guide
128.	Marshall Islands Investment and Business Guide
129.	Mauritania Investment and Business Guide
130.	Mauritius Investment and Business Guide
131.	Mayotte Investment and Business Guide
132.	Mexico Investment and Business Guide
133.	Micronesia Investment and Business Guide
134.	Moldova Investment and Business Guide
135.	Monaco Investment and Business Guide
136.	Mongolia Investment and Business Guide
137.	Monserrat Investment and Business Guide
138.	Morocco Investment and Business Guide
139.	Mozambique Investment and Business Guide

140. Myanmar Investment and Business Guide
141. Namibia Investment and Business Guide
142. Nauru Investment and Business Guide
143. Nepal Investment and Business Guide
144. Netherlands Investment and Business Guide
145. New Caledonia Investment and Business Guide
146. New Zealand Investment and Business Guide
147. Nicaragua Investment and Business Guide
148. Niger Investment and Business Guide
149. Nigeria Investment and Business Guide
150. Niue Investment and Business Guide
151. Northern Mariana Islands Investment and Business Guide
152. Norway Investment and Business Guide
153. Oman Investment and Business Guide
154. Pakistan Investment and Business Guide
155. Palau Investment and Business Guide
156. Palestine (West Bank & Gaza) Investment and Business Guide
157. Panama Investment and Business Guide
158. Papua New Guinea Investment and Business Guide
159. Paraguay Investment and Business Guide
160. Peru Investment and Business Guide
161. Philippines Investment and Business Guide
162. Pitcairn Islands Investment and Business Guide
163. Poland Investment and Business Guide
164. Polynesia French Investment and Business Guide
165. Portugal Investment and Business Guide
166. Qatar Investment and Business Guide
167. Romania Investment and Business Guide
168. Russia Investment and Business Guide
169. Rwanda Investment and Business Guide
170. Saint Kitts and Nevis Investment and Business Guide
171. Saint Lucia Investment and Business Guide
172. Saint Vincent and The Grenadines Investment and Business Guide
173. Samoa (American) A Investment and Business Guide
174. Samoa (Western) Investment and Business Guide
175. San Marino Investment and Business Guide
176. Sao Tome and Principe Investment and Business Guide
177. Saudi Arabia Investment and Business Guide
178. Scotland Investment and Business Guide
179. Senegal Investment and Business Guide
180. Serbia Investment and Business Guide
181. Seychelles Investment and Business Guide
182. Sierra Leone Investment and Business Guide
183. Singapore Investment and Business Guide
184. Slovakia Investment and Business Guide
185. Slovenia Investment and Business Guide
186. Solomon Islands Investment and Business Guide
187. Somalia Investment and Business Guide
188. South Africa Investment and Business Guide
189. Spain Investment and Business Guide
190. Sri Lanka Investment and Business Guide

191. St. Helena Investment and Business Guide
192. St. Pierre & Miquelon Investment and Business Guide
193. Sudan Investment and Business Guide
194. Sudan South Investment and Business Guide
195. Suriname Investment and Business Guide
196. Swaziland Investment and Business Guide
197. Sweden Investment and Business Guide
198. Switzerland Investment and Business Guide
199. Syria Investment and Business Guide
200. Taiwan Investment and Business Guide
201. Tajikistan Investment and Business Guide
202. Tanzania Investment and Business Guide
203. Thailand Investment and Business Guide
204. Togo Investment and Business Guide
205. Tonga Investment and Business Guide
206. Trinidad and Tobago Investment and Business Guide
207. Tunisia Investment and Business Guide
208. Turkey Investment and Business Guide
209. Turkmenistan Investment and Business Guide
210. Turks & Caicos Investment and Business Guide
211. Tuvalu Investment and Business Guide
212. Uganda Investment and Business Guide
213. Ukraine Investment and Business Guide
214. United Arab Emirates Investment and Business Guide
215. United Kingdom Investment and Business Guide
216. United States Investment and Business Guide
217. Uruguay Investment and Business Guide
218. Uzbekistan Investment and Business Guide
219. Vanuatu Investment and Business Guide
220. Vatican City Investment and Business Guide
221. Venezuela Investment and Business Guide
222. Vietnam Investment and Business Guide
223. Virgin Islands, British Investment and Business Guide
224. Wake Atoll Investment and Business Guide
225. Wallis & Futuna Investment and Business Guide
226. Western Sahara Investment and Business Guide
227. Yemen Investment and Business Guide
228. Zambia Investment and Business Guide
229. Zimbabwe Investment and Business Guide

**To order and for additional analytical and marketing information, please contacts
International Business Publications, USA at:**
P.O. Box 15343, Washington, DC 20003, USA. Phone: (202) 546-210 Fax: (202) 546-32
E-mail: ibpusa@comcast.net
Global Business Information Catalog: http://wwww.ibpus.com

www.ingramcontent.com/pod-product-compliance
Lightning Source LLC
Chambersburg PA
CBHW080515220326
41599CB00032B/6093